FAIRFAX COUNTY

VIRGINIA

DEED BOOK, J-2

August 1808–March 1810

Transcribed by
Jane Haile Dawkins and Joyce Browning

WILLOW BEND BOOKS

2004

WILLOW BEND BOOKS
AN IMPRINT OF HERITAGE BOOKS, INC.

Books, CDs, and more—Worldwide

For our listing of thousands of titles see our website
at
www.HeritageBooks.com

Published 2004 by
HERITAGE BOOKS, INC.
Publishing Division
65 East Main Street
Westminster, Maryland 21157-5026

International Standard Book Number: 0-7884-2590-0

PREFACE

This is a verbatim transcript of Fairfax County, Virginia, Deed Book J-2, August 16, 1808 through March 23, 1810. William Moss was Clerk of Court during these years.

The Editors recognize the need to provide federal-era records in verbatim text and anticipate that it will be a useful tool for historians and legal title searches as well as serve the needs of family historians and genealogists. The original Deed Book J-2 contains 423 pages, which are reduced in this verbatim transcript to 182 pages, with full name and location indices attached.

Inasmuch as authenticity is important, the Editors transcribed the original spelling of people and locations, while they regularized the spelling of such common words as tree, small, receipt, etc. Original punctuation is generally retained except when added to separate a series of people, places, or actions.

FAIRFAX COUNTY, VIRGINIA with portions of Neighboring Virginia Counties of Loudoun and Prince William and the State of Maryland

[Map of John Wood by order of the Governor of Virginia, James P. Preston, completed in Spring 1826 and revised 'by order of the Executive" in 1859]

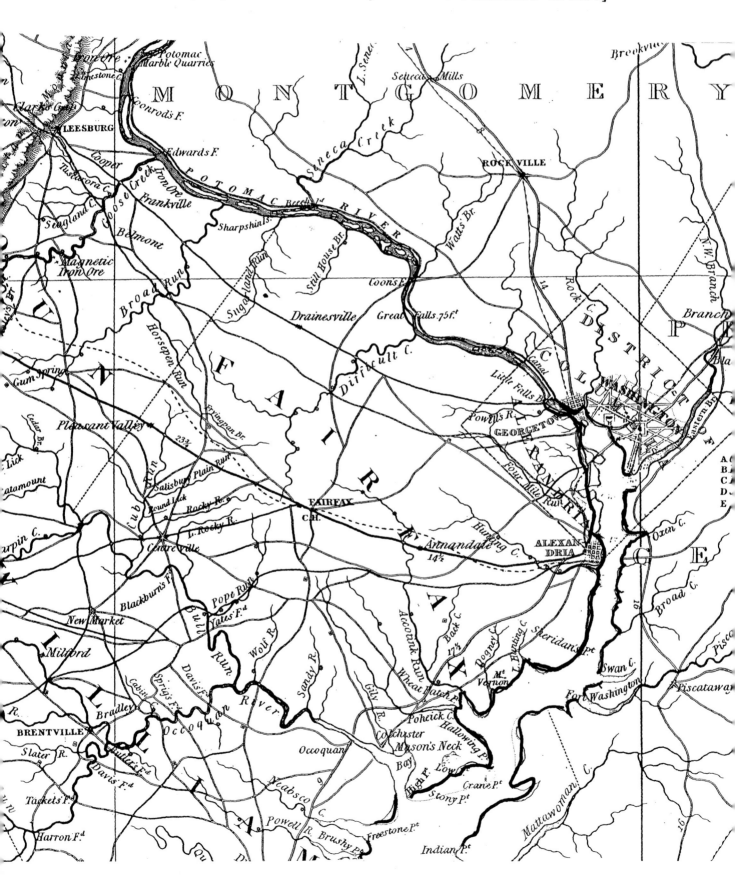

Fairfax County, Virginia
Deed Book J-2

Pages 1-5. THIS INDENTURE this sixteenth day of August in the Year of our Lord one thousand Eight hundred and eight between MOSES HOPWOOD & MARY his wife of Fairfax County and State of Virginia of the one part and EDMD. DENNEY of the same of the other part. WITNESSETH that the said MOSES HOPWOOD & MARY his wife for & in consideration of the sum of one Hundred Pounds Current money of Virginia to them in hand paid at and before the Sealing & delivery of these presents the receipt whereof we do hereby acknowledge and of every part & parcel thereof doth acquit, exonerate & discharge the said EDMD. DENNEY & his Heirs forever Have granted, bargained, sold & Confirmed and by the presents do grant, bargain, sell & Confirm unto the said EDMD. DENNEY to his heirs & assigns forever All that parcel or lot of Land situate in the County aforesaid in the Town of Centreville known by the lot No. 124 on the East side of the Turnpike Road & bounded as follows: Beginning at a stone on the main Street & running thence North 47 degrees East eight poles & twenty one links, thence South 48 degrees & eight poles & twenty one links, thence South 47 degrees West eight poles & twenty one links, thence North 48 degrees West eight poles and twenty one links to the beginning containing half one acre of land & all Houses, Orchards, fences, ways, waters, profits, commodities, hereditaments and appurtenances whatsoever to the said Premises hereby granted or any part thereof belonging or in anywise appertaining and the Reversion & Reversions, Remainder & remainders, rents, issues and profits thereof & all the Estate right, Title, Interest, property claim & demand whatsoever of them the said MOSES HOPWOOD and MARY his wife or either of them in and to the Premises & all Deeds, evidences & writings touching or in anywise concerning the same. To have and To Hold the aforesaid half acre of Land hereby Conveyed with all and Singular the premises hereby bargained & Lots and every part and parcel thereof with their & every of their appurtenances unto the [said] EDMD. DENNEY his heirs and assigns forever to the only proper use and behoof of him the said EDMD. DENNEY & his heirs & assigns forever. And the said MOSES HOPWOOD & MARY his wife for themselves, their heirs, Executors & adms do covenent, promise, grant & agree to and with the said EDMD. DENNY his Heirs, Executors, Administrators and assigns by these presents that they the said MOSES & MARY his wife now at the time of sealing & delivering of these presents and seized of a good, sure, perfect & Indisputable Estate of inheritance in fee simple of, in and to the premises hereby bargained and sold & that they have good power & lawful and absolute authority to grant & Convey the same to the said EDMD. DENNY in manner & form aforesaid and that the said Premises now are and so forever hereafter shall remain free of and from all former and other gifts, grants, bargains, sales, Dowers & right or Title of dowers, Judgments, Executions, Titles, Troubles charges & incumbrancy whatsoever made, done, commited or suffered to be done by the sd. MOSES HOPWOOD & MARY his wife or either of them and that the said MOSES HOPWOOD & MARY his Wife & their heirs all & Singular the premises hereby bargained and sold with the appurtenances unto the said EDMD. DENNEY his heirs & assigns against the claim or claims of themselves or either of them and against the claim or claims of any other person or persons whatsoever shall and will warrant & forever defend by these presents & lastly that they the said MOSES HOPWOOD & MARY his wife and their Heirs shall & will from time to time and at all times hereafter upon the reasonable request & at the proper costs & charges in the Law of the said EDMD. DENNEY his heirs or assigns make, do & execute or cause to be made, done & executed all and every such further and other lawful & other reasonable act & acts, thing and things, conveyances, assurances & assignments for the further better & more perfect conveying & securing the premises aforesaid with their & every appurtenances unto the said EDMD. DENNEY his heirs & assigns as by the said EDMD. DENNEY his heirs & assigns or by his or their council learned in the Law shall be reasonably required or advised; In WITNESS whereof the said MOSES HOPWOOD & MARY his wife hath hereunto set their hands & Seals the day, month & year above Written.

Signed, Sealed & delivered
In the presence of   MOSES HOPWOOD   (seal)
HUMPH. PEAKE   MARY her X mark HOPWOOD   (seal)
FRANCIS ADAMS
SPENCER BALL

At a Court held for Fairfax County the 19th Day of September 1808 this Deed from MOSES
HOPWOOD & MARY his wife to EDMUND DENNEY was proved to be the Act and Deed of the said
MOSES HOPWOOD by the oaths of HUMPHREY PEAKE and FRANCIS ADAMS Witnesses hereto and
ordered to be certified. And at a Court held for the said County the 19th day of December 1808
the same was further proved by the oath of SPENCER BALL, another witness hereto which
together with a Commission & return hereto annexed for taking the acknowledgment & privy
examination of the said MARY are ordered to be recorded.

Teste WM. MOSS Cl.

FAIRFAX COUNTY:

The CommonWealth of Virginia, to WILLIAM LANE JR, FRANCIS ADAMS & HUMPHREY
PEAKE Gentlemen Justices of the County of Fairfax Greeting: Whereas MOSES HOPWOOD &
MARY his wife by their certain Indenture of bargain & sale bearing date the sixteenth day of
August, have Sold & Conveyed unto EDMUND DENNEY the fee simple estate of a Certain Lot of
ground in the Town of Centreville, designated in the plat of the Town as Lot No. 124 with its
appurtenances situate, lying and being in the sd. Town & County of Fairfax. and whereas the
said MARY cannot conveniently travel to our said Court to make acknowledgement of the said
conveyance therefore we do give unto you or any two or more of you power to receive the
acknowledgment which the said MARY shall be willing to make before you of the conveyance
aforesaid contained in the said Indenture which is hereunto annexed and we do therefore
desire you or any two or more of you personally to go to the said MARY and receive her
acknowledgment of the same and examine her privily and apart from the said MOSES her
husband whether she doth the same freely and voluntarily without his persuasions or threats
& whether she be willing the said indenture together with this commission should be
recorded in our said Court and when you have received her acknowledgment and examined
her as aforesaid that you distinctly and openly certify us thereof in our said court under your
hands & seals sending there this Indenture and this Writ: WITNESS WILLIAM MOSS Clerk of
the said Court, this sixteenth day of August 1808.

WM. MOSS Cl.

FAIRFAX:

In obedience to the within commission we the subscribers waited on the within named
MARY HOPWOOD & having examined her privily and apart from her husband touching the
conveyance of a lott of ground in the Town of Centreville and do find that she hath done the
same freely & voluntarily without the persuasion or threats of her husband and that she is
willing that the Deed for the same together with this commission shall be recorded in the
County Court of Fairfax. Given under our hands & seals this 16th August 1808.

FRANCIS ADAMS   (seal)
HUMPH. PEAKE   (seal)

Pages 5 & 6. Know all men by these presents that I CHARLES L. BROADWATER of the County of
Fairfax & State of Virginia for and in consideration of the natural love and affection which I
have & bear to my Son WILLIAM E. BROADWATER (now living with me) as well as for the
further consideration of one Dollar to me in hand paid by the said WILLIAM E. BROADWATER
at or before the ensealing & delivery of these presents (the receipt whereof is hereby
acknowledged) have given & granted & by these presents do give & grant unto the said
WILLIAM E. BROADWATER his heirs & assigns forever Two certain Negro slaves (to wit) JULIA
aged 7 Years and JAMES aged about nine months (both being children of PEGGY my old house
Woman). To Have and To Hold the said Two Negroes before recited and all their increase unto
him the said WILLIAM E. BROADWATER his heirs and assigns forever. In WITNESS whereof I
have hereunto set my hand & affixed my seal this fifteenth day of October one Thousand Eight
Hundred and Eight.
Signed Sealed & delivered   CHARS L. BROADWATER (seal)

In presence of
WILLIAM JOHNSTON
JOHN MOORE
THOMAS HOOD

Received 15th October 1808 of WILLIAM E. BROADWATER one Dollar the consideration within mentioned.

WITNESS   CHARS. L. BROADWATER (seal)
JOHN MOORE
THOMAS HOOD JR
WILLIAM JOHNSON

At a Court held for Fairfax County the 19th day of December 1808 CHARLES L. BROADWATER acknowledged this Deed of Gift to WILLIAM E. BROADWATER to be his act and Deed which is ordered to be recorded.   Teste WM. MOSS Cl.

Pages 6 & 7. THIS INDENTURE made the nineteenth day of July in the Year of Lord one Thousand eight Hundred and eight between WILLIAM MAFFITT of the County of Fairfax and CommonWealth of Virginia of the one part and ELIZABETH LEE wife of RICHARD BLAND LEE of the County and CommonWealth aforesaid of the other part. WITNESSETH that for and in consideration of five dollars lawful money of Virginia to him the said WILLIAM MAFFITT in hand paid by the said ELIZABETH LEE and receipt whereof he doth hereby acknowledge hath granted, bargained and sold, aliened, conveyed and by these presents doth grant, bargain & sell, alien & convey unto the said ELIZABETH LEE her heirs and assigns forever all that certain tract or parcel of land situate, lying & being in the County of Fairfax and CommonWealth aforesaid being all that farm lying on the south or South east side of the road leading from the Town of Turberville and in the said County to the Little Falls of the Potowmack and which is now in the occupation of J. C. SCOTT commonly called Langley Farm, being part of a larger Tract Sold & conveyed to the before mentioned RICHARD BLAND LEE by HENRY LEE SR and HENRY LEE JR as will fully appear by their deed to the said RICHARD BLAND LEE bearing date on the fifth day of June in this present Year of our Lord one thousand eight hundred & eight, reference being had thereto now on the records of the Court of the said County of Fairfax and which said Tract hereby intended to be sold & conveyed by the said WILLIAM MAFFITT was conveyed unto him the said WILLIAM MAFFITT by Deed of Indenture from the said RICHARD BLAND LEE and ELIZABETH his wife bearing date on the day preseding the date of these presents as will fully appear by reference thereto on the records of the Court of the said County of Fairfax and which said tract hereby intended to be sold & conveyed contains by estimation three hundred acres be the same more or less. To Have and To Hold unto the said ELIZABETH LEE her heirs & assigns forever all the above described Tract or parcel of land with all and every of the appurtenances thereunto belonging or in any manner appertaining. And the said WM. MAFFITT for himself & his Heirs all the above described tract or parcel of land unto her the said ELIZABETH LEE her heirs & assigns, against the claim or claims of him the said WILLIAM MAFFITT & the claim or claims of all and every person claiming by, from or thro him the said WILLIAM MAFFITT, shall, will & doth forever warrant and defend by these presents. In testimony whereof he the said WILLIAM MAFFITT hath hereunto set his hand and seal the day & year first above written.

Signed, Sealed & delivered   WM. MAFFITT (seal)
In the presence of us [No witnesses listed]

At a Court held for Fairfax County the 19th day of December 1808 WILLIAM MAFFITT acknowledged this Deed to ELIZABETH LEE wife of RICHARD B. LEE, to be his act and deed which is ordered to be recorded.   Teste WM. MOSS Cl.

Pages 8-11. THIS INDENTURE made this Twenty eighth day of April one thousand eight hundred & eight between AMELIA BROCAS of the County of Alexandria and District of Columbia of the one part and MICHAEL O'MEARA of the County of Fairfax & State of Virginia of the other part. WITNESSETH that the said AMELIA BROCAS for and in consideration of the sum of Ten Pounds sixteen shillings Current money of Virginia to her the said AMELIA BROCAS in hand paid by the said MICHL. O'MEARA before the ensealing & delivery of these presents the

receipt whereof she the said AMELIA BROCAS doth hereby acknowledge have given, granted, bargained, Sold, Aliened & Confirmed and by these presents do give, grant, bargain, sell, Alien and Confirm unto the aforesaid MICHL. O'MEARA his heirs and assigns forever a certain piece or parcel of Ground situate, lying and being in the County of Fairfax & State of Virginia (near the Town of Alexandria) bounded as follows to wit: beginning at a stone on the North side of the Turnpike road leading into Duke Street, running thence Northwardly ten poles to a locust post, thence Westwardly to the Widow SUMMERVILLE'S line three poles one foot six inches, thence Southwardly along said SUMMERVILLE line ten poles, thence eastwardly along the turnpike road one pole eight feet six inches to the beginning, it being a part of a large piece of ground formerly sold and conveyed by the aforesaid MICHL. O'MEARA to a certain EDMUND DELAHUNTY of Prince George County Maryland which was since sold and conveyed to me by Deed from said DELAHUNTY bearing date May the fifteenth one Thousand eight hundred and four as will more fully appear, reference being had to the records of the County Court of Fairfax with all the improvements and profits thereof; To Have & To Hold the said piece or parcel of Ground with all the improvements thereunto belonging unto the sd. MICHL. O'MEARA his heirs & assigns forever and the said AMELIA BROCAS for herself her heirs, Executors, Administrators and assigns doth Covenant, Grant to and with the said MICHL. O'MEARA his heirs & assigns that she the sd. AMELIA BROCAS is seized in her own right of a good, sure, perfect, absolute and indefeasible estate of Inheritance in Fee simple in all and singular the premises hereby granted and their appurtenances without any manner of condition, mortgage, limitation of use or uses or other matters cause, or thing to alter, change, cause or determine the same. And also that she the said AMELIA BROCAS and her Heirs shall and will from time to time and at all times forever hereafter at the reasonable request and at the cost & charges in the law for him the said MICHL. O'MEARA his heirs or assigns make, do, execute and suffer or cause to procure or be made, done, levied, executed and suffered all and every such further and other lawful and reasonable Act and Acts, thing and things, Device and Devices, conveyances and assurances in the law, for the further better and more perfect assuring & sure making & conveying, all and Singular the Premises hereby granted, with their and every of their appurtenances unto him the said MICHL. O'MEARA his heirs & assigns as by the sd. MICHL. O'MEARA his heirs or assigns or their or any of their council learned in the Law, shall or may be reasonably advised, devised or required. And lastly that the said AMELIA BROCAS & her heirs or assigns the said piece or parcel of Ground, Hereditaments and all and singular the premises hereby granted with their and every of their appurtenances unto him, the sd. MICHAEL O'MEARA his heirs and assigns against the claim and demand of her the sd. AMELIA BROCAS her heirs or assigns and from the claim and claims, demand and demands of all and every other person or persons whatsoever shall & will warrant & forever defend by these presents. In testimony whereof the said AMELIA BROCAS hath hereunto set her hand & affixed her seal the day & Year first within Written.
Signed, Sealed & delivered
in Presence of   AMELIA BROOKES (seal)
R. MOSS, FREDERICK KOONES
IGNATIUS FUNIGAL
EDM. J. LEE
GEO. YOUNGS
THO. SWANN, N. HERBERT
       Recd. of MICHAEL O'MEARA Ten Pounds sixteen shillings Current money of Virginia, it being the full consideration within mentioned.
WITNESS   AMELIA BROCKES
R. MOSS
FREDERICK KOONES
       DISTRICT OF COLUMBIA To Wit:
             I GEORGE DENEALE Clerk of the United States Circuit Court of the District of
(SEAL)   Columbia for the County of Alexandria do hereby certify that at a Court
             continued and held for the said County the seventeenth day of December
eighteen Hundred & eight, this Deed from AMELIA BROCAS to MICHAEL O'MEARA was proved by the oath of EDM. J. LEE and GEORGE YOUNGS and NOBLET HERBERT to be the act and Deed of

the said AMELIA BROCAS and ordered to be certified to the County Court of Fairfax in the CommonWealth of Virginia. In testimony whereof I have hereunto set my hand and affixed my seal of office the day & Year above.   G. DENEALE Cl.
DISTRICT OF COLUMBIA:
I WILLIAM CRANCH, Chief Judge of the Circuit Court of the District of Columbia, do certify that the attestation hereunto annexed of GEORGE DENEALE Clerk of the said Court for Alexandria County in the District aforesaid is in due form given under my hand this 17th day of December 1808.   W. CRANCH
At a Court held for Fairfax County the 19th December 1808 this Deed from AMELIA BROCAS to MICHAEL O'MEARA having been duly proved before the United States Circuit Court of the District of Columbia held for the County of Alexandria and Certified by GEO. DENEALE Clerk of the said Court and under the seal of his office, also by WILLIAM CRANCH Chief Judge of the said court, is on motion of the said MICHAEL O'MEARA together with a receipt and the certificates thereon endorsed, ordered to be recorded.
Teste WM. MOSS Cl.

Pages 11-17. THIS INDENTURE made this twentieth day of September in the Year of our Lord one thousand eight hundred and six between PHINEAS JANNEY and ANDREW SCHOLFIELD of the Town & County of Alexandria in the District of Columbia of the one part & JONATHAN SCHOLFIELD and MAHLON SCHOLFIELD of the same Town, County and District of the other part. Whereas DANIEL McCARTY of the County of Fairfax in the State of Virginia, being indebted to the said JOHNATHAN and MAHLON SCHOLFIELD in a sum of money, he the said DANIEL McCARTY and MATILDA MARGARET SNOWDEN his wife in order to secure the Payment thereof did by their Indenture bearing date the fourth day of February one thousand eight hundred and six convey unto them the said PHINEAS JANNEY and ANDREW SCHOLFIELD their heirs, Executors, Administrators & assigns forever a Tract of land situate, lying and being upon Accotinque Run and Creek in the County of Fairfax and bounded as followeth to wit: begining upon the second line of the tract of land of which he the said DANIEL McCARTY was at that time seized three hundred & twenty poles from the beginning of that line and running thence South twenty six Degrees West two hundred and sixty poles to the main Accotinque Creek, then down the main creek with the several courses and meanders thereof and binding therewith to the end of the third line of the said Tract, thence with that line reversed North three hundred and twenty poles to the beginning of that line, thence with the second line of the said Tract to the beginning within which limits were contained thirty acres sold to DEANE & GARDINER and one hundred acres adjoining thereto secured to them by Mortgage which were excepted in the Conveyance made to the said PHENIAS JANNEY and ANDREW SCHOLFIELD, the land so conveyed to them being in Trust for the following purposes to wit: that if he the said DANIEL McCARTY his Heirs, Executors, Administrators or assigns should fail and neglect to pay to the said JONATHAN & MAHLON SCHOLFIELD the money so owing by him together with Interest thereupon from the date of the said Indenture on or before the first day of May then next following, then that they the said PHENIAS JANNEY and ANDREW SCHOLFIELD or the survivor of them or the Executors or Administrators of such survivor whenever after such failure thereto required should expose all and singular the Premises so conveyed with their appurtenances or such part of them as might be necessary for the purpose to sale at public auction for ready money giving three weeks notice of the time and place of such sale in the Alexandria Advertizer and with the money arising from such sale satisfy and pay the Costs thereof and the money and interest so owing to the said JOHNATHAN and MAHLON SCHOLFIELD and Whereas the said DANIEL McCARTY failed to pay unto the said JONATHAN and MAHLON SCHOLFIELD the money and Interest owing by him to them upon the said first day of May and the said PHENIAS JANNEY and ANDREW SCHOLFIELD, having been by them required to make sale of the lands so conveyed to them according to the terms expressed in the said convey-ance, they the said PHENIAS JANNEY and ANDREW SCHOLFIELD did on the [left blank] Day of August one Thousand eight Hundred and six insert an advertisement in the Alexandria Advertiser that they would on the seventeeth day of September then next ensuing expose to sale upon the Premises the land so conveyed to them by the said DANIEL McCARTY for ready money which advertisement was continued in the said Advertiser to the said seventeenth day of September on which day the lands so conveyed them were exposed to sale at public Auction for ready money and struck off to CHARLES STEUART as the highest bidder at the price of eight hundred and eighty dollars who hath directed the said PHENIAS JANNEY and ANDREW SCHOLFIELD to convey the lands so purchased by him to the said JONATHAN SCHOLFIELD & MAHLON SCHOLFIELD their heirs & assigns. Now this indenture WITNESSETH that the said PHENIAS JANNEY and ANDREW SCHOLFIELD for and in consideration of the said sum of eight Hundred and eighty Dollars to them in hand paid by the said JONATHAN SCHOLFIELD and MAHLON SCHOLFIELD, at or the ensealing & delivery of these presents the receipt whereof they the said PHENIAS JANNEY and ANDREW SCHOLFIELD do hereby acknowledge and thereof and of every part and parcel thereof do acquit, release and discharge them the said JONATHAN SCHOLFIELD and MAHLON SCHOLFIELD their Heirs, Executors and Administrators by these presents have given, granted, bargained, sold, aliened and confirmed and by these presents do give, grant, bargain, sell, alien & confirm unto them the said JONATHAN SCHOLFIELD and MAHLON SCHOLFIELD their heirs and assigns forever as Tenants in Common, all the lands contained within the boundaries expressed in the said Indenture made between the said DANIEL McCARTY and MATILDA MARGARET SNOWDEN his wife of the one part and the said PHENIAS JANNEY and ANDREW SCHOLFIELD of the other part and the said JONATHAN SCHOLFIELD and MAHLON SCHOLFIELD of a third part bearing date the said fourth day of February one Thousand eight hundred and six, except thirty acres within the said boundaries which had been sold to DEAN and GARDNER and one hundred acres conveyed them to secure the payment of a sum of money owing them and all Houses, buildings, Trees, Woods, waters, water-courses, profits, commodities, Hereditaments and appurtenances whatsoever to the said premises belonging or in anywise appertaining and the Reversion and Reversions, Remainder and Remainders, Rents, Issues and profits thereof and of every part and parcel thereof. To have and To Hold all and singular the premises hereby granted with their appurtenances unto them the said JONATHAN SCHOLFIELD and MAHLON SCHOLFIELD their heirs and assigns as Tenants in Common, to the only proper use and behoof of them the said JONATHAN SCHOLFIELD and MAHLON SCHOLFIELD their heirs and assigns forever as Tenants in Common and not as joint Tenants and the said PHENIAS JANNEY and ANDREW SCHOLFIELD do for themselves their heirs, Executors and Administrators covenant, grant and agree to and with the said JONATHAN SCHOLFIELD and MAHLON SCHOLFIELD their heirs and assigns that they the said PHENIAS JANNEY and ANDREW SCHOLFIELD will at any time during their lives and upon the request and at the cost and charge of them the said JONATHAN SCHOLFIELD & MAHLON SCHOLFIELD their heirs and assigns execute and acknowledge any further lawful act and Deed for the more certain assuring & conveying all and singular the said premises with their appurtenances unto them the said JONATHAN SCHOLFIELD and MAHLON SCHOLFIELD their heirs and assigns as by them or any of them, their or any of their Council learned in the law shall or may be advised or required. And Lastly that they the said PHENIAS JANNEY and ANDREW SCHOLFIELD and their heirs all and singular the said premises with their appurtenances unto them the said JONATHAN SCHOLFIELD and MAHLON SCHOLFIELD and their heirs and assigns against the claim and Demand of them the said PHENIAS JANNEY and ANDREW SCHOLFIELD and their heirs and all and every other person or persons whatsoever claiming by, from or under them shall and will warrant and forever defend by these presents. In WITNESS whereof the said PHENIAS JANNEY and ANDREW SCHOLFIELD have hereunto set their hands and seals the day and Year first herein before mentioned.

Sealed and Delivered   PHINEAS JANNEY   (seal)
In Presence of [No witnesses listed]   ANDREW SCHOLFIELD   (seal)

    Received of JONATHAN SCHOLFIELD and MAHLON SCHOLFIELD eight Hundred & eight Dollars, the consideration herein mentioned.

WITNESS   PHINEAS JANNEY
                                               ANDREW SCHOLFIELD

    DISTRICT OF COLUMBIA To Wit:

    I GEORGE DENEALE Clerk of the United States Circuit Court of the District of Columbia for the County of Alexandria do hereby certify that at a United States Circuit Court of the District aforesaid continued & held for the said County the sixth day of December Eighteen Hundred and six, PHINEAS JANNEY and ANDREW SCHOLFIELD acknowledged this Deed and receipt to

JONATHAN SCHOLFIELD and MAHLON SCHOLFIELD to be their Act and Deed and ordered to be Certified to the County Court of Fairfax in the CommonWealth of Virginia.

In testimony whereof I have hereunto set my hand and Affixed the
(SEAL)   Public Seal of my Office on this 7th day of December 1806.
G. DENEALE Cl.

DISTRICT OF COLUMBIA To Wit:

I WILLIAM CRANCH Chief Judge of the United States Circuit Court of the District of Columbia, do hereby certify that the above Attestation of GEORGE DENEALE Clerk of the Court for Alexandria County is in due form. Given under my hand this 17th day of December 1808.
W. CRANCH

At a Court held for Fairfax County the 19th December 1808 this Deed from PHINEAS JANNEY and ANDREW SCHOLFIELD to JONATHAN and MAHLON SCHOLFIELD having been duly acknowledged before the United States Circuit Court of the District of Columbia held for the County of Alexandria and Certified by GEORGE DENEALE Clerk of the said Court and under the seal of his office, also by WILLIAM CRANCH Chief Judge of the said Court, is on motion of the said JONATHAN SCHOLFIELD and MAHLON SCHOLFIELD together with a receipt and the Certificates hereon endorsed ordered to be recorded.
Teste WM. MOSS Cl.

Pages 18-20. THIS INDENTURE made this eighteenth day of July in the Year of our Lord one Thousand eight Hundred and eight between RICHARD BLAND LEE and ELIZABETH his wife of the County of Fairfax & CommonWealth of Virginia of the one part and WILLIAM MAFFITT of the said County and CommonWealth of the other part. Whereas the said ELIZABETH hath consented on this said eighteenth day of July to join the said RICHARD BLAND LEE in sealing and conveying to ZACCHEUS COLLINS of the City of Philadelphia a certain house and lot situate in the said City in Vine Street which house and Lot was bequeathed to the said ELIZABETH by the last Will and Testament of her Father STEPHEN COLLINS and the proceeds of which sale are paid by the said ZACCHEUS COLLINS to the said RICHARD BLAND LEE and whereas a Deed for the said House and lot in the City of Philadelphia to the said ZACCHEUS COLLINS hath this day been executed in due form by the said RICHARD BLAND LEE and ELIZABETH his wife and whereas the said RICHARD BLAND LEE is desirous and has agreed with the said ELIZABETH to convey to the said ELIZABETH certain other real property in lieu of the said House and lot to sold to the said ZACCHEUS COLLINS and of the value thereof a conveyance of which other real property the said WILLIAM MAFFITT is willing to receive for the purpose of reconveying the same to the said ELIZABETH. Now this Indenture WITNESSETH that for and in consideration of the premises and in further consideration of the sum of Three Thousand Dollars lawful Money of Virgina to them the said RICHARD BLAND LEE and ELIZABETH his wife in hand paid by the said WILLIAM MAFFITT the receipt whereof they do hereby acknowledge, they the said RICHARD BLAND LEE and ELIZABETH his wife have granted, bargained and sold, aliened & conveyed and by these presents do grant, bargain and sell, alien and convey unto the said WILLIAM MAFFITT his heirs and assigns forever all that certain Tract or parcel of land situate, lying and being in the said County of Fairfax and CommonWealth aforesaid being all that farm lying on the south or southeast side of the Road leading from the Town of Turberville in the said County to the Little Falls of the Potomac and which is now in the occupation of J. C. SCOTT commonly called Langley farm, being part of a larger Tract sold and conveyed to the said RICHARD BLAND LEE by HENRY LEE SR and by HENRY LEE JR as will fully appear by their Deed to the said RICHARD BLAND LEE bearing date on the fifth day of June in this present Year of our Lord one Thousand Eight Hundred & eight reference being had thereto now on the records of the Court of the said County of Fairfax which said Tract by these premises intended to be sold and Conveyed to the said WILLIAM MAFFITT contains by estimation Three Hundred acres be the same more or less. To Have and To Hold unto the said WILLIAM MAFFITT his heirs and assigns forever all the above described Tract or Parcel of land with all and every the appurtenances thereunto belonging or in any manner appertaining. And he, the said RICHARD BLAND LEE for himself and his Heirs, all the above described Tract or parcel of land unto him the said WILLIAM MAFFITT his heirs and assigns with all and every of the appurtenances thereunto belonging or in any manner appertaining against the claim of him the said RICHARD BLAND LEE and of all and every person whatsoever shall, will and doth forever warrant and defend by these presents. In testimony whereof the said RICHARD BLAND LEE and ELIZABETH his wife have hereunto set their hands and seals the Day & Year first above written.

Signed Sealed & Delivered   RICHARD BLAND LEE   (seal)
In the Presence of us [No witnesses listed]   (seal)
        At a Court held for Fairfax County the 19th day of December 1808 RICHARD BLAND LEE acknowledged this Deed to WILLIAM MAFFITT to be his act and Deed which is ordered to be Recorded.   Teste WM. MOSS Cl

Pages 20-24. THIS INDENTURE made this fourteenth day of December in the Year of our Lord one Thousand eight Hundred and seven between JOHN KORN and ROSANNAH KORN his wife of the Town and County of Alexandria in the District of Columbia of the one part and JACOB WISEMILLER of the same Town, County and District of the other part. Whereas JOHN WEST and SARAH his wife did by their Indenture made the eighteenth day of March one Thousand seven hundred and ninety four sell and convey unto him the said JOHN KORN his heirs and assigns forever a Tract or Parcel of land situate, lying and being upon Great Hunting Creek in the County of Fairfax and State of Virginia and bounded as followeth to wit: beginning at a small ash one pole from the sd. creek and running thence North four Degrees, East one hundred and twelve poles to the Turnpike Road, thence with that road South seventy five Degrees East twenty six poles, thence South one hundred and ten poles to the said Creek, thence up the meanders of the said creek and binding therewith North seventy seven degrees West twenty one poles to the beginning containing fifteen acres three Roods and six poles. And whereas JOHN THOMAS RICKETTS and MARY his wife did by their Indenture bearing date the twentieth day of October one Thousand seven Hundred and ninety six sell and convey unto him the sd. JOHN KORN his heirs and assigns forever a Tract or Parcel of land situate, lying and being upon the Drains of Great Hunting Creek in the said County of Fairfax and State of Virginia and bounded as followeth to wit: beginning upon the south side of the road leading from the Turnpike Gate to Colchester at that part of the said Road where the eastern line of the Tract or parcel of land sold by WILLIAM DUVALL to WILLIAM HERBERT crosses the same and running thence with the line of that land and binding upon the Western line of that tract or parcel of land sold and conveyed by JOHN WEST and SARAH his wife unto him the said JOHN KORN, north six Degrees west twenty poles and three quarters of a pole to the Turnpike Road, thence with that road North seventy five Degrees West seven poles ten links, South six Degrees East twenty poles to the South side of the road leading from the Turnpike Road to Colchester, thence with that road north eighty eight Degrees East seven poles eight links to the beginning containing fifty two perches being more than seven eighths of an acre. Now this indenture WITNESSETH that the said JOHN KORN and ROSANNAH KORN his wife for and in consideration of the sum of one Dollar to him the said JOHN KORN in hand paid by him the said JACOB WISEMILLER at or before the sealing and delivery of these presents the receipt whereof he the said JOHN KORN doth hereby acknowledge have given, granted, bargained, sold, aliened & confirmed and by these presents do give, grant, bargain, sell, alien and Confirm unto him the said JACOB WISEMILLER his heirs and assigns forever one equal undivided moiety or half part of the said Tracts of land with their appurtenances and all Houses, buildings, Trees, Woods, Waters, Water-courses, profits, Commodities, Hereditaments and appurtenances whatsoever to the said premises or any part of them belonging or in anywise appertaining and the Reversion and Reversions, Remainder and Remainders, Rents, Issues and Profits thereof and of every Part and Parcel thereof. To have and To Hold all and singular the said premises with their and every of their appurtenances unto him the said JACOB WISEMILLER his heirs and assigns to the only proper use and behoof of him the said JACOB WISEMILLER his Heirs and assigns forever. And the said JOHN KORN doth for himself, his Heirs, Executors and Administrators, covenant, grant and agree to & with the said JACOB WISEMILLER his heirs & assigns that he the said JOHN KORN and his Heirs will at any time hereafter upon the request and at the costs and charges of him the said JACOB WISEMILLER his heirs and assigns execute and acknowledge any further lawful act and Deed for the more certain assuring and conveying all and singular the sd. premises with their appurtenances unto him the said JACOB WISEMILLER his Heirs and assigns as by him the said JACOB WISEMILLER his heirs and assigns his, their or any of their council learned in the Law, shall or may be advised or required. And Lastly that he the said JOHN KORN and his Heirs all and singular the said premises with their appurtenances unto him the said JACOB WISEMILLER his heirs and assigns against the claim and Demands of him the said JOHN KORN and his Heirs and all and every other person or persons whatsoever claiming by, from or under him shall and will warrant and forever defend by these presents. In WITNESS whereof the said JOHN KORN and ROSANNAH KORN his wife have hereunto set their hands and seals the Day & Year first herein before mentioned.

Sealed and Delivered

In Presence of [No witnesses listed]   JOHN KORN   (seal)

DISTRICT OF COLUMBIA To Wit:

I GEORGE DENEALE Clerk of the United States Circuit Court of the District of Columbia for the County of Alexandria do hereby certify that at a Court continued and held for the District and County aforesaid the twenty second day of December Eighteen hundred and seven JOHN KORN acknowledged this Deed to JACOB WISEMILLER to be his Act and Deed and ordered to be Certified to the County Court of Fairfax in the CommonWealth of Virginia.

In testimony whereof I have hereunto set my hand and affixed the
(SEAL)   Public seal of my office on the aforeseaid 22nd day of December 1807.

G. DENEALE Cl.

DISTRICT OF COLUMBIA To Wit:

I WILLIAM CRANCH Chief Judge of the Circuit Court of the District of Columbia, do hereby Certify that the above attestation of GEORGE DENEALE Clerk of the said Court for Alexandria County, is in due form. Given under my hand this 23rd day of December 1807.

W. CRANCH

At a Court held for Fairfax County the 19th December 1808 this Deed from JOHN KORN to JACOB WISEMILLER having been duly acknowledged before the United States Circuit Court of the District of Columbia held for the County of Alexandria and Certified by GEORGE DENEALE Clerk of the said Court and under the Seal of his Office, also by WILLIAM CRANCH Chief Judge of the said Court is on motion of the said JACOB WISEMILLER together with the Certificate hereon endorsed ordered to be recorded.   Teste WM. MOSS Cl.

Pages 25-31. THIS INDENTURE TRIPARTITE made this twenty fourth day of October in the Year of our Lord one Thousand eight hundred and eight between ELIAS B. CALDWELL Esqr. of George Town in the district of Columbia, Trustee of the Estate of GUSTAVUS SCOTT Esqr. late of the said District decd of the first part, ROBERT RANKIN of the City Washington in the District aforesaid and ELIZABETH his wife of the second part and WILLIAM SWINK of the County of Fairfax and CommonWealth of Virginia of the third part. Whereas JOHN C. SCOTT of the County of Fairfax aforesaid pursuant to the decree of the County Court of Fairfax hath lately conveyed to ELIAS B. CALDWELL and his Heirs forever a tract or parcel of land situated in the said County of Fairfax and being Part of the tract of land whereon the sd. JOHN C. SCOTT resides and which said Parcel of Land conveyed as aforesaid by the said JOHN C. SCOTT to the said ELIAS B. CALDWELL containing six hundred acres and was conveyed to the said ELIAS B. CALDWELL in Trust for the use and benefit of the sd. ELIZABETH wife of the said ROBERT RANKIN her Heirs and assigns forever. And whereas it is conceived conducive to the interest of the said ELIZABETH that one Hundred and sixty three and half acres or thereabouts of the land conveyed for her benefit as aforesaid should be sold and the Proceeds thereof vested in some other Security for the use and benefit of the said ELIZABETH and the said Trustee together with the said ROBERT RANKIN and ELIZABETH his Wife have agreed to make the said sale and accordingly have sold to the said WM. SWINK one hundred sixty three and one half acres or thereabouts of the said Land. Now this Indenture WITNESSETH that the said ELIAS B. CALDWELL, ROBERT RANKIN and ELIZABETH his wife as well as in consideration of the Premises as for and in consideration of the sum of nine hundred Dollars to them in hand paid by the said WILLIAM SWINK at and before the ensealing and delivery of these presents the receipt whereof they do hereby acknowledge and thereof and of every part thereof doth exonerate and acquit the said WILLIAM SWINK his Heirs, Executors and Administrators by these presents they the said ELIAS B. CALDWELL and ROBERT RANKIN and ELIZABETH his wife have granted, bargained and sold, Aliened, Released and Confirmed and by these presents Do grant, bargain and sell, alien, Release & confirm unto the said WILLIAM SWINK his heirs and assigns forever a tract or parcel of land situated in the County of Fairfax and CommonWealth of Virginia, being Part of the land conveyed by JOHN C. SCOTT to the said ELIAS B. CALDWELL as aforesaid and bounded as follows to wit: beginning at a red oak tree standing in the line of SCOTT'S Original Patent near a branch also corner tree of the land of HENRY GUNNELL that he purchased of said ELIAS B. CALDWELL, ROBERT RANKIN and Wife, thence with said H. GUNNELL line South 49° & 284 poles to a corner of SCOTT'S Original Patent near a branch called JENKINS' spring branch and near JENKINS old Orchard, thence with SCOTT'S Original Patent South 88° & 89 poles to a red oak in deep glen corner of said SCOTT'S, thence North 37° & 54 poles to another red oak, another of said SCOTT'S Corners, thence North 23 1/2° West 62 poles to pile of Stones and small white oak bush on the side of a hill near a branch shewn by DANIEL JENKINS and others to be Corner of SCOTT'S, thence North 75.36° West 365 poles to the beginning containing one hundred sixty three & half acres according to a survey made by COLO. WM. PAYNE as will more fully appear by the records of Fairfax County together with all houses, buildings, ways, Waters, Water Courses, Profits, commodities and appurtenances to the said piece or parcel of land belonging or in any wise appertaining and the Reversion and Reversions, Remainder and Remainders, Rents, Issues and Profits thereof and all the estate right, Title, interest, property claim and demand of them the said ELIAS B. CALDWELL and ROBERT RANKIN and ELIZABETH his Wife of, in and to the same and every part thereof. To Have and To Hold the said piece or parcel of land with all and singular the appurtenances thereto belonging unto the SWINK his heirs and assigns to the only proper use and behoof of the said WILLIAM SWINK his heirs and assigns forever and the said ROBERT RANKIN and ELIZABETH his Wife for themselves, their heirs and Executors and Administrators do covenant, promise and agree to and with the said WILLIAM SWINK his heirs and assigns that they the said ELIAS B. CALDWELL, ROBERT RANKIN and ELIZABETH his wife now at the time of sealing and delivering of these presents are seized of a good, sure, perfect and Inheritance in Fee simple and of & in the premises hereby granted and that they have good power and Lawfull and absolute authority to grant and convey the same to the said WM. SWINK his heirs and assigns in manner and form aforesaid and that the premises now, are and so forever hereafter shall be, free and clear of and from all former and other gifts, grants, bargains, Sales, Dower right and title of Dower Judgments, Executions, Titles, Troubles, Charges and incumbrances whatsoever made, done, committed or suffered by the said ELIAS B. CALDWELL, ROBERT RANKIN and wife ELIZABETH or any other Person or Persons Whatsoever and Lastly the said ROBERT RANKIN and ELIZABETH his wife and their heirs, the said hereby granted premises with all and singular the appurtenances hereunto belonging unto the said WILLIAM SWINK his heirs and assigns forever against the claim and demand of him the said ELIAS B. CALDWELL and the said ROBERT RANKIN and ELIZABETH his wife and JOHN C. SCOTT and their and each of their heirs and of all and every Person or Persons claiming by, from or under him, them or any of them, shall & will warrant and forever defend by these presents. In WITNESS whereof the said ELIAS B. CALDWELL and the said ROBERT RANKIN and ELIZABETH his Wife have hereunto set their Hands and Affixed their seals the Day and Year first before written.

Sealed and delivered
in the Presence of
WM. GUNNELL JR
JOHN SWINK
SPENCER MOXLEY
JOHN C. SCOTT
WILLIAM SWINK JR
JOHN JACKSON

ELIAS B. CALDWELL   (seal)
ROBERT RANKIN   (seal)
ELIZA C. RANKIN   (seal)

October 24th 1808 Recd. of MR. WILLIAM SWINK the grantee within named nine Hundred Dollars the Consideration money within mentioned.
Teste

WM. GUNNELL JR   E. B. CALDWELL
SPENCER MOXLEY   ROBERT RANKIN

At a Court held for Fairfax County the 19th December 1808 this deed from ELIAS B. CALDWALL and ROBERT RANKIN and ELIZABETH his wife to WM. SWINK was proved to be the Act and Deed of the said ELIAS B. CALDWELL and ROBERT RANKIN by the oaths of WILLIAM GUNNELL JR, JOHN SWINK & WM. SWINK which together with a Commission and Return hereto annexed for taking the acknowledgment and privy examination of the said ELIZABETH are ordered to be Recorded.   Teste WM. MOSS Cl.

FAIRFAX COUNTY To Wit:

The CommonWealth of Virginia to JAS. COLEMAN, WM. GUNNELL JR Gentlemen justices of the County of Fairfax Greeting: WHEREAS ELIAS B. CALDWELL, ROBERT RANKIN and ELIZA wife of the sd. RANKIN by their certain indenture of bargain & sale bearing date the 20th day of October in this present month have sold and conveyed unto WM. SWINK the fee simple Estate of one hundred sixty three and one half acres land with the appurtenances situate, lying and being in the said county of Fairfax and whereas the said ELIZA RANKIN cannot conveniently travel to our said County Court of Fairfax to make acknowledgment of the said conveyance therefore we do give unto you or any two or more of you power to receive the acknowledgment which the said ELIZA RANKIN shall be willing to make before you of the conveyance aforesaid contained in the said indenture which is hereunto annexed and we do thereof desire you or any two or more of you personally to go to the said ELIZA RANKIN and receive her acknowledgment of the same and examine her privily and apart from the said ROBERT RANKIN her husband whether she doth the same freely and voluntarily without his persuasions or threats and whither she be willing the said indenture together with this Commission shall be recorded in our said Court; And when you have received her acknowledgment and examined her as aforesaid that you distinctly and openly certify us thereof in our said Court under your hands and seals sending then there the said indenture and this Writ. WITNESS WILLIAM MOSS Clerk of the said Court and the Courthouse of the County aforesaid this 30th day of October 1808 and in the Thirty third year of the CommonWealth.   WM. MOSS Cl.

FAIRFAX COUNTY To Wit:

In pursuance to the within Dedimus to us directed we waited on ELIZA RANKINS wife of the said ROBERT RANKINS and proceeded to examine the sd. ELIZA RANKIN her said husband who acknowledged the hereunto annexed instrument of writing as her act and Deed and relinquished all her rights of the same as also all her Dower of the same, in and unto the Premises therein conveyed and described in the said Deed together with this Dedimus might be recorded and further declared that she made said acknowledgment freely, Voluntarily & of her own accord & that she was not induced thereto by threats of her said husband or the fear of said husband or his displeasure. Given under our hands & seals this 31st October 1808.

WM. GUNNELL JR   (seal)
JOHN JACKSON   (seal)
Teste WM. MOSS Cl.

Pages 32-38. THIS INDENTURE TRIPARTITE made this fifteenth day of December in the Year of our Lord one Thousand eight hundred and eight between FREDERICK TRYTALL and MARY his wife of the County of Fairfax in the State of Virginia of the first part, RICHARD LEWIS and ELIZA his wife of the Town and County of Alexandria in the District of Columbia of the second part and WILLIAM S. MOORE and JOHN MUNCASTER, Church Wardens of the Episcopal Church in the said Town of Alexandria of the third part. Whereas ROBERT PATTON JR did, by his indenture bearing date the thirty first day of October one Thousand eight hundred and one, sell and convey unto JOHN DUFF his heirs and assigns a tract or parcel of land situate, lying and being upon the west side of that parcel of land granted by WILLIAM THORNTON ALEXANDER and LUCY his wife unto JOHN GILL the East side of Fayette lane, South side of Green lane and North side of Hunting creek in the said County of Fairfax and bounded as followeth To wit: beginning at the intersection of Green lane with the line of GILL and running thence with that line Southwardly to Hunting Creek, thence Westwardly with the meanders of Hunting Creek and binding therewith to Fayette lane, thence Northwardly with that lane to its intersection with Green lane, thence Eastwardly with that lane to the beginning, being an entire Square of that tract of land known by the name of Spring Garden farm & in the platt and Subdivisions thereof distinguished by the numbers (13, 14, 15, 16). Also one other tract or parcel of land lying upon the South side of Wolf lane, North side of Wilks lane, West side of Hamilton lane and East side of Mandeville lane in the said County and bounded as followeth to wit: beginning at the intersection of Hamilton lane with Wolf lane and running thence Southwardly with Hamilton lane to its intersection with Wilk's lane, thence Westwardly with that lane to its intersection with Mandeville lane, thence north-wardly with that lane to its intersection with Wolf lane, thence Eastwardly with that lane to the beginning it being one other Square of the aforesaid tract of land and in the said platt distinguished by the numbers (97, 98, 110, 111) and whereas the said JOHN DUFF and SARAH his wife did by their indenture bearing date the fourth day of August one Thousand eight hundred and two sell and convey unto him the said FREDERICK TRYTALL his heirs and assigns forever that tract or parcel of land lying upon Wolf, Wilks, Hamilton and Mandevilles lanes who instead of recording it in the County of Fairfax where the land lay had it recorded in the County of Alexandria in the District of Columbia and by one other indenture bearing date the fifth day of April one Thousand eight Hundred and five sold and conveyed unto the said FREDERICK TRYTALL his heirs and assigns by certain metes and bounds a part of that other tract of land lying upon Gills lane, Green lane, Fayette lane and Hunting Creek after which several sales so made by the said JOHN DUFF, he sold the residue of the said tract of land lying upon Gills lane, Hunting Creek, Fayette and Green lanes unto the said RICHARD LEWIS and by an indenture bearing date the Sixth day of December eight hundred and Six conveyed the same unto him and by some improper directions given for drawing the same he also conveyed unto him that other tract of land lying upon Wolfe, Wilkes, Hamilton and Mandeville lanes which he had formerly sold to the said FREDERICK TRYTILLE; now this Indenture WITNESSETH that the said FREDERICK TRYTILL and MARY his wife for and in consideration of the sum of three hundred and Ten Dollars to him in hand paid by the said WILLIAM S. MOORE and JOHN MUNCASTER at or before the Sealing and Delivery of these presents the receipt whereof he the said FREDERICK TRYTILL doth hereby acknowledge and thereof and of every part and parcel thereof doth acquit, release and discharge them the said WILLIAM S. MOORE and JOHN MUNCASTER their heirs, Executors and Administrators, by these presents have given, granted, bargained, sold, aliened and confirmed and by these presents Do give, grant, bargain, Sell, alien and Confirm unto them the said WILLIAM S. MOORE and JOHN MUNCASTER and their Successors in Office forever all that part of the said tract or parcel of land lying upon Wolfe, Wilks, Hamilton and Mandeville lanes contained within the following boundaries to wit: beginning at the intersection of Wilks and Hamilton lanes and running thence Northwardly with Hamilton lane to its intersection with Wolfe lane, thence Westwardly with that lane to a ten foot alley laid off in the centre of the Square formed by Hamilton and Mandeville lanes, thence Southwardly with the said alley and parallel to Hamilton and Mandeville lanes to its intersection with Wilkes lane, thence Eastwardly with that lane to the beginning and all Houses, buildings, Trees, Woods, Waters, Watercourses, lanes, alleys, profits, commodities, Hereditaments and appurtenances whatsoever to the said premises, belonging or in anywise appertaining and the Reversion & Reversions, Remainder and Remainders, Rents, Issues and Profits thereof and of every part and parcel thereof and the said RICHARD LEWIS and ELIZA his wife for and in consideration of one Dollar to him the said RICHARD LEWIS in hand paid by the said WILLIAM S. MOORE at or before the Sealing and delivery of these presents the receipt whereof he doth hereby acknowledge have given, granted, bargain, Sold, Aliened and Confirmed and by these presents Do give, grant, bargain, Sell, Alien & Confirm unto the said WILLIAM S. MOORE & JOHN MUNCASTER and their Successors in Office forever all the estate right, Title, use, Trust, Interest, property, claim and Demand as will in Law as Equity of them the said RICHARD LEWIS and ELIZA his wife of, in and to all and singular the premises hereby granted with their appurtenances To Have and To Hold all and singular the premises hereby granted with their appurtenances unto them the said WILLIAM S. MOORE and JOHN MUNCASTER and their Successors in Office forever for the use of the Episcopal Inhabitants of the said Town of Alexandria and to and for no other use or purpose whatever. And the said FREDERICK TRYTALL doth for himself his Heirs, Executors and Administrators, covenant, grant and agree to and with the said WILLIAM S. MOORE and JOHN MUNCASTER and their Successors in Office that he the said FREDERICK TRYTILL is now at the time of the Sealing and Delivery of these presents seized in his own right of a good, sure, perfect, absolute and indefeasible Estate of inheritance in fee Simple in all and Singular the Premises hereby granted with their appurtenances without any manner of Condition, Mortgage, Limitation of use or uses or any other matter, cause or thing to alter, change, charge or determine the same And also that he the said FREDERICK TRYTILL & his Heirs will at any time hereafter upon the request and at the Cost and charge of them the said WILLIAM S. MOORE and JOHN MUNCASTER and their Successors in Office execute and acknowledge any further lawfull Act and Deed for the more certain assuring and conveying all and singular the said premises with their appurtenances unto them the said WILLIAM S. MOORE and JOHN MUNCASTER and their Successors in Office as by them the said WILLIAM S. MOORE and JOHN MUNCASTER or their Successors in Office, their or any of their Council learned in the Law shall or may be advised or required and also that he the said FREDERICK TRYTILLE and His Heirs all and Singular the said premises with their appurtenances unto them the said WILLIAM S. MOORE and JOHN MUNCASTER and their Successors in Office against the claim and Demand of him the said FREDERICK TRYTILL and his Heirs and all and every other person or persons whatsoever shall and will warrant and forever defend by these presents; and Lastly that he the said FREDERICK TRYTILL will lay off an alley ten feet wide in the centre of the Square formed by Hamilton and Mandeville lanes for the use & benefit of the Episcopal Inhabitants of the Town of Alexandria in common with those holding any part of the said Square and that he, his Heirs or assigns will at no time hereafter stop up or interrupt the passage of it. In WITNESS whereof the said FREDERICK TRYTLE and MARY his wife And RICHARD LEWIS and ELIZA his wife have hereunto set their Hands and Seals the Day & Year first herein before mentioned.

Sealed and Delivered   FREDERICK TRYTLE   (seal)
In Presence of [No witnesses listed]   MARY her X mark TRYTLE (seal)

Received of WILLIAM S. MOORE and JOHN MUNCASTER three hundred and Ten Dollars the consideration herein mentioned.

WITNESS [No witnesses listed]   FREDERICK TRAITLE

At a Court held for Fairfax County the 16th day of January 1809 FREDERICK TREITLE and MARY his wife (she being first privately and again in open Court examined and thereto consenting) acknowledged this Deed and receipt to WILLIAM S. MOORE and to JOHN MUNCASTER to be their Act and deed and the said FREDERICK TREITLE acknowledged the receipt hereon endorsed to be his act and deed which are ordered to be recorded.

Teste WM. MOSS Cl.

Pages 38-45. THIS INDENTURE TRIPARTITE made this fifteenth day of December in the Year of our Lord one thousand eight hundred and eight between FREDERICK TRYTLE and MARY his wife of the County of Fairfax in the State of Virginia of the first part, RICHARD LEWIS and ELIZA his wife of the Town and County of Alexandria in the District of Columbia of the second part and JACOB HOFFMAN, JOSEPH SMITH, WILLIAM RHODES, JOHN SLOAN and THOMAS PRESTON of the same Town, County and District of the third part. Whereas ROBERT PATTON JR did by his indenture bearing date the thirty first Day of October one thousand and eight Hundred and one Sell and Convey unto JOHN DUFF his heirs and assigns a tract or parcel of land situate, lying and being upon the west side of that piece of ground granted by WILLIAM THORNTON ALEXANDER unto JOHN GILL the East side of Fayette lane South side of Green lane and North side of Hunting Creek in the said County of Fairfax and bounded as followeth to wit: beginning at the intersection of Green lane with the line of GILL and running thence Southwardly with that line to Hunting Creek and binding therewith to Fayette lane, thence Northwardly with that lane to its intersection with Green lane, thence Eastwardly with that lane to the Beginning being an entire Square of that tract of land known by the same of the Spring Garden Farm and on the Platt and subdivisions thereof distinguished by the numbers (13, 14, 15, 16). Also one other tract or parcel of land lying upon the South side of Wolfe lane, North side of Wilks lane, West side of Hamilton lane and East side of Mandeville lane in the aforesaid County and bounded as followeth To wit: Beginning at the intersection of Hamilton lane with Wolf lane and running thence Southwardly with Hamilton lane to its intersection with Wilks lane, thence Westwardly with Wilks to its intersection with Mandeville lane, thence Northwardly with that lane to its intersection with Wolf lane, thence Eastwardly with that lane to the beginning it being one other Square of the aforesaid tract of land and in the said Platt distinguished by the numbers (97, 98, 110, 111) and whereas the said JOHN DUFF and SARAH his wife did by their Indenture bearing date the fourth day of August one Thousand eight hundred and two Sell and Convey unto the said FREDERICK TRYTILLE his heirs and assigns forever that tract or parcel of land lying on the South side of Wolfe lane, North side of Wilks lane, West side of Hamilton lane and East side of Mandeville lane and by one other Indenture bearing date the fifth day of April one Thousand eight hundred and five also sold and conveyed unto him the said FREDERICK TRYTILLE his heirs and assigns by certain metes and bounds a part of that other parcel of land lying upon the West side of Gills lane, North side of Hunting Creek and east side of Fayette lane and South side of Green lane which Deed for the land lying upon Wolfe, Wilkes, Hamilton and Mandeville lanes the said FREDERICK TRYTILL instead of recording it in the County of Fairfax in which the land lay had it recorded in the County of Alexandria after which several transactions the said JOHN DUFF sold the residue of that parcel of land lying upon Gills lane, Hunting Creek and Fayette and Green lanes unto the said RICHARD LEWIS and by an indenture bearing date the sixth day of December one Thousand eight hundred and six conveyed the same to him and through some improper directions also conveyed to him and his Heirs and assigns that other tract of land lying upon Wolf, Wilkes, Hamilton and Mandeville lanes which he had formerly sold to the said FREDERICK TRYTLE. Now this Indenture that the said FREDERICK TRITELL and MARY his wife for and in consideration of the Sum of three hundred and forty dollars to him the said FREDERICK TRYTILL in hand paid by them the said JACOB HOFFMAN, JOSEPH SMITH, WILLIAM RHODES, JOHN SLOAN and THOMAS PRESTON at or before the Sealing and delivery of these presents the Receipt whereof he the said FREDERICK TRYTILL doth hereby acknowledge and thereof and of every part and parcel thereof doth acquit, release them their heirs, Executors and Administrators by these presents and the further consideration of the trusts herein after contained and expressed on the part and behalf of them the said JACOB HOFFMAN, JOSEPH SMITH, WILLIAM RHODES, JOHN SLOAN and THOMAS PRESTON to be executed, fulfilled and performed: Have given, granted, bargained, Sold, Aliened and Confirmed and by these presents do give, grant, bargain, Sell, Alien and Confirm unto them the said JACOB HOFFMAN, JOSEPH SMITH, WILLIAM RHODES, JOHN SLOAN and THOMAS PRESTON their heirs & assigns forever all that part of the said tract or parcel of Land lying upon Wolf, Wilkes, Hamilton and Mandeville lanes contained within the following Boundaries to wit: beginning at the intersection of Wilks and Mandeville lanes and running thence Northwardly with Mandeville lane to its intersection with Wolf lane, thence Eastwardly with Wolf lane to a ten foot alley laid off in the centre of the Square formed by Hamilton and Mandeville lanes, thence Southwardly with the said alley and Parrallel to Hamilton and Mandeville lanes to its intersection with Wilks lane, thence Westwardly with that lane to the beginning and all Houses, Buildings, Trees, Woods, Waters, Water Courses, lanes, Allies, Profits, Commodities, Hereditaments and appurtenances whatsoever to the said premises belonging or in anywise appertaining and the Reversion and Reversions, Remainder and Remainders, Rents, issues and Profits thereof and of every part and parcel thereof and the said RICHARD LEWIS and ELIZA his wife for and in consideration of the sum of one Dollar to him the said RICHARD LEWIS in hand paid by them the said JACOB HOFFMAN, JOSEPH SMITH, WILLIAM RHODES, JOHN SLOAN and THOMAS PRESTON at or before the sealing and delivery of these presents the receipt whereof he the said RICHARD LEWIS doth hereby acknowledge Have given, granted, bargained, sold, aliened and confirmed and by these presents Do give, grant, bargain, Sell, Alien and Confirm unto them the said JACOB HOFFMAN, JOSEPH SMITH, WILLIAM RHODES, JOHN SLOAN and THOMAS PRESTON their heirs and assigns forever all the estate right, Title, Use, Trust, interest, Property claim and Demand as well in law as Equity of them the said RICHARD LEWIS and ELIZA his wife of, in and to all and Singular the premises hereby granted with their appurtenances. To have and to hold all and singular the premises hereby granted with their appurtenances unto them the said JACOB HOFFMAN, JOSEPH SMITH, WILLIAM RHODES, JOHN SLOAN and THOMAS PRESTON their heirs and assigns forever in trust to and for the uses and purposes herein after mentioned and to and for no other use or purpose whatever that is to say for the use and Benefit the Methodist

Episcopal Church in the Town of Alexandria to be made use of and applied to such purposes as that Church shall think proper and also upon this further Trust that whenever the said JACOB HOFFMAN, JOSEPH SMITH, WILLIAM RHODES, JOHN SLOAN and THOMAS PRESTON shall by death or discontinuing to be members of that Church (from whatever cause such discontinuance proceeds) shall be reduced to two Persons only, then that the said two persons or the Survivor of them in case of a death taking place after such a reduction of the members before a conveyance could be prepared and executed do convey all and Singular the said Premises with their appurtenances to such other Persons as they shall be directed by the members of the said Church in Trust for the same purposes the said Premises are hereby conveyed to the said JACOB HOFFMAN, JOSEPH SMITH, WILLIAM RHODES, JOHN SLOAN and THOS. PRESTON and the said FREDERICK TRYTILL doth for himself, his Heirs, Executors and Administrators, covenant, grant and agree to and with the said JACOB HOFFMAN, JOSEPH SMITH, WILLIAM RHODES, JOHN SLOAN and THOMAS PRESTON their heirs and assigns, that he the said FREDERICK TRYTILL is now at the time of the Sealing and Delivery of these presents seized in his own right of a good, sure, perfect, absolute and indefeasible Estate of inheritance in fee Simple in all and Singular the sd. premises with their appurtenances without any manner of condition, mortgage, limit-ation of use or uses or any other matter cause or thing to alter, change, charge, or determine the same. And also that he the said FREDERICK TRYTILL and his Heirs will at any time here-after upon the request and at the cost and charge of them the said JACOB HOFFMAN, JOSEPH SMITH, WILLIAM RHODES, JOHN SLOAN and THOMAS PRESTON their heirs and assigns execute and acknowledge any further lawful Act and Deed for the more certain assuring and conveying all and Singular the said premises with their appurtenances unto them their heirs and assigns as by them their heirs and assigns their or any of their council learned in the law shall or may be advised or required. And Lastly that he the said FREDERICK TRYTILL and his Heirs all and Singular the said Premises with their appurtenances unto them the said JACOB HOFFMAN, JOSEPH SMITH, WILLIAM RHODES, JOHN SLOAN and THOMAS PRESTON their heirs and assigns against the claim and Demand of him the said FREDERICK TRYTILL and his Heirs and all & every other person or persons whatsoever shall and will warrant and forever defend by these presents. And also that he will lay off an alley ten feet wide in the centre of the Square formed by Hamilton & Mandeville lanes for their use and benefit in common with those holding any part of the said Square and that he his heirs and assigns will at no time hereafter stop up or interrupt the passage of it. In WITNESS whereof the said FREDERICK TRYTLE and his wife and RICHARD LEWIS and ELIZA (sic) his wife have hereunto set their Hands and Seals the Day and Year first herein before mentioned.

Sealed and Delivered	FREDERICK TREITLE (seal)
in Presence of [No witnesses listed]	MARY her + mark TRIDLE (seal)

        Received of JACOB HOFFMAN, JOSEPH SMITH, WILLIAM RHODES, JOHN SLOAN and THOMAS PRESTON three Hundred and forty Dollars the consideration herein mentioned.
Witness   FREDERICK TREUTLE

        At a Court held for Fairfax County the 16th January 1809 FREDERICK TREITLE and MARY his wife (she being privately and again in open Court examined and thereto consenting) acknowledged this Deed to JACOB HOFFMAN, JOSEPH SMITH, WILLIAM RHODES, JOHN SLOAN and THOMAS PRESTON to be their act and Deed and the said FREDERICK TREITLE acknowledged the Receipt hereon endorsed which are ordered to be recorded.
                                Teste WM. MOSS Cl.

Pages 46-48. THIS INDENTURE made this fifteenth day of March in the Year of our Lord one Thousand eight Hundred and eight between EDWARD DULIN of the County of Fairfax and CHARLES LITTLE of the same County. WITNESSETH that the said EDWARD DULIN as well for and in consideration of the sum of one Dollar to him in hand paid by the said CHARLES LITTLE at and before the Sealing and delivery of these presents the receipt whereof he doth hereby acknowledge as to secure the Payment of the sum of Five hundred Dollars loaned by HENRY WHALEY to the said EDWARD DULIN hath granted, bargained & Sold, aliened & confirmed and by these presents Doth grant, bargain & Sell, Alien & confirm unto the said CHARLES LITTLE his heirs & assigns all that Tract or parcel of land situate, lying and being in the County of Fairfax containing four Hundred & Seventy acres which was devised by the last Will &

Testament of EDWARD DULIN decd to the said EDWARD DULIN as by the said last Will & Testament duly proved & recorded in the County Court of Fairfax will more fully & at large appear and all and Singular the appurtenances to the said Tract of land belonging or in anywise appertaining. To have and to Hold the said tract or parcel of land with all and Singular the appurtenances thereunto belonging unto the said CHARLES LITTLE his heirs and assigns to the following uses and Trusts that is to say to the use of the said EDWARD DULIN his heirs and assigns until default shall be made in the payment of the said Sum of five hundred Dollars with legal interest thereon and if the said EDWARD DULIN his heirs and assigns Executors or Administrators shall fail to pay to the said HENRY WHALEY his Executors or Administrators on the fifteenth day of June in the Year of our Lord one Thousand eight Hundred and eight the said sum of money then the said CHARLES LITTLE his Executors or Administrators shall at any time thereafter when requested by the said HENRY WHALEY his Executors or Administrators sell and dispose of the said Tract or parcel of land at Public Auction for ready money to the highest bidder having first advertised the same for the space of thirty days in the Alexandria News paper and at Fairfax Court House and the said CHARLES LITTLE his Executors or Administrators shall out of the Money arising from the Sale of said lands first satisfy and pay the expense of said sale and satisfy and pay to the said HENRY WHALEY his Executors or Administrators the said Sum of five Hundred Dollars with legal interest thereon from the date hereof and shall pay the surplus if any remains to the said EDWARD DULIN his Executors and Administrators and the said CHARLES LITTLE for himself his Executors & Administrators doth covenant, Promise & grant to and with the said EDWARD DULIN and the said HENRY WHALEY severally & respectively that he will well and faithfully perform and execute the aforesaid Trust and the sd. EDWARD DULIN for himself, his Heirs, Executors and Administrators Doth Covenant, Promise and grant to and with the said CHARLES LITTLE his heirs & assigns that he the said tract or parcel of land with all & singular the appurtenances thereunto belonging he the said EDWARD DULIN his heirs & assigns unto the said CHARLES LITTLE his heirs & assigns shall & will warrant & forever defend by these presents. In WITNESS whereof the said EDWARD DULIN and the said CHARLES LITTLE have hereunto set their hands & affixed their Seals the Day and Year first before written.

Sealed & Delivered
In Presence of
CH. SIMMS
JOSEPH POWELL
GEO. YOUNGS

E. DULIN   (seal)
CHARLES LITTLE   (seal)

    At a Court held for Fairfax County the Nineteenth December 1808 this Deed between EDWARD DULIN & CHARLES LITTLE for the use of HENRY WHALEY was acknowledged by the Parties hereto to be their act & Deed & ordered to be recorded.
                                        WM. MOSS Cl.

Pages 49-56. THIS INDENTURE made the 31st day of December in the Year one Thousand eight hundred & eight between GEORGE D. ALEXANDER, AUGUSTIN ALEXANDER, PHILIP ALEXANDER & CHARLES ALEXANDER all of the County of Alexandria in the District of Columbia of the one part & GEORGE CHAPMAN JR of Fauquier County in the State of Virginia of the other part. WITNESSETH that whereas GERARD ALEXANDER did in his lifetime possess and enjoy a tract of land which he bought of BENJAMINE SEBASTINE which said Tract was Originally granted unto WILLIAM SCUTT by LORD FAIRFAX the proprietor of the Northern Neck of Virginia bearing date the seventeenth day of December One thousand seven hundred & thirty lying & being in the County of Stafford now Fairfax for three hundred & Sixty seven acres which said Tract of land was Willed and devised by the said GERARD unto his Son GEORGE ALEXANDER which said Will bears date the Ninth day of August, One Thousand seven hundred & Sixty and by the said GEORGE ALEXANDER devised unto his two brothers ROBERT ALEXANDER and PHILIP ALEXANDER at the Death of there mother which said Will of the said GEORGE bears date the Sixteenth day of September, one thousand seven hundred & sixty seven and recorded in Fairfax County, one moiety of which the said PHILIP did will & devise unto his three Sons to wit: the said GEORGE D. ALEXANDER, AUGUSTIN ALEXANDER and GERARD ALEXANDER which said will was recorded in Fairfax County and bears the [left blank] day [left blank] one Thousand seven hundred and [left blank] reference being thereunto had will appear and whereas GERARD ALEXANDER the Son and devisee of the said last mentioned PHILIP from bodily infirmities and from other causes his intellect or mind is so infirmed as to unfit him forever in Law to dispose of his Estate either by Deed or Will and in consequence of which his Moiety or proportion of the said land which he is or may be entitled to under his father the said last mentioned PHILIP'S Will will & must fall unto his brothers the said GEORGE D. ALEXANDER, AUGUSTIN ALEXANDER, PHILIP ALEXANDER and CHARLES ALEXANDER and the said PHILIP ALEXANDER and CHARLES ALEXANDER Sons of the said PHILIP & brothers to the said GERARD ALEXANDER are willing to convey those parts or proportions of the said land which they may be entitled to at the death of their said brother GERARD ALEXANDER as aforesaid unto the said GEORGE CHAPMANN JR and are willing to join their aforesaid brothers to wit: the said GEORGE D. ALEXANDER and AUGUSTIN ALEXANDER in this deed to complete the title of the said Land and whereas from a recent survey made of the said tract of land it is found that the sd. tract of land containeth four Hundred and thirty four acres in the whole (the other moiety which belonged unto the said ROBERT ALEXANDER as aforementioned which he claimed held and enjoyed under his said brother the said GEORGE ALEXANDER's Will as aforementioned and which he the said ROBERT ALEXANDER, devised unto his Son, ROBERT ALEXANDER by will which said Will bears date the ninth day of January one Thousand seven hundred & ninety three & sold by his Son the said ROBERT under an Order of Court held for the County of Alexandria in the District of Columbia at their March adjoining session in the Year eighteen hundred & six to satisfy a Debt due unto the said GEORGE CHAPMAN JR and the said GEORGE CHAPMAN JR became the purchaser of the moiety aforesaid with two other Tracts of land sold under the said decree and conveyed to him the said GEORGE CHAPMAN JR by THOMAS SWANN, EDMUND J. LEE and GEORGE DENEALE commissioners appointed by the said Court under the said Decree by deed bearing date the eighteenth day of December One thousand eight hundred and seven and recorded in the General Court of Richmond & Fairfax County. Now this indenture WITNESSETH that for and in consideration of the sum of eight hundred & sixty eight Dollars unto the said GEORGE D. ALEXANDER, AUGUSTIN ALEXANDER, PHILIP ALEXANDER and CHARLES ALEXANDER in hand paid by the said GEORGE CHAPMAN JR at the ensealing & delivery of these presents the receipt whereof they do hereby acknowledge & thereof release, acquit and discharge the said GEORGE CHAPMAN JR his Heirs, Executors & administrators, by these presents they the said GEORGE D. ALEXANDER, AUGUSTIN ALEXANDER, PHILIP ALEXANDER and CHARLES ALEXANDER have granted, bargained, sold, Aliened, enfeoffed and Confirmed and by these presents do give, grant, bargain, Sell, alien, enfeoff & Confirm unto the said GEORGE CHAPMAN JR and his heirs & assigns one undivided moiety of a tract of land which said moiety containeth by a recent Survey made two hundred and Seventeen acres as aforesaid situate, lying and being in the said County of Stafford, now Fairfax & being a part of a tract of land granted unto WM. SCUTT by a proprietors Deed bearing date the said seventeenth day of December seventeen hundred & thirty, for three hundred and Sixty seven acres as aforementioned the said messuage or tract of land lying and being near CHARLES BROADWATER'S and on a branch of Difficult run, commonly called Wolf Trap branch and opposite to the land surveyed for EPHRAHAM THORN now the land of STEPHEN LEWIS and bounded as follows Vizt: beginning at a small red oak standing between a red and white oak on the South side of the said branch and extending thence North 87° West 12 poles to a white oak in a glade, thence South 3° West 180 poles along a line of the land of CAPT. BROADWATER to a red oak his corner tree, thence along another of his lines South 65° East 113 poles to another of his corner trees, thence South 85° East 65 poles to a white oak and a red oak on the South side of a branch, thence North 59° East 86 poles to a red oak nigh a branch of Ackotink, thence North 28° East 56 poles to a white oak in a large glade, thence South 88° East 28 poles to a chesnut saplin in a Poison field, thence North 40° East 46 poles, to a small red oak and three chesnut trees in a glade, thence North 3° East 48 poles to a white oak saplin on the side of the old Sugar land path, thence North 25° 30' West 62 poles to two white oaks on the side of a tract that leads from EDWARD EDWARDS' to PATRICK DUNKINS, thence North 54° West 26 poles to a white oak on the side of the aforesaid branch being the corner beginning tree to the aforesaid land of STEPHEN LEWIS, thence down the said branch the several courses and meanders thereof reduced to a right line South 86° West 245 poles to the first station and all houses, buildings, Ways, Waters and Watercourses, profits, commodities, Hereditaments and appurtenances whatsoever to the said premises hereby granted or in any part thereof belonging or in anywise appertaining and the Reversion and Reversions, Remainder & Remainders, Rents, issues and Profits thereof and also all the estate right, title, interest, use, trust, property, claim and demand, whatsoever of them the said GEORGE D. ALEXANDER, AUGUSTIN ALEXANDER, PHILIP ALEXANDER and CHARLES ALEXANDER of, in and to the said premises and all other Deeds, evidences and writing or in any wise touching or concerning the same. To Have & To hold the said undivided Moiety of two Hundred & Seventeen acres of land hereby Conveyed & all and Singular the Premises hereby bargained and Sold and every part thereof with their and every of their appurtenances unto the said GEORGE CHAPMAN JR his heirs and assigns forever to the only proper use and behoof of him the said GEORGE CHAPMAN JR and his heirs & assigns forever. And the said GEORGE D. ALEXANDER, AUGUSTIN ALEXANDER, PHILIP ALEXANDER and CHARLES ALEXANDER for themselves and their Heirs, Exors and Admrs do covenant, Promise and grant to and with the said GEORGE CHAPMAN JR his heirs & assigns by these presents that the said GEORGE D. ALEXANDER, AUGUSTIN ALEXANDER, PHILIP ALEXANDER and CHARLES ALEXANDER now & at the time of Sealing & delivery of these presents are seized of good, sure, perfect and indefeasible estate of inheritance in the fee simple of the said undivided Moiety of two hundred and seventeen acres of and in the Premises hereby bargained & Sold and that they have good power lawfull & absolute authority to grant & convey unto the said GEORGE CHAPMAN JR in manner & form aforesaid and that the said Premises of the said undivided Moiety of two hundred & seventeen acres of land now are and so for ever shall remain and be free & clear of and from all former & other gifts, grants, bargains, sales, dower right and title of dower, Judgments, Executions, titles, troubles, charges and incumbrances made, done, committed or suffered, by the said GEORGE D. ALEXANDER, AUGUSTIN ALEXANDER, PHILIP ALEXANDER and CHARLES ALEXANDER or any other person or persons whatsoever and that the said GEO. D. ALEXANDER, AUGUSTIN ALEXANDER, PHILIP ALEXANDER & CHARLES ALEXANDER and their heirs & all & singular the premises of the said undivided Moiety of two hundred and seventeen acres of land hereby bargained & sold with the appurtenances unto the said GEORGE CHAPMAN JR his heirs & assigns against them the said GEORGE D. ALEXANDER, AUGUSTIN ALEXANDER, PHILIP ALEXANDER & CHARLES ALEXANDER and their Heirs & all and every other Person and persons whatsoever shall warrant and forever defend by these presents. And further if the said PHILIP ALEXANDER and CHARLES ALEXANDER or either of them will not warrant & defend the premises aforesaid then the said GEORGE D. ALEXANDER and AUGUSTINE ALEXANDER have particularly agreed & covenanted to & with the said GEORGE CHAPMAN JR his heirs and assigns to warrant and forever defend the whole of the said undivided moiety of two Hundred & seventeen acres of land hereby conveyed against themselves, their respective heirs & against all other Person or Persons whatsoever by these presents: In WITNESS whereof the said GEORGE D. ALEXANDER, AUGUSTIN ALEXANDER, PHILIP ALEXANDER & CHARLES ALEXANDER have hereunto set their hands & Seals the day Month & Year first above written.

Signed Sealed & Delivered	GEORGE D. ALEXANDER	(seal)
in Presence of	AUGUSTIN ALEXANDER	(seal)
R. J. TAYLOR, to G.D.A.& A.A. & C.	CH. ALEXANDER	(seal)
WM. HERBERT JR do do do		(seal)
GEO. YOUNGS		

At a Court held for Fairfax County the 16th Day of January 1809 this Deed from GEORGE D. ALEXANDER, AUGUSTIN ALEXANDER and CHARLES ALEXANDER to GEORGE CHAPMAN JR was proved to be the act & Deed of the said GEORGE D. ALEXANDER, AUGUSTIN ALEXANDER and CHARLES ALEXANDER by the oaths of ROBERT J. TAYLOR, WILLIAM HERBERT JR and GEORGE YOUNGS Witnesses hereto & ordered to be recorded.

Teste WM. MOSS Cl.

Pages 56-59. THIS INDENTURE made this eighteenth day of June in the Year one thousand eight hundred & eight between LEWIS SUMMERS of the County of Fairfax and CommonWealth of Virginia of the first part, ROBERT MOSS now resident of the Town of Alexandria in the District of Columbia of the second Part and ROBERT J. TAYLOR of the same Town and District of the third Part: WITNESSETH whereas the said LEWIS SUMMERS did on the 5th day of September in the Year one Thousand eight hundred and seven join a certain THOMAS PETERKIN as his security in a forthcoming bond to ARMSTEAD LONG for the delivery of certain property at a certain time, which bond has since become forfeited and whereas the said ROBERT MOSS is now special bail for the said SUMMERS in a suit brought by the President, Directors & Company of the Bank of Alexandria, agt. said SUMMERS in the Circuit Court of the District of Columbia for the County of Alexandria which said several responsibilities the said LEWIS SUMMERS is desirous of securing to the said ROBERT MOSS and against any damage that may result to him from the same. Now this indenture WITNESSETH that the said LEWIS as well to afford the said security as for & in consideration of the sum of one Dollar in hand paid the receipt whereof he doth hereby acknowledge has granted, bargained & sold & does by these presents, grant, bargain & sell, alien & confirm unto the said ROBERT J. TAYLOR a certain tract or parcel of land in the County of Fairfax situate on the old and new turnpike roads from Alexandria and about five miles distant from said town containing thirty six and one quarter acres as will more fully appear by reference to the deed of conveyance from FRANCIS SUMMERS JR and wife to the said LEWIS dated the 15th day of December 1805 also one other Lot or Parcel of ground situate in the City of Washington being lot number 8 in Square number eleven hundred & thirty as will more fully appear by reference to the deed of the super-intendant MUNROE and to the said LEWIS dated the 23 of October in the Year 1802. To have and To Hold unto the said ROBERT his heirs & assigns forever in Trust however for the following uses and purposes that is to say that if the said LEWIS SUMMERS & his representatives shall not within a reasonable time to be judged of by the said ROBERT J. TAYLOR relieve the said ROBERT MOSS from his liability by paying the debt due to the Bank and whatever amt. may be recovered against him the said LEWIS on the forthcoming bond aforementioned and for which the said ROBERT may be deemed responsible by the said Trustee on the ground of the security being insufficient then that the said ROBERT or his heirs shall proceed to Sell the said Premises on a Credit of sixty & ninety days at Public sale having advertised the same a reasonable time and after defraying the expences of the said Sale shall apply the Money arising therefrom to the relieving of the said ROBERT MOSS from his afore recited respons-ibility and the ballance remaining shall be paid over to the said LEWIS SUMMERS his heirs &c and the said LEWIS SUMMERS and his heirs covenent to warrant & forever defend the hereby granted Premises unto the said ROBERT J. TAYLOR his heirs & assigns agt. the claims or demands of all Persons whatsoever and the said ROBERT J. TAYLOR for himself, his Heirs &c doth hereby covenant & agree with the other parties aforementioned that he will faithfully discharge the trust hereby created. In Testimony whereof the several parties have hereunto set their hands and Seals this day & Year first mentioned.

Signed Sealed & Delivered   LEWIS SUMMERS   (seal)
in Presence of   R. J. TAYLOR   (seal)
SAMMUEL SUMMERS
THOMPSON VIOLETT
W. MILLAN
G. DENEALE to R. J. TAYLOR
N. HERBERT to R. J. T.
GEO. YOUNGS to R. J. T., WM. MOSS to L. S.

    At a Court held for Fairfax County the 19th day of December 1808 this Deed from LEWIS SUMMERS to ROBERT J. TAYLOR in trust for the use of ROBERT MOSS was proved to be the Act and deed of the said LEWIS SUMMERS by oath of WILLIAM MILLAN a Witness hereto and ordered to be certified and at a Court continued & held for the said County the 17th January 1809 the same was further proved to be the act and Deed of the said LEWIS SUMMERS by oaths of THOMPSON VIOLETT and WM. MOSS two other Witnesses hereto and the said ROBERT J. TAYLOR acknowledged the Covenant herein contained to be binding on his part and ordered to be recorded.   Teste WM. MOSS Cl.

Pages 59-61. THIS INDENTURE made this tenth day of January in the Year of our Lord eighteen hundred & nine between EDWARD GANTT of the County of Fairfax & CommonWealth of Virginia of the one part & WILLM. STOUGHTON GANTT of Leesburg in the County of Loudoun &

CommonWealth afsd of the other part. WITNESSETH whereas the said WILLIAM S. GANTT became bound as the security of the sd. EDWARD GANTT for the payment of the following sums of money to wit: to STEWART BROWN of the City of Baltimore two Thousand Dollars with interest from the 1st of February 1805, To T. W. PRATT of the City of Washington for one thousand Dollars with interest since 1805 and to the Bank of Columbia for one hundred and eighty dollars with interest since 1805 and hath moreover paid to and advanced for the said EDWARD GANTT the sum of two thousand two hundred and six dollars and whereas the said EDWARD GANTT being willing to secure the said WILLIAM S. GANTT from all damage and loss that shall or may happen to him the said WILLIAM S. GANTT or his Heirs from the Payment of the said Debts & now this indenture WITNESSETH that for and in Consideration of the said WILLIAM S. GANTT having assumed the Payment of the said Debts and having acquited the said EDWARD GANTT of the payment of the said Sum of two thousand two Hundred & six Dollars and for and in consideration of the sum of one dollar to him the said EDWARD GANTT in hand paid the receipt whereof is hereby acknowledged the said EDWARD GANTT hath granted, bargained and Sold and by these presents doth grant, bargain & sell to the said WILLIAM S. GANTT all and Singular the following Property Viz: Negroes, BENNET, LOUDER, NANCY, ISAIAH, SOMERSET, TUBMAN, JOE, DILLY and her two children: LUCY 4 Years old and LEAH 2 Years old; NELL and her four children: ELIZA 8 Years old, JAMES 6 Years old, GEORGE 4 Years old and HARRIOT 2 Years old and KESSEY; 3 Horses and a mare, 8 head of black cattle, 20 Hogs, a small horse cart, 4 Ploughs, 2 Harrows, 12 hoes, 4 mattoxes, 2 picks, 1 X cut saw, 2 Bill hooks, 100 bushels Wheat in the Straw, 50 barrells corn, 5 beds and furniture, 1 mahogany side-board, 5 do tables, 18 chairs, 24 knives and forks, 1 clothes press, 1 cupboard, looking glass, 24 silver spoons, 1 Do cann, 1 Cabinet, 4 Pr and Irons, 2 Pr tongs and shovels, 1 fender, 5 Bedsteads, 3 Dozen china cups & saucers, 24 Plates & dishes, some glass ware, one dressing glass, 2 Carpets, 8 window curtains, 4 suits, bed ditto, pots, 2 Dutch ovens, 1 Bell Mettle skillet, Salamander, pothooks &c, 1 copper, 40 gallons, 2 Linen and 1 Wollen or Cotton wheel, 1 Iron Mortar and Pestle, 100 lbs 1 spice mortar & pestle, 1 tea table, 1 wash stand, 1 Desk & writing ditto, 4 Doz mahogany chairs, one Easy chair, 2 looking glasses, 1 crib, one Walnut table to have & To Hold forever and the said EDWARD GANTT his Heirs &c shall forever warrant & defend the title & right in and to all and singular the above named property free from the claim of all persons whatsoever except the above named Negroes SOMERSET, TUBMAN and ISAIAH who have been secured to HENRY GANTT of Jefferson County Virginia for the payment of five hundred & sixteen dollar, as will appear from record in the Office of the Clerk of Fairfax County Virginia which sum of five hundred & sixteen dollars the sd. WILLIAM S. GANTT hereby assumes the Payment of. In WITNESS whereof the said EDWARD GANTT hath hereunto set his hand & seal, the day and Year first above written.

Signed Sealed & Delivered   EDWARD GANTT   (seal)
in the Presence of
DANIEL GOODING
EDWARD S. GANTT
SAMUEL SMITH

　　　　At a Court held for Fairfax County the 16th day of January 1809 this bill of Sale from EDWARD GANTT to WILLIAM S. GANTT was proved to be the Act and Deed of the said EDWARD GANTT by the oaths of DANIEL GOODING, EDWARD S. GANTT and SAMUEL SMITH Witnesses hereto and Ordered to be Recorded.   Teste WM. MOSS Cl.

Pages 61-66. THIS INDENTURE made the 17th day of November one thousand eight hundred & eight between MARMADUKE B. BECKWITH and REBECKAH his wife of the County of Fairfax in the State of Virginia of the one part and BERNARD BRYAN of the Town of Alexandria & District of Columbia of the other Part. WITNESSETH that the said MARMADUKE B. BECKWITH & REBECKAH his wife for and in consideration of the sum of three Thousand four Hundred & forty Dollars specie to them in hand paid by the said BERNARD BRYAN before the ensealing & delivery of these presents the receipt whereof the said MARMADUKE B. BECKWITH and REBECKAH his wife doth hereby acknowledge they the said MARMADUKE B. BECKWITH & REBECKAH his wife have granted, bargained & Sold, aliened & confirmed and do by these presents grant, bargain, Alien & confirm unto the said BERNARD BRYAN and to his Heirs and assigns all that tract & parcel of land containing four hundred & thirty acres of land be the same more or less situate & being in the County & State aforsd and lying on the head branches of Jonnymore Run and bounded as follows: beginning at a large white oak corner to WAUGH now GIBSON, also a Hickory and Gum marked pointing to said oak on the North side of sd. Jonnymore Run and extending thence along the line of sd. WAUGH South sixty seven degrees West one hundred & twenty nine poles to two black oak saplings a (corner) in sd. line, thence North 29° West 104 poles to a Hickory and white oak the Hickory now down and rotten, thence North 35° East 58 poles to a small black oak (a corner), thence South 87° East 69 poles to a white oak corner on the side of a ridge now down and a white & red oaks marked, pointing to the same, near the Root thereof and by the fence side, thence North 3° East 110 poles to a Hickory and white oak, (corner), thence South 68° 12 East 82 poles to a white oak (corner), thence South 28° East 71 poles to a Gum & water-oak marked the Corner between the two in a drain of sd. Jonnymore Run, thence South 22° West 165 poles to where an elm formerly stood the Corner two white oak saplings marked in its stead in a drain of the aforesaid run, thence South 25° East 98 poles to a stake of several white oak Saplings in a lane of sd. WAUGHS line, thence North 78° West 156 poles to the Beginning. Also all Houses, Trees, Woods, underwoods, Profits, advantages, Hereditaments, Ways, Waters & appurtenances whatsoever to the Messuage or tract of land & Tenement above mentioned, belonging or in anywise appertaining and also the Reversion & Reversions and every part and parcel and all the Estates, Right, Title, interest, claim & demand whatsoever of & in the said four Hundred & thirty acres of land and Premises of, in and to the said messuage & Tenement & Premises and every part thereof. To Have and to hold the said Messuage, Tenement and Tract of land and all & Singular the premises above mentioned and every Part & parcel thereof with the appurtenances unto the said BERNARD BRYAN his heirs & assigns forever and the said MARMADUKE B. BECKWITH & REBECKAH his wife do for themselves & their Heirs the said Messuage, Tenement & tract of land & premises and every part thereof against them & their Heirs & against all and every other Person or Persons whatsoever to the said BERNARD BRYAN & his heirs & assigns, shall & will warrant & forever defend by these presents. In WITNESS the said MARMADUKE B. BECKWITH & REBECKAH his Wife have hereunto set their hands & Seals the date above written.

Signed Sealed and delivered	MARMADUKE B. BECKWITH	(seal)
In the Presence of	REBECKAH BECKWITH	(seal)

JAS. S. TRIPLETT
FRANCIS ADAMS
TRAVIS PRITCHART

    Received this [left blank] day of November, One Thousand eight Hundred & eight of BERNARD BRYAN the Sum of three Thousand four Hundred & forty Dollars Specie being the Consideration mentioned for the within lands & Premises and is in full for the same.

Teste   Recd. by me MARMADUKE B. BECKWITH
FRANCIS ADAMS
JAS S. TRIPLETT
TRAVIS PRITCHARTT

    At a Court held for Fairfax County the 16th day of January 1807 MARMADUKE B. BECKWITH acknowledged this Deed and Receipt to BERNARD BRYAN which together with the Commission & Return hereto annexed for taking the acknowledgment & privy examination of REBECCA BECKWITH wife of the said MARMADUKE B. are ordered to be recorded.

Teste WM. MOSS Cl.

FAIRFAX COUNTY To Wit:

    The CommonWealth of Virginia to FRANCIS ADAMS, JAMES S. TRIPLETT and HUMPHREY PEAKE Gentlemen Justices of the County of Fairfax Greeting: Whereas MARMADUKE B. BECKWITH and REBECKAH his wife by their certain Indenture of Bargain and Sale bearing date the seventeenth day of November 1808 have sold and Conveyed unto BERNARD BRYAN the fee simple estate of four hundred & thirty acres of land more or less bounded as per said indenture hereunto annexed with the appurtenances situate, lying and being on the waters of Jonnymore Run in the said County of Fairfax and whereas the said REBECKAH cannot conveniently travel to our said County Court of Fairfax to make acknowledgment of the said

Conveyance therefore we do give unto you or any two or more of you power to receive the acknowledgment which the said REBECKAH BECKWITH shall be willing to make before you of the conveyance aforesaid contained in the said indenture which is hereunto annexed and we do therefore desire you or any two or more of you personally to go to the said REBECKAH BECKWITH and receive her acknowledgment of the same & examine her privily and apart from the said MARMADUKE B. BECKWITH her husband whither she doth the same freely & voluntarily without his persuasions or threats and whether she be willing the said indenture together with this commission, shall be recorded in our said Court and when you have received her acknowledgment & examined her as aforesaid that you distinctly and openly Certify us thereof in our said Court under your hands & Seals sending then there the said indenture & this Writ. Witness WILLIAM MOSS Clerk of the said Court at the Courthouse of the County aforesaid this 17th day of November 1808 and in the 33rd Year of the CommonWealth.
WM. MOSS Cl.

  FAIRFAX COUNTY To Wit:

  In Obedience to the within Commission, We the undersigned two of the CommonWealths justices of the said County Personally attended the said REBECKAH BECKWITH the wife of MARMADUKE B. BECKWITH the party to the indenture Hereunto annexed & have examined her Privately and apart from her said Husband as directed by the within Commission and she acknowledged the same to be her Act and Deed and freely & voluntarily relinquishes all right of dower in the lands in said indenture hereto annexed and is willing the same shall be recorded. Given under our hands & Seals this 17th day of November 1808.

     FRANCIS ADAMS (seal)
     JAS S. TRIPLETT (seal)

Pages 66-68. THIS INDENTURE made the thirteenth day of January in the Year of our Lord one thousand eight hundred & nine between GEORGE TILLET and ANNA his wife of the County of Loudoun and CommonWealth of Virginia of the one part and JAMES TILLET of the County of Fairfax & CommonWealth aforesaid of the other part. Whereas GEORGE TILLET late of the County of Fairfax aforesaid (father of the said GEORGE TILLET party hereto) died possessed of a certain Tract of land lying in the said County of Fairfax and whereas the said GEORGE TILLET the elder before he departed this life duly made & Published his last Will & testament in writing bearing date the ninth day of March One Thousand eight hundred & Six whereby he devised unto the said GEORGE TILLET the younger after payment of all his just debts and legacies, one ninth part of all the residue of his Estate both Real & Personal. Now this indenture WITNESSETH that the said GEORGE TILLET & ANNA his wife for & in consideration of the sum of Eighty Dollars lawful Money of the United States to them in hand paid by the said JAMES TILLET at & before the ensealing & delivery hereof the receipt whereof they do hereby acknowledge and thereof & of every part thereof do forever exonerate, acquit and dishcarge the said JAMES TILLET his Heirs, Executors and Administrators by these presents have granted, bargained & Sold, aliened, enfeoffed, released & confirmed and by these presents Do grant, Bargain & Sell, alien, enfeoff, release and confirm unto, the said JAS. TILLET his heirs and assigns all his the said GEORGE TILLET the Youngers one ninth part or share of and in the said tract of land lying in the said County of Fairfax of which the said GEORGE TILLET the elder died Possessed of and devised to the said GEORGE TILLET the Younger by the above in part recited Will together with all and Singular the rights, members, Liberties, Privileges, improvements, Hereditaments and appurtenances thereunto belonging or in anywise appertaining and the Reversions and Remainders, Rents, issues and Profits thereof also all the estate right, Title, possession, property, claim and demand of them the said GEORGE TILLET and ANNA his wife in Law, Equity or otherwise howsoever of, in, to or out of the premises and every part thereof. To have and To hold the said one ninth part or share of and in the Premises hereby granted with the appurtenances unto the said JAMES TILLET his heirs & assigns forever to the only proper use, benefit and behoof of the said JAMES TILLET his heirs & assigns forever. And the said GEORGE TILLET for himself and his Heirs the hereby granted premises with the appurtenances unto the said JAMES TILLET his heirs and assigns against the claim or claims of them the said GEORGE TILLET and ANNA his wife or any Person or Persons claiming by, from or under them or either of them and by, from and against all and every other Person or Persons whatsoever shall and will Warrant and forever defend by these. In WITNESS whereof the said GEORGE TILLET and ANNA his wife have hereunto set their hands & Seals the day and Year first above written.

Sealed & delivered in   GEORGE TILLET   (seal)
Presence of us   ANNA her X mark TILLET (seal)
JN. MATHIAS
BLINCOE as to GEO. TILLET
WM. CHILTON
RICHD. H. HENDERSON

At a Court held for Fairfax County the 16th day of January 1809 this Deed from GEORGE TILLET & ANN his wife to JAMES TILLET was acknowledged by the said GEORGE TILLET to be his Act and Deed and ordered to be recorded.   Teste WM. MOSS Cl.

Pages 68-73. THIS INDENTURE made this twenty eighth day of May one Thousand eight Hundred & eight between NATHANIEL ELLICOTT & ELIZABETH his wife of the Town of Occoquan, JAMES CAMPBELL & VICTORIA his wife of the Town of Petersburg and LUKE WHEELER of the Town of Norfolk, all in the State of Virginia of the one part and EDWARD WASHINGTON of the County of Fairfax State of Virginia of the other Part. WITNESSETH that the said N. ELLICOTT and ELIZABETH his wife, J. CAMPBELL and VICTORIA his wife and LUKE WHEELER, for & in consideration of the sum of two Thousand five hundred and thirty one Dollars & sixty three Cents to the said N. ELLICOTT and JAS. CAMPBELL & LUKE WHEELER in hand paid by the said EDWARD WASHINGTON the receipt whereof is hereby acknowledged have granted, bargained, Sold, Aliened and Confirmed and by these presents do grant, bargain, Sell, Alien & Confirm unto the said EDWARD WASHINGTON all that tract or Parcel of land containing three hundred & eighty three acres situate in the County of Fairfax being part of a larger tract containing five hundred and thirteen acres sold & conveyed by HENRY LEE to CHARLES LEE, three Hundred & eighty three acres of which the said CHARLES LEE sold & Conveyed to one JOHN FISHER who sold & Conveyed the same to N. ELLICOTT & ISAAC McPHERSON; the said ISAAC McPHERSON sold & conveyed his moiety of the same three hundred & eighty three acres with other property to said JAMES CAMPBELL and LUKE WHEELER by deed bearing date the 19th day of August 1799 duly recorded in the District Court at Hay Market the whole of which tract of 513 acres had been sold under a decree of the High Court of Chancery obtained against the Representatives of JOHN SEMPLE (Decd) which said three hundred & eighty three acres are bounded as follows to wit: beginning at a white oak on the north side of a drain of a branch, Corner to GODFREY as shewn to WILLIAM PAYNE the Surveyor in the Year 1789, thence South fifty five degrees East two hundred and eleven poles to a stake and near a box oak corner to land purchased by ROBERT LAWSON, thence along LAWSON'S line South thirty degrees West two hundred and fifty four poles to a red oak Corner to said LAWSON'S land on the West of the Ox Road, thence North forty eight degrees West two hundred and seventy six poles to the line of the patent, thence along the said Patent line North forty seven degrees East Twenty five poles to Corner of land sold to EDWARD WASHINGTON and the beginning of PAYNE'S Survey, thence in a straight line to the beginning; and the Reversion and Reversions, Rents, Issues and Profits thereof together with all Houses, Woods, Ways, Water Courses, Commodities, advantages and Hereditaments to the said tract of land belonging or in any manner appertaining. To have and To Hold the said Tract of land hereby granted together with all Singular the Premises and appurtenances thereunto belonging unto him the said EDWARD WASHINGTON his heirs and assigns forever to the only use and behoof of him the said EDWARD WASHINGTON and his heirs & assigns forever and the said N. ELLICOTT, JAMES CAMPBELL & LUKE WHEELER for themselves & their Heirs unto the said EDWARD WASHINGTON & his heirs & assigns the said Tract of land & its appurtenances hereby granted will warrant against them the said N. ELLICOTT, JAS. CAMPBELL & LUKE WHEELER & their Heirs & all persons whatsoever claiming by, from, through or under them & forever defend agt all & every person or persons whatsoever. In WITNESS whereof the parties hereunto have to these presents severally set their Hands & Seals the day & Year first above written.
Signed Sealed & delivered

In Presence of	N. ELLICOTT	(seal)
BENNIAH WILLETT to L. W.	ELIZABETH ELLICOTT	(seal)
BERNARD GILPIN L.W. & N. E. & E. E.	JAMES CAMPBELL	(seal)
ALFRED P. GILPIN for L.W. & N.E. & E.E.	VICTORIA CAMPBELL	(seal)
ROBERT WELSH	LUKE WHEELER	(seal)

Recd. this 28th May 1808 of EDWARD WASHINGTON the consideration in the within Deed mentioned.

Teste   ELLICOTT, CAMPBELL & WHEELER
ALFRED P. GILPIN
B. G. GILPIN
ROBERT WELSH

TOWN OF PETERSBURG To Wit:

I certify that JAMES CAMPBELL one of the grantors in the above Deed of Indenture personally appeared before [me] as Mayor of the said Town of Petersburgh & acknowledged the Signing & Sealing by him thereto made to be his Act & Deed & that he delivered it as such & the said VICTORIA the wife of the said JAS. CAMPBELL also acknowledged the signing of the same to be her Act & Deed July 2nd 1808.   JAS. BYRNE Mayor

At a Court held for Fairfax County the Sixteenth day of January 1809 this Deed from NATHANIEL ELLICOTT and ELIZABETH his wife, JAMES CAMPBELL and VICTORIA his wife and LUKE WHEELER to EDWARD WASHINGTON and a receipt hereon endorsed were proved to be the act & Deed of the said NATHANIEL ELLICOTT and LUKE WHEELER by the oaths of BERNARD GILPIN, ALFRED P. GILPIN and ROBERT WELSH and the same having been duly acknowledged by the said JAMES CAMPBELL and VICTORIA his wife before JAMES BYRNE Mayor of the Town of Petersburg and Certified by him is on motion of the said EDWARD WASHINGTON together with the certificate hereon endorsed and a Commission & Return hereto annexed for taking the acknowledgment and privy examination of the said ELIZABETH are ordered to be recorded
Teste WM. MOSS Cl.

FAIRFAX COUNTY To Wit:

The CommonWealth of Virginia to ROBT. H. HOOE & BERNARD HOOE JR Gentlemen Justices of the County of Prince William Greeting: Whereas NATHANIEL ELLICOTT and ELIZABETH his wife by their certain indenture of Bargain & Sale bearing date the second day of May 1805 have Sold & Conveyed unto EDWARD WASHINGTON of Fairfax County the fee simple estate of a certain tract of land containing Three Hundred & eighty three acres with the appurtenances situate, lying & being in the said County of Fairfax and Whereas the said ELIZABETH ELLICOTT cannot conveniently travel to our said County Court of Fairfax to make acknowledgment of the sale conveyance therefore we do give unto you or any two or more of you Power to receive the acknowledgment which the said ELIZABETH ELLICOTT shall be willing to make before you of the Conveyance aforesaid contained in the said indenture which is hereunto annexed and we do therefore desire you or any two or more of you personally to go to the said ELIZABETH ELLICOTT & receive her acknowledgment of the same and examine her Privily and apart from the said NATHANIEL ELLICOTT her Husband whither she doth the same freely and voluntarily without his Persuasions or threats and whether she be willing the said indenture together with this Commission shall be recorded in our said Court & when you have received her acknowledgment & examined her as aforesaid that you distinctly & openly certify us thereof in our said Court under your hands & Seals sending them there the said indenture & this Writ. Witness WILLIAM MOSS Clerk of our said Court at the Courthouse of the County aforesd. this 14th day of January 1809 & in the 33rd year of the CommonWealth.
WM. MOSS Cl.

PRINCE WILLIAM COUNTY To Wit:

Pursuant to the within Dedimus we ROBT. H. HOOE & BERNARD HOOE JR two justices of the Peace for the County afsd waited on the within named ELIZABETH ELLICOTT and she acknowledged the annexed indenture to be her act & Deed & we further examined her Privily and apart from the sd. NATHL. ELLICOTT her husband & she declared the same to have been done freely & voluntarily without the persuasion or threats of him the sd. NATHL. & that she is willing the same together with this commission shall be recorded in the County Court of Fairfax. Given under our hands & Seals this 14th day of January 1809.

Truly Recorded and   ROBERT H. HOOE   (seal)
Examined Teste WM. MOSS Cl.   BERND. HOOE JR   (seal)

Pages 73-75. THIS INDENTURE made the twenty sixth day of August in the year of our Lord one Thousand eight hundred & eight between JAMES WAUGH SR of the County of Fairfax & State of Virginia of the one part and JOSEPH HICKMAN of Prince George's County in the State of Maryland of the other Part. WITNESSETH that the said JAMES WAUGH for & in consideration of the sum of Three Hundred twenty two Pounds Money of Virginia Currency to him the said JAMES WAUGH in hand well & truly paid the receipt whereof is hereby acknowledged he the said JAMES WAUGH hath granted, bargained & Sold and by these presents doth grant, bargain & Sell unto the said JOSEPH HICKMAN his heirs & assigns all that messuage, tenement, tract or Parcel of land situate, lying & being in the County of Fairfax and bounded as follows (Viz:) Beginning at a cedar (a parcel of stones around it) corner of MAUZEY, running thence South nineteen East two Hundred and six poles to an Hickory on the Bank of Popeshead below and near the Mouth of a small branch another corner to said MAUZEY, thence down the said Popeshead Run and binding there with agreeable to the several Courses and Meanders thereof, South seventy one West sixty four poles, thence South nine East eleven Poles, thence South sixty eight West eighteen Poles, thence South fifteen & half degrees East twelve Poles, thence South fifty two West twenty nine and an half poles, thence leaving the said run North Nineteen West two hundred & twenty two poles to a red oak sapling the East side of small branch and near the same, thence North sixty three and an half degrees East one Hundred and twenty poles to the beginning containing one hundred & sixty one acres and also all Trees, Woods and under Woods, water, water courses, profits, Commodities, advantages, hereditaments and appurtenances whatsoever to the said Messuage, tenement, tract or parcel of land belonging or in anywise appertaining and the Reversion and Reversions, Remainder & Remainders, issues, Profits and Rents (the Rents now due and unpaid and for the Present Year excepted) of the sd. premises and of every Part & Parcel thereof and all the estate right, Title, interest, claim and demand (except the Rents before excepted) and the right & privilege of a Road or passway through the said Tract or parcel of land for the use the said JAMES WAUGH his Heirs &c to pass through the upper or north end following the present Road which passes by a blacksmiths Shop now on the said Messuage, Tenement, Tract or Parcel of Land, whatsoever of him the said JAMES WAUGH of, in and to the said Messuage, Tenement, Tract or Parcel of land & Premises and every part thereof To Have and To Hold the said Messuage, Tenement, Tract or Parcel of land & all and Singular other the Premises above mentioned and every part & parcel thereof with the appurtenances unto the said JOSEPH HICKMAN his heirs & assigns to the only Proper use and behoof of the said JOSEPH HICKMAN his heirs & assigns forever. And the said JAMES WAUGH, for himself & his heirs the said Messuage, Tenement, tract or parcel of land and premises & every part thereof against him & his heirs to the said JOSEPH HICKMAN his heirs & assigns shall & will warrant & forever defend by these presents. In WITNESS whereof the said JAMES WAUGH hath hereunto set his hand & Seal the day and Year first written.
WITNESSES   JAS. WAUGH (seal)
TOWNSHEND WAUGH
ALEXN. WAUGH
WM. KINCHELOE
        At a Court held for Fairfax County the 16th day of January 1809 JAMES WAUGH acknowledged this Deed to JOSEPH HICKMAN to be his Act & Deed which is ordered to be Recorded.   Teste WM. MOSS Cl.

Pages 75-77. THIS INDENTURE made this eighteenth day of April in the year of our Lord one Thousand Eight hundred & eight between LEONARD BARKER & ANNA his wife of the County of Fairfax & State of Virginia of the one part and THOMAS PARSONS of the other part: WITNESSETH that the said LEONARD BARKER & ANNA his wife for & in consideration of the Sum of one hundred & ten Dollars to them in hand paid by the said THOMAS PARSONS before the Sealing and delivery of these presents the Receipt whereof is hereby acknowledged have granted, bargained & Sold, aliened & conformed and by these presents do grant, bargain &

Sell, Alien and Confirm unto the said THOMAS PARSONS his heirs & assigns forever the upper part of the Lott No. 22 in the Town of Colchester beginning at a Peach tree marked TB and running thence on the West side of a line of fence to a Gate-Post standing on Essex Street, thence up the said Street to the corner of Lott No. 24, thence with Lott 24 to the corner of Lott 28, thence with Lott 28 to the aforesaid peach tree marked TB and also all Houses, Buildings, improvements, advantages and appurtenances whatsoever to the said upper part of said Lott of land belonging or in anywise appertaining and also the Reversion & Reversions, Remainder & Remainders, Rents & profits of the said Premises and also all the estate right, Title, claim & Demand whatever of them the said LEONARD BARKER & ANNA his wife of, in & to the said Lott of land and every part thereof as above bounded. To have and To hold the said Lott of land and Premises above mentioned and every part and parcel thereof with the appurtenances unto the said THOMAS PARSONS his heirs & assigns to the only proper use & behoof of him the said THOMAS PARSONS his heirs & assigns forever. And the said LEONARD BARKER and ANNA his wife for them and their Heirs the said Lott of land and premises and every Part thereof against the claim of themselves & their Heirs and against all & every other person and persons whatever to the said THOMAS PARSONS his Heirs and assigns shall and will warrant and defend forever by these presents. In WITNESS whereof the said LEONARD BARKER and ANNA his Wife have hereunto set their hands & Seals the day & Year first above written.   LEONARD BARKER   (seal)
                                                           ANNA BARKER   (seal)
        At a Court held for Fairfax County the 16th day of January 1809 LEONARD BARKER and ANNE his wife (she being first privately and again in open Court examined and thereto consenting) acknowledged this Deed to THOMAS PARSONS to be their act and Deed which is ordered to be Recorded.   Teste WM. MOSS Cl.

Pages 77-80. THIS INDENTURE made this twenty ninth day of May in the Year of our Lord Christ One Thousand eight Hundred & eight between EDWARD WASHINGTON & ELIZABETH his wife of the County of Fairfax State of Virginia of the one part ALFRED P. GILPIN of the second part and NATHANIEL ELLICOTT of the Town of Occoquan in the County of Prince William, JAMES CAMPBELL of the Town of Petersburg and LUKE WHEELER of the Borough of Norfolk, Merchants and Partners trading at the aforesaid Town of Occoquan under the Style and firm of ELLICOTT, CAMPBELL & WHEELER of the third & last part. Whereas the said ELLICOTT C. & WHEELER on or about the 28th day of this same Month April in conformity to Public notice thereof given set to Sale at Public Auction certain Lotts, Lands and other Estates in & about the said Town of Occoquan the terms of which Sale were "that the purchaser should give Bonds for the Purchase Money Payable in one, two & three Years and to secure the Payment thereof by Deed in Trust upon the purchased premises" at which Sale the aforesaid EDWD. WASHINGTON became the Purchaser of one of the Tracts of land so sold Situated in the County of Fairfax as will be herein after described estimated to contain three hundred & Eighty three acres at the Price of six Dollars & sixty one cents pr. acre which amounts to the Sum of $2531 62/100 agreeable to the Bonds which the said EDWARD WASHINGTON hath therefore given. Now this indenture WITNESSETH that the aforesaid EDWARD WASHINGTON & ELIZABETH his wife for the objects aforesaid and for and in the further consideration of one Dollar to him in hand paid by the aforesaid ALFRED P. GILPIN the receipt whereof is hereby acknowledged hath granted, bargain'd, Sold, aliened and by these presents doth grant, bargain, Sell, Alien and Confirm unto the said ALFRED P. GILPIN all that tract or parcel of land containing three hundred & Eighty three acres situated in the County of Fairfax about three Miles from the Occoquan Mills the History and titles whereof will be found particularly described in a certain Deed of Indenture from the said ELLICOTT C. & WHEELER bearing date the 25th of the present Month May to the said EDWARD WASHINGTON. Beginning for the boundaries thereof at a white oak on the north side of a drain of a branch corner to GODFREY as shewn to WILLIAM PAYNE the Surveyor in the year 1789, thence South fifty five degrees east two hundred and eleven poles to a stake and near a box oak corner to Land Purchased by ROBERT LAWSON, thence along LAWSONS line South thirty Degrees West two Hundred fifty four poles to a red oak another Corner of LAWSONS on the West of the Ox road, thence North forty eight degrees, West two Hundred & Seventy six poles to the line of the patent, thence along the said

Patent line North forty seven degrees east twenty five poles to corner of land sold EDWARD WASHINGTON and the beginning of PAYNES survey, thence in a straight line to the beginning and the reversion & reversions, rents, issues and profits thereof together with all Houses, Woods, Ways, water courses, commodities, advantages and hereditaments to the said tract of land belonging or in anywise appertaining. To have and to Hold the said Tract of land hereby granted with all singular the Premises and appurtenances thereto belonging unto to him the said ALFRED P. GILPIN and his heirs & assigns forever to the only proper use and behoof of him the said ALFRED P. GILPIN and his heirs forever upon Trust nevertheless and it is hereby declared to be the true intent and meaning of these presents that if the said EDWARD WASHINGTON & ELIZABETH his wife, his Heirs, Executors or Administrators, shall well & truly pay and satisfy the said ELLICOTT, CAMPBELL & WHEELER their heirs, Executors, Administrators or assigns the several Bonds which he has given them for the payment of the said Lands at the times and periods which the same are made payable then this indenture is to cease & to be of no effect and the property hereby conveyed or meant to be conveyed shall revert to the said EDWARD WASHINGTON and ELIZABETH his wife in as full and ample a manner as if this Deed had never been made. But if the said EDWARD WASHINGTON, his Heirs, Executors or Administrators shall fail to pay the Bonds for the purchase money or either of them as they respectively fall due then it shall be Lawfull and full power & authority is hereby given to the said ALFRED P. GILPIN if thereto required by the said ELLICOTT, CAMPBELL & WHEELER or either of them or their Legal representatives to advertize, set up and Sell after Two Months previous Public Notice all or so much of the said Tract of land with its appurtenances as shall & May be sufficient to Pay the Debt or part of the Debt then due and any surplus if any after the Bonds aforesaid be fully paid remain it is to be paid the said EDWARD WASHINGTON his Heirs, Executors, Administrators or assigns. In WITNESS whereof the Parties to these presents have hereunto Subscribed their names and affixed their Seals on the day & Year first above written.

Signed Sealed & Delivered	EDWARD WASHINGTON (seal)
In Presence of	BETSY WASHINGTON (seal)
G. B. GILPIN	ALFRED P. GILPIN (seal)
BENNIAH WILLETT	ELLICOTT, CAMPBELL & WHEELER (seal)
ROBERT WELSH	

At a Court held for Fairfax County the 16th day of January 1809 this Deed from EDWARD WASHINGTON and BETSY his wife to ALFRED P. GILPIN in Trust for the use of ELLICOTT, CAMPBELL & WHEELER was proved to be the Act & Deed of the said EDWARD WASHINGTON, ALFRED P. GILPIN and NATHANIEL ELLICOTT for ELLICOTT, CAMPBELL & WHEELER by the oaths of BERNARD GILPIN, BENNIAH WILLETT & ROBERT WELCH which together with the Commission & Return hereto annexed for taking the acknowledgment & privy examination of the said BETSEY are ordered to be Recorded.

Teste WM. MOSS Cl.

PAGE 81. [Page left blank]

Pages 82 & 83. THIS INDENTURE made this fifteenth day of June in the Year one Thousand eight hundred & eight between LEWIS SUMMERS of the County of Fairfax and CommonWealth of Virginia of the one part & FRANCIS KEENE of the same County & State of the other part. WITNESSETH that the said LEWIS SUMMERS for and in consideration of the sum of Twelve Hundred Dollars lawfull Money to him in hand paid the receipt whereof he doth hereby acknowledge (and as will more fully appear by reference to an agreement entered into between the said LEWIS SUMMERS and a certain JAMES WAUGH JR dated the twenty first day of November in the Year One Thousand Eight Hundred & one for the land hereafter granted & demised & which said agreement hath been since assigned by the said JAMES WAUGH JR to the said FRANCIS KEENE) hath granted, bargained & Sold and by these presents do bargain & Sell unto the said FRANCIS KEENE his heirs & assigns a certain tract or parcel of land situate, lying and being upon the upper side of Bull Run in the County of Fairfax in the State aforesaid containing one hundred & sixty six acres be the same more or less and bounded as follows Viz: beginning at the Mouth of a branch called Johny More at a marked black Walnut tree standing on the bank of the lower side of the Mouth of said branch being a corner tree to a

tract of land formerly taken up by a certain JOHN WAUGH and extending along his line North Twenty eight degrees east two Hundred & twenty six poles to a small red oak on the side of a Stony Hill in the said WAUGH'S line, thence West one hundred & Twenty poles to a small Hickory & box oak on the side of a stony Hill, thence South seventeen degrees West thirty poles wanting nine links to a small black oak on a level, thence South fifty two degrees West one hundred & forty poles to a white oak on the side of Bull Run, from thence down the said run the several Courses & Meanders thereof to the first station & in the same tract of land which GEORGE SUMMERS & ANN SMITH SUMMERS his wife by Deed bearing date the fifteenth day of February in the year one Thousand eight hundred conveyed to the said LEWIS SUMMERS as reference being had thereunto will more fully appear. To Have and To Hold the said Tract or Parcel of land and premises with all and singular the appurtenances thereunto appertaining or in anywise belonging unto the said FRANCIS KEENE his heirs & assigns & to his & their own proper use and behoof forever and the said LEWIS SUMMERS and his Heirs the aforesaid tract or parcel of land & premises with all and Singular the appurtenances unto the said FRANCIS KEENE his heirs & assigns doth hereby warrant and forever will defend against the claim or demand of the said LEWIS SUMMERS his heirs or assigns and all and every other person or persons whatsoever. In WITNESS whereof the said LEWIS SUMMERS hath hereunto set his hand & affixed his Seal this day & date first mentioned.
Signed Sealed & Delivered in
the Presence of   L. SUMMERS (seal)
WILLI. PADGETT
GEO. SUMMERS
JAS. H. BLACK, CHARLES OGDEN
        At a Court held for Fairfax County the 10th day of January 1800 LEWIS SUMMERS acknowledged this Deed to FRANCIS KEENE to be his Act and Deed which is ordered to be recorded.   Teste WM. MOSS Cl.

Pages 84 & 85. THIS INDENTURE made this seventh Day of June in the year of our Lord one thousand eight hundred & eight between HENRY LEE SR and HENRY LEE JR both of the County of Westmoreland and CommonWealth of Virginia of the one part and RICHARD BLAND LEE of the County of Fairfax & CommonWealth aforesaid of the other part. WITNESSETH that for & in consideration of the sum of twenty five Thousand dollars lawfull Money of Virginia to them the said HENRY LEE SR & HENRY LEE JR in hand paid by the said RICHARD BLAND LEE the receipt whereof they the said HENRY LEE SR & HENRY LEE JR do hereby acknowledge they the said HENRY LEE SR and HENRY LEE JR have granted, bargained & Sold, Aliened & Confirmed and by these presents do grant, bargain & Sell, alien & Confirm unto the said RICHARD BLAND LEE his heirs & assigns forever all that tract or parcel of land situate, lying and being in the County of Fairfax and CommonWealth aforesaid commonly called Langley Farm containing sixteen hundred acres be the same more or less being all the estate in the said County of Fairfax which was settled on the said HENRY LEE JR by his sd. father HENRY LEE SR and his Mother MATILDA by a Deed bearing date of the tenth day of August in the year of our Lord one Thousand seven hundred and ninety as will more fully appear by reference thereto on record in the office of the general Court of said CommonWealth. To have and To hold all the above described tract or parcel of land with all and every its appurtenances unto him the said RICHARD BLAND LEE his heirs & assigns forever. And for themselves and their heirs the said HENRY LEE SR and HENRY LEE JR unto the said RICHARD BLAND LEE his heirs and assigns all the above described tract or parcel of land with all & every its appurtenances against the claim or claims of them the said HENRY LEE SR and HENRY LEE JR & against the claim or claims of all and every Person whatsoever will, shall and do forever warrant & defend by these presents. In testimony of the Premises the Parties have hereunto set their Hands & Seals the Day and Year first above mentioned.
Signed Sealed & delivered   HENRY LEE   (seal)
in the Presence of   HENRY LEE JR   (seal)
CUTHBERT POWELL
WM. CHILTON
CHS. FENTON MERCER as to H. LEE

JN. B. ARMISTEAD
WM. MAFFITT
BURDET ESKRIDGE as to HENRY LEE JR
McCARTY FITZHUGH
JOHN KING, WALK MUSE, JOHN RANDALL
BAILEY POWELL, THOS. DARNE JR as to H. LEE JR
JOHN HOGLAND

At a Court held for Fairfax County the twentieth December 1808 this Deed from HENRY LEE SR and HENRY LEE JR to RICHARD B. LEE was proved to be the act & Deed of the said HENRY LEE JR by the oath of WILLM. MAFFITT, BAYLEY POWELL and JOHN HOGLAND Witnesses hereto & ordered to be certified. And at a Court held for the sd. County the 16th January 1809 the same was proved to be the act and Deed of the said HENRY LEE by the oaths of WILLIAM CHILTON & JOHN B. ARMISTEAD and ordered to be certified as to the said HENRY LEE and recorded as to the said HENRY LEE JR and at a Court continued & held for the said County the 17th January 1809 the same was further proved to be the act & deed of the said HENRY LEE by the oath of CUTHBERT POWELL another Witness hereto & ordered to be recorded.
Teste WM. MOSS Cl.

Pages 86-88. THIS INDENTURE made this Eleventh day of October in the Year of our Lord one Thousand Eight hundred and eight between WILLIAM HERBERT, NICHOLAS FITZHUGH and EDMUND J. LEE of the Town & County of Alexandria in the District of Columbia excutors of the last Will & Testament of RICHARD CONWAY deceased of the one part and WILLIAM DEVAUGHN of the County of Fairfax State of Virginia of the other Part. WITNESSETH: Whereas the said RICHARD CONWAY did by his last will and Testament bearing date the 5th Day of June in the Year One Thousand eight hundred and four order, authorise, empower and direct the said WILLIAM HERBERT, NICHOLAS FITZHUGH and EDMUND J. LEE (who by his last Will & Testament as aforesaid were appointed his executors) should sell certain parts of his Real estate therein left to be sold and which was not otherwise disposed of by the Codicil attached to the same and bearing date the seventeenth day of November in the year eighteen hundred & six which together with the said Will was duly proven and recorded in the Orphans Court of the County of Alexandria. Now this indenture withesseth that the said WILLIAM HERBERT, NICHOLAS FITZHUGH and EDMUND J. LEE Executors as aforesaid for and in consideration of the Premises & of the sum of Five hundred & twenty five 00/100 Dollars to him in hand paid at and before the Sealing and delivery of these presents the receipt whereof is hereby acknowledged have granted, bargained & Sold and by these presents do grant, bargain & Sell unto the said WILLIAM DEVAUGHN his heirs & assigns forever a certain Tract or parcel of land situate, lying and being in the County of Fairfax and State of Virginia adjoining the Ravensworth Tract and bounded as follows to wit: beginning in the line of Ravensworth at two small Spanish oaks corner to the land Sold MRS WASHINGTON of Hayfield, thence along said Ravensworth line North seventy six poles to a stake, thence North eighty eight and half West one hundred & thirty seven poles to a stake and several Saplins, thence South seventy six poles to a stake and several marked Hickorys in the line of the land Sold [to] MRS WASHINGTON, thence along said line South eighty eight & a half West one hundred & thirty seven poles to the beginning containing sixty five acres. To Have and To Hold the said premises with all and Singular the appurtenances thereto unto him the said WILLIAM DEVAUGHN his heirs & assigns to the only use and behoof of him his heirs and assigns forever and the said WILLIAM HERBERT, NICHOLAS FITZHUGH and EDMUND J. LEE executors as aforesaid do Covenant, Promise and agree to and with the said WILLIAM DEVAUGHN his heirs and assigns that they will forever warrant and defend the said premises against the claim and demand of all and every person or persons claiming by, through, from or under them or either of them in testimony whereof the said WILLIAM HERBERT, NICHOLAS FITZHUGH and EDMUND J. LEE have hereunto set their Hands & Seals the day & Year before written.
Sealed & Delivered in
Presence of   WM. HERBERT   (seal)
GEO. YOUNGS   NS. FITZHUGH   (seal)
WM. HERBERT JR all three   EDM J. LEE   (seal)

N. HERBERT
R. J. TAYLOR
C. G. BROADWATER to E. J. L.

At a Court held for Fairfax County the 17th day of October 1808 this Deed from WILLIAM HERBERT, NICHOLAS FITZHUGH and EDMUND J. LEE Executors of RICHARD CONWAY deceased to WILLIAM DEVAUGHN was proved to be the Act and Deed of the said Executors by the oaths of WILLIAM HERBERT JR and ROBERT J. TAYLOR Witnesses hereto and ordered to be Certified. And at a Court continued & held for the said County the 17th Day of January 1809 the same was further proved by the oath of GEORGE YOUNGS another Witness hereto and ordered to be recorded.   Teste WM. MOSS Cl.

Pages 88-91. THIS INDENTURE made this 7th day of November in the Year of our Lord eighteen hundred & eight between CUTHBERT POWELL & CATHARINE his wife of the one part and JOHN JACOB FROBEL of the other part, the first party resident in the Town of Alexandria, the last in the county of Fairfax. WITNESSETH that the said CUTHBERT POWELL & CATHARINE his wife for and in consideration of the Sum of Two hundred & forty three Dollars & seventy five Cents to them in hand paid by the said JN. JACOB FROBEL the receipt whereof is hereby acknowledged and of which they do hereby forever acquit the said JN. JACOB FROBEL his heirs, Executors and Admins by these presents have granted, bargained, Sold, aliened, enfeoffed and confirmed and by these presents do grant, bargain & Sell, alien, enfeoff & confirm unto the said JN. JACOB FROBEL his heirs & assigns forever all that tract or parcel of Ground lying and being in the County of Fairfax & State of Virginia and bounded as follows: beginning at a mark'd black Gum standing in or near the line of MATTHEWS Patent, a corner of said POWELLS Purchase of THOMAS RICHARDS, running thence North eighty three west ninety seven & 3/4 poles to a stake in the line of said FROBELS Purchase of JAMES H. HOOE and opposite to the barn Door of said FROBELL, thence with the line of JAMES H. HOOE'S Purchase of said POWELL North 1°, West 22 1/2 poles to a stake in the line of HOOES Purchase of SANFORD, thence with said line South 89° East Ninety eight & 1/2 poles to a stake in an old field, thence South thirty one & a half poles to the beginning containing sixteen & a quarter acres, the same being the balance of my Purchase of RICHARDS after the sale of Ten & a half acres thereof to JAMES H. HOOE and embracing in addition thereto one and a quarter acres of of the lott Purchased by me of JAMES H. HOOE adjoining it. To have and To Hold the aforesaid tract of land & premises & all and Singular the appurtenances thereunto belonging or in anywise appertaining to him the said JN. JACOB FROBEL his Heirs and assigns forever. And the said CUTHBERT POWELL & CATHARINE his wife for themselves and their Heirs the said Parcel of land with all and singular the premises & appurtenances aforementioned unto the said JN. JACOB FROBEL his heirs & assigns forever free from the claim or claims of them the said CUTHBERT POWELL & CATHARINE his wife or either of them, their or either of their heirs and of all & every other person or persons claiming under them or either of them shall, will & do warrant & forever defend by these presents and also further bind themselves & their heirs to the said JN. JACOB FROBEL his heirs & assigns to repay the purchase Money if said title is not good & sufficient or in the same proportion for any part thereof of which the said JN. JACOB FROBEL his heirs or assigns may be legally dispossessed of on account of such defect. In WITNESS whereof the said CUTHBERT POWELL & CATHARINE his wife have hereunto set their hands & Seals the Day & Year first before written.

Signed, Sealed & Delivered   CUTHBERT POWELL   (seal)
in the Presence of   CATHARINE POWELL   (seal)
EDM J. LEE
N. HERBERT
CH. SIMMS
THO. SWANN

At a Court continued and held for Fairfax County the Seventeenth Day of January 1809 CUTHBERT POWELL acknowledged this Deed to JOHN J. FROBEL to be his Act and Deed which together with a Commission & Return hereto annexed for taking the acknowledgment & privy examination of CATHARINE POWELL wife of the said CUTHBERT are ordered to be Recorded.
                    Teste WM. MOSS Cl.

FAIRFAX COUNTY To Wit:

The CommonWealth of Virginia to GEORGE GILPIN, JOSEPH DEAN & JONAH THOMPSON Gentlemen justices of the County of Alexandria Greeting: Whereas CUTHBERT POWELL and CATHARINE his wife by their Certain indenture of Bargain & Sale bearing date the Seventh Day of November 1808 have Sold & conveyed unto JOHN JACOB FROBEL the fee simple Estate of a certain Tract or Parcel of land containing 16-1/4 acres with the appurtenances situate, lying and being in the said County of Fairfax and whereas the said CATHARINE cannot conveniently travel to our Court in the said County of Fairfax to make acknowledgment of the said convey-ance therefore we do give unto you or any two or more of you Power to receive the acknow-ledgment which the said CATHARINE shall be willing to make before you of the conveyance aforesaid contained in the said indenture which is hereunto annexed; and we do therefore desire you or any two or more of you personally to go to the said CATHARINE and receive her acknowledgment of the same and examine her privily and apart from the said CUTHBERT POWELL her husband whither she doth the same freely and voluntarily without his persuasions or threats And whither she be willing the said indenture together with this Commission shall be recorded in our said Court and when you have received her acknow-ledgment and examined her as aforesaid that you distinctly and openly certify us thereof in our said Court under your hands & seals sending then & there the said indenture and this writ. WITNESS WM. MOSS Clerk of our said Court at the Courthouse of the County aforesaid this 9th Day of November 1808 and in the 33rd Year of the CommonWealth.

WM. MOSS Cl.

DISTRICT OF COLUMBIA, County of Alexandria To Wit:

Agreeable to the within Commission to us directed we did Proceed Privately to examine the said CATHARINE the wife of CUTHBERT POWELL separate & apart from her husband and she avow'd to us that she made the Conveyance within mentioned freely and voluntarily without the threats or persuasions of her husband and was willing that the indenture together with the Commission be recorded. Given under our Hands & Seals this 11th Day of November 1808.

GEORGE GILPIN (seal)
JOSEPH DEAN

Pages 92-94. THIS INDENTURE made this twentieth Day of February in the Year of Our Lord one Thousand eight hundred & Nine between GILES FITZHUGH of the County of Fairfax and State of Virginia of the one part and NICHOLAS FITZHUGH of the Town & County of Alexandria and District of Columbia of the other part. WITNESSETH that the said GILES FITZHUGH for and in consideration of the sum of Two Thousand two hundred & seventeen Dollars to him in hand paid by the said NICHOLAS FITZHUGH before the Sealing & Delivery of these presents the Receipt whereof is hereby acknowledged & the said NICHOLAS FITZHUGH hereby exonerated and acquitted from the payment thereof Hath granted, bargained & Sold and by these presents doth bargain & Sell unto the said NICHOLAS FITZHUGH a certain Tract or Parcel of land situate, lying and being in the County of Fairfax and State of Virginia and bounded as follows to wit: beginning at a stake in the line of WEST, PEARSON & HARRISON where it crosses the Rolling Road and corner to the land Sold by the Executors of RICHARD CONWAY Deceased to CHARLES SIMMS, thence along the line of the said WEST, PEARSON and HARRISON South one & three quarter Degrees East for nine poles to an ancient corner white oak now dead around which are marked three saplings as pointers. thence South twenty nine and one quarter degrees West two hundred & forty five poles to an antient corner marked white oak which is a corner to ASHFORD & marked "MA" & also a corner to the land Purchased by LUND WASHINGTON deceased from the aforesaid RICHARD CONWAY, thence along the said WASHINGTON'S line South eighty eight and an half degrees West one hundred & Seventy nine & an half poles to a stake around which are marked several Hickories Corner to the land bought of WILLIAM POTTER from the aforesaid Executors of the said CONWAY & by the said POTTER sold to WILLIAM DEVAUGHN, thence North seventy six poles along the said POTTERS line to a stake and several marked Saplings, thence along another of the said POTTERS lines South eighty eight & an half Degrees West one hundred & thirty seven poles to a stake in the line of the tract of land called Ravensworth, thence along the Ravensworth line North seventy six poles to COOKS corner near a marked Spanish oak, thence along the said COOKS line North seventy seven & an half

degrees East one hundred & ninety four & an half poles to two marked small Hickories, COOKS Corner & in the line of the aforesaid SIMMS, thence along the said SIMMS' line to his corner in the middle of the aforesd. Rolling Road, thence binding with the said SIMMS' lines down the said Road along the meanders & in the middle thereof to wit: North sixty Degrees East twenty two poles, thence North eighty one & an half East twenty four poles, thence South seventy six Degrees East thirty one poles, thence North eighty three & an half Degrees East thirty two poles, thence North Seventy five Degrees East twenty poles, thence North thirty nine Degrees East eighteen Poles, thence North thirty five and an half Degrees East fourteen poles, thence North fifty three Degrees East twelve poles, thence North seventy six Degrees East thirty two poles, thence North seventy four and an half Degrees East fifty four poles, thence North fifty-five Degrees East eight poles to the beginning containing three hundred & ninety eight and an half acres be the same more or less with all and Singular the appurtenances to the same in any manner appertaining or belonging which said tract of land the said GILES FITZHUGH purchased from the aforesaid Executors of RICHARD COUNTY (*sic*) and was conveyed to him by Deed dated the fifteenth day of February 1809. To have and To hold the said Tract of land with its appurtenances to the said NICHOLAS FITZHUGH his heirs & assigns forever to the only proper use and behoof of the said NICHOLAS FITZHUGH his heirs & assigns forever. And the said GILES FITZHUGH hereby convenants and agrees to & with the said NICHOLAS FITZHUGH his heirs & assigns forever that he the said GILES FITZHUGH will forever warrant & Defend the said tract of land with its appurtenances to the said NICHOLAS FITZHUGH his heirs and assigns forever against the claim or Demand of any person or Persons claiming by, through, from or under him the said GILES FITZHUGH. In testimony whereof the said GILES FITZHUGH hath hereunto set his Hand & Seals the Day & Year first within written.
Signed Sealed & Delivered
in Presence of   GILES FITZHUGH (seal)
RCHD. FITZHUGH
SM. MOSS
WM. HERBERT JR
HUGH W. MINOR
    At a Court held for Fairfax County the Twentienth Day of February 1809 GILES FITZHUGH acknowledged this Deed to NICHOLAS FITZHUGH to be his Act and deed which is ordered to be recorded.   Teste WM. MOSS Cl.

Pages 95-97. THIS INDENTURE made this twenty seventh day of August in the Year of our Lord one Thousand Eight Hundred and Eight between JOSEPH HIGHMAN of Prince Georges County & State of Maryland of the one part and ALEXANDER WAUGH of the County of Fairfax and State of Virginia of the other part. WITNESSETH that the said JOSEPH HIGHMAN in order to secure the payment of the following debt to wit: the sum of five hundred & ninety nine Dollars Current Money of the United States due to JAMES WAUGH JR of Fairfax County & State of Virginia aforesaid. And in Consideration of the sum of one Dollar to him in hand paid by the said ALEXANDER WAUGH at & before the ensealing and Delivery of these presents the receipt whereof is hereby acknowledged he the said JOSEPH HIGHMAN hath given, granted, bargained & Sold and by these presents doth grant, bargain & Sell unto the said ALEXANDER WAUGH all that Messuage, Tenement, Tract or Parcel of Land situate, lying and being in the said County of Fairfax and bounded as follows Vizt: beginning at a Cedar bush (a parcel of stones around it) Corner of MAUZEY, running thence South nineteen east two hundred & six poles to an Hickory on the bank of Popeshead Run below and near the Mouth of a small branch, another corner to said MAUZEY, thence down the said Popeshead Run & binding therewith agreeable to the several courses & Meanders thereof South Seventy one west sixty four poles, thence South nine east Eleven poles, thence South sixty eight West eighteen poles, thence South fifteen & an half Degrees east twelve poles, thence South fifty two West twenty nine & an half poles, thence leaving the said run North nineteen West two hundred & twenty Poles to a red oak sapling on the east side of a small branch & near the same, thence North sixty three & an half Degrees east one hundred and twenty poles to the beginning containing one hundred & sixty one acres also all the Trees, Woods, under woods, Ways, Waters,

WaterCourses, profits, commodities & advantages, Hereditaments & appurtenances to these Messuage, Tenement, Tract or Parcel of Land belonging or in anywise appertaining and the Reversion & Reversions, Remainder & Remainders, Rents, Issues & Profits thereof and of every part & parcel thereof and also all the estate right, Title, interest, Trust, property claim & demand whatsoever both at Law & in equity of him the said JOSEPH HICKMAN in, to or out of the said lands, Tenements, Hereditaments & premises. To Have and To Hold the said messuage, Tenement, tract or parcel of Land and all & Singular other the Premises herein before mentioned to be hereby granted with their & every of their appurtenances unto the said ALEXANDER WAUGH his Heirs, Executors, Administrators & assigns forever upon Trust nevertheless that the said ALEXN. WAUGH shall as soon as conviently he can after the expiration of two Years from the date hereof (having first advertised the time & place of the said Property aforementioned in some Public News paper published in the Town of Alexandria) proceed to sell the same to the highest bidder for the best price that can be obtained and out of the monies arising from the sale in the first place, to pay & satisfy all reasonable charges attending such sale and then the Debt above mentioned of five hundred & ninety nine Dollars due or to become due to the said JAMES WAUGH JR on the twenty seventh Day of August in the Year of our Lord One Thousand and eight hundred & Ten and the residue of the monies arising from such sale as aforesaid to the use of the said JOSEPH HICKMAN his heirs & assigns Provided that if the sd. JOSEPH HICKMAN his Heirs, Executors or Administrators shall well & truly pay or cause to be paid unto the said JAMES WAUGH JR his heirs or assigns on or before the said twenty seventh day of August in the Year eighteen hundred & Ten the aforesaid sum of five hundred & Ninety Nine Dollars Current Money of the United States then & in that case these presents & all contained therein shall be null & void to all intents and Purposes whatsoever any thing herein to the contrary notwithstanding. In testimony whereof the said JOSEPH HICKMAN hath hereunto set his hand and affixed his seal the day & Year first above written.

Signed Sealed & Delivered
in the Presence of   JOSEPH HICKMAN (seal)
WM. KINCHELOE
TOWNSHEND WAUGH
JAS. WAUGH

    At a Court held for Fairfax County the Seventeenth Day of October 1808 this Deed from JOSEPH HICKMAN to ALEXANDER WAUGH was proved to be the Act and Deed of the said JOSEPH HICKMAN by the oath of JAMES WAUGH a witness hereto & ordered to be certified. And at a Court continued & held for the said County the 17th January 1809 the same was further proved by the oath of TOWNSHEND WAUGH another witness hereto & ordered to be certified & at a Court held for the said County the 20th February 1809 the same was further proved by the oath of WILLIAM KINCHELOE another witness hereto & ordered to be recorded.
                                     Teste WM. MOSS Cl.

Pages 98-100. THIS INDENTURE made this sixteenth day of April in the Year of our Lord Eighteen hundred & eight between WILLIAM HERBERT, NICHOLAS FITZHUGH and EDMUND J. LEE of the Town & County of Alexandria in the District of Columbia executors of the last Will & Testament of RICHARD CONWAY deceased of the one part and PHENIAS JANNEY of the Town, County and District aforesaid of the other part. WITNESSETH whereas the said RICHARD CONWAY did by his last Will & Testament bearing date the fifth Day of June in the Year of our Lord eighteen hundred and four order, authorize, empower and Direct the said WILLIAM HERBERT, NICHOLAS FITZHUGH and EDMUND J. LEE, who by his last Will & Testament as afore-said were appointed his executors to sell certain parts of his real estate therein designated and not otherwise disposed of by the Codicil attached to the same and bearing date the seventeenth day of November in the Year of our Lord eighteen hundred & six which together with the said Will has been duly Proven & Recorded. Now this indenture WITNESSETH that the said WILLIAM HERBERT, NICHOLAS FITZHUGH and EDMUND J. LEE executors as aforesaid for and in consider-ation of the Promises and of the Sum of thirty five Dollars and forty Cents to them in hand paid by the said PHENIAS JANNEY at and before the Sealing and Delivery of these presents the receipt whereof is hereby acknowledged hath granted, bargained & Sold and by these

presents doth grant, bargain and Sell unto him the said PHENIAS JANNEY his heirs & assigns a certain Tract or parcel of land situate, lying and being in the County of Fairfax and State of Virginia being part of that tract of Land called Stump Hill and designated on the Platt of the same by the No. 39 and bounded as follows to wit: beginning at a stake on the edge of the outlet on the fourth line of the said Tract of Land twenty three poles to the Westward of the inter-section of the second lane or avenue with that outlet corner to that lott or dividend of the said Tract described by the No. 35 and running thence with the line of said Lott No. 35 and the line of lott No. 34 forty seven poles & a half to a stake in the line of Lott No. 33 corner to the Lott No. 34, thence with the line of Lott No. 33 North seventy seven Degrees West seventeen poles to a stake in the line of Lott No. 40, thence North thirty eight degrees East fifty three to a stake on the edge of the said outlet corner to the said Lott No. 40, thence with the said outlet South sixty six Degrees East sixteen Poles to the beginning containing five acres with all and Singular the appurtenances thereto belonging or in any manner appertaining. To have and To Hold the said Premises with the appurtenances as aforesaid unto him the said PHENIAS JANNEY his heirs & assigns to the only use & behoof of him his heirs & assigns forever and the said WILLIAM HERBERT, NICHOLAS FITZHUGH and EDMUND J. LEE executors as aforesaid do covenant & agree to & with the said PHENIAS JANNEY his heirs and assigns that they will forever warrant & defend the said Premises against the claim & demand of all & every person or persons whatsoever claiming by, through, from, or under them or any of them. In testimony whereof the said Parties have hereunto set their hands and affixed their Seals the Day & Year before written.
Sealed & Delivered
In Presence of   WM. HERBERT   (seal)
R. J. TAYLOR   N. FITZHUGH   (seal)
W. HERBERT   EDM. J LEE   (seal)
WM. HERBERT JR.
      At a Court held for Fairfax County the Sixteenth Day of January 1809 this Deed from WILLIAM HERBERT, NICHOLAS FITZHUGH and EDMUND J. LEE Executors of RICHARD CONWAY deceased to PHENIAS JANNEY was proved to be the Act & Deed of the said WILLIAM HERBERT, NICHOLAS FITZHUGH and EDMUND J. LEE by the oaths of ROBERT J. TAYLOR and WILLIAM HERBERT JR and ordered to be Certified. And at a Court held for Fairfax County the twentieth Day of February 1809 the same was further proved by the oath of NOBLET HERBERT another Witness hereto and ordered to be recorded.
                                          Teste WM. MOSS Cl.

Pages 100 & 101. To all whom these presents shall come Know Ye that I MARY TALBOTT of the County of Fairfax and State of Virginia in the County & CommonWealth of aforesaid do hereby constitute and appoint WILLIAM S. TALBOTT of the County of Fairfax & State of aforesaid in the County & State of aforesaid my attorney in all cases real, personal & mixed, moved or to be moved, for me or against me in any Court of Law in my name to appear, plead & pursue unto final judgment & execution with Power of Substitution. In WITNESS whereof I hereunto set my hand & Seal this 17th Day of October Anno Domina 1808.
Teste   MARY TALBUT   (seal)
COLEMAN LEWIS
BENJAMIN BERKLEY
      At a Court held for Fairfax County the 20th Day of February 1809 this Power of Attorney from MARY TALBUT to WILLIAM S. TALBUT was proved to be the Act & Deed of the said MARY TALBUT by the oaths of COLEMAN LEWIS & BENJAMIN BERKLEY & ordered to be Recorded.
                                          Teste WM. MOSS Cl.

Pages 101-103. THIS INDENTURE made this Seventeenth day of October in the Year of our Lord one Thousand eight Hundred & eight between RICHARD BLAND LEE and ELIZABETH his wife of the County of Fairfax & State of Virginia of the one Part and FRANCIS KEENE of the same County & State of the other part: Whereas the said FRANCIS KEENE did by indenture dated the 28th Day of June in the year eighteen hundred and Six convey unto the said RICHARD BLAND LEE his heirs & assigns forever a tract of land in the said County of Fairfax on Pohick Run

bounded and Described in said Deed as follows: beginning at a stake on a hill side where there has formerly been a marked red oak running South 53° West 135 poles to a white oak corner to KEENE & SIMPSON, passing a white oak corner of the land the said KEENE purchased of NICHOLAS KEENE at 45 poles, thence South 21° West 65 poles to a Spanish oak and dogwood SIMPSON'S corner, thence South 62° East 80 poles to a red oak, thence South 83° East 165 Poles to a Stake said to be VIOLETS corner, thence North 4° West 113 Poles to Box oak & gum sapling in the line of ROBERTS the elder, thence with said ROBERTS'S now VIOLETS line South 40° East 48 Poles to marked maple & Gum in the head of a branch of Pohick, thence down the said branch of Pohick & binding therewith to Pohick Run, thence up the said run with the meanders thereof to two white oaks corner to ROBERTS & BEAVERS at the mouth of a small branch just below JAMES KEENES mill, thence South 78° West 162 poles to the line of WILLIAM KEENE the land he purchased of the aforesaid NICHOLAS KEENE, thence to the beginning containing three hundred & fifty acres; and whereas the said RICHARD BLAND LEE and ELIZABETH are desirous of reconveying the above described land to the said FRANCIS KEENE now this indenture WITNESSETH that the said RICHARD BLAND LEE and ELIZABETH his wife in consideration of the sum of five Dollars to the said RICHARD BLAND LEE in hand paid the receipt whereof he doth hereby acknowledge and of other good considerations Have granted, bargained and Sold, Aliened & Confirmed and by these presents do grant, bargain & Sell, alien & Confirm unto the said FRANCIS KEENE his heirs & assigns forever all the right, Title and interest of the said RICHARD BLAND LEE and ELIZABETH his wife to the above described tract or parcel of land, To Hold the said FRANCIS KEENE his heirs & assigns forever and the said RICHARD BLAND LEE for himself, his Heirs, executors and administrators unto the said FRANCIS KEENE his heirs & assigns all the Right, Title and Interest of him the said RICHARD BLAND LEE and ELIZABETH his wife in and to the above described piece or Tract of Land Doth and will forever warrant and defend against claim and Demand of all & every Person or Persons claiming by, from, through or under him. In testimony whereof the said RICHARD BLAND LEE and ELIZABETH his wife have hereunto set their hands and seals the day & Year first before written.
Sealed & Delivered in
the Presence of   RICHARD BLAND LEE (seal)
R. RATCLIFFE (R.B.L.)   [signature of ELIZABETH not showing]
JAS. WAUGH
GEO. SUMMERS
     At a Court held for Fairfax County the 16th Day of January 1800, this Deed from RICHARD B. LEE to FRANCIS KEENE was proved to be the Act & Deed of the said RICHARD B. LEE by the oaths of JAMES WAUGH and GEORGE SUMMERS witnesses hereto & ordered to be certified. And at a Court held for the said County the 10th February 1809 the same was further proved by the oath of RICHARD RATCLIFFE another Witness hereto and ordered to be Recorded.   Teste WM. MOSS Cl.

Pages 103-106. THIS INDENTURE made this tenth Day of November in the year of our Lord one Thousand eight hundred & eight between CHARLES LITTLE executor of the last Will and Testament of JOHN WEST late of the County of Fairfax and State of Virginia of the one Part and MICHAEL (sic) QUIGLEY of the County and State aforesaid of the other part. WITNESSETH whereas JOHN WEST late of the County aforesaid by his last will & Testament bearing date the first day of June in the Year one Thousand eight hundred & six did for the payment of his debts devise to be Sold his moiety of a Tract of land of two Hundred and thirteen acres in the County aforesaid which was devised to him & his brother THOMAS WEST by their father JOHN WEST as will appear by his last WILL & Testament bearing date the 17th day of April in the year 1775 one half to each and which has been laid off and divided since the death of the said JOHN and THOMAS WEST by and between the said CHARLES LITTLE Executor of the said JOHN WEST and THOMAS WEST Son and devisee of THOMAS WEST as will appear by their indenture of partition bearing date the first day of November in the year of our Lord one Thousand eight hundred & eight. And Whereas the said CHARLES LITTLE having in pursuance of the authority given him by the will of his Testator & for the Payment of his Debts caused the said Moiety to be laid off in Lotts and Sold at Public Auction when & where the lott No. 5 as laid down in a platt of the same made by ROBERT RATCLIFFE Deputy Surveyor of the County of Fairfax and which is now of Record was struck off to PATRICK QUIGLEY as the highest bidder. Now this indenture WITNESSETH that the said CHARLES LITTLE executor as aforesaid for and in consideration of the Premises and of the Sum of one hundred Dollars and Seventy seven cents to him in hand paid by the said PATRICK QUIGLEY at and before the Sealing and delivery of these presents the receipt whereof is hereby acknowledged have granted, devised, leased and to farm let and by these presents do devise, lease and to farm let unto the said PATRICK QUIGLEY his Executors, Administrators and assigns the aforesaid Lott number Five which lies within the following boundaries to wit: beginning at a stake corner to Lott number four, thence with a line of said lott South Seventy West fifty one & a half Poles to a white oak Sapling in the division line, thence South twenty six Degrees Twenty Minutes East thirty two and three quarter poles to a stake, thence North Seventy East forty one & one third poles to a stake in the outline, thence with said line North eight Degrees thirty Minutes West thirty three poles to the beginning containing nine acres and Sixty poles with the appurtenances thereto, the said Lott being part of the said Moiety of two hundred & thirteen acres so devised as aforesaid by JOHN WEST to his two Sons THOMAS & JOHN one half to each being a tract of land that was patented in the name of CAPTAIN SIMON PEARSON by Deed from the proprietor dated the seventeenth Day of February Seventeen hundred and twenty nine; and was devised by the said PEARSON to his Daughter MARGARET (who intermarried with WILLIAM H. TERRETT) by his last will & Testament bearing date the seventeenth day of December seventeen Hundred and thirty one and Recorded in Stafford Court Liber M folio 101; and was afterwards conveyed by WILLIAM H. TERRETT and MARGARET his wife to HUGH WEST by indenture bearing date the twentieth day of August Seventeen Hundred & forty five in consideration of the Sum of fifty Pounds which indenture recites the courses and distances of the original Patent. To Have and To Hold the said Lott with the appurtenances thereto unto the said MICHAEL (*sic*) QUIGLEY his executors, Adminstrators and assigns from the day of the date hereof for and during and to the full end and term of One Thousand Years fully to be completed & ended yielding therefor yearly & every Year the rent of one pepper corn. And the said CHARLES LITTLE executor aforesaid for himself and his heirs doth covenant with the said PATRICK QUIGLEY his heirs & assigns that he will forever warrant the said premises with the appurtenances against the claim & demand of all Persons or person whomsoever claiming through or under him. In WITNESS whereof the said CHARLES LITTLE executor as aforesaid has set his hand & Seal the Day & Year before written.

Sealed & delivered   CHARLES LITTLE (seal)
in Presence of [No witnesses listed]

  At a Court held for Fairfax County the 20th Day of February 1809 CHARLES LITTLE, executor of JOHN WEST deceased acknowledged this Deed to MICHAEL (*sic*) QUIGLEY to be his Act and Deed which is ordered to be recorded.

             Teste WM. MOSS Cl.

Pages 106-110. THIS INDENTURE made this fifth day of July in the year of our Lord one thousand eight Hundred & eight between DYER HUBBARD and CHARLOTTE his wife of the Town and County of Alexandria in the District of Columbia of the one part and CARROLL BARKER of the County of Fairfax in the State of Virginia of the other part. WITNESSETH that the said DYER HUBBARD & CHARLOTTE his wife for and in consideration of the sum of one hundred & forty four Dollars to him the said DYER HUBBARD in hand paid by him the said CARROLL BARKER at or before the Sealing & Delivery of these presents the receipt whereof he the said DYER HUBBARD doth hereby acknowledge and thereof and of every part and parcel thereof doth acquit, release and discharge him the said CARROLL BARKER his heirs, Executors and Administrators by these presents Have given, granted, bargained, Sold, aliened and Confirmed and by these presents Do give, grant, bargain, Sell, alien and Confirm unto him the said CARROLL BARKER his heirs and assigns forever a piece or parcel of Ground situate, lying and being upon the South side of Duke Street extended and to the Eastward of George Street in the said County of Fairfax and State of Virginia and bounded as followeth to wit: beginning upon Duke Street sixty eight feet six inches to the Eastward of George Street and running thence Eastwardly with Duke Street binding thereupon twenty four feet, thence Southwardly with a

line parallel to George Street one hundred & twenty feet, thence Westwardly with a line parallel to Duke Street twenty four feet, thence Northwardly with a line parallel to George Street one hundred & twenty feet to the beginning it being that piece of Ground Sold and conveyed by PRESLEY JACOBS and ELIZABETH his wife unto the said CHARLOTTE her heirs & assigns by the name of CHARLOTTE RIGG by an indenture bearing date the twenty first day of June one Thousand eight Hundred & two and a part of that Lott of Ground granted by JOHN WEST unto THOMAS RICHARDS his heirs & assigns by an indenture bearing date the twenty seventh day of March one Thousand seven hundred & ninety seven, subject to the payment of an annual Rent of Twenty five Dollars and forty two cents unto the said JOHN WEST, which lott of ground subject to the payment of the said Rent the said THOMAS RICHARDS and NANCY his wife afterwards Sold to JOHN LIMERICK to whom the said JOHN WEST released the said annual rent after which the said JOHN LIMERICK by an indenture bearing date the twelfth day of October one Thousand seven hundred & ninety eight Sold all that part of the said Lott of Ground contained within the limits herein expressed unto the said PRESLEY JACOBS his heirs and assigns and all Houses, buildings, Streets, lanes, allies, profits, Commodities, Hereditaments and appurtenances whatsoever to the said premises belonging or in anywise appertaining and the Reversion and Reversions, Remainder and Remainders, Rents, Issues and profits thereof and of every part and parcel thereof. To have and To hold all and Singular the premises hereby granted with their appurtenances unto him the said CARROLL BARKER his heirs & assigns to the only proper use and behoof of him the said CARROLL BARKER his heirs and assigns forever and the said DYER HUBBARD and CHARLOTTE his wife do for themselves their heirs, Executors and Administrators covenant, grant and agree to & with the said CARROLL BARKER his heirs and assigns that they the said DYER HUBBARD and CHARLOTTE his wife are now at the time of the Sealing and Delivery of these presents seized in their own right of a good, sure, perfect, absolute and indefeasible estate of inheritance in fee simple in all and Singular the premises hereby granted with their appurtenances without any manner of Condition, Mortgage, Limitation of use or uses, or any other matter, cause or thing to alter, change, charge, or determine the same and also that they the said DYER HUBBARD and CHARLOTTE his wife and their Heirs will at any time hereafter upon the request and at the costs and charges of him the said CARROLL BARKER his heirs & assigns execute and acknowledge any further Lawfull Act and Deed for the more certain assuring & conveying all and Singular the said Premises with their appurtenances unto him the said CARROLL BARKER his heirs & assigns as by him the said CARROLL BARKER his heirs & assigns his, their or any of their council learned in the law shall or may be advised or required and lastly that they the said DYER HUBBARD & CHARLOTTE his wife & their Heirs all & Singular the said premises with their appurtenances unto him the said CARROLL BARKER his heirs & assigns against the claim & demand of them the said DYER HUBBARD & CHARLOTTE his wife and their Heirs and all and every other person or persons whatsoever shall & will warrant and forever defend by these presents. In WITNESS whereof the said DYER HUBBARD & CHARLOTTE his wife have hereunto set their hands & seals the Day & Year first herein before mentioned.
Sealed & Delivered
Presence of   DYER HUBBARD   (seal)
RICHD. LIBBY   CHARLOTTE her X mark HUBBARD (seal)
DANL. MINOR
CHAS. SLADE
      Received of CARROLL BARKER one hundred & forty four Dollars the consideration herein mentioned.
WITNESS
RD. LIBBY   DYER HUBBARD
DANL. MINOR
      At a Court held for Fairfax County the 20th Day of February 1809 DYER HUBBARD acknowledged this Deed and a receipt hereon endorsed to CARROLL BARKER to be his Act & Deed which together with a commission & Return hereto annexed for taking the acknowledgment & privy examination of CHARLOTTE HUBBARD wife of the said DYER HUBBARD are ordered to be recorded.   Teste WM. MOSS Cl.

FAIRFAX COUNTY To Wit:

The CommonWealth of Virginia to CUTHBERT POWELL, JOSEPH DEAN & RICHARD LIBBY Gentlemen Justices of the County of Alexandria in the District of Columbia Greeting: Whereas DYER HUBBARD and CHARLOTTE his wife by their certain indenture of Bargain & Sale bearing date the fifth Day of July 1808 have Sold & conveyed unto CARROLL BARKER the fee Simple estate of a piece of Ground with the appurtenances situate, lying & being upon the South side of Duke Street and to the eastward of George Street in the said County of Fairfax and whereas the said CHARLOTTE cannot conveniently travel to our said County Court of Fairfax to make acknowledgment of the said conveyance therefore we do give unto you or any two or more of you power to receive the acknowledgment which the sd. CHARLOTTE shall be willing to make before you of the conveyance aforesaid contained in the said indenture which is hereunto annexed and we do therefore desire you or any two or more of you personally to go to the said CHARLOTTE and receive her acknowledgment of the same and examine her privily and apart from the said DYER her husband whither she doth the same freely & voluntarily without his persuasions or threats; And whither she be willing the said indenture together with this commission shall be recorded in our said Court. And when you have received her acknowledgment & examined her as aforesaid that you distinctly and openly certify us thereof in our said Court under your hands and Seals sending then there the said indenture and this writ. WITNESS WILLIAM MOSS Clerk of our said Court at the Courthouse of the County aforesaid this sixth Day of July 1808 and in the 33rd Year of the CommonWealth.

WM. MOSS Cl.

DISTRICT OF COLUMBIA, County of Alexandria To Wit:

In obedience to the within commission we did examine the said CHARLOTTE privily & apart from the said DYER her husband who declared that she executed the said indenture freely and voluntarily without his persuasions or threats & that she is willing the same together with this Commission should be recorded in the said Court. Given under our hands and Seals this sixth Day of July one Thousand eight Hundred & eight.

CUTHBERT POWELL (seal)
RICD. LIBBY   (seal)

Page 111. KNOW ALL MEN by these presents that I DRUMMOND WHEELER of the County of Fairfax and State of Virginia hath bargained & Sold to THOS. WHEELER of the County of Campbell and State of Tennessee one Negro boy named TOM now in possession of my Father RICHARD WHEELER for the valuable consideration of three hundred Dollars in hand paid by the said THOS. WHEELER for which I do warrant and defend the said boy from me, my heirs and from the claim of every other person whatsoever as Witness my hand & Seal this twenty seventh Day of December 1808.

Teste   DRUMMOND WHEELER (seal)
EDWARD BATES
WILLIAM WHEELER
FRANCIS MONTGOMERY

At a Court held for Fairfax County the 20th day of February 1809 DRUMMOND WHEELER acknowledged this bill of sale to THOMAS WHEELER to be his Act & Deed which is ordered to be recorded.   Teste WM. MOSS Cl.

Pages 111-114. THIS INDENTURE made the twenty fourth Day of June in the Year of our Lord one Thousand eight hundred & eight between ROBERT BOGGESS of the County of Fairfax & CommonWealth of Virginia of the first part, RICHARD RATCLIFFE & WILLIAM MOSS of the said County & CommonWealth of the second Part & ROBERT J. TAYLOR of the County of Alexandria in the District of Columbia of the third part. Whereas the said RICHARD RATCLIFFE and WILLIAM MOSS did on the [left blank] day of May 1808 Jointly become Security in a Prison Bounds Bond for the said ROBERT BOGGESS at the suit of RICHARD SIMPSON, he the said ROBERT BOGGESS then being in Custody by Nature of an Execution from the Haymarket District Court against a certain SAMUEL BAILEY and the said BOGGESS; and Whereas the said ROBERT BOGGESS is desirous of fully indemnifying & saving harmless them the said RICHARD RATCLIFFE & WILLIAM MOSS from all Risk, Cost & trouble on account of their undertaking aforesaid. Now this indenture WITNESSETH that the said ROBERT BOGGESS as well to effect the purposes aforesaid as for and in consideration of the Sum of one Dollar to him in hand paid by him the said ROBERT J. TAYLOR the receipt whereof he the said ROBERT BOGGESS doth hereby acknowledge the said ROBERT BOGGESS hath given, granted, bargained & Sold and by these presents Doth Give, grant, bargain, Sell & deliver unto him the said ROBERT J. TAYLOR his heirs, Executors, Administrators or assigns forever a certain piece, parcel or Tract of Land, Situate, lying and being in the County aforesaid containing about four Hundred acres be the same more or less, it being that Tract of land on which he the said ROBERT BOGGESS now lives, also two Negro men Slaves to wit: HANSON and GEORGE. To have and to Hold unto him the said ROBERT J. TAYLOR his Heirs, Executors, Administrators or assigns forever the aforesaid piece, parcel or Tract of land together with all and Singular its appurtenances & every part and Parcel thereof also the aforesaid negro Men Slaves to and for the uses and Purposes hereinafter mentioned and to and for no other use or purpose whatsoever that is to say that whenever they the said RICHARD RATCLIFFE and WILLIAM MOSS their heirs, executors, or admors shall feel themselves in Danger of suffering by reason of their undertaking aforesaid of them the said RICHARD RATCLIFFE & WILLIAM MOSS as Securities as aforesaid that he the said ROBERT J. TAYLOR his Heirs, exors, or administrators being thereto required by them the said RICHARD RATCLIFFE and WILLIAM MOSS their heirs, exors, or admors, upon giving twenty Days Public notice of the time and place of Sale do expose to Public Sale for ready Money the aforesaid Property or so much thereof as will be sufficient to satisfy and pay the amount of the Execution aforesaid and all such interest & Costs as have or may accrue on the same together with such costs as may be necessary to carry this trust into effect; and that the Money arising from the said Sale be applied by him the said ROBERT J. TAYLOR his heirs, executors or admors, to satisfy the Costs attending the same and then to the satisfaction of the execution, interest & Costs as aforesaid of him the said RICHARD SIMPSON and the overplus (if any should remain) unto him the said ROBERT BOGGESS his heirs, executors, administrators, or assigns & the said ROBERT J. TAYLOR do for himself, his Heirs, executors, or admors, covenant to and with the said ROBERT BOGGESS, RICHARD RATCLIFFE & WILLIAM MOSS their heirs, executors, or administrators that he will well and truly execute, fulfill & perform the several Trusts hereby Reposed in him and the said ROBERT BOGGESS do for himself, his heirs, executors & admors Covenant & grant to and with the said RICHARD RATCLIFFE & WILLIAM MOSS & ROBERT J. TAYLOR their heirs, executors, admors or assigns severally that he will fully satisfy and pay the aforesaid Execution interest & Costs and fully indemnify & save harmless them the sd. RICHD RATCLIFFE and WILLIAM MOSS their heirs, Executors and admors, from all trouble, costs & charges on account of their undertaking as his Securities aforesaid and that he has full right & Lawfull authority to sell and convey the aforesaid Property and that he will at any time hereafter execute and acknowledge any further or other conveyance of the more perfect assurance of the Premises & Slaves aforesaid and that he will forever warrant and defend the same against the claim of all and every Person or Persons whatsoever. In WITNESS whereof the parties to these presents have hereunto set their hands & affixed their seals the Day Month & Year in this indenture first written.

Sealed, Delivered & acknowledged
In the Presence of
ROBERT RATCLIFFE, R.B.   ROBERT BOGGESS   (seal)
GIDEON M. MOSS   do   R. J. TAYLOR   (seal)
DANIEL BRADLEY   do
CHARLES LITTLE to R.J.T.
W. DENEALE to R.J.T.
HUGH W. MINOR, R.J.T.

    At a Court contd. & held for Fairfax County the 20th Day of September 1808 this Deed from ROBERT BOGGESS to ROBERT J. TAYLOR in trust for the use of RICHARD RATCLIFFE and WILLIAM MOSS was proved to be the Act and Deed of the said ROBERT BOGGESS by the oaths of GIDEON M. MOSS and DANIEL BRADLEY witnesses hereto and acknowledged by the said ROBERT J. TAYLOR to be his act & Deed and ordered to be certified and at a Court held for the said County the twentieth Day of February 1809 the same was acknowledged by the said ROBERT BOGGESS to be his act and Deed which is ordered to be Recorded.

Teste WM. MOSS Cl.

Pages 115-117. THIS INDENTURE made the twenty fourth Day of June in the Year eighteen hundred & eight between ROBERT BENSON & ELIZABETH his wife of the one part and WM. JOHNSTON of the other part, all of the County of Fairfax and State of Virginia. WITNESSETH that the said ROBERT and ELIZABETH his wife for and in consideration of one dollar to them in hand paid by said WM. and for the further consideration that DENNIS JOHNSTON hath this Day become the Security of the said ROBERT in a forthcoming bond given to TOWNSHEND DADE of Prince William County for the Sum of eighty eight Dollars & sixty six cents have bargained, Sold, aliened, enfeoffed and confirmed and by these presents do bargain, Sell, alien, enfeoff and confirm unto the said WILLIAM all that Tract or Parcel of land now occupied by the said ROBERT and devised to the said ELIZABETH by her brother GEO. JOHNSTON containing about twenty five acres. To Have and To Hold the said Tract of land to him the said WILLIAM his heirs & assigns forever to the only proper use and behoof of him the said WILLIAM in trust; nevertheless that if the said ROBERT shall fail to pay the amount due by said forthcoming bond with all costs attending the same the said DENNIS be compelled to pay the same or any part thereof then the said WILLIAM is to proceed to Sell said Tract of land to the highest bidder at Public Sale having first advertized the time & place of sale for twenty days in some Public Newspaper published in the Town of Alexr. & shall apply the Money arising from such sale which is to be for cash first to the payment of the debt due to said DADE aforementioned with all Costs & Officers' fees attending the same then to the payment of the costs of advertising & selling & the surplus to be paid to the said ROBERT or his order. In Testimony whereof the said parties have hereunto set their hands & affixed their Seals the Day above written.

Signed Sealed & Delivered

in presence of		
EDW SUMMERS	ROBERT BENSON	(seal)
DANL. BRADLEY	BETTY BENSON	(seal)
RICHD. H. HENDERSON	WM. JOHNSTON	(seal)

At a Court continued and held for Fairfax County the 17th Day of January 1809 this Deed from ROBERT BENSON & ELIZABETH his wife to WILLIAM JOHNSTON, in trust for the use [of] DENNIS JOHNSTON was proved to be the Act and Deed of the said ROBERT BENSON by the oaths of DANIEL BRADLEY and RICHARD H. HENDERSON WITNESSES hereto and ordered to be certified and at a Court held for the said County the twentieth Day of February 1809 the same was further proved by the oath of EDWARD SUMMERS another Witness hereto which together with a Commission & return hereto annexed for taking the acknowledgment & privy examination of the said ELIZABETH are Ordered to be Recorded.

Teste WM. MOSS Cl.

FAIRFAX COUNTY To Wit:

The CommonWealth of Virginia to WILLIAM DENEALE, WM. PAYNE & RICHARD RATCLIFFE Gentlemen Justices of the County of Fairfax Greeting: Whereas ROBERT BENSON & BETTY or ELIZABETH his wife by their certain indenture of Bargain & Sale bearing date the 24th Day of June 1808 have Sold and conveyed unto WM. JOHNSTON the fee simple estate of twenty five acres of land with the appurtenances situate, lying and being in the said County of Fairfax and whereas the said ELIZABETH or BETTY cannot conveniently travel to our said County Court of Fairfax to make acknowledgement of the said conveyance therefore we do give unto you or any two or more of you Power to receive the acknowledgment which the said BETTY or ELIZABETH shall be willing to make before you of the conveyance aforesaid contained in the said indenture which is hereunto annexed and we do therefore desire you or any two or more of you personally to go to the said ELIZABETH and receive her acknowledgement of the same and examine her privily and apart from the said ROBERT her husband whither she Doth the same freely and voluntarily without his persuasions or threats and whither she be willing the said indenture together with this commission shall be recorded in our said Court. And when you have received her acknowledgment & examined her as aforesaid that you distinctly and openly certify us thereof in our said Court under your hands &

Seals sending then there the said indenture & this writ. WITNESS WILLIAM MOSS Clerk of the said Court at the Courthouse of the County aforesaid this 24th Day of June 1808 and in the 32nd Year of the CommonWealth.   WM. MOSS Cl.

FAIRFAX COUNTY:

Pursuant to the within commission to us directed we the Subscribers have called on the within named BETTY (or ELIZABETH) wife of the within named ROBERT BENSON touching her Relinquishment of her Dower to the Land in the annexed Deed Described separate & apart from her said husband who declared her willingness to Relinquish the same and that she was not induced thereto from coercive measures used by her said husband and was willing the said Deed should be recorded in Fairfax County Court. Certified under our hands & Seals this 24th Day of June 1808.   W. DENEALE   (seal)
                                                           RD. RATCLIFFE   (seal)

Pages 118-123. THIS INDENTURE made this 17th Day of May in the Year of our Lord Eighteen hundred & eight between ROBERT YOUNG & ELIZABETH his wife of the District of Columbia and County of Alexandria of the one part and ROBERT OBER of the District of Columbia & County of Washington of the other part. Whereas a certain ROBERT ALLISON in his life time was seized in fee of a track of Land Containing two hundred & seventy acres, three Roods & thirty seven Poles or thereabouts in the County of Fairfax and State of Virginia and in order to sell the same to advantage laid the same off into Twenty small divisions of different sizes and containing different quantities of land the same being numbered from one to twenty several of which divisions he sold & Conveyed unto RICHARD LEWIS his heirs & assigns and who sold the hereafter mentioned track (part of the above) to a certain PIERCE LACY TANNER his heirs & assigns who sold the same to THOMAS PATTON his heirs & assigns and by him Sold to the said ROBERT YOUNG as will more fully and at large appear reference being had to the Indenture of the said THOMAS PATTON and MARY his wife bearing date the nineteenth day of August in the Year of our Lord 1806. Now this indenture WITNESSETH that the said ROBERT YOUNG & ELIZABETH his wife for and in consideration of the sum of two Hundred & fifty Dollars to him the said ROBERT in hand paid by the said ROBERT OBER at and before the sealing & Delivery of these presents the receipt whereof & therefrom doth forever acquit & Release the said ROBERT OBER his Heirs & assigns have granted, bargained, Sold, aliened, set over & confirmed and by these presents do give, grant, bargain, Sell, Alien, set over, assign & confirm unto him the sd. ROBERT OBER his heirs & assigns forever all that dividend, piece or parcel of the said Track of Land laid off as aforesaid by the said ROBERT ALLISON Described & designated in the said division by the number (eighteen) the same being bounded as followeth to wit: beginning at an Hickory bush corner to the lott number (fifteen) and running thence with the line of the said Lott or Dividend north eighty six Degrees West forty Poles, to two small saplings blazed corner to Lotts numbered 14: 15: 17 and the lot 18, thence South four degrees West forty poles to a stake corner to Lotts No. 17: 19: 20 and the said lot 18, thence with the line of lot number twenty, South eighty six Degrees East forty Poles to several Saplings blazed near the North side of an old Road corner to the said Lot No. 18, thence North four degrees East forty poles to the beginning containing Ten acres. To have & To hold all & Singular the Premises with their & every of their appurtenances in any manner thereunto belonging unto the said ROBERT OBER his heirs & assigns forever and the said ROBERT YOUNG for himself, his Heirs, Executors & Administrators Covenants, grants & agrees to & with the said ROBERT OBER his heirs & assigns the Right, Title and Interest of and to the said Ten acres of Land here before conveyed to the said ROBERT OBER and also all & singular the Premises against the Right, Title & Interest, Claim & Demand of all & every Person or Persons whatsoever and the said ROBERT YOUNG for himself & his heirs doth further covenant & agree to and with the said ROBERT OBER his heirs & assigns that he the said ROBERT YOUNG and his Heirs will at any and at all times hereafter (at the costs & charges of the said ROBERT OBER his Heirs or assigns) execute any other Deed or Deeds assuring the said Property unto the said ROBERT OBER his heirs & assigns. In testimony whereof the said ROBERT & ELIZABETH have hereunto set their Hands & Seals the Day & Year first above Written.
Signed, Sealed & Delivered
In the Presence of

THOS. COLE   ROBERT YOUNG   (seal)
A. GREEN   ELIZABETH YOUNG (seal)
MARIA GROVERMAN
      DISTRICT OF COLUMBIA To Wit:

             I GEORGE DENEALE Clerk of the United States Circuit Court of the District of
(SEAL)   Columbia for the County of Alexandria do hereby Certify that at a United States
             Circuit Court of the District & County aforesaid continued & held the first Day of
December in the Year eighteen Hundred & eight ROBERT YOUNG acknowledged this Deed to
ROBERT OBER to be his Act and Deed which together with a Commission & Return for the Privy
examination of ELIZABETH YOUNG wife of the said ROBERT are ordered to be Recorded and
Certified to the County Court of Fairfax in the CommonWealth of Virginia. In Testimony
whereof I have hereunto set my hand & affixed the Public Seal of my Office on this 14th Day
of January in the Year 1809.   G. DENEALE Cl.
      At a United States Circuit Court of the District of Columbia Continued & held for the
County of Alexandria the 1st day of December 1808 ROBERT YOUNG acknowledged this Deed to
ROBERT OBER to be his Act & Deed which together with a commission & Return for the Privy
examination of ELIZABETH YOUNG wife of the said ROBERT are ordered to be Recorded &
Certified the County Court of Fairfax in the CommonWealth of Virginia.
                    Teste G. DENEALE Cl.
      DISTRICT OF COLUMBIA WASHINGTON COUNTY:
      I hereby certify that GEORGE DENEALE before whom the above acknowledgment
appears to have been taken was at the time of taking thereof & now is the Clerk of the Circuit
Court of the District of Columbia for the County of Alexandria duly qualified & Sworn & that to
all his acts as such due faith should be given & that the above attestation by him is in due
form.   WILLIAM CRANCH
                  Chief Judge of the said Court
      At a Court held for Fairfax County the 10th day of March 1809: this Deed from ROBERT
YOUNG & ELIZABETH his wife to ROBERT OBER having been duly acknowledged before the
United States Circuit Court of the District of Columbia held for the County of Alexandria &
admitted to record and certified by GEORGE DENEALE Clerk of the said Court & under the seal of
his office also by WILLIAM CRANCH Chief Judge of the said Court is on motion of the said
ROBERT OBER together with the certificates hereon endorsed & a Commission & Return hereto
annexed for taking the acknowledgment & privy examination of the said ELIZABETH are
ordered to be recorded.   Teste WM. MOSS Cl.
      FAIRFAX COUNTY To Wit:
      The CommonWealth of Virginia to ABRAHAM FAW, AMOS ALEXANDER & JOHN McKINNEY
Gentlemen justices of the County of Alexandria Greeting: Whereas ROBERT YOUNG &
ELIZABETH his wife by their certain indenture of Deed bearing date the Seventeenth day of
May 1808 have Sold & Conveyed unto ROBERT OBER the fee simple estate of a certain Piece or
parcel of Land with the appurtenances situate, lying & being in the said County of Fairfax &
whereas the said ELIZABETH cannot conveniently travel to our said County Court of Fairfax to
make acknowledgment of the said conveyance therefore we do give unto you or any two or
more of you power to receive the acknowledgment which the said ELIZABETH shall be willing
to make before you of the conveyance aforesaid contained in the said indenture which is
hereunto annexed; and we do therefore desire you or any two or more of you personally to go
to the said ELIZABETH and receive her acknowledgment of the same and examine her privily
& apart from the said ROBERT YOUNG her husband whether she doth the same freely &
voluntarily without his persuasions or threats & whether she be willing the said indenture
together with this Commission shall be recorded in our said Court and when you have
received her acknowledgment & examined her as aforesaid that you distinctly and openly
certify us thereof in our said Court under your hands & seals sending then there the said
indenture & this writ. WITNESS WILLIAM MOSS Clerk of our said Court at the Courthouse of the
County aforesaid this fourth day of August 1808 and in the 33rd Year of the CommonWealth.
                  WM. MOSS Cl.
      COUNTY OF ALEXANDRIA District of Columbia:
      By the authority of the within commission to us directed we waited on the within

mentioned ELIZABETH and did examine her privily & apart & out of the hearing of ROBERT YOUNG her said husband touching the execution of the within mentioned Deed when she declared to us that it was her own voluntary act done with her own own free will & accord without having been induced thereto by either the threats or persuasion of her said husband & that she was willing that the said Deed together with this Commission should be admitted to record thereby to pass away her right of Dower. Given under our hands & Seals the fourth Day of August 1808.   A. FAW   (seal)
                                       AMOS ALEXANDER   (seal)

Pages 123 & 124. KNOW ALL MEN by these presents that I THOMAS MILLAN of Fairfax County for & in consideration of the natural love & affection I bear my two only Daughters JANE and ANN MILLAN as well as in consideration of one Dollar to me in hand paid the receipt whereof I do hereby acknowledge Hath and Do by these presents give, grant, bargain, Sell & confirm unto my said Daughter JANE MILLAN now about twelve Years of age my Negro girl PENELOPE Daughter of ANN with her future increase forever to be held & enjoyed by my said Daughter JANE and her heirs forever; and to my said Daughter ANN I do Hereby give, grant, bargain, Sell & confirm, my Negro girl Slave named PATIENCE Daughter of ANN with her future increase forever to be held & enjoyed by my said Daughter ANN & her heirs forever. And I do hereby for myself my Heirs &c declare that my said Two Daughters JANE & ANN are to enjoy & possess the above conveyed property independent of and in addition to any other or further part of my estate they or either of them may be hereafter entitled to by devise or desent. In testimony whereof I have hereunto set my hand & affixed my Seal the 15th day of March 1809.   THOS. MILLAN   (seal)
     At a Court held for Fairfax County the 20th Day of March 1809 THOMAS MILLAN acknowledged this Deed of Gift to JANE & ANN MILLAN to be his act & Deed which is ordered to be Recorded.   Teste WM. MOSS Cl.

Pages 124-129. THIS INDENTURE made this 28th day of February in the Year of our Lord eighteen Hundred & nine between WILLIAM SIMPSON of the County of Fairfax & JANE his wife of the one part & EDWARD W. SIMPSON of the same County of the other part. WITNESSETH that said WILLIAM SIMPSON and JANE his wife for and in consideration of the Sum of five hundred and twenty eight Dollars which said sum is to be deducted out of the Legacy of the said EDWARD W. SIMPSON left him by the aforesaid WILLIAM SIMPSON his father, as a part of his Father's estate after his Decease the receipt whereof they doth hereby acknowledge & thereof doth acquit & discharge the said EDWARD W. SIMPSON his executors & Administrators Hath granted, bargained & Sold, aliened, Releas'd & Confirmed & by these presents Doth grant, bargain & Sell, alien, Release & confirm unto the said EDWARD W. SIMPSON his heirs & assigns all that tract or Parcel of Land that belongs to the said WILLIAM SIMPSON & JANE his wife all that tract or parcel of land that the aforesaid WILLIAM SIMPSON purchased of JOHN MILLS and ANN his wife situate on the Ox Road & on the waters of Sandy Run in the County aforesaid beginning at a Stump & small red oak shewn by MRS. WILLIAM SIMPSON SR corner of BAXTER SIMPSON and extending from thence South nine degrees east thirty two poles to a white oak corner of THOMAS SIMPSON'S Land, then with his line South thirteen Degrees West sixty six poles to another corner of sd. SIMPSONS Land a Stump two Red oaks & Hickory marked inwards as also corner of GILES TILLETTS land, thence with TILLETTS line South thirty one Degrees East forty three poles to a red oak on a hill corner of JAMES ROBERTS, then with ROBERTS' line North eighty five degrees East eighty six poles cornering in a Road called Hendersons Road on the West side of a small drain of Sandy Run, then with the Road North Seventy eight Degrees east thirty three & a half poles to a white oak standing in the aforesaid Road, thence North sixty seven degrees east Sixty four Poles to a black oak on the West side of the Ox Road, thence up the Road & binding there with North forty three degrees West eighty poles, then North 31 degrees West seventy six Poles to a small path, thence with a straight line to the beginning which said line divides this land from WILLIAM OFFUTTS land it being the other part of of a said larger tract containing one Hundred & thirty two acres be the same more or less and all Houses, buildings, Orchards, Gardens, Pastures, Meadows, Woods, underwoods, Ways, Waters & watercourses, Profits, Commodities, hereditaments, appurtenances whatsoever to the same belonging or in any wise appertaining and the Reversion & Reversions, Remainder & Remainders, Rents, issues & Profits thereof and also all the estate right, title & interest of the said WILLIAM SIMPSON & JANE his wife of, in & to the same. To Have & to hold the said Parcel of Land hereby granted & conveyed with all & Singular the appurtenances thereunto belonging unto the said EDWARD W. SIMPSON his heirs & assigns to the only proper use & behoof of the sd. EDWARD W. SIMPSON his heirs & assigns forever and the said WILLIAM SIMPSON and JANE his wife for themselves their heirs, Executors and Administrators Doth covenant Promise & Grant to & with the said EDWARD W. SIMPSON his heirs & assigns in manner following that is to say that the said Parcel of land hereby granted & conveyed now is & so forever hereafter shall remain and be free & clear of & from all former & other Gifts & grants, bargains, Sales, Mortgages, Judgments, executions, charges & encumberances what-soever & that the said WILLIAM SIMPSON & JANE his wife their heirs and every person or persons whatsoever claiming by, from, or under them shall & will from time to time and at all times forever hereafter upon the request and at the Cost & charges in the Law of the said EDWARD W. SIMPSON his heirs or assigns make, do and execute or cause or procure to be made, done & executed and every such further & other Lawful & Reasonable Act & acts, Deed or Deeds, Conveyances or assurances in the Law whatsoever for the further better & more perfect granting, conveying and assuring the said Parcel of Land with the appurtenances unto the said EDWARD W. SIMPSON his heirs & assigns as by the said EDWARD W. SIMPSON his heirs & assigns or his or their Council learned in the Law shall be reasonably advised, devised or Required; and Lastly that the said WILLIAM SIMPSON & JANE his wife their heirs the said parcel of land with the appurtenances unto the said EDWARD W. SIMPSON his heirs & assigns shall and will warrant & forever defend. In WITNESS Whereof the said WILLIAM SIMPSON & JANE his wife hath hereunto set their Hands & affixed their Seals, the Day & Year first above written.

Seal'd & Delivered
In Presence of   WILLIAM SIMPSON   (seal)
W. PAYNE   JANE her mark SIMPSON   (seal)
W. DENEALE
RD. SIMPSON
THOMAS COFFER

  Received of EDWARD W. SIMPSON the Sum of five hundred and twenty eight Dollars (as specified in the Deed) in consideration within mentioned in full as Witness my hand this 28th Day of February1809.
Teste
W. PAYNE   WILLIAM SIMPSON
W. DENEALE
RD. SIMPSON
THOMAS COFFER

  At a Court held for Fairfax County the 20th day of March 1809 this Deed from WILLIAM SIMPSON & JANE his wife to EDWARD W. SIMPSON and a receipt hereon endorsed were proved to be the Act and Deed of the said WM. SIMPSON by the oaths of WILLIAM PAYNE, THOMAS COFFER and RICHARD SIMPSON which together with a commission & return hereto annexed for taking the acknowledgment and privy examination of the said JANE are ordered to be Recorded.   Teste WM. MOSS Cl.

  FAIRFAX COUNTY To Wit:
  The CommonWealth of Virginia to CHARLES LITTLE, WM. PAYNE, WM. DENEALE & RICHARD RATCLIFFE Gentlemen justices of the County of Fairfax Greeting: Whereas WILLIAM SIMPSON & JANE his wife by their certain indenture of bargain & Sale bearing date the 28th Day of February 1809 have sold & conveyed unto EDWARD W. SIMPSON the fee simple estate of one hundred & thirty two acres of land with the appurtenances situate, lying & being in the said County of Fairfax and whereas the said JANE cannot conveniently travel to our said County Court of Fairfax to make acknowledgment of the said conveyance therefore we do give unto you or any two or more of you power to receive the acknowledgment which the said JANE shall be willing to make before you of the conveyance aforesaid contained in the said indenture which is hereunto annexed; and we do therefore desire you or any two or more of

you personally to go to the said JANE & receive her acknowledgment of the same & examine her Privily & apart from the said WILLIAM SIMPSON her husband whither she doth the same freely & voluntarily without his persuasions or threats and whither she be willing the said indenture together with this commission shall be recorded in our said Court and when you have received her acknowledgment and examined her as aforesd. that you distinctly & openly certify us thereof in our said Court under your hands & seals sending then there the said indenture & this writ. WITNESS WILLIAM MOSS Clerk of our said Court at the Courthouse of the County aforesd. this 28th Day of February 1809 and in the 33rd Year of the CommonWealth.

WM. MOSS Cl.

FAIRFAX COUNTY:

Pursuant to the within Commission to us directed we the Subscribers have waited on JANE SIMPSON and proceeded to take her privy examination separate and apart from her husband when the said JANE voluntarily & freely relinquished all her right of Dower in & to a cerain Tract of Land which is this day conveyed by the said WILLIAM SIMPSON which Deed is hereunto annexed and also the said JANE consented that the same may be recorded as Given under our hands & Seals this 28th day of February 1809.

W. PAYNE   (seal)
W. DENEALE   (seal)

Pages 129 & 130. KNOW ALL MEN by these presents that I SAMUEL S. HARWOOD of the County of Fairfax & State of Virginia for and in consideration of the Sum of four hundred & ninety five Dollars to me in hand paid hath bargained & Sold unto WILLIAM S. BELT of the County & State aforesaid the following Property, viz: two black Horses, 1 Mare, 1 Cow & Calf, all my stock of Hogs, Cart & Gears, 1 bed & bedstead, 1 Desk, 1 Table, all my farming utensils & all my part of the wheat & the Corn now growing, all which Property I warrant & defend to the said BELT and his Heirs forever. Witness my hand & Seal this 5th Day of August 1808.

Teste   SAML. S. HARWOOD (seal)
MIDDLETON BELT
EPHRAIM CARTER
JESSE WADE

Received the within consideration Sum of four Hundred and Ninety five Dollars in full.

Teste
MIDDLN. BELT   SAML. S. HARWOOD
EPHRAIM CARTER
JESSE WADE

At a Court continued & held for Fairfax County the 21st Day of March 1809 this Bill of Sale from SAMUEL S. HARWOOD to WILLIAM S. BELT was proved to be the act & Deed of the said SAMUEL S. HARWOOD by the oaths of MIDDLETON BELT & EPHRAIM CARTER Witnesses hereto and ordered to be Recorded.   Teste WM. MOSS Cl.

Pages 130-134. THIS INDENTURE made the third Day of September in the Year of our Lord one Thousand eight hundred & eight between JOHN STANHOPE and ANN STANHOPE his wife of the one part and ROBERT GUNNELL of the other part both the parties being of Fairfax County & CommonWealth of Virginia. Whereas in the Year of our Lord one Thousand eight hundred & one in the Month of February THOMAS GUNNELL the father of the aforesaid ANN STANHOPE died intestate seized & possessed of a certain Tract or Parcel of Land which was conveyed to the said THOMAS GUNNELL by his father by Deed of Gift bearing date the 11th Day of April 1782 and afterwards the better to confirm the same was willed to the said THOMAS GUNNELL by his said father at his Decease. And the said THOMAS GUNNELL at his decease leaving five surviving Children Viz: HENRY GUNNELL JR THOMAS GUNNELL JR WILLIAM GUNNELL (of THOMAS), JAMES GUNNELL JR and ANN STANHOPE and in the same year which his father died THOMAS GUNNELL JR also died intestate leaving no issue and the remaining four Children & their mother [are] at Present the only surviving heirs who succeeded to the inheritance of said Land as the Law directs. The said tract or Parcel of Land is part of a larger tract that was originally taken up by the Grandfather of the aforesaid THOMAS GUNNELL laying on the waters of Difficult Run and is bounded as follows agreeable to the Deed of Gift (to wit):

beginning at a red oak now down but the stump thereof is still standing on the North side of a glade (about ten & an half Yards from a marsh) being corner to the original tract and to Fairfax (and no vacancy adjoining as hath been recently reported), running thence North 27° 156 Poles binding on Fairfax to two red oaks standing some distance apart not far from DOCTR. GANTT's Mill road, being corner to said GANTT'S, thence with said GANTT'S line South 87° & West 38 Poles to a Hickory corner to said GANTT, thence continuing with the line of said GANTT North 52° West 144 Poles to a large white oak now dead on a glade side corner to said GANTT and to NEALE & likewise to the original, thence South 30° West 114 Poles with the line of said NEALE to a white oak in a bottom corner to said NEALE & the original, thence South 7° West 82 Poles to a white oak standing rather on the South side of a high hill and thence South 70° East 224 Poles to the beginning containing two hundred & four acres be the same more or less; and the said ANN STANHOPE being one of the lawful heirs of her Deceased father and likewise heir to her legal Proportion of the share of her Deceased brother THOMAS GUNNELL JR which shares in the said Tract amounting to fifty one acres including her rights and interests aforesaid together with her rights thereby in her Mothers Dower. Now this indenture WITNESSETH that the aforesaid JOHN STANHOPE & ANN STANHOPE his wife for and in consideration of the sum of seventy seven Pounds lawful money of Virginia to them in hand paid by the said ROBERT GUNNELL before the Sealing & Delivery of these presents the receipt whereof the said JOHN STANHOPE & ANN STANHOPE his wife doth hereby acknowledge and thereof doth acquit and discharge the said ROBERT GUNNELL his heirs, executors & administrators & the said JOHN STANHOPE & ANN STANHOPE his wife hath given, granted, bargained, alien'd, Sold, enfeoffed and confirmed & by these presents doth give, grant, bargain, Sell, alien, enfeoff and confirm to the said ROBERT GUNNELL his heirs & assigns all the rights, title, interest, claim, or demand which the aforesaid JOHN STANHOPE & ANN STANHOPE his wife has or may have in Law of equity of, in, or to the said Tract of Land as heir or Heirs to THOMAS GUNNELL or THOMAS GUNNELL JR including the Dower thereof in the same. To have and to hold the said fifty one Acres of Land be the same more or less and all & singular the Premises and appurtenances to the said ROBERT GUNNELL his heirs & assigns forever and the said JOHN STANHOPE & ANN STANHOPE his wife doth hereby for themselves their heirs, executors & Administrators, covenant & agree to & with the said ROBERT GUNNELL his heirs & assigns to warrant and forever defend all & every of their several rights & claims in and to the aforesaid Tract of land to the said ROBERT GUNNELL his heirs & assigns forever against the claim or claims or demands of all & every person or persons claiming by, from, or under the said JOHN STANHOPE & ANN STANHOPE his wife & against the claim & demand of all and every Person or persons whatever. In WITNESS whereof the said JOHN STANHOPE & ANN STANHOPE his wife have hereunto set their hands & affixed their Seals this Day & Year first above written.
Signed Sealed & Delivered
In Presence of   JOHN STANHOPE   (seal)
WM. GUNNELL JR.   ANN STANHOPE   (seal)
JAMES WILEY
WM. GUNNELL of THOS.

    At a Court held for Fairfax County the 20th day of February 1809 this Deed from JOHN STANHOPE and ANN his wife to ROBERT GUNNELL was proved to be the Act & Deed of the said JOHN STANHOPE by the oaths of WILLIAM GUNNELL of THOS. & WM. GUNNELL JR Witnesses hereto & ordered to be certified and at a Court held for the said County the 20th day of March 1809 the same was acknowledged by the said JOHN STANHOPE to be his act & Deed which together with a commission & Return hereto annexed for taking the acknowledgment & privy examination of the said ANN are ordered to be recorded.
Teste WM. MOSS Cl.

    FAIRFAX COUNTY To Wit:
    The CommonWealth of Virginia to WM. GUNNELL JR, JAMES WILEY & SPENCER JACKSON Gentlemen Justices of the County of Fairfax Greeting: Whereas JOHN STANHOPE and ANN STANHOPE his wife by their certain indenture of Bargain & Sale bearing date the 3rd day of September 1808 have sold and conveyed unto ROBERT GUNNELL all their claims and Interest in and to the fee simple estate of a certain Tract of Land as described and expressed in the indenture to which this commission is annexed with the appurtenances situate, lying and

being in the said County of Fairfax and whereas the said ANN STANHOPE cannot conveniently travel to our said County Court of Fairfax to make acknowledgment of the said Conveyance therefore we do give unto you or any two or more of you Power to receive the acknowledgment which the said ANN STANHOPE shall be willing to make before you of the conveyance aforesaid contained in the said Indenture which is hereunto annexed and we do therefore desire you or any two or more of you personally to go to the said ANN STANHOPE and receive her acknowledgment of the same and examine her privily & apart from the said JOHN STANHOPE her husband whither she doth the same freely and voluntarily without his persuasions or threats And whither she be willing the said indenture together with this commission shall be recorded in our said County. And when you have received her acknowledgment and examined her as aforesaid that you distinctly and openly certify us thereof in our said Court under your hands & Seals sending then there the said Indenture and this writ. WITNESS WILLIAM MOSS Clerk of the said Court at the Court House of the county aforesaid this 3rd day of September 1808 and in the 33rd Year of the CommonWealth.

WM. MOSS Cl.

FAIRFAX COUNTY:

In Obedience to the within commission we the Subscribers did on the 3rd day of September 1808 wait on the within mentioned MRS ANN STANHOPE and did privately and apart from the said JOHN STANHOPE her husband examine the said ANN STANHOPE whether she was willing to execute the within named indenture and upon her declaring she was willing to do the same freely without the threatening or persuasion of her said husband she the said ANN STANHOPE did then & there in our Presence execute the said INDENTURE and did freely & voluntarily acknowledge & convey all her right of Dower and inheritance to the said ROBERT GUNNELL and his heirs forever in & to the said Land as therein mentioned. Certified under our hands & Seals this 3rd Day of September 1808.

WM. GUNNELL JR   (seal)
JAMES WILEY   (seal)

Pages 135-139. THIS INDENTURE made this thirtieth day of July in the Year one Thousand eight hundred and eight between HENRY ROSE of the County of Fairfax and State of Virginia of the one part and RICHARD STUART Guardian of the Co-Heirs of DANIEL McCARTY decd of the County of Westmoreland and State aforesaid of the other part. WITNESSETH that the said HENRY ROSE in consideration of four hundred pounds of Lawful money of this State to him in hand paid by the said RICHARD STUART Guardian aforesd. at or before the ensealing & delivery of these presents (the receipt whereof is hereby acknowledged) Have bargained & Sold and by these presents doth bargain & sell unto the said RICHARD STUART aforesaid his heirs & assigns a certain Tract or parcel of Land situate, lying and being in the County of Fairfax containing eight Hundred & twenty acres of Land and bounded as follows: Beginning at "D" (as marked in the Plat) a chesnut dividing corner between AUGUSTIN J. SMITH and HENRY ROSE, North 23° 36' West 279 1/2 Poles to "E" a chesnut a corner to MORDICAI & FITZHUGH, thence North 62 1/4° East 191 Poles to "F" a Spanish oak, thence South 80 3/4° East 52 Poles to "G" a chesnut and red oak saplin, thence North 45° East 95 Poles to "H" a large red oak, thence North 96 1/2° West 98 1/2 Poles to "I" a stake near several marked Saplins, thence North 15 1/4°, East 73 Poles to "J" a stake in CRUMPS old fields corner to GILES FITZHUGH, thence North 65 3/4° East 190 Poles to "K" a white oak on the West side of the Church road, thence South 72° East 40 poles to "L" several marked saplings on the east side of a branch, thence North 12° East 16 poles to "M" on the North bank of Middle Run, thence North 34 Poles to "N" a small white oak on the east side of a branch, thence North 78° East 94 poles to "O" a Stake in the South line of Ravensworth, thence along the same line South 38° West 402 poles to "S" several white oak bushes corner to said SMITH and ROSE, thence South 78° West 26 poles to "R" a red oak, thence South 31 1/2° West 150 poles to "Q" a black oak, thence South 31 1/2° West 148 1/2 poles to "P" a black oak, thence South 28° West 205 poles to the beginning. Together with all the Singular houses, dove houses, Barnes, buildings, stables, yards, gardens, orchards, lands, tenements, meadows, pastures, feedings, commons, Woods, under Woods, Ways, Waters, Watercourses, fishings, privileges, profits, easements, commodities, advantages, emuluments, hereditaments and appurtenances whatsoever to the said certain Tract or parcel

of Land belonging or appertaining or with the same used or enjoyed or accepted, reputed taken or known as part, parcel or member thereof or as belonging to the same or any Part thereof and the reversion and reversions, remainder & remainders, Yearly and other Rents, Issues and Profits thereof and of every part and parcel thereof. To have and To Hold the said Tract or Parcel of Land with the Tenements, hereditaments and all and Singluar other premises herein before mentioned or intended to be bargained & Sold and every part and parcel thereof with every of their rights, members and appurtenances unto the said RICHARD STUART aforesaid his heirs and assigns forever to & for the proper use & behoof of him the said RICHARD STUART only his heirs and assigns forever provided always and upon condition that if the said HENRY ROSE his Heirs, executors, or Administrators shall well & truly pay or cause to be paid unto the aforesaid RICHARD STUART his Heirs, Executors, administrators, or assigns the full & just sum of four hundred Pounds of Lawfull Money of the United States on or before the first day of January one Thousand eight hundred & twelve next ensuing the date of these presents at Popes Creek in the County of Westmoreland and Legal Interest annually thereon as it becomes due from Year to Year then and in such case and at all times from thence forth these presents and all the estate hereby granted and every clause and sentence herein contained shall cease, determine and be utterly void to all intents and purposes any thing herein contained to the contrary notwithstanding. And the said HENRY ROSE doth hereby for himself, his Heirs, executors and Administrators covenant & agree with the said RICHARD STUART his executors, administrators and assigns that the said HENRY ROSE his Heirs, executors or administrators shall & will well & truly pay or cause to be paid unto the said RICHARD STUART his executors, Administrators or assigns the said sum of four hundred pounds of Lawfull Money of the United States at such time as is herein before mentioned and legal interest annually thereon as it becomes due from the date of these presents from Year to Year and further that it shall & may be lawful to & for the said RICHARD STUART his executors, Administrators & assigns from time to time and at all times from & after default shall happen to be made in the Payment of the said Sum of four hundred Pounds of Lawful Money aforesaid or any part thereof or the legal interest as it becomes due annually thereon from the date of these presents as aforesaid contrary to the form and effect of the aforesaid proviso & covenant of the same peaceably & quietly to enter into, have, hold, occupy, possess & enjoy the said Tract or Parcel of Land and to receive and take the Rents & Profits thereof without the lawful let, suit, trouble, denial, eviction, or interruption of or by the said HENRY ROSE his heirs or assigns or of or by any other person or persons whatsoever. And it is hereby declared & agreed by and between the said parties to these presents that in the mean time and untill default shall happen to be made of or in payment of the said Sum of four hundred pounds of lawful money aforesaid contrary to the form & effect of the aforesaid proviso and covenant for payment of the same it shall & may be lawful to and for the said HENRY ROSE & his Heirs peaceably and quietly to have, hold and enjoy all the said Tract or Parcel of Land, Messuages or dwelling Houses, buildings, hereditaments & Premises & to receive and take the Rents and Profits thereof and of every part thereof to & for his and their use & benefit without lawful let, suit, trouble or interruption of the said RICHARD STUART his executors, administrators, or assigns or any other Person or Persons Lawfully claiming or to claim by, from, or under him or them or any of them. In WITNESS Whereof the Parties to these presents have hereunto set their hands & affixed their Seals the day and Year first above Written. Signed Sealed and Delivered
In Presence of
R. J. TAYLOR   HENRY ROSE   (seal)
THO. SWANN as to R.S.   RICHARD STUART   (seal)
EDM. J. LEE as to R.S.
WM. MOSS to H. ROSE
        ALEXANDRIA CORPORATION:
        HENRY ROSE and RICHARD STUART Personally appeared before me the Subscriber, Mayor of Alexandria, and acknowledged the above to be their Hands and Seals and Delivered this Instrument of Conveyance as their act and Deed for the purposes therein mentioned. In

testimony whereof I have hereunto affixed my hand and the seal of the Corporation October 18th 1808.   CUTHBERT POWELL
                                                                Mayor of Alexandria
     At a Court Held for Fairfax County the 16th Day of January 1809 this Deed from HENRY ROSE to RICHARD STUART Guardian of the Heirs of DANL. McCARTY Deceased was proved to be the Act and Deed of the said HENRY ROSE by the oath of WILLIAM MOSS a Witness hereto & ordered to be certified. And at a Court continued & held for the said County the 21st Day of March 1809 the same was acknowledged by the said HENRY ROSE to be his his act and Deed & proved to be the act & deed of the said RICHARD STUART by the oath of THOS. SWANN, another Witness hereto which together with the Certificate hereon endorsed are ordered to be recorded.   Teste WM. MOSS Cl.

Pages 139-143. THIS INDENTURE made this 20th day of September in the Year of our Lord one Thousand eight Hundred & eight between JOHN B. BARKER & ANN his wife of the County of Fairfax and CommonWealth of Virginia of the one part & WILLIAM BARKER of the County and State aforesaid of the other part: WITNESSETH that the said JOHN B. BARKER & ANN his wife for and in consideration of the Sum of Nine hundred & Sixty Dollars current Money in hand paid to the said JOHN B. BARKER by the said WILLIAM BARKER at and before the Sealing & delivery of these presents the receipt whereof he doth hereby acknowledge and thereof doth acquit and Discharge the said WILLIAM BARKER his heirs, executors and Administrators and the said JOHN B. BARKER and ANN his wife by these presents have granted, bargained & Sold, aliened, Released & Confirmed and by these presents Doth grant, bargain and Sell, alien, release and Confirm unto the said WILLIAM BARKER his heirs and assigns a certain tract or parcel of Land containing one hundred & ninety two acres and four poles being a part of a larger tract of Land which the said JOHN B. BARKER purchased of WM. LYLES of the State of Maryland and the said LYLES purchased that with other lands from WILLIAM AYLITE LEE and FRANCIS LIGHTFOOT LEE which said land lying & being on both sides of Difficult Run in the County of Fairfax which said Land hereby conveyed is bounded as follows: beginning at a box white oak, thence North 4° East 98 poles to a stake, thence North 18° East 14 poles to a stake, thence North 67 3/4° East 145 1/2 poles to a red oak, thence South 590° West 26 poles to a stake on West side of Difficult Run, thence South 7° West 38 poles to a stake, thence South 87° West 7 1/2 poles, thence South 19° East 12 poles to a Spanish oak on the West side of Difficult Run, thence South 39° East 42 poles crossing said run to a stake, thence South 28° West 80 poles near a red oak and pine, thence North 56° West 171 poles to a red oak, thence to the beginning containing one hundred & ninety two acres and four poles and all houses, buildings, Yards, gardens, orchards, meadows, pastures, Ways, Waters, Watercourses, Woods and Underwoods, Profits, commodities, hereditaments and apertenances to the same belonging or in anywise apper-taining and reversion & Reversions, Remainder & Remainders, Rents, Issues & Profits thereof and all the estate right, title and Interest of the said JOHN B. BARKER and ANN his wife of, in and to the same either in Law or equity. To have and To Hold the said tract or parcel of Land hereby granted & conveyed with all and singular the appurtenances thereunto belonging unto the said WILLIAM BARKER his heirs and assigns to the only proper use and behoof of the said WILLIAM BARKER his heirs and assigns forever and the said JOHN B. BARKER for himself, his Heirs, executors and Administrators doth covenant, Promise and grant to and with the said WILLIAM BARKER his heirs, executors, Administrators and assigns that the said JOHN B. BARKER at the time of Sealing and delivering of these presents is seized of a good, sure, perfect and indefeasible estate of Inheritance of, in and to the said tract or parcel of Land hereby granted & conveyed and that the said tract of Land now is and so forever hereafter shall remain and be free and clear of and from all former and other gifts, Grants, bargains, Sales, Mortgages, Dower rights and titles of Dower, Judgments, executions, Titles, troubles, charges and incumbrances whatever. And that the said JOHN B. BARKER his Heirs, executors and Administrators the said tract or parcel of Land with all and Singular the appurtenances thereunto belonging unto the said WILLIAM BARKER his heirs and assigns shall and will warrant & forever defend by these presents. In WITNESS whereof the said JOHN B. BARKER & ANN his wife have hereunto set their their Hands and affixed their Seals this Day & Year first above written.

Signed Sealed & Delivered
In Presence of   JNO. B. BARKER   (seal)
JNO. C. HUNTER   ANN BARKER   (seal)
HANCOCK LEE
JOSEPH BENNETT

At a court contd. & held for Fairfax County the 17th January 1809 this Deed from JNO. B. BARKER & ANNE his wife to WILLM. BARKER was proved to be the act and Deed of the said JOHN B. BARKER by the oath of JNO. C. HUNTER a Witness hereto & ordered to be Certified. And at a Court continued & held for the said County the 25th day of March 1809 the same was acknowledged by the said JNO. B. BARKER to be his Act and Deed which together with the commission & Return hereto annexed for taking the acknowledgment & privy examination of the said ANNE are ordered to be Recorded.   Teste WM. MOSS Cl.

FAIRFAX COUNTY To Wit:

The CommonWealth of Virginia to JOHN C. HUNTER, HANCOCK LEE & CHARLES LITTLE Gentlemen of the County of Fairfax Greeting: Whereas JOHN B. BARKER and ANN BARKER his wife by their certain Indenture of bargain & Sale bearing date the 20th day of September 1808 have Sold & Conveyed unto WM. BARKER the fee Simple estate of 192 acres and 4 poles of Land lying on both sides of Difficult Run with the appurtenances situate, lying and being in the County of Fairfax and Whereas the said ANN BARKER cannot conveniently travel to our said County Court of Fairfax to make acknowledgment of the said conveyance therefore we do give unto you or any two or more of you power to receive the acknowledgment which the said ANN BARKER shall be willing to make before You of the Conveyance aforesaid contained in the said Indenture which is hereunto annexed and we do therefore desire You or any two or more of You Personally to go to the said ANN BARKER and receive her acknowledgments of the same and examine her privily and apart from the said JOHN B. BARKER her husband whither she doth the same freely and voluntarily without his persuasions or threats and whither she be willing the said Indenture together with this commission shall be recorded in our said Court and when you have received her acknowledgment and examined her as aforesaid that you distinctly and openly certify us thereof in our said Court under your hands & Seals sending then there the sd. Indenture and this Writ. WITNESS WILLIAM MOSS Clerk of the said Court this 20th Day of September 1808 and in the 33rd Year of the CommonWealth.
                                                          WM. MOSS Cl.

FAIRFAX COUNTY To Wit:,

In pursuance of the within commission to us directed We the Subscribers two of the justices of the Peace for the County aforesaid do hereby certify that we did Personally go to the within named ANN BARKER wife of the within named JOHN B. BARKER and did privately and apart from her said Husband examine her touching the execution of the within Deed which was by us read and explained to her & she declared to us that she executed the same freely and voluntarily without the treats, persuasion or undue influence of her said Husband and that she relinquished all right to Dower in the Property therein conveyed and was willing the same together with this commission and acknowledgment should be recorded in the Court of the said County. Given under our hands & Seals this 20th day of September 1808.
                                                          JNO. C. HUNTER   (seal)
                                                          HANCOCK LEE   (seal)

Pages 143 & 144. FAIRFAX COUNTY:

Agreeable to the 7th Section of an Act of Virginia Legislature passed the 28th of January 1804 entitled "an Act to amend and reduce into one the several Acts of the General Assembly for regulating the Militia of this CommonWealth" I certify that FRANCIS HAMERSLY JR this day came before me a justice of the Peace for the County aforesaid and took the oath Prescribed by the said Act of Assembly to execute the Office of Lieutenant in the Militia of the CommonWealth of Virginia. Given under my Hand this 19th of May 1808.
                                                          THOMSON MASON

To The Clerk, Fairfax Court:

At a Court held for Fairfax County the 20th Day of March 1809 FRANCIS HAMMERSLEY JR Produced to the Court this Certificate of his qualification as Lientenant in the 60th Regiment Virginia Militia which is ordered to be recorded

Teste WM. MOSS Cl.

Pages 144-149. THIS INDENTURE made this twenty Seventh day of April in Year of our Lord one thousand eight Hundred & seven between THOMAS RICHARDS of the County of Fairfax and CommonWealth of Virginia and NANCY his wife of the one part and JAMES H. HOOE of the Town of Alexandria of the other part. Whereas the said THOMAS RICHARDS by his Indenture bearing date the [left blank] Day of [left blank] in the Year one thousand eight Hundred and [left blank] did Convey unto THOMAS SWANN Esquire of the Town of Alexandria two Tracts or Parts of Land situated in the County of Fairfax upon the Drains of Great Hunting Creek one of which said Tracts contained eighty two Acres the other five acres and an half which said conveyance was made in Trust that he the said THOMAS SWANN should upon the terms and conditions in the said conveyance mentioned sell the said Tracts or Parcels of Land for the purpose of paying a Debt mentioned in the said Deed due from him to the said THOMAS RICHARDS to ROBERT T. HOOE & Company of Alexandria. And whereas the said THOMAS RICHARDS having failed to pay the Debt in the said Deed mentioned to the said THOMAS SWANN according to the terms & conditions of the said Deed proceeds sell the said Tract of Land and the aforementioned JAS. H. HOOE at the sale aforesaid became the purchaser thereof in consequence of which he the said THOMAS SWANN as Trustee aforesaid conveyed the said Tract of Land to the said JAMES H. HOOE in fee. And whereas the said THOS. RICHARDS notwith-standing the said sale & conveyances still retains Possession of the said Lands alledging that the Houses & Gardens now in his tenure and occupation were not contained in his aforesaid Deed of Trust to the said THOMAS SWANN and that his wife the said NANCY had not relin-quished her Dower in the said Lands. And Whereas the said THOMAS RICHARDS & NANCY his wife for the consideration herein after mentioned have agreed to give up the possession of the said Land and confirm the title thereof to him the said JAMES H. HOOE. Now this indenture WITNESSETH that the said THOMAS RICHARDS and NANCY his Wife for and in consideration of the Sum of two Hundred and fifty Dollars to him the said THOMAS RICHARDS in hand paid by the said JAMES H. HOOE and before the ensealing and Delivery of these presents the receipt whereof the said THOMAS RICHARDS doth hereby acknowledge and thereof doth exonerate & acquit the said JAMES H. HOOE his executors and Administrators by these presents have Granted, Bargained and Sold, Aliened, released, confirmed and given up and by these presents Do grant, bargain and Sell, alien, release, confirm and give up to the said JAMES H. HOOE his heirs and assigns forever the said two tracts of land sold and conveyed to the said JAMES H. HOOE by the said THOMAS SWANN as trustee aforesaid which said tracts of land are bounded as follows to wit: the said Tract containing eighty two acres beginning at a Stake supposed to stand in or near the lane of MATHEWS Patent corner to WM. JONES, thence with the line of MATTHEWS Patent north 53 degrees and a half West 158 Poles and a half to a Stake in or near the said line to HENRY TUCKERS, thence with TUCKERS Line South forty two degrees west 40 1/2 Poles to a stake another corner of the said TUCKER in or near the line of WILLIAM SIMMS, thence with SIMMS' line South 61 degrees east 143 Poles and a quarter to a Corner of SIMMS' land near two black oaks standing on the North side of the Road leading from Colchester to Alexandria, thence up the Meanders of the Road South seventy six Degrees East sixteen Poles, North eighty Seven Degrees East eighteen Poles, North Sixty two Degrees east fifteen Poles, North forty five Degrees east sixteen Poles, North Seventy five Degrees east eighteen Poles, North Sixty Degrees east fifteen Poles opposite to a ditch corner of the said JONES' Land, then with his line North twenty seven Degrees West Sixty one Poles to the Beginning. The other tract or parcel of Land containing as before stated five acres and a half beginning at the corner of a Ditch near a Dead red oak said to be a corner of RICHARD SANFORD'S land and supposed to stand in or near the line of MATTHEWS Patent corner of JAMES SAVAGES land & running thence with his line South ten Degrees West 28 1/4 Poles to two small white oak saplins corner of said SAVAGE and WILLIAM SIMMS' land, thence with a line of SIMMS' South sixty one Degrees east seventeen poles and three quarters to a Stake in or near the said line corner to the above tract, thence with a line of that tract reversed North forty two Degrees east 40 poles and an half to a stake in or near the line of MATTHEWS' Patent, Corner to the said Tract, thence with the line of MATTHEWS' North eighty three Degrees and an half West 38 poles to the beginning which said Tracts or parcels of land adjoin each other. And all Houses, buildings, Gardens, Ways, Waters, Watercourses, profits, commodities and advantages to the said Tracts or Parcels of Land belonging or in anywise appertaining and the reversion and Reversions, remainder and Remainders, Rents, Issues and Profits thereof also all the estate right, title, Interest, property claim & demand of them the said THOS. RICHARDS and NANCY his wife of, in and to the same and every part and parcel thereof. To have and to Hold the said hereby granted premises with all and singular the appurtenances thereunto belonging unto the said JAMES H. HOOE his heirs & assigns forever to the only proper use and behoof of him the said JAS. H. HOOE his Heirs and Assigns for ever. And the said THOMAS RICHARDS for himself and his heirs the said hereby granted premises with all and Singular the appurtenances thereunto belonging unto the said JAS. H. HOOE his heirs & assigns forever against the claim and demand of all and every person and persons whatsoever shall and will Warrant & forever Defend by these presents. In WITNESS whereof the said THOMAS RICHARDS & NANCY his wife have hereunto set their hands & affixed their Seals the Day and Year first before Written.

Sealed and Delivered
In Presence of
PHILIP HENRY SEIDER
RICHD. M. SCOTT
JOHN J. FROBLE
GUSTAVUS H. SCOTT

THOS. RICHARDS   (seal)
ANN RICHARDS   (seal)

    At a Court held for Fairfax County the Nineteenth Day of October1807 this Deed from THOMAS RICHARDS and ANN his wife to JAMES H. HOOE was proved to be the Act and Deed of the said THOMAS RICHARDS by the oaths of PHILIP HENRY SEIDER and JOHN J. FROBEL Witnesses hereto and ordered to be Certified. And at a Court held for the said County the Seventeenth Day of April 1809 the same was further proved by the oath of RICHARD M. SCOTT another Witness hereto which together with a Commission & Return hereto annexed for taking the acknowledgment and privy examination of the said ANN and Ordered to be Recorded.   Teste WM. MOSS Cl.

    FAIRFAX COUNTY To Wit:

    The CommonWealth of Virginia to RICHARD M. SCOTT, THOMSON MASON & JAMES H. BLAKE Gentlemen justices of the Courty of Fairfax Greeting: Whereas THOMAS RICHARDS and NANCY his wife by their certain Indenture of bargain and Sale bearing date the 27th Day of April 1807 have Sold and conveyed unto JAMES H. HOOE the fee simple estate of two tracts or parcels of Land with the appurtenances situate, lying & being in the County of Fairfax and whereas the said NANCY wife of the said THOMAS cannot conveniently travel to our said County Court of Fairfax to make acknowledgment of the said conveyance therefore we do give unto you or any two or more of you power to receive the acknowledgment which the said NANCY shall be willing to make before you of the conveyance aforesaid contained in the said Indenture which is hereunto annexed. And we do therefore desire You or any two or more of You Personally to go to the said NANCY and receive her acknowledgment of the same and examine her privily and apart from the said THOMAS RICHARDS her husband whither she doth the same freely and voluntarily without his persuasions or threats. And whither she be willing the said Indenture together with this commission shall be recorded in our said Court; and when you have received her acknowledgment and examined her as aforesaid that You distinctly and openly certify us thereof in our said Court under Your hands and Seals sending then there the said Indenture and this Writ. WITNESS WILLIAM MOSS Clerk of our said Court, at the Court House of the County aforesaid this twenty Seventh Day of April 1807 and in the 31st Year of the CommonWealth.

    FAIRFAX COUNTY To Wit:

    In Obedience to the within Commission we the under sign'd Justices of the Peace for the County of Fairfax aforesaid went to the within mentioned NANCY RICHARDS wife of the within mentioned THOS. RICHARDS and examined her privily and apart from the said THOMAS her Husband and the said NANCY did then and there acknowledge that she had executed and Delivered the Deed in the within Commission mentioned freely and voluntarily without the Persuasions or threats of the said THOMAS her Husband and Declared that she was willing that the said Deed together with this Commission should be recorded in the County Court of Fairfax. Given under our hands and Seals this twenty seventh Day of April 1807.

RICHD. M. SCOTT   (seal)
JAMES H. BLACK   (seal)

Pages 149-158. [Marginal Note: Examined and Delivered to MARSHALL SMITH upon order from SAMUEL G. GRIFFIN of Baltimore who pd. me the fees for Recording. NASH]

THIS INDENTURE made this second Day of September in the Year of our Lord Christ eighteen Hundred & eight between NATHANIEL ELLICOTT of the Town of Occoquan County of Prince William, JAMES CAMPBELL of the Town of Petersburg and LUKE WHEELER of the Borough & Town of Norfolk in the CommonWealth of Virginia of the one part and JOHN ROBERTS and EDMUND JENNINGS LEE both of the Town of Alexandria in the District of Columbia of the other Part. WITNESSETH that the said NATHANIEL ELLICOTT, JAMES CAMPBELL and LUKE WHEELER trading & carrying on business under the Style, name & firm of ELLICOTT, CAMPBELL and WHEELER, stands justly indebted to a certain SAMUEL GOLDSMITH GRIFFITH of the Town of Baltimore State of Maryland in the full Sum of fifteen thousand Dollars Lawful Money of the United States and Whereas the said SAMUEL G. GRIFFITH and [left blank] of the Town of Baltimore have become endorsers for the said ELLICOTT, CAMPBELL and WHEELER upon their accommodation notes in the [left blank] of the said Town of Baltimore amounting to the sum of Twelve thousand Dollars and whereas it is right and just that the said ELLICOTT, CAMPBELL & WHEELER should secure the repayment to the said SAMUEL G. GRIFFITH of the aforesaid Sum of fifteen Thousand Dollars with legal Interest on the same from the first Day of January last past and that they should also secure & save harmless the said SAMUEL G. GRIFFITH and [left blank] for their endorsment aforesaid. And whereas the true intent and meaning of this Indenture is fully to secure the repayment with Interest of the said Sum of Fifteen Thousand Dollars to the said SAMUEL G. GRIFFITH and fully to indemnify & save harmless the said SAML G. GRIFFITH and [left blank] for their endorsment aforesaid and Whereas the said NATHANIEL ELLICOTT and a certain ISAAC McPHERSON now in the said Town of Baltimore were on the seventeenth Day of August in the Year of our Lord one thousand seven Hundred & ninety nine seized in fee Simple as tenants in Common of the following pieces or Parcels of land situate, lying & being in the County of Prince William and Fairfax and upon and on each side of the River Occoquan and in the State of Virginia to wit: one tract containing two hundred and fifty acres (two acres of which hath been Previously conveyed in fee to a certain DANIEL DAUGHERTY) one other piece or Parcel containing twenty five acres, one other piece or parcel of land containing seventy nine acres and also one other piece or parcel containing Three Hundred and Eighty three acres and whereas the said ISAAC McPHERSON and JACY his wife did by their Indenture bearing date on the Seventeenth day of August in the Year of our Lord one thousand & seven hundred & ninety nine and now of Record of this Office of the District Court held at the Town of Haymarket in the State of Virginia all which together with history of the title to the said several tracts of land will more fully & at large appear convey the aforesaid tracts of land in fee simple to the said NATHANIEL ELLICOTT & whereas the said NATHANIEL ELLICOTT did by his Indenture bearing date [left blank] on the day of [left blank] in the Year of our Lord one thousand [left blank] duly executed & Recorded convey two undivided third parts of the Right, title and interest which he the said NATHANIEL had in and to all and each of the aforesaid several tracts of land unto the said JAMES CAMPBELL and LUKE WHEELER to hold as tenants in common with the said NATHANIEL ELLICOTT as will more fully and at large appear by reference to the said Indenture last mentioned. Now this Indenture WITNESSETH that the said NATHANIEL ELLICOTT, JAMES CAMPBELL and LUKE WHEELER as well for and in consideration of the Premises as for and in consideration of the sum of five Dollars to them in hand paid by the said JOHN ROBERTS and EDMUND JENNINGS LEE at & before the Sealing and Delivery of these presents the receipt whereof the said NATHANIEL ELLICOTT, JAMES CAMPBELL & LUKE WHEELER do hereby acknowledge and thereof doth acquit, release and Discharge them the said JOHN ROBERTS and

EDMUND JENNINGS LEE their heirs, executors and Administrators by these presents have Granted, bargained, Sold, aliened & confirmed & by these presents do grant, bargain, Sell, alien & confirm unto them the said JOHN ROBERTS and EDMUND JENNINGS LEE and to the Survivor of them and their Heirs and assigns and to the Heirs and assigns of the Survivor forever all the estate right, title, use and Trust, Interest and Property of them the said NATHANIEL ELLICOTT, JAMES CAMPBELL & LUKE WHEELER in and to as much of all and each of the aforesaid several Tracts or Parcels of Land as the said NATHANIEL ELLICOTT, JAMES CAMPBELL & LUKE WHEELER have not heretofore for a valuable and sufficient consideration conveyed or heretofore covenanted to convey to any other persons or person by a good, legal and sufficient Deed or Deeds. Sealed & delivered in full & due form of Law to wit: Lot Number thirty eight to THOMAS TROOPE, Lot No. thirty nine to WILLIAM ROBEY, Lot number twenty four to GEORGE SELCKMAN, Lot number fifty three to ADAM KREMER and Lot number six to THOMAS SELCKMAN. And the Distant Fairfax Tract of Land containing [left blank] acres Sold to EDWARD WASHINGTON saving and reserving to the above persons their heirs and Assigns full and complete titles to the aforesaid Lotts, Parcels or tracts of Land together with the rights of Waters of the River Occoquan which shall be included within the boundaries of the Lands or any part of the Lands heretofore conveyed or intended to be conveyed and also all Mills, Mill Dams, Houses, buildings and improvements of every sort or kind in and upon any part of the hereby granted premises made & erected or to be made or to be erected on the same together with the bridge over the said River Occoquan at the Mill now held and used by the said NATHANIEL ELLICOTT, JAMES CAMPBELL and LUKE WHEELER and all the trees, Woods, Timber, Profits, commodities, Hereditaments and appurtenances Whatsoever to the premises hereby granted or any part of them belonging or any wise appertaining and the Reversion and Reversions, Remainder and Remainders, Rents, Issues and Profits thereof and of every part and parcel thereof in any manner belonging. To have and to hold all and Singular the premises hereby granted with the appurtenances unto them the said JOHN ROBERTS and EDMUND JENNINGS LEE & the Survivor of them & their Heirs & assigns & the Heirs & assigns of the Surivor of them forever. Nevertheless upon the Condition and Trust following and none other that is to say to the use & benefit of the said NATHANIEL ELLICOTT, JAMES CAMPBELL and LUKE WHEELER & the survivor of them untill a sale be made of the hereby granted premises under the authority of this Deed & after sale shall be made then to the use and benefit of the purchaser or purchasers untill a conveyance shall be made to such purchaser or purchasers under the authority of this Deed. And if the said NATHANIEL ELICOTT, JAS. CAMPBELL & LUKE WHEELER or either of them shall not within four Months after notice is given in writing by the said SAMUEL G. GRIFFITH to the said NATHANIEL ELLICOTT, JAMES CAMPBELL & LUKE WHEELER or to either of them or to either of the Heirs, Executors or Administrators of them or either of them that he the said SAML. G. GRIFFITH desires & wishes that a contract dated on the twenty seventh day of November in the year one thousand eight hundred and seven (1807) between him and the said NATHANIEL ELLICOTT, JAMES CAMPBELL and LUKE WHEELER under the firm of ELLICOTT, CAMPBELL & WHEELER to cease and be at an end (by which contract the said SAMUEL G. GRIFFITH agrees to lend to the said ELLICOTT, CAMPBELL & WHEELER the said sum of Fifteen Thousand Dollars) pay to the said SAMUEL G. GRIFFITH his Executors, Administrators, or assigns or to his or their Legally authorized agent or agents the aforesaid Sum of Fifteen Thousand Dollars with all Interest which shall or may at the time when such notice is given be due and owing from the said ELLICOTT, CAMPBELL & WHEELER to the said SAMUEL G. GRIFFITH. And also at any time it should so happen that the said [left blank] should give the said SAMUEL G. GRIFFITH and [left blank] endorses as aforesaid upon the aforesaid notes of the said ELLICOTT, CAMPBELL & WHEELER or either of them notice that the Amount of the said notes so endorsed by them must be paid, that then and in case either of the above events or defaults on the part of the said ELLICOTT, CAMPBELL & WHEELER should happen or take place, the said JOHN ROBERTS or EDMUND JENNINGS LEE or the Survivor of them or the Heirs, Executors or Administrators of the Survivor of them shall upon being required by the said SAMUEL G. GRIFFITH his Executors, Administrators or assigns by a request in writing Signed by him or them after giving three Months Public Notice in any NewsPaper Published in the District of Columbia or State of Virginia of the time and place Sell at Public Sale on the premises or in the Town of Occoquan upon such terms as shall be expressed and directed by the said SAMUEL G. GRIFFITH his Executors, Administrators or Assigns in and by his or their aforesaid written request the hereby granted premises or so much thereof as shall or may be necessary to pay after deducting the charges of the said Sale not only whatever may be due on Account of the aforesaid loan of Fifteen thousand Dollars and on Account of the Endoresement aforesaid on the aforesaid notes to the [left blank] but also whatever may be due from the said ELLICOTT, CAMPBELL & WHEELER upon the accounts. And the Money arising from the said sale is to be applied as aforesaid and the surplus if any to be paid over to the said ELLICOTT, CAMPBELL & WHEELER or their Legally authorized Representatives. And the said NATHANIEL ELLICOTT, JAMES CAMPBELL & LUKE WHEELER do each for themselves and for their and each of their Heirs Covenant & agree to & with the said JOHN ROBERTS & EDMUND JENNINGS LEE their heirs & assigns & with the Survivor of them that they the said NATHANIEL ELLICOTT, JAMES CAMPBELL and LUKE WHEELER and their Heirs will at any time hereafter at the request and at the Cost and charges of them the said JOHN ROBERTS and EDMUND JENNINGS LEE their heirs and assigns execute and acknowledge any other or further lawful Deed for the more certain assuring and conveying all and every part of the hereby granted Premises with their appurtenances unto them the said JOHN ROBERTS and EDMUND JENNINGS LEE in Trust as aforesaid or their heirs Heirs and Assigns as by them the said JOHN ROBERTS and EDMUND JENNINGS LEE their heirs or assigns or any of their Council learned in the Law shall devise or advise. And lastly that they the said NATHANIEL ELLICOTT, JAMES CAMPBELL and LUKE WHEELER and their Heirs all and Singular the hereby granted premises unto them the said JOHN ROBERTS and EDMUND JENNINGS LEE and the Survivors of them and their or his Heirs and assigns against the claim and demand of all and every Person or Persons whomsoever shall and will forever defend by these presents. And the said JOHN ROBERTS and EDMUND JENNINGS LEE do for themselves severally and not jointly covenant & agree with the said SAMUEL GOLDSMITH GRIFFITH and his Heirs and Assigns that they will well and truly execute the trust vested in them by this indenture. In WITNESS whereof the said parties to this Deed have on the Day and Year first above written set their hands & affixed their Seals.

Signed Sealed & delivered		N. ELLICOTT	(seal)
In Presence of		JAMES CAMPBELL by his	(seal)
JOHN ELLICOTT	Witnesses to the	attorney L. WHEELER	
B. G. GILPIN	Signatures of Ellicott,	LUKE WHEELER	(seal)
ALFRED P. GILPIN	Campbell & Wheeler	JOHN ROBERTS	(seal)
		EDM. J. LEE	(seal)
		JAMES CAMPBELL	(seal)

PRINCE WILLIAM COUNTY Court April 4th 1809 this Indenture between N. ELLICOTT, JAMES CAMPBELL by his Attorney LUKE WHEELER and LUKE WHEELER for himself, JOHN ROBERTS, EDMUND J. LEE and JAMES CAMPBELL was acknowledged by N. ELLICOTT & Proved as to the Execution by LUKE WHEELER by the oaths of JOHN ELLICOTT, B. GILPIN and ALFRED P. GILPIN and ordered to be certified to the County Court of Fairfax to be Recorded.
Teste J. WILLIAMS Cl.

CORPORATION OF ALEXANDRIA To Wit:
JOHN ROBERTS and EDMUND J. LEE personally appeared before me the Subscriber, Mayor of Alexandria and acknowledged their Signatures & Seals to the foregoing Deed.
Given under my hand and the Seal of the Corporation this 8th
(SEAL)   day of September 1808.   CUTHBERT POWELL
Mayor

VIRGINIA To Wit:
At a general Court held at the Capitol in Richmond the 12th Day of November 1808 this Indenture was acknowledged by JAS. CAMPBELL party thereto and together with the certificate from under the hand and Seal of CUTHBERT POWELL Mayor of the Corporation of Alexandria thereafter written On the Motion of JOHN ROBERTS and EDMUND J. LEE Parties thereto was ordered to be Recorded.   Teste WILSON ALLEN Cl.

At a Court held for Fairfax County the 17th day of April 1809 this Deed from NATHANIEL ELLICOTT, JAMES CAMPBELL and LUKE WHEELER to JOHN ROBERTS and EDMUND JENNINGS LEE in Trust for the use of SAMUEL G. GRIFFITH having been duly acknowledged by the several parties hereto is on motion together with the several Certificates hereon endorsed and powers of attorney's annexed ordered to be Recorded.

Teste WM. MOSS Cl.

KNOW ALL MEN by these presents that I JAMES CAMPBELL Partner in the firm of ELLICOTT, CAMPBELL and WHEELER at Occoquan and residing at Fleet Mills in Chesterfield County all in the State of Virginia having special Trust and confidence in LUKE WHEELER of the Borough of Norfolk my Partner in the aforesaid Firm Do hereby constitute and appoint the said LUKE WHEELER my true and lawful attorney in my name to sell and convey or otherwise dispose of all and Singular the Real estate and other Property held and owned by me as Partner in the aforesaid firm of ELLICOTT, CAMPBELL & WHEELER or as tenants in Common or as joint tenants lying in Prince William or Fairfax County or elsewhere hereby binding and obliging myself my Heirs, Executors and Administrators to abide by, ratify and perform all such Covenants and agreements for the sale or Disposal of all such Property Real or Personal as is held by me in conjunction with NATHANIEL ELLICOTT of Prince William County & LUKE WHEELER of the Borough of Norfolk my Partners as aforesaid under the firm of ELLICOTT, CAMPBELL & WHEELER. In testimony whereof I have hereunto set my hand and affixed my Seal at the Place first above mentioned to this Instrument this first Day of September eighteen hundred & Eight (1808). JAMES CAMPBELL (seal)

VIRGINIA TOWN OF PETERSBURG To Wit:

(SEAL)   Before me JAMES BYRNE the present MAYOR or Chief Magistrate of the Town aforesaid personally appeared JAMES CAMPBELL of the trading House of CAMPBELL and WHEELER and acknowledged the annexed Power of Attorney to be his Act & Deed & desired that it might be so Certified to all whom it may or doth concern. In Testimony whereof I have hereto subscribed my name and caused to be affixed the Seal of the said Town of Petersburg this thirteenth day of September, eighteen Hundred and eight and in the 33rd [year] of American Independence.   JAS. BYRNE Mayor

Know all Men by these presents that I JAMES CAMPBELL Partner in the firm of ELLICOTT, CAMPBELL and WHEELER at Occoquan and residing at Fleet Mills in Chesterfield County all in Virginia having special Trust and confidence in LUKE WHEELER of the Borough of Norfolk my Partner in the aforesaid Firm do hereby constitute and appoint the said LUKE WHEELER my true and lawful attorney in my name to sell and convey or otherwise dispose of all and Singular the Real estate and other Property held and owned by me as Partner in the aforesaid firm of ELLICOTT, CAMPBELL & WHEELER or as Tenants in Common or as joint Tenants lying in Prince William or Fairfax Counties or elsewhere hereby binding and obliging myself, my Heirs, Executors and Administrators to abide by, ratify and perform all such Covenants and agreements for the sale or Disposal of all such Property Real or Personal as is held by me in conjunction with NATHANIEL ELLICOTT of Prince William County & LUKE WHEELER of the Borough of Norfolk my Partners as aforesaid under the firm of ELLICOTT, CAMPBELL & WHEELER. In Testimony whereof I have hereunto set my hand and affixed my Seal at the Place first above mentioned to this Instrument all in my own hand writing this first day of September eighteen hundred & Eight.

JAMES CAMPBELL (seal)

Pages 158-162. THIS INDENTURE made this seventeenth Day of April in the Year one thousand eight hundred & nine between JAMES SANGSTER of the County of Fairfax and State of Virginia of the one part and WILLIAM DENEALE of the State and County aforesaid attorney in fact for JANE HAMMOND formerly JANE SANGSTER of the County of Nelson and State of Kentucky of the other Part. WITNESSETH that the said DENEALE attorney as aforesaid in consideration of the sum of Ninety Dollars to him in hand paid the receipt whereof he doth hereby acknowledge hath granted, bargained Sold, Aliened, enfeoffed & Confirmed and by these presents Doth grant, Bargain, Sell, alien, enfeoff & Confirm unto the said SANGSTER all that part of the Land of THOS. SANGSTER deceased lying in the County of Fairfax to which the said JANE as one of the Representatives of said THOMAS is entitled it being clearly understood that he the said WILLIAM attorney as aforesaid does not convey any part of the Widow's third Part either immediately or in Reversion. To have and To Hold the said undivided distributory ninth Part of the said Lands of said THOMAS SANGSTER deceased excepting said Widow's Portion to him the said JAMES SANGSTER his heirs and assigns forever with all the appurtenances and improvements, to the only proper use and behoof of him the said JAMES SANGSTER his Heirs and assigns. And the said WILLIAM as attorney aforesaid the said Land to the said JAMES SANGSTER his heirs & assigns against the Claim of him the said WILLIAM and of the said JANE his principal and against the Claims of those deriving title from or under them or either of them doth by these presents forever warrant and defend. In testimony whereof the said WILLIAM DENEALE attorney as aforesaid hath hereunto set his hand and affixed his Seal the Day & year aforementioned.

Signed Sealed & delivered   W. DENEALE attorney for
in Presence of [No witnesses listed]   JANE HAMMOND   (seal)
    Received of JAMES SANGSTER the Sum of Ninety Dollars this 17th of April 1809.
                                   W. DENEALE

    At a Court continued and held for Fairfax County the 18th Day of April 1808 this Deed from WILLIAM DENEALE Attorney in fact for JANE HAMMOND to JAMES SANGSTER and a receipt hereon endorsed was acknowledged by the said WILLIAM DENEALE to be his Act and Deed & ordered to be Recorded.   Teste WM. MOSS Cl.

    To all whom these presents may Concern, Know Ye that we JANE HAMMOND executrix and THOMAS S. HAMMOND Executor to the last will and Testament of GERVIS HAMMOND Decd late of Nelson County State of Kentucky for good causes us thereunto moving have constituted and appointed and do by these presents constitute, authorise and appoint our trusty friend WILLIAM DENEALE of Fairfax County state of Virginia our Attorney in fact for the Purpose of making a compleat and final settlement for and in behalf of the Heirs, legatees or Representatives of the said GERVIS HAMMOND deceased with the Administrators to the Estate of the late THOMAS SANGSTER of the said County of Fairfax State of Virginia and we the said JANE and THOMAS S. HAMMOND as aforesaid do hereby fully authorize and empower our said Attorney to ask, Demand, sue for, Recover, Receipt for and receive all or any Part or Parts of whatever may be in anywise Due to the Heirs of the said GERVIS HAMMOND from any Person or Persons whatever or by whatever legal claim the same may be so due either in money or in any Species of Property of any kind or name and whereas the said JANE HAMMOND it is supposed claims and is justly entitled to a Proportion of the Landed Estate of the aforesaid THOMAS SANGSTER of the County of Fairfax as aforesaid she the said JANE doth hereby jointly with the said THOMAS S. HAMMOND fully authorise our said attorney to sell, transfer and convey to whom and in what manner he may think proper all the right, title, Interest and Claim she the said JANE can or could have in the said County of Fairfax as one of the heirs of the said THOMAS SANGSTER together with any title of Dower that be vested in the said JANE by any law of Kentucky or Virginia and we the said JANE and THOMAS S. HAMMOND finally hereby authorize and empower our said attorney in fact to Act in any and every thing relating to the premises herein mentioned in whatsoever manner may to him seem right, hereby Compleatly and finally Ratifying what our said attorney may so do in as full and ample a manner as if we Ourselves either jointly or separately had been present and had done the same Ourselves. Witness our hands & Seals this twenty sixth Day of November one Thousand Eight Hundred and Eight.   JANE her + mark HAMMOND   (seal)
                                   THOS S. HAMMOND   (seal)

    STATE OF KENTUCKY NELSON COUNTY To Wit:
    We AUSTIN HUBBARD and JOHN SNEED two of the justices of the Peace in for the County aforesaid do hereby Certify that on this Day the above named JANE HAMMOND and THOMAS S. HAMMOND personally appeared before us and acknowledged the foregoing letter of Attorney to be their voluntary Act and Deed for the Purposes therein mentioned. Given under our hands this 26th Day of November 1808 and in the 17th Year of the CommonWealth.
                                   A. HUBBARD (seal)
                                   JOHN SNEED (seal)

    STATE OF KENTUCKY and NELSON COUNTY To Wit:
    To all whom it may concern, I BENJAMIN GRAYSON Clerk of the County Court of the County aforesaid do certify that AUSTIN HUBBARD and JOHN SNEED Esqr. whose names are subscribed to the above Certificate are two of the justices of the Peace within the County aforesaid duly Commissioned and sworn to discharge the duties of their said office. In

(SEAL)   Testimony whereof I have hereunto set my hand & affixed the Seal of the said County this 29th Day of November in the Year of our Lord one thousand eight hundred & Eight.   BEN. GRAYSON

NELSON COUNTY To Wit:

I HENRY MILES Presiding justice of the said County Court do Certify that the above attestation of BENJAMIN GRAYSON Clerk of the said Court is in due form. Witness my hand and Seal this 29th Day of November 1808.   H. MILES J.P.N.C   (seal)

At a Court continued & held for Fairfax County the 18th April 1809 this power of Attorney from JANE HAMMOND and THOMAS S. HAMMOND to WILLIAM DENEALE having been duly acknowledged before AUSTIN HUBBARD and JOHN SNEED two justices of the Peace for the County of Nelson in the State of Kentucky and Certified by them, also by BENJAMIN GRAYSON Clerk of the said Court and under the Seal of his office and by HENRY MILES Presiding justice of the Court is on motion of the said WILLIAM DENEALE together with the Certificates hereon endorsed ordered to be Recorded.   Teste WM. MOSS Cl.

Pages 162 & 163. THIS INDENTURE made the 17th day of April in the Year of our Lord one thousand Eight Hundred & nine between FRANCIS ADAMS of the County of Fairfax and State of Virginia of the one part and THOMAS PEAKE and MARY ANN ADAMS of the County and State aforesaid of the other Part. WITNESSETH that for and in consideration of the Sum of thirty five Pounds eleven Shillings and one Penny Current money of Virginia to the said FRANCIS ADAMS in hand paid by ABEDNIGO ADAMS at or before the Sealing and delivery of these presents the receipt whereof he doth hereby acknowledge and thereof Doth Release, acquit and discharge the said THOMAS PEAKE and MARY ANN ADAMS their heirs, Executors and Administrators by these presents the said FRANCIS ADAMS Hath granted, bargained, Sold, aliened, released and Confirmed and by these presents Doth bargain, Sell, alien, Release and Confirm unto the said THOMAS PEAKE and MARY ANN ADAMS their heirs and assigns two certain Lots of ground situate in the Town of Centreville designated and known by the plan thereof by the names of Lot No. 95 and fronting on Mary & Adams Streets, Lot No. 96 & fronting on Mary Street; reference being had to said Plan will more fully and at large appear Together also with all and Singular the Rights, members, liberties, Privileges, Improvements, hereditaments and appurtenances whatsoever thereunto belonging or in anywise appertaining and the Reversion and Reversions, Remainders, rents, Issues and Profits thereof also all the estate right, Title, Interest, use, Possession, Property, claim and Demand whatsoever of him the said FRANCIS ADAMS his Heirs or Executors In Law, equity or otherwise however, of, into or out of all and Singular the Premises and every Part thereof. To Have and To Hold all and Singular the Premises hereby granted with the appurtenances unto the said THOMAS PEAKE and MARY ANN ADAMS their heirs and assigns to the only Proper use, benefit and behoof of them the said THOMAS PEAKE and MARY ANN ADAMS their heirs and assigns forever subject however to the condition of building on each Lot agreeable to the Act of Assembly establishing said Town. In WITNESS whereof the said FRANCIS ADAMS hath hereunto set his hand & Seal the date above.

                  FRANCIS ADAMS (seal)

At a Court held for Fairfax County the 17th day of April 1809 FRANCIS ADAMS acknowledged this Deed to THOMAS PEAKE and MARY ANN ADAMS to be his Act and Deed which is Ordered to be Recorded.   Teste WM. MOSS Cl.

Pages 164 & 165. KNOW ALL MEN by these presents that I THOMAS WEST of the County of Fairfax & State of Virginia for and in consideration of the natural Love and affection which I bear to my Daughter NANCY WEST as well as for the further consideration of one Dollar to me in hand paid by the said NANCY WEST at or before the ensealing and delivery of these presents the receipt whereof is hereby acknowledged have given and granted and by these presents do give and grant unto the said NANCY WEST her heirs and assigns forever one full fifth part of a Tract of Land in the State of Kentucky containing five Thousand acres in the whole taken up by a certain Person by the Name of COX and HENRY BANKS which said BANKS sold the whole to GILBERT FINLAY who sold the same to WILLIAM HINDMAN who gave a power of Attorney to HENRY LEE Esqr. to sell the said Land which said HENRY LEE made Sale to me the

said THOMAS WEST by virtue of the said Power of Attorney which is recorded in the State of New York the said land lying on the Waters of Salt River beginning at POWELL'S trace and bounded by Beach Fork and Long Lick Run it being part of the land on which JOHN WEST JR the Son of the said THOMAS WEST now lives it being in the Neighbourhood of JOHN DOUDLE which Property she shall have full right, title and possession of when she arrives to the age of eighteen Years or on the day of her marriage. To have and to hold the said land with the appurtenances unto her the said NANCY WEST her heirs and assigns forever and the said THOMAS WEST for himself his heirs, executors and administrators the above one fifth of the said Land in quantity and quality unto the said NANCY WEST her heirs and assigns, against the claim of him the said THOMAS WEST, his heirs, executors, Administrators, or any person or persons whatsoever claiming by, from or under him the said THOMAS WEST will warrant and forever by these presents. In WITNESS whereof I have hereunto set my hand and affixed my Seal this twenty first day of April one thousand eight hundred and one.
Signed, Sealed and delivered before us
JOHN BRONAUGH   THOS. WEST   (seal)
JOHN WEST
BEAL FOWLER
        April 21st 1801 Received the within Consideration in full of one Dollar.
Teste
JOHN BRONAUGH   THOS. WEST
JOHN WEST
        At a Court continued and held for Fairfax County the 22nd day of September 1801 this Deed of Gift and receipt from THOMAS WEST to NANCY WEST were proved by the oaths of JOHN BRONAUGH and JOHN WEST witnesses hereto and ordered to be Certified. And at a Court continued & held for the said County of Fairfax the 18th day of April 1809 this Deed from the said THOMAS WEST to NANCY WEST having been heretofore duly Proved by two WITNESSES and Certified it appearing to the Court that BEAL FOWLER the only other subscribing Witness to the said Deed & the said THOMAS WEST have both since the execution of the same departed this life and AMOS ALEXANDER being sworn to state his knowledge of the hand Writing of the said BEAL FOWLER and THOMAS WEST declares that the Signature of the said BEAL FOWLER as a Witness and the Signature of the said THOMAS WEST the grantor he believes to be in the true hand Writing respectively of the said BEAL FOWLER and THOMAS WEST upon which evidence the said Deed is ordered to be recorded and then to be Certified to the Proper Court of record in the State of Kentucky.   Teste WM. MOSS Cl.

Pages 165-167. KNOW ALL MEN by these presents that we THOMAS WEST and ELIZABETH his wife both of the County of Fairfax and State of Virginia for and in consideration of the Natural love and affection which we bear to FRANCIS MARTIN Son in law of THOMAS WEST and NANCY his daughter the wife of said MARTIN both of the County of Fauquier in said State of Virginia as well as for the further Consideration of one Dollar to us in hand paid by the said FRANCIS MARTIN at or before the ensealing and delivery of these presents (the receipt whereof is hereby acknowledged) Have given and granted and by these presents do give and grant unto the said FRANCIS MARTIN & NANCY his wife their executors, administrators and Assigns a Parcel of land lying in the said County of Fairfax and near Cameron beginning at the upper Corner of a Parcel of land Conveyed by the said THOMAS WEST to his daughter KITTY WEST and lying on the Leesburgh Road including the House and buildings where DOCTR. HAUCK now lives together with all other improvements thereon running, thence eastwardly and binding with said line down the spring branch untill it intersects with MICHAEL FIELDINGS lease, then along his line Northwardly and binding therewith, thence returning to the beginning and running with the main road and binding therewith so far on said road it being parallel with FIELDINGS line so that the head line shall be directed from a stake on the road, thence at right angles to FIELDINGS line so that this land now conveyed to my Daughter NANCY and her husband FRANCIS MARTIN shall contain as many acres, rods and purches as KITTY WEST holds and no more. To have and To Hold the said Land unto them, the sd. FRANCIS MARTIN and NANCY his wife, their executors, administrators & assigns forever. And the said THOMAS WEST and ELIZABETH his wife for themselves, their executors &

administrators, the said land unto the said FRANCIS MARTIN & NANCY his wife, their executors, administrators and assigns, against the claim of them the said THOMAS WEST and ELIZABETH his wife, their executors & administrators & against the claim or claims of all and every Person whatsoever claiming from & under him the said THOMAS WEST & ELIZABETH his wife unto them these presents. In WITNESS whereof we have hereunto set our hands and Seals this Nineteenth day of August One thousand eight hundred and one.
Signed Sealed & delivered   THOS. WEST   (seal)
in the Presence of us   ELIZA. WEST   (seal)
W. PAYNE as to T.W.
HENRY TIMMERMAN
JOHN BRONAUGH, BEAL FOWLER
        At a Court continued and held for Fairfax County the 22nd day of September 1801 this Deed of Gift from THOMAS WEST and ELIZABETH his wife to FRANCIS MARTIN and NANCY his wife was Proved to be the act & deed of the said THOMAS WEST by the oaths of WILLIAM PAYNE and JOHN BRONAUGH Witnesses thereto and ordered to be Certified and at Court continued and held for the said County of Fairfax the 18th day of April 1809 this Deed from THOMAS WEST to FRANCIS MARTIN & NANCY his wife having been heretofore proved by two of the Subscribing witnesses and Certified and it appearing to the Court that HENRY TIMMERMAN and BEAL FOWLER the only other Subscribing Witnesses to the said Deed & the said THOMAS WEST have since the execution of the said Deed departed this life. And AMOS ALEXANDER being sworn to state his knowledge of the hand writing of the said BEAL FOWLER and THOMAS WEST, declares that the Signature of the said BEAL FOWLER as a Witness and the Signature of the said THOMAS WEST the grantor he believes to be in the true hand writing respectively of the said FOWLER and THOMAS WEST upon which evidence the Court Ordered the deed to be Recorded.
                                        Teste WM. MOSS Cl.

Pages 167-169. THIS INDENTURE made this twenty Seventh day of March in the Year of our Lord Christ one thousand eight hundred and Nine between JONATHAN DENTY of the County of Fairfax in the state of Virginia and SIBEY his wife of the one Part and LEONARD BARKER of the County and State aforesaid of the other Part. WITNESSETH that the said JONATHAN DENTY and SIBEY his wife for and in consideration of the sum of two hundred and Seventy five dollars Current Money to them in hand Paid before the Sealing and delivery of these presents the receipt whereof they do hereby acknowledge and the said JONATHAN DENTY his heirs and assigns therefrom acquit and discharge, have granted, bargained, aliened and confirmed & by these presents do grant, bargain & sell, alien and confirm unto the said LEONARD BARKER his heirs and assigns that tract or Parcel of land Containing sixty one acres by estimation be the same more or less (Vizt:) beginning at JOHN ROBERTS SR'S line opposite to the Poplar spring and running thence to and with the said Spring branch the several meanders thereof to Pohick Run, thence up the said Run the several meanders thereof to the mouth of ROGERS' spring branch near a large rock Stone, thence up the said branch the several meanders thereof to the said line of the said ROBERTS' near the School-House spring to a hickory and from thence with said ROBERTS line to the beginning including the Plantation whereon MARY ROGERS lately lived which said Sixty one acres of land be it more or less we have granted, bargained and Sold unto the said LEONARD BARKER and all Houses, buildings, Orchards, Meadows, Yards, gardens, Woods, Ways, Waters, Water-courses, easements, Profits or advantages whatsoever unto the said tract of land belonging or appertaining thereto and the Reversion and Reversions, Remainder and Remainders, Rents and Services of the said Premises and also all the estate right and Title of them the said JONATHAN DENTY and SIBEY his wife of, in and to the said premises and of, in and to every part or Parcel thereof with the appurtenances. To have and To hold the said Tract & Premises above mentioned and every Part and Parcel thereof with the appurtenances unto the said LEONARD BARKER his heirs and assigns to the only Proper use and behoof of him the said LEONARD BARKER his heirs & assigns forever. And the said JONATHAN DENTY and SYBEY his wife for themselves, their heirs & assigns do Covenant and grant to & with the said LEONARD BARKER his heirs and assigns that they the said JOHNATHAN DENTY and SIBEY his wife their heirs and assigns all and Singular the Premises above mentioned with the appurtenances against the right and title of us, ourselves, our Heirs and assigns forever. In WITNESS whereof the said JONATHAN DENTY and SIBEY his wife have hereunto set their hands & seals the day & Year above written. Sealed and delivered in

| Presence of us | JONATHAN DENTY | (seal) |
| Teste | SIBEY DENTY | (seal) |

ZEBEDEE COMPTON
JOHN H. BARKER
JOHN COMPTON

Recd. the within sum of two Hundred & Seventy five Dollars in full for the within Land by me.

Teste JOHN COMPTON
Teste JOHN H. BARKER   JONATHAN DENTY
Teste ZEBIDEE COMPTON

At a Court continued & held for Fairfax County the 18th day of April 1809 this Deed from JONATHAN DENTY and SIBEY his wife to LEONARD BARKER and a receipt hereon endorsed was proved to be the act and Deed of the said JONATHAN DENTY by the oaths of ZEBEDEE COMPTON, JOHN H. BARKER and JOHN COMPTON and the said SIBEY being first Privately and again in open Court examined and thereto consenting acknowledged the same to be her Act and Deed which is Ordered to be Recorded.   Teste WM. MOSS Cl.

PAGES 169-171. THIS INDENTURE made this eighth day of April in the Year of our Lord Christ one thousand eight hundred and nine between SAMUEL BAYLY of the Town of Colchester in the County of Fairfax and State of Virginia and MARY his wife of the one part and JOHNATHAN DENTY of the County and State aforesaid of the other Part: WITNESSETH that the said SAMUEL BAYLEY and MARY his wife for and in Consideration of the sum of three hundred & forty Dollars Current Money to them in hand paid before the Sealing and Delivering of these presents the receipt whereof they do hereby acknowledge and the said JONATHAN DAINTY his heirs & assigns therefrom acquit and discharge, have granted, bargained, alien and confirm and by these presents do grant, bargain and sell, alien and confirm unto the said JONATHAN DENTY his heirs & assigns a Parcel of land being a part of JOHN MERCER'S Patent lying and being in the County aforesaid containing forty one and one fourth acres by survey be the same more or less and the boundaries are as follows (Vizt:) beginning at a Corner at the junction of Pohick Road with the back line of the patent running thence down the said Pohick road with the meanders thereof South Eighty four Degrees East thirty six poles to HOOE's road the same course continued in all sixty two poles, from thence South seventy Degrees East twenty eight Poles to two marked black oaks and two box oaks, then leaving the Road North three degrees West forty nine poles to the said HOOE's road a white oak marked half a pole to the right of the corner, then with the said road and with the meanders thereof north fifty eight degrees east sixteen poles, north thirty three degrees east fifty eight poles to a white oak on the said Road, then leaving the road North thirty seven degrees West thirty four poles to a marked hickory in the line of the Patent, then with the said line one hundred and fifty nine and a half poles to the beginning which said forty one and one fourth acres of land be it more or less we have granted, bargained and Sold unto the said JONATHAN DENTY and all Houses, buildings, Orchards, Meadows, Yards, gardens, Woods, Ways, Waters, Water-Courses, easements, Profits or advantages whatsoever unto the said tract of land belonging or appertaining thereto; and the Reversion and Reversions, Remainder and Remainders, Rents and services of the said Premises and also all the estate, right and title of them the said SAMUEL BAYLEY & MARY his wife of, in and to the said Premises and of, in and to every part or Parcel thereof with the appurtenances. To Have and to Hold the said Tract and Premises above mentioned and every Part or Parcel thereof with the appurtenances unto the said JOHNATHAN DENTY his heirs and assigns unto the only Proper use and behoof of him the said JONATHAN DENTY his heirs & assigns forever; and the said SAMUEL BAYLY and MARY his wife for themselves their heirs & assigns do Covenant and grant to and with the said JONATHAN DENTY his heirs and assigns that they the said SAMUEL BAYLEY and MARY his wife their heirs & assigns all and Singular the Premises above mentioned with the appurtenaces against the claim, right and title of us, ourselves, our heirs and Assigns and all other Person or

Persons whatever claiming under, by or through us forever. In WITNESS whereof the said
SAMUEL BAYLEY & MARY his wife have hereunto set their hands & Seals the day and Year
above written.
Sealed and delivered in
Presence of us   SAML. BAYLY   (seal)
JOHN COMPTON   MARY BAYLEY   (seal)
LEONARD BARKER
JOHN H. BARKER
     Received the within Consideration in full by me.
Teste
LEONARD BARKER   SAML. BAYLEY
JOHN COMPTON
JOHN H. BARKER
     At a Court continued and held for Fairfax County the 18th day of April 1809 this Deed
from SAMUEL BAYLEY and MARY his wife to JONATHAN DENTY and a receipt hereon endorsed
was proved to be the act and deed of the said SAMUEL BAYLEY by the oaths of JOHN COMPTON,
LEONARD BARKER and JOHN H. BARKER and Ordered to be Recorded.
                         Teste WM. MOSS Cl.

Pages 171 & 172. THIS INDENTURE made this seventeenth day of April in the Year of our Lord
one thousand eight hundred and nine between ZEBEDEE COMPTON of the County of Fairfax and
State of Virginia of the one part and LEONARD BARKER and BARBARA BARKER of the same
County and State. WITNESSETH that for and in Consideration of certain priviledges granted
unto the said LEONARD and BARBARA BARKER (Viz) that the said ZEBEDEE COMPTON his heirs
or assigns shall make a good and sufficient fence from two persimmon bushes formerly
where two white oaks stood and corner to COMPTONS Land to a birch on the bank of Pohick
Run and Corner to said COMPTONS land Purchased of WILLIAM VIOLETT and to keep the said
fence in good repair except it should be removed by water or destroyed by fire when the said
COMPTON his heirs or assigns shall be allowed six days to replace said fence again and that the
said LEONARD and BARBARA BARKER their heirs and Assigns shall have liberty to join their
fence to said COMPTONS fence at the aforesaid two persimmon bushes or any where within
thirty Yards thereof on either side of said Corner & also at the said birch on the bank of the
Run or any where within twenty Yards thereof to the fence of the said COMPTON which
liberty shall be granted to them their heirs and Assigns forever. And for and in Consideration
thereof the said LEONARD and BARBARA BARKER have bargained, Sold & Conveyed and Do
hereby bargain, sell and Convey unto the said ZEBEDEE COMPTON his heirs and assigns forever
a certain piece of land lying and being in the County aforesaid on the North branch of
Pohick Run and on the North side thereof and bounded as follows: beginning at the aforesaid
two persimmon bushes, thence South thirty two degrees West nine Poles to the middle of the
old track of the run, then with the meanders of said old Run and in the middle thereof to two
small Sycamores, thence a straight line to the beginning containing as supposed by both
parties about half an acre of Land which land the said LEONARD and BARBARA BARKER doth
warrant and defend unto the said ZEBEDEE COMPTON his heirs and assigns forever against the
claim of them the said LEONARD and BARBARA BARKER their heirs and assigns and all other
persons whatsoever. And Whereas there is a difference between the binding Courses of said
COMPTON and BARKERS land it is agreed that a straight course shall be established between
them from the red oak Corner of said BARKERS land and also Corner of COMPTONS land, thence
to the aforesaid two persimmon bushes formerly where two white oaks stood & Corner also of
said COMPTONS land which shall remain as an established line between the said Parties their
heirs & assigns forever. In WITNESS whereof both parties have hereunto set their hands &
Seals the day & Year above written.
Teste
JOHN COMPTON   ZEBEDEE COMPTON   (seal)
SIBEY DENTY   LEONARD BARKER   (seal)
JOHN H. BARKER   BARBARA BARKER   (seal)

At a Court continued & held for Fairfax County the 18th day of April 1809 this Deed between ZEBEDEE COMPTON, LEONARD BARKER and BARBARA BARKER was proved to be the act and Deed of the Parties by the oaths of JOHN COMPTON, SIBEY DENTY and JOHN H. BARKER and ordered to be Recorded.   Teste WM. MOSS Cl.

Pages 173-175. IN THE COUNTY COURT of Fairfax the twenty third Day of March 1809
JAMES TILLETT....Complaintant
against   IN CHANCERY
TILLET'S Representatives....Defendants.

It appearing to the satisfaction of the Court that JAMES TILLETT, ANN TILLET, SUSANNA TILLET, JOHN TILLETT, ELIZABETH TILLETT, MARY TILLETT and LYDIA TILLET children and Heirs at Law of JOHN TILLETT deceased; and that SAMUEL TILLETT, WILLIAM DAWSON and NANCY his wife MILDRED POWELL, NATHAN WALDEN and MARY his wife and JONATHAN JACKSON and JANE his wife are not Inhabitants of this CommonWealth and that the order of Publication in this case made at August Court last has been duly executed by inserting the same for two Months successively in the Impartial Journal in Leesburgh & by posting the same at the front Door of the Courthouse of this County. The Court doth thereupon Order and Decree that the Complainants bill be taken for confessed as to the said absent defendants & it appearing further to the satisfaction of the Court that the Complainant has purchased the shares of JONATHAN JACKSON and JANE his wife, SOLOMAN BEACH & MARGARET his wife, of GEORGE TILLETT and ANN his wife in the Land in the Bill mentioned, it is thereupon further ordered and decreed that the said Land be equally divided according to Quantity and Quality amongst the Devisees of the said GEORGE TILLETT deceased and those claiming under them and that WILLIAM DENEALE, FRANCES COFFER, CHARLES THRIFT and EDWARD WASHINGTON be appointed Commissioners to make the said Division and allott to the several Devisees their respective proportions and that they or any three of them have Power to Act and that they do make report of their proceedings to the next Court.
                    A Copy from the Minutes
                    Teste WM MOSS Cl.

Page 174.   [MAP OF THE PLAT]

At the instance of MR. RICHARD RATCLIFFE for the Heirs of GEO TILLETT decd and by the directions of Messrs EDWARD WASHINGTON, WILLIAM DENEALE and CHARLES THRIFT, Gentl Commrs, I surveyed, laid off & divided the Land as represented by and on the above Plat and bounded as follows: Lotts No. 1, 2, 3 & 4 beginning at "a" stake and Pile of Stones corner of RICHARD SIMPSONS Land, thence with his line North 75° 30' West 38 1/2 Poles to "b" a red oak corner of JAMES KEITH'S land, thence with his lines North 26° East 100 Poles to "c" a pile of Stones, thence North 45° 16' West 37 poles to "d" the intersection with the out line, thence North 27° 12' East 45 1/2 Poles to"e" a stump, thence North 86° East 65 Poles to "f" a small hiccory bush at the intersection with the next line, thence along with the said line South 33° East 77 1/2 Poles to "g" a stake three feet Northwest from a red oak saplin, thence South 45° 40' West 151 3/4 Poles to the Beginning, including four Lotts Containing Eighty three acres forty one poles.
Lotts No. 5, 6 & 7 beginning at "g" corner of Lotts No. 1, 2, 3 & 4, thence South 35° East 79 Poles to "h" a pile of Stones, thence South 66° East 38 Poles to "i" a white oak sapling, thence South 41° West 138 poles to "k," thence North 47° 15' West 30 Poles to "l" a box oak, thence North 7° 40' East 153 1/2 Poles to "m" a pile of Stones in the line of Lotts No. 1, 2, 3 & 4, thence with said line North 45° 41' East 20 Poles to the beginning containing 62 acres 71 Poles.
Lott No. 8, beginning at "m," a pile of Stones corner of Lotts 5, 6 & 7, thence South 25° 65' West 139 3/4 Poles to a pile of Stones in the out line, thence along said line South 58° 27' East 48 poles to "l" a box oak corner of lotts 5, 6 & 7, thence along a line of said lotts North 7° 48' East 153 1/2 poles to the beginning, twenty acres & 135 poles.
Lott No. 9 beginning at "n," a Corner of Lott No. 8, thence along a line of said Lott North 25° 43' East 139 3/4 Poles to "m," a pile of Stones in a line of Lotts No. 1, 2, 3 & 4, thence along a line of said Lotts South 45° 41' West 181 3/4 Poles to a stake and pile of Stones corner of

RICHARD SIMPSONS land, thence with his line South 5° West 14 Poles to "o," the intersection with the out line, thence along said line South 58° 27' East 38 Poles to the beginning containing twenty acres 131 poles.   ROBT. RATCLIFFE Deputy Cl.

  In obedience to an order of the County Court of Fairfax to us directed we the Subscribers did go on the Land of said TILLETT and then and on the Land of the Deceased did cause the same to be laid of into Lotts as it appears on the within platt drawn by ROBERT RATCLIFFE which different Parts is designated on the face of the Plat by the Surveyor. Given under our hands this 17th April 1809.   EDWARD WASHINGTON
                         W. DENEALE
                         CHARLES THRIFT

  At a Court continued & held for Fairfax County the 18th day of April 1809 this Platt Survey & division of Land between the Representatives of GEORGE TILLETT decd & the report of the Commissioners appointed to divide the same, is returned & ordered to be Recorded.
                    Teste WM. MOSS Cl.

Pages 175-178. THIS INDENTURE made this thirty first day of May in the Year one Thousand eight hundred and Six between THOMAS FAIRFAX Esqr. of the one part and JOHN STANHOPE of other part. WITNESSETH that the said THOMAS FAIRFAX for and in consideration of the Rents & Covenenats hereinafter expressed by the said JOHN STANHOPE to be paid and performed doth by these presents grant, demise and to farm let unto the said JOHN STANHOPE a certain Lott of Land situate in the County of Fairfax near the land of ROBERT CARTER deceased and bounded as follows: beginning at a red oak Stump near which formerly stood two small white oaks corner to RICHARD THOMPSONS Lott formerly held by ALLEN DAVIS, thence with the given line of said Lott North 77° West 120 Poles to a large Chesnut corner to said THOMPSON and JOB MOXLEY lots, thence with MOXLEY'S line South 84 12° West 150 Poles to the line of ROBT. CARTER, Deceased, thence with his line corrected South 33° West 58 poles to JOHN HARPERS corner of his lot, supposed and intended to be in the line of said CARTER, thence with HARPERS line South 59° 4' East 126 Poles to a black Jack corner to said HARPER'S lot and also a corner to the Lot held by WM. LATIMER, thence with LATIMER'S line North 25° East 48 Poles to a white oak stump, another corner of LATIMERS lot, then with another of his lines South 87° East 195 Poles to two small Spanish oak sprouts in the line of the Lot lately held by CAPTN. WM. STANHOPE decd, thence with the line of that lott North 13 34° East 45 Poles to a stake in a field, thence to the beginning containing one hundred & 62 3/4 acres more or less. To have and To Hold the said Lott of land from and after the thirty first day of December, in the Year 1803 unto him the said JOHN STANHOPE his heirs and assigns for and during the natural lives of him the said JOHN STANHOPE, ANN his wife and LEWIS his Son. He the said JOHN STANHOPE his heirs and assigns Yielding and paying therefore unto the said THOMAS FAIRFAX his heirs and assigns on the thirty first day of December in the Year one Thousand eight hundred and four, the rent of ten pounds eighteen Shillings in gold or Silver coin and on the thirty first day of December in every Year thereafter, during the Continuance of this demise, the like rent of ten Pounds eighteen Shillings and also paying all taxes of whatsoever nature or kind which shall become payable for the said Lot of Land during the continuance of this demise and the said THOMAS FAIRFAX doth for himself his heirs and assigns covenant and agree with the said JOHN STANHOPE his heirs and assigns that he the said JOHN STANHOPE, will not cut down or clear up for cultivation or pasture any part of that portion of said Lot which is bounded as follows: beginning at a small spanish oak in the fifth line of the Lot and Eight Poles from the stump corner of the Lot and on the South side of the Falls road, thence with said road North 88° West 59 Poles to a red oak on the north side of the aforesd. road, thence North 12° East to the intersection of the line of the lot thence with the lines of the Lot to the beginning containing about thirty one & 34 acres, but will leave the same standing as a reserve for fuel and timber for the use of the said Lot and that he will not take any wood or timber from that part of the Lot so reserved while it can be got on any other part; That he will not during the time he his heirs and assigns may hold the said Lot of Land, cut down any green wood for fuel while the tops or bodies of trees cut down for other purposes or any dead or dry wood fit for fuel can be obtained on the same; and that whenever he has occasion to fell green trees on the said reserve, either for rails or other uses of the Plantation, he will not fell them all in one Place so as to make an opening or clearing, but will cut them in such manner as to thin the standing wood and give it the better room to grow; that he will not sell nor dispose in any way whatever of any kind of wood or timber from the said Lot of Land, either for services rendered in lieu thereof or upon any other pretext; That he will not make any assignment of the term hereby granted him without the consent of the said THOMAS FAIRFAX his heirs or assigns or his or their agent; That he will not place any sub tenant upon the said Lot of Land nor admit any person not living with him as one of his own family, to cultivate any part of the same for a share of the crop to be raised thereon, or other consideration to be paid to the said JOHN STANHOPE; that he will not raise Tobacco upon any ground except such as is manured or except one crop upon new ground in order to Prepare it for small grain or grass seed; that he will not Plant Indian Corn on any part of the said Lot where it was planted the Preceeding Year and that when ever any field on said Lot is Planted with indian corn he will sow it down the same season with either wheat or Rye; that he will, within three Years from the date of these presents, build on some convenient Part of the Premises a good dwelling House at least sixteen feet Square, provided the same is not already built; that if it shall so happen that all or Part of the Rent aforesaid be unpaid for the space of Thirty days after the same shall become due, if lawfully demanded and no sufficient distress can be found whereby the same may be levied, that then it may and shall be lawfull for the said THOMAS FAIRFAX his heirs or assigns to render and hold the same as if this indenture had never been made; that he the said JOHN STANHOPE his heirs and assigns will by the expiration of this lease leave the Buildings, Fences and Orchards in good Rentable repair and the said THOMAS FAIRFAX doth for himself his heirs & assigns covenant and agree with the said JOHN STANHOPE his heirs & assigns that he the said JOHN STANHOPE his heirs and assigns shall, during the time for which the said Lot of Land is hereby demised, or he or they Paying and performing the Rents, Taxes and Stipulations herein contained, peaceably and quietly occupy and Possess the said Lot of Land without the molestation or interruption of him the said THOMAS FAIRFAX, or any other person whatsoever and for the due and faithful performance of all and Singular the Stipulations herein contained, the said Parties bind themselves their heirs and Assigns, to each other, in the Penal Sum of one Thousand Dollars, to be paid by the party failing to Perform to the other. In WITNESS whereof the said Parties have hereunto set their hands and Seals the Day and Year first above mentioned.

The name and Seal of the said THOMAS FAIRFAX being hereto set by his agent.

JNO. C. HUNTER	THOMAS FAIRFAX (seal)
Sealed and Delivered	JOHN STANHOPE (seal)
In Presence of	
JACOB HUGUELY	
CHARLES HUGUELY	
JAMES HUGUELY	

At a Court continued & held for Fairfax County the 18th day of April 1809 this Deed of Lease between THOMAS FAIRFAX and JOHN STANHOPE was acknowledged by JOHN C. HUNTER, Attorney in fact for the said FAIRFAX and the said JOHN STANHOPE to be their Act and Deed and Ordered to be Recorded.   Teste WM. MOSS Cl.

Pages 178-181. THIS INDENTURE made the eighth Day of April in the Year one thousand seven hundred and ninety six between BALDWIN DADE and CATHARINE his wife of the one part and HENRY LEE of the County of Westmoreland of the other part. WITNESSETH that the said BALDWIN DADE for and in consideration of the sum of five Pounds Current Money of Virginia to him in hand paid by the said HENRY LEE the receipt whereof he doth hereby acknowledge & from the same doth acquit and discharge the said HENRY LEE, his heirs, executors & administrators, by these presents hath granted, bargained & Sold, aliened & conveyed and by these presents doth Grant, bargain and sell, alien and convey unto the said HENRY LEE his heirs and assigns forever a tract, or Parcel of Land situate, lying & being in Fairfax County near the Falls Church, containing by estimation one hundred and Ninety seven acres be the same more or less which tract of Land was conveyed to the said BALDWIN DADE by RICHARD CONWAY & MARY his wife by Deed of Record in the County Court of Fairfax, as by reference therto will more fully & at large appear and bounded as follows Vizt: Beginning at a Poplar on

Pimmitts Run and Running thence North thirty eight Degrees West one hundred & fifteen Poles to an old Locust stake, then North eighty three degrees West one hundred and fifty seven Poles to a burn'd red oak in a line, then South nineteen degrees East two hundred & forty one Poles to Pimmits run, then down the said run & binding therewith to the beginning. To have and To Hold the said Tract or Parcel of Land, with all & singular its appurtenances, to the said HENRY LEE his heirs & assigns to the only Proper use and behoof of him the said HENRY LEE, his heirs and assigns forever and the said BALDWIN DADE for himself his heirs, executors & Administrators doth covenant, grant and agree to & with the sd. HENRY LEE his heirs & assigns that he the said BALDWIN DADE hath full power & authority to sell & convey the said tract or Parcel of Land & that he the said HENRY LEE, shall peaceably & quietly have, hold, occupy & possess the said tract or Parcel of Land freely & clearly, exonerated of & from all former other gifts, grants, sales, or encumbrances whatsoever had, made, suffered or done or to be had, made, suffered or done by him the said BALDWIN DADE his heirs or assigns or by any Person or Persons claiming by, thro', from or under him, them or any of them and the said BALDWIN DADE for himself & his heirs, the sd. tract or Parcel of land with its appurtenances to the said HENRY LEE his heirs & assigns against the claim or claims of him the said BALDWIN DADE & his heirs & against the claim or claims of all persons claiming from or under him or them, will forever warrant & defend by these presents. In WITNESS whereof the parties to these presents have hereunto set their hands & Seals the day & Year first above written.
Signed Sealed & delivered in
Presence of
THOS. LEE JR
EDM. J. LEE
SAML. LAMKIN

B. DADE	(seal)
CATHA. DADE	(seal)

    FAIRFAX COUNTY:
    The CommonWealth of Virginia to WILLIAM HERBERT, JOHN POTER Gentlemen justices of the Peace of the County of Fairfax Greeting: Whereas BALDWIN DADE and CATHARINE his wife by their certain indenture of bargain & Sale bearing date the eighth day of April 1796, have sold and conveyed unto HENRY LEE the fee simple estate of a certain tract of Land containing by estimation one hundred & ninety seven Acres with the appurtenances situate, lying & being in the County aforesaid and whereas the said CATHARINE cannot conveniently travel to our said Court to make acknowledgment of the said conveyance therefore we do give unto you or any two or more of you Power to receive the acknowledgment which the said CATHARINE shall be willing to make before You, of the conveyance aforesaid contained in the said Indenture which is hereto annexed and we do therefore desire you or any two or more of you personally to go to the said CATHARINE and receive her acknowledgment of the same and examine her privily and apart from the said BALDWIN her husband whither she doth the same freely and voluntarily without his persuasions or threats and whither she be willing the said indenture together with this Commission should be recorded in our said Court & when you have received her acknowledgment and examined her as aforesaid that you distinctly and openly certify us thereof in our said Court under your hands and seals sending then there this indenture and this Writ. WITNESS PETER WAGENER Clerk of the said Court this 10th day of November 1796.   P. WAGENER Cl.
    FAIRFAX COUNTY:
    In Pursuance of the within commission, we the subscribers have waited upon the within named CATHARINE wife of the within named BALDWIN DADE and have received her acknowledgment of the within Deed and that she is willing it should be Recorded as her act & Deed. Given under our Hands and Seals this 12th day of November in the Year 1796.

JOHN POTER	(seal)
WM. HERBERT	(seal)

    At a Court held for Fairfax County the 19th day of December 1796, this Deed from BALDWIN DADE and CATHARINE his wife to HENRY LEE was Proved to be the Act and Deed of the said BALDWIN DADE by the Oaths of EDMUND J. LEE and SAMUEL LAMKIN Witnesses thereto and ordered to be certified and at a Court contind. & held for the said County the 18th day of April 1809 the same having been theretofore proved by two Witnesses and and Certified by

THOMAS LEE SR the only other subscribing witness to the said Deed having since the execution of the same departed this life and it appearing to the Court by the affadavit of EDMUND J. LEE and JAS. WIGGINTON that the Signature to the said Deed is in the true hand writing of the sd. THOS. LEE SR on which Proof the same together with the Commission & return thereto annexed for taking the acknowledgment and privy examination of the said CATHARINE are ordered to be Recorded.   Teste WM. MOSS Cl.

Pages 181-184. THIS INDENTURE made this fourteenth Day of February in the Year of our Lord one thousand eight hundred and Nine between WILLIAM HARTSHORNE, receiver of the social Effects of SUTTON and MANDEVILLE, Merchants and Partners and acting under a Decree of the Superior Court of Chancery for the District of Richmond of the one part and JOHN STUMP of the County of [left blank] in the State of Maryland and DAVID RICKETTS of the County of Fairfax in the State of Virginia of the other Part; Whereas JOHN MANDEVILLE did during the Copartnery of SUTTON & MANDEVILLE together with JOHN STUMP and JOHN THOMAS RICKETTS, Purchase of and from [left blank] a tract of Land containing ten acres situate, lying and being in the said County of Fairfax and State of Virginia, near the ford of Cameron Run on Great Hunting Creek, one moiety thereof appertaining to the said JOHN MANDEVILLE, the other moiety to the said JOHN STUMP and JOHN THOMAS RICKETTS after which a misunder-standing taking place between the said SUTTON and MANDEVILLE, suits were instituted by each of them in the High Court of Chancery against the other which on the second Day of October one Thousand eight hundred and seven, came in to be heard in the Superior of Chancery for the District of Richmond when it was adjudged, Ordered and Decreed that all the social Property of JOHN SUTTON and JOHN MANDEVILLE in anywise appertaining to them as Merchants & Partners in trade from the Year one thousand seven hundred and eighty three to the close of the Partnership accounts which commenced at that period and from the Year one Thousand seven hundred & ninety three to the close of the Partnership accounts which commenced at that Period should be sold at Public Auction by the receiver formerly appointed to Receive and take charge of the social effects of the said SUTTON & MANDEVILLE after a reasonable Public Notice thereof in compliance with which Order and Decree the said WILLIAM HARTSHORNE who had been, by an order of the High Court of Chancery, formerly appointed receiver of the said effects advertized the Moiety of the said Ten acres of Land so Purchased by the said JOHN MANDEVILLE and JOHN STUMP and JOHN THOMAS RICKETTS for sale on the [left blank] day of [left blank] one thousand eight hundred and seven, on which day the Moiety of the said ten acres of Land was exposed to sale at Auction and struck off to JONAH THOMPSON as the highest bidder at the Price of one hundred and ten Dollars who hath directed the said WILLIAM HARTSHORNE to convey the same to the said JOHN STUMP and DAVID RICKETTS who in compliance with the said Decree and the Directions of the said JONAH THOMPSON and for and in consideration of the said sum of one hundred and ten Dollars to him the said WILLIAM HARTSHORNE in hand paid at or before the Sealing and delivery of these presents the receipt whereof he doth hereby acknowledge and thereof and of every part and Parcel thereof doth acquit the said JONAH THOMPSON and them the said JOHN STUMP and DAVID RICKETTS and each and every of them their heirs and each and every of their Heirs, Executors and administrators by these presents hath Granted, bargained & Sold, aliened and confirmed and by these presents doth grant, bargain, sell, alien & Confirm unto them the said JOHN STUMP and DAVID RICKETTS their heirs and assigns forever as tenants in Common, all the Estate right, Title, use, Trust, Interest, Property, claim and Demand as well in Law as equity of them the said JOHN SUTTON and JOHN MANDEVILLE and each of them of, in and to one equal undivided Moiety of the said ten acres of Land so Purchased by the said JOHN MANDEVILLE and JOHN STUMP and JOHN THOMAS RICKETTS and to all Houses, buildings, trees, Woods, waters, Watercourses, Profits, commodities, hereditaments & appurtenances whatsoever to the said Premises belonging or in anywise appertaining and the Reversion and Reversions, remainder & remainders, Rents, Issues and Profits thereof. To have and to hold all and Sing-ular the premises hereby bargained and Sold with their appurtenances unto them the said JOHN STUMP and DAVID RICKETTS their heirs and Assigns, as Tenants in common to the only Proper use and behoof of them the said JOHN STUMP and DAVID RICKETTS their heirs and Assigns forever as Tenants in Common and not as joint Tenants. In WITNESS whereof the said

WILLIAM HARTSHORNE hath hereunto set his hand and Seal the day and Year first herein before mentioned.

Sealed and Delivered
in Presence of   WM. HARTSHORNE (seal)
R. J. TAYLOR
GEO. YOUNGS
THO. SWANN
JOHN DUNDAS
    Received one hundred and ten Dollars the consideration herein mentioned.
WITNESS   WM. HARTSHORNE
R. J. TAYLOR
    At a Court held for Fairfax County the 15th Day of May 1809 this Deed from WILLIAM HARTSHORNE to JOHN STUMP & DAVID RICKETTS was Proved by the oaths of ROBERT J. TAYLOR, GEORGE YOUNGS & THOMAS SWANN three of the Witnesses thereto to be the Act and Deed of the said WILLM. HARTSHORNE and ordered to be Recorded.
Teste WM. MOSS Cl.

    PAGES 184 & 185. THIS INDENTURE made this first Day of October one thousand eight hundred & eight between JAMES COLEMAN of the County of Fairfax of the one part & THOMAS COLEMAN his Son of the same County of the other part. WITNESSETH that the said JAMES COLEMAN for and in consideration of the Natural love and affection which he hath and beareth unto his said Son THOMAS COLEMAN doth by these presents give and grant unto his said Son THOMAS COLEMAN a certain tract or parcel of land situate, lying & being in the County of Fairfax, all that tract or parcel of Land containing one hundred and fifty three acres or there about which Land is part of a larger tract of Land called ABRAHAM BARNES'S which Land of one hundred fifty three acres is part of the Land Devised by JOHN EVANS in his last Will and Testament bearing date the 4th day of October 1766 and was recorded in the County Court of Loudoun the [left blank] day of [left blank] who gave and devised unto his Son DAVID EVANS the lot between LAY and CRISWELL on the Folley Lick branch and the half of CRISWELL Lot joining next to it and by the same will gave unto his Son GRIFFITH EVANS, ABRAHAM LAY lot upon the Folley lick branch and GRIFFITH EVANS, by this last will and Testament dated the 12th day of December 1767 and recorded in the [left blank] office in the State of Pennsylvania, the [left blank] day [left blank] 176_ [left blank] gave and Devised to his brother DAVID EVANS the Lot or tract of Land where ABRAHAM LAY lives upon (for which LAY holds a lease from the before mentioned ABRAHAM BARNES for lives) and DAVID EVANS by his last Will and Testament dated the 4th day of June 1771 and Recorded in the Register Generals office in Philadelphia in the State of Pennsylvania the 21st day of August 1771, gave and Devised one third part of the aforesaid described lands unto his Daughter MARY wife of GEORGE JEWELL and the said GEORGE JEWELL and MARY his wife to JAMES COLEMAN, by Deed bearing date the fourteenth day of April 1798 and Recorded in the County Court of Loudoun. To have and To Hold the said tract or parcel of Land with all and Singular the appurtenances hereunto belonging unto the said THOMAS COLEMAN his heirs and assigns to the only proper use and behoof of the said THOMAS COLEMAN his Heirs and assigns forever. In testimony whereof the said JAMES COLEMAN hath hereunto set his hand & affixed his Seal the day and Year first before written.

Signed Sealed and
Delivered in Presence of   JAMES COLEMAN   (seal)
DANL. McCARTY CHICHESTER
WM. COLEMAN
JAMES COLEMAN JR
    At a Court held for Fairfax County the 15 day of May 1809 this Deed of Gift from JAMES COLEMAN to THOMAS COLEMAN was in open Court acknowledged by the said JAMES COLEMAN to be his act & deed & is therefore ordered to be recorded.
Teste WM. MOSS Cl.

Pages 185 & 186. THIS INDENTURE made this first November 1808 between CHRISTOPHER NEALE of the County of Fairfax and State of Virginia of the one part and CHARLES TYLER JR of the County of Prince William and State aforesaid of the other part. WITNESSETH that the said CHRIS. NEALE for and in consideration of the Sum of Three hundred and twelve Dollars lawful Money of Virginia to him in hand paid by the said CHARLES TYLER JR the receipt whereof he doth hereby acknowledge have bargained and Sold & by these presents doth bargain and Sell, alien & confirm unto the said CHARLES TYLER JR a certain piece or parcel of Land lying & being in the County of Fairfax & bounded as follows Vizt: beginning at a large red oak, thence North 172° East 85 Poles to a white oak sapling, thence North 47° West 64 Poles to a stake in the old fields, thence South 8° West 103 poles to 3 small Hiccorys, thence to the beginning containing twenty six acres be the same more or less also all his right, Title, interest, property & claim to the one sixth part of the Dower land of his mother ANN SIMPSON formerly ANN NEALE Widow and relict of THOMAS NEALE deceased, containing forty one and two thirds acres be the same more or less with all & Singular the appurtenances thereunto belonging or in any wise appertaining for and in consideration of the sum of one hundred Pounds Current Money of Virginia to him the said CHRIST. NEALE in hand paid the receipt whereof he doth hereby acknowledge and the said CHRISTO. NEALE the said Pieces or Parcels of Land will forever defend against the claim of him or his heirs, his Exors, Admors or Assigns to him the said CHARLES TYLER JR his heirs or Assigns forever. In WITNESS whereof he hath hereunto set his hand & affixed his Seal the day & Year above Written.
DANIEL HARRINGTON
NIMROD GRIGSBY   CHR. NEALE   (seal)
EDWARD FORD
       At a Court held for Fairfax County the 15th day of May 1809 this Deed from CHRISTOPHER NEALE to CHARLES TYLER JR was acknowledged by the said CHRISTO. NEALE to be his Act and Deed ordered to be Recorded.   Teste WM. MOSS Cl.

Pages 186 & 187. THIS INDENTURE made this the first day of November in the Year of our Lord God eighteen hundred and eight between CHRISTO. NEALE Attorney in fact for his Brother HAMLET NEALE and as such duly constituted & appointed by Power of Attorney bearing date the 30th August 1808 of the County of Fairfax and State of Virginia of the one part and CHARLES TYLER JR of the County of Prince William and State aforesaid of the other part. WITNESSETH that the said CHRISTOPHER NEALE Attorney in fact aforesaid hath this day bargained and Sold and by these presents doth bargain and Sell, Alien and confirm unto the said CHARLES TYLER JR all the right, title, interest, Property and claim of his said Brother HAMLET in and to Lott No. 2 as described and given to him as one childs part in the tract of Land formerly owned by his father THOS. NEALE deceased and bounded as follows Vizt: beginning at a white oak and red oak, thence North 13° West 77 Poles to a white and red oak sapling, thence South 17° West 43 Poles to a red oak, thence South 30° Eest 44 poles to two white oak and red oak saplings, thence South 14° West 144 Poles to a Stake in the Dower line, thence along said line North 79 1/2° East 62 poles to a stake in the said line corner of Lott No. 1, thence to the beginning containing 99 acres more or less. Also all his said Brothers right, title, interest and claim to the one sixth part of the Dower Land of his Mother ANN SIMPSON formerly ANN NEALE widow and Relict of THOS. NEALE decd containing forty one and two thirds acres be the same more or less. Also all his right, title, property & claim in and to Lott No. 6 as described and given to his brother JOHN NEALE decd for his share in the tract of Land formerly owned by his father, THOS. NEALE decd reference being had to the Platt and Division of said estate now on Record in the County Court of Loudoun will more fully appear for and in consideration of the sum of Eighteen hundred Dollars to him the said CHRISTOPHER NEALE in hand paid the receipt whereof he doth hereby acknowledge and the said CHRISTOPHER NEALE attorney in fact as aforesaid the said Pieces or Parcels of Land with all and Singular the appurtenances, Profits and commodities thereunto belonging or in anywise appertaining unto the said CHARLES TYLER JR his heirs or assigns will forever defend free from the claim of him the said CHRISTOPHER NEALE, attorney in fact as aforesaid his Heirs, Exors, Admors or assigns. In WITNESS whereof the said CHRISTOPHER NEALE attorney in fact as aforsaid hath set his hand and affixed his Seal the Day and Year above Written.

Signed Sealed and acknowledged
in presence of   CHR. NEALE Atty in fact   (seal)
NIMROD GRIGSBY   for HAMLET NEALE
EDWARD FORD
DANIEL HARRINGTON
 At a Court held for Fairfax County the 15th day of May 1809 this Deed from
CHRISTOPHER NEALE (attorney in fact for HAMLET NEALE) to CHARLES TYLER JR was
acknowledged by the said CHRISTOPHER NEALE attorney in fact as aforesaid to be his Act and
Deed and ordered to be Recorded.   Teste WM. MOSS Cl.

Pages 187 & 188. ARTICLES of agreement, made and entered into this seventh day of October
1808 between ROBERT THOMAS JR and ANN DODD, both of the County of Fairfax and
CommonWealth of Virginia. WITNESSETH that Whereas a marriage is intended to be had and
solemnized between the aforesaid Parties and they have mutually agreed that they are to hold,
enjoy and dispose of such estate as they are now Possessed of without the claim or
interruption of the other; therefore the said ROBERT THOMAS JR doth for himself his heirs,
Exors &c, covenant, Promise and agree to and with the said ANN DODD her heirs &c, that he
will not attempt to sell or dispose of any Property that she now has or may have in her
Possession, or be in any manner entitled to, except for the joint use or support of them during
their Coverture aforesaid but that the said ANN DODD may dispose of the same in such manner
as she may think proper and in default of such disposition that the same shall go and descend
to her child or children, or in default of such child or children attaining of legal age in such
manner as the Laws describing the course of decent shall direct, as to her family and the said
ANN DODD doth for herself her heirs &c, Covenant to and with the said ROBERT, his heirs &c,
that in case she should survive him, that she will not claim any Dower in his estate, but the
same may go and descend in such manner as he may direct, or in case of no direction to such
person or Persons of his family as under the Law are legally entitled to receive and enjoy the
same. In WITNESS whereof the Parties have hereunto set their hands and Seals the Day and
Year first within written.
Signed & acknowledged
in Presence of   ROBERT THOMAS JR   (seal)
GEORGE WHALEY   ANN her X mark DODD   (seal)
SANFORD PAYNE
ANN WHALEY
FIELDER THOMAS
 At a Court held for Fairfax County the 15th day of May 1809 this Instrument of Writing
in the Nature of a Marriage contract between ROBT. THOMAS JR and ANN DODD was proved by
the oaths of GEO. WHALEY, SANFORD PAYNE & FIELDER THOMAS, three of the Witnesses thereto
and ordered to be Recorded.   Teste WM . MOSS Cl.

Pages 189-192. THIS INDENTURE made this twenty sixth day of November in the Year of our
Lord one thousand eight hundred and eight between CHARLES J. LOVE and FRANCES PEYTON
his wife of the County of Fairfax and State of Virginia of the one part and DANIEL
HARRINGTON of the County and State aforesaid of the other part. WITNESSETH that the said
CHARLES J. LOVE and FRANCES PEYTON his wife for and in consideration of the sum of Four
thousand Dollars to them in hand paid by the said DANIEL HARRINGTON at or before the
enseeling & delivery of these presents (the receipt whereof is hereby acknowledged) Have
bargained & Sold & by these presents do and each of them doth bargain & Sell unto the said
DANL. HARRINGTON, his Heirs or assigns forever a certain piece, parcel or Lot of Land laying
and being in the County and State aforesaid and bounded as follows Vizt: beginning at a red
oak on the South side of the Mill Pond near the Mill Dam and running South thirty two West
fifty poles to a branch of Hiccory sprouts or Grubs, thence South eighty seven West twenty
seven poles to a white oak stump at Rocky Run (sometimes called Great Rockey Cedar Run),
thence up the said Run North ten poles, thence again with said Run North fourteen East 15
poles, thence again with said Run North twenty East ten Poles, thence again with the said Run
North thirty seven East eighteen Poles, thence again with the said Run North fifty one East

twenty eight Poles, thence again with the said Run North nine East ten poles, thence again with the said Run North thirty one West fourteen poles, thence again with the said Run North fifteen East sixteen poles, thence again with said Run North seventy four East eight poles, thence again with said Run South fifty one East fourteen Poles, thence again with said Run North seventy four East six Poles, thence again with said Run South sixteen East ten Poles, thence again with said Run South fifteen West twenty poles, thence again with said Run South twenty five West six Poles, thence leaving said Run South fifty six East ten Poles to the side of the Mill Pond, thence with the Northern side of the Mill Pond North sixty one East seven poles, thence again with said Northern side of the Pond North twenty five East Ten Poles, thence again with said Northern side of the Pond And across the aforesaid Rockey Run North seventy four East twelve poles, thence again in a straight line South fifty six West about forty six poles to the beginning at a red oak near the Mill Dam, containing in all Twenty one acres and twenty four Poles more or less. The said piece, Parcell or Lott of Ground is joined on the Southern and eastern side by the Land of WILLIAM LANE SR and on the Northern & Western side by the aforesaid Rockey Run (sometimes called Great Rockey Cedar Run) which divided it from the Lands of COLEMAN BROWNE; the Road from Centreville to Frying-Pan Passes through the said Piece, Parcell or Lot of Ground and this Indenture is intended to convey all the land formerly held by SAMUEL LOVE deceased together with all the houses, buildings, Pastures, Waters, Water Courses, Priviledges, Profits, hereditaments and appurtenances thereunto belonging or in anywise appertaining, or with the same used & enjoyed or known as part, parcell or member thereof and the Reversion and Reversions and profits thereof and every part and parcel thereof. To have and to hold the said piece, parcell or Lott of Land with the tenements, hereditaments and all & Singular the Premises before mentioned and every part and parcel thereof with every of their rights, members and appurtenances unto the said DANIEL HARRINGTON, his Heirs and assigns forever. And the said CHARLES J. LOVE and FRANCES PEYTON his wife, for themselves and their Heirs, the said piece, parcell or Lot of Land with all and singular the Premises and appurtenances before mentioned unto the said DANIEL HARRINGTON his heirs and assigns free from the claim or claims of them the said CHARLES J. LOVE and FRANCES PEYTON his wife their heirs & assigns and of all and every Person or persons whatsoever shall, will & do warrant & forever defend by these presents. In WITNESS whereof the said CHARLES J. LOVE & FRANCES PEYTON his wife have hereunto set their hands and Seals the day and Year first above Written.

Signed Sealed and acknowledged
& delivered in Presence of
JAS. S. TRIPLETT
HUMPH. PEAKE
WM. MOSS
JNO. G. LADD
THO. R. MOTT

CH. J. LOVE   (seal)
FRANCES P. LOVE   (seal)

At a Court held for Fairfax County the 18th day of April 1809 this Deed from CHARLES J. LOVE & FRANCES PEYTON his wife to DANIEL HARRINGTON was Proved to be the Act & Deed of the said CHARLES J. LOVE by the oaths of WILLIAM MOSS and THOMAS R. MOTT, two of the Witnesses thereto & ordered to be certified. And at a Court held for the said County the 15th day of May in Year aforesaid this Deed was further Proved by the oath of HUMPHREY PEAKE, another Witness thereto to be the act and Deed of the said CHARLES J. LOVE which together with a Commission and return hereto annexed for taking the acknowledgment and Privy examination of the said FRANCES PEYTON are ordered to be Recorded.

Teste WM. MOSS Co. Cl.

FAIRFAX COUNTY To Wit:
The CommonWealth of Virginia to FRANCIS ADAMS, JAMES S. TRIPLETT and HUMPHREY PEAKE Gentlemen Justices of the County of Fairfax Greeting: Whereas CHARLES J. LOVE and FRANCES P. LOVE his wife by their certain Indenture of bargain & Sale bearing date the twenty sixth day of November 1808 have sold and conveyed unto DANIEL HARRINGTON the fee simple estate of twenty one acres & twenty four poles more or less, situated on Great Rockey Cedar Run, it being the Lott on which the Rockey Run mill stands with the appurtenances situate, lying and being in the said County of Fairfax and whereas the said FRANCES P. LOVE

cannot conveniently travel to our said County Court of Fairfax to make acknowledgment of the said conveyance therefore we do give unto You or any two or more of You Power to receive the acknowledgment which the said FRANCES P. LOVE shall be willing to make before you of the conveyance aforesaid contained in the said indenture which is hereunto annexed; and we do therefore desire You or any two or more of You personally to go to the said FRANCES P. and receive her acknowledgment of the same and examine her privily and apart from the said CHARLES J. LOVE her husband whither she doth the same freely and voluntarily without his persuasions or threats; And whether she be willing the said Indenture together with this Commission shall be Recorded in our said Court. And when You have received her acknow-ledgment and examined her as aforesaid that You distinctly and openly certify us thereof in our said Court under Your hands and seals sending then there the sd. indenture this Writ. WITNESS WILLIAM MOSS Clerk of the said Court at the Courthouse of the County aforesaid this twenty sixth Day of November 1808 and in the 33rd Year of the CommonWealth.

WM. MOSS Cl.

FAIRFAX COUNTY:

In obedience to the within Commission to us directed we the subscribers waited on the within named FRANCES P. LOVE and having examined her privily and apart from her said Husband CHARLES J. LOVE touching the conveyance of the Land within mentioned and do find that She hath done the same freely & voluntarily without the persuasions or threats of her said Husband and that she is willing that the Deed for the same together with this Commission be recorded in the County Court of Fairfax. Given under our hand & seals this 26th day of November 1808.

HUMPH. PEAKE   (seal)
JAS. S. TRIPLETT   (seal)

Pages 192-195. [Marginal Note: Delivered to N. FITZHUGH]

THIS INDENTURE made this fifteenth day of February in the Year of our Lord one thousand eight hundred and nine between WILLIAM HERBERT, NICHOLAS FITZHUGH and EDMUND J. LEE of the Town of Alexandria and District of Columbia, Executors of the last Will and Testament of RICHARD CONWAY deceased, of the one part and GILES FITZHUGH of the County of Fairfax and State of Virginia of the other part; WITNESSETH whereas the said RICHARD CONWAY did by his last will and Testament bearing date the fifth day of June in the Year 1804 order, authorise, empower & direct the said WILLIAM HERBERT, NICHOLAS FITZHUGH and EDMUND J. LEE who by his last will and Testement aforesaid were appointed his executors to sell certain parts of his Real estate therein designated and which was not otherwise disposed of by the Codicil attached to the same and bearing Date the 17th day of November 1806 which together with the said Will has been duly proved & recorded. Now this indenture WITNESSETH that the said WILLIAM HERBERT, NICHOLAS FITZHUGH and EDMUND J. LEE Executors as aforesaid for and in consideration of the premises and of the sum of Two thousand two Hundred and seventeen Dollars to them in hand paid by the said GILES FITZHUGH at & before the sealing & delivery of these presents the receipt whereof is hereby acknowledged have granted, bargained & Sold and by these presents do grant, bargain and sell unto the said GILES FITZHUGH his heirs & assigns forever a certain tract or parcel of Land situate, lying and being in the County of Fairfax and State of Virginia and bounded as follows to wit: Beginning at a Stake in the line of WEST, PEARSON and HARRISON where the same crosses the Rolling Road and corner to COLO. CHARLES SIMMS' purchase from the said Executors, thence along the said WEST, PEARSON & HARRISONS line south one & three quarter Degrees east forty nine poles to an antient corner marked white oak now dead, around which are marked three saplings as pointers, thence South twenty nine and one quarter Degrees West two hundred and forty five poles to an ancient corner marked white oak corner to ASHFORD & marked "MA" and also corner to LUND WASHINGTONS purchase from the aforesaid RICHARD CONWAY, thence along the said WASHINGTON line South eighty eight and an half Degrees West one hundred & seventy nine & an half poles to a stake around which are marked several Hickories, Corner to the Land Purchased by WILLIAM POTTER from the aforesaid Executors & by him sold to WILLIAM DEVAUGHN, thence North seventy six poles along the said POTTERS line to a stake and several marked saplings, thence along another of the said POTTERS lines South eighty eight and an half degrees West one hundred & thirty seven poles to a stake

in the line of the Tract of Land called Ravensworth, thence along the said line of Ravensworth North seventy six poles to COOKES corner near a marked spanish oak, thence along the said COOKES line North seventy seven & an Half Degrees East one hundred & ninety four & an half poles to two small Hickories, COOKES Corner and in COLO. SIMMS'S line, thence along said SIMMS' line to the Road two poles COLO. SIMMS' corner, thence binding with his lines along the meanders and middle of the said Rolling Road as follows to wit: down the said Road North sixty Degrees East twenty two poles, thence North eighty one & an half East twenty one poles, thence North eighty three and half Degrees east thirty two poles, thence North twenty five Degrees East twenty Poles, thence North thirty nine degrees East eighteen Poles, thence North thirty five & half Degrees East fourteen poles, thence North fifty three Degrees East twelve poles, thence North twenty six degrees East thirty two poles, thence North Seventy four & half Degrees East fifty four Poles, thence North fifty five Degrees East eight poles to the beginning containing three hundred and ninety eight & half acres with all and Singular the appurtenances thereto belonging or in any manner appertaining. To have and To Hold the said Tract of Land and all & Singular its appurtenances unto him the said GILES FITZHUGH his heirs & assigns forever. And the said WILLIAM HERBERT, NICHOLAS FITZHUGH and EDMUND J. LEE do covenant & agree to & with the said GILES FITZHUGH his heirs & assigns that they will forever warrant & defend the said Tract of Land with its appurtenances to the said GILES FITZHUGH his heirs & assigns forever against the claim or demand of all & every person or persons whatsoever, claiming by, through, from, or under them or either of them. In Testimony whereof the said WILLIAM HERBERT, NICHOLAS FITZHUGH and EDMUND J. LEE have hereunto set their hands & Seals the Day & Year first within written.
Sealed & Delivered
in Presence of   WM. HERBERT   (seal)
WM. HERBERT JR.   N. FITZHUGH   (seal)
R. J. TAYLOR   EDM. J. LEE   (seal)
G. DENEALE
WM. DENEALE

At a Court continued and held for the County of Fairfax the 18th day of April 1809 this Deed from WILLIAM HERBERT, NICHOLAS FITZHUGH & EDMUND J. LEE, executors of RICHARD CONWAY deceased to GILES FITZHUGH was proved to be the Act and Deed of the said WILLIAM HERBERT & NICHOLAS FITZHUGH by the oaths of ROBERT J. TAYLOR and WILLIAM DENEALE and acknowledged by the said EDMUND J. LEE to be his act & Deed & ordered to be certified. And a Court held for the said County the 15th day of May 1809 this Deed was further proved to be the act and Deed of the said WILLIAM HERBERT & NICHOLAS FITZHUGH by the oath of GEORGE DENEALE and Ordered to be Recorded.   Teste WM. MOSS Cl.

Pages 195 & 196. THIS INDENTURE had, made, enter'd into & fully concluded this 21st day of December in the Year of our Lord 1808 between WILLIAM SETTLE of the County of Richmond in the State of Virginia of the one part and BENJAMIN HUTCHISON and ELIZABETH his wife of the County of Fairfax in the said State of the other part. WITNESSETH that the said SETTLE for and in consideration of the love and natural affection that he has for the said BENJAMIN & ELIZABETH his wife have loan'd, given, granted & possessed and do by these presents loan, give, grant & possess the said BENJAMIN & ELIZABETH, for their & each of their joint & several lives, one Negro girl named JUDAH & her future increase. To have and to hold the said JUDAH & her future increase for the full term & time of their & each of their joint & several lives. And the said BENJAMIN HUTCHISON for himself his heirs, Executors, administrators & assigns doth Covenant & agree to & with the said WILLIAM, his Heirs, Executors, administrators & assigns, that the said JUDAH with all her increase shall at the Death of him the said BENJAMIN & ELIZABETH which ever shall be the survivor, be returned to the said WILLIAM, his heirs, Executors, administrators or assigns well clothed. In WITNESS whereof the said parties have here unto put their hand & affixed their Seals the day & Year above written.
Signed Sealed & delivered
In presence of   WM. SETTLE   (seal)
J. HUTCHISON JR   BEN. HUTCHISON   (seal)
WILLIAM AMBLER JR

THOMAS ODEN
JOSHUA HUTCHISON
    At a Court held for Fairfax County the 15th day of May 1809 this Deed of Gift between WILLIAM SETTLE & BENJAMIN HUTCHISON & ELIZABETH his wife was proved to be their Acts & deeds by the oaths of J. HUTCHISON SR & WILLIAM AMBLER JR two of the Witnesses thereto & ordered to be Recorded.   Teste WM. MOSS Cl.

Pages 196-200. THIS INDENTURE made this fourth day of August in the Year of our Lord one Thousand eight hundred & two between JOHN DUFF and SARAH his wife of the County of Fairfax in the State of Virginia of the one part and FREDERICK DRYDELL (*sic*) of the same County & state of the other part. WITNESSETH that the said JOHN DUFF and SARAH his wife for and in consideration of the sum of one hundred & fifty Pounds current money of Virginia to him the said JOHN DUFF in hand paid by him the said FREDERICK DRYDELL (*sic*) at or before the Sealing & Delivery of these presents the receipt whereof he the said JOHN DUFF doth hereby acknowledge and thereof & of every Part and parcel thereof doth acquit, release and discharge him the said FREDERICK DRYDELL (*sic*), his Heirs, Executors and administrators, by these presents have, given, granted, Bargained, Sold, Aliened & confirmed and by these presents do give, grant, bargain, Sell, alien & confirm unto him the said FREDERICK DRYDELL (*sic*), his heirs & assigns for ever, a tract or parcel of Land situate, lying & being in the said County and State contiguous to the Town of Alexandria and upon the South side of Wolfe lane, North side of Wilks Lane, West side of Hamilton Lane and East side of Mandeville Lane & bounded as followeth to wit: beginning at the intersection of Wolf Lane with Hamilton Lane and running thence Southwardly with Hamilton Lane to the intersection thereof with Wilks Lane, thence Westwardly with Wilks lane to the intersection thereof with Mandeville Lane, thence Northwardly with Mandeville lane to the Intersection thereof with Wolf Lane, thence Eastwardly with Wolfe Lane to the beginning, it being one of those squares into which the Tract of Land called Spring Garden Farm was laid off & in the subdivisions of the said Square distinguished by the numbers (97, 98, 110, 111) which tract or parcel of Land was sold & conveyed by JESSE SIMMS unto JESSE GREEN his heirs & assigns who sold and conveyed the same unto ROBERT PATTON JR his heirs & assigns by whom it was Sold & Conveyed unto him the said JOHN DUFF his heirs & assigns by an indenture bearing date the thirty first day of October one thousand eight hundred and one; And all Houses, Buildings & Trees, Woods, Waters, Watercourses, Lanes, allies, Profits, Commodities, Hereditaments & appurtenances whatsoever, to the said presmises belonging or in anywise appertaining and the Reversion & Reversions, Remainder and Remainders, Rents, Issues & Profits thereof and of every part and parcel thereof To Have and To Hold the said Tract of Land, Hereditaments and all & singular the Premises hereby granted with the appurtenances unto him the said FREDERICK DRYDELL (*sic*) his heirs and assigns to the only proper use & behoof of him the said FREDERICK DRYDELL (*sic*) his heirs & assigns forever & the said JOHN DUFF doth for himself his Executors & administrators, covenant, grant & agree to & with the said FREDERICK DRYDELL (*sic*) his heirs & assigns that he the said JOHN DUFF is now at the time of the Sealing & delivery of these presents, seized in his own right of a good, sure, perfect, absolute and indefeasible estate of Inheritance in fee simple in the said Tract or parcel of Land, hereditaments and all & Singular the Premises hereby granted with the appurtenances without any manner of condition, Mortgage, Limitation of use or uses, or any other matter, cause or thing to alter, change, charge or determine the same and also that he the said JOHN DUFF & his Heirs will at anytime hereafter at the request and at Cost & charges of him the said FREDERICK DRYDELL (*sic*) his heirs & assigns execute and acknowledge any further and other lawfull act and Deed for the more certain assuring and conveying the said Tract or parcel of Land, hereditaments and all and Singular the said premises with the appurtenances unto him the said FREDERICK DRYDELL (*sic*) his heirs & assigns as by him the said FREDERICK DRYDELL (*sic*) his heirs & assigns his, their or any of their council learned in the Law shall or may be advised or required and lastly that he the said JOHN DUFF and his Heirs all and Singular the said premises with the appurtenances unto him the said FREDERICK DRYDELL (*sic*) his heirs and assigns against the claim and demand of him the said JOHN DUFF and his heirs and all and every other person or persons whatsoever shall & will warrant & forever defend by these presents. In

WITNESS whereof the said JOHN DUFF & SARAH his wife have hereunto set their hands & Seals the day & Year first herein before mentioned.

Sealed & Delivered

In presence of   JOHN DUFF   (seal)
JAS. KEITH   SARAH her X mark DUFF   (seal)
ARCH. McCLEAN
THOMAS R. KEITH

 Received of FREDERICK DRYDELL (*sic*) one hundred and fifty Pounds, current Money of Virginia. the consideration herein mentioned.

WITNESS [No witnesses listed]   JOHN DUFF

 At a Circuit Court of the District of Columbia continued & held for the County of Alexandria the 24th of November 1802 JOHN DUFF acknowledged this Deed & receipt to FREDERICK TRYDELL (*sic*) to be his Act and Deed which together with a Commission & return hereto annexed for taking the acknowledgment & privy examination of SARAH DUFF wife of the said JOHN are ordered to be recorded. Teste G. DENEALE Cl.

 DISTRICT OF COLUMBIA To Wit:

 I GEORGE DENEALE Clerk of the United States circuit Court of the District of Columbia for the County of Alexandria do hereby certify that at a United States Circuit Court of the District aforesaid continued & held for the County aforesaid the Seventeenth day of July 1804, this Deed and receipt from JOHN DUFF to FREDERICK TRYDELL (*sic*) having been heretofore acknowledged by the said JOHN DUFF to be his act and Deed which together with a commission & return hereto annexed for taking the acknowledgment and privy examination of SARAH DUFF wife of the said JOHN was recorded whereupon it is ordered that the same be certified to the County Court of Fairfax in the CommonWealth of Virginia.

(SEAL) In testimony whereof I hereunto set my hand & Seal of office this 25th
  day of July 1804. G. DENEALE Cl.

 DISTRICT OF COLUMBIA To Wit:

 I WILLIAM CRANCH Chief Judge of the Circuit Court of the District of Columbia, do hereby certify that the annexed certificate of GEORGE DENEALE Clerk of the said Court for the County of Alexandria, is in due form. Given under my hand this 26th day of April 1808.

      W. CRANCH

 At a Court held for Fairfax County the 15th day of May 1809 this Deed from JOHN DUFF and SARAH his wife to FREDERICK TRYDELL (*sic*) & a recipt thereon endorsed having been duly acknowledged by the said JOHN DUFF, before the United States circuit court for the District of Columbia held for the County of Alexandria & Certified by GEORGE DENEALE Clerk of the said Court, under the Seal of his office, also by WILLIAM CRANCH Chief Judge of the said Court, is on motion of the said FREDERICK TRYDELL (*sic*) together with the Certificates thereon endorsed & a commission & return thereto annexed for taking the acknowledgment & Privy exmination of the said SARAH are ordered to be recorded.

     Teste WM. MOSS Cl.

 FAIRFAX COUNTY:

 The CommonWealth of Virginia to ABRAHAM FAW, JACOB HOFFMAN and GEORGE GILPIN, Gentleman of the County of Alexandria in the District of Columbia Greeting: Whereas JOHN DUFF & SARAH his wife by their certain indenture of bargain and Sale bearing date the fourth day of August 1802 have sold and conveyed unto FREDERICK DRYDELL (*sic*) the fee simple estate of a tract or parcel of Land with the appurtenances situate, lying and being in the said County of Fairfax & State of Virginia and whereas the said SARAH cannot conveniently travel to our said County Court to make acknowledgment of the said conveyance therefore we do give unto You or any two or more of you power to receive the acknowledgment which the said SARAH shall be willing to make before You of the conveyance aforesaid contained in the said indenture which is hereto annexed and we do thereof desire You or any two or more of you personally to go to the said SARAH and receive her acknowledgment of the same & examine her privily & apart from the said JOHN her husband whether she doth the same freely & voluntarily without his persuasions or threats & whether she be willing the said indenture together with this Commission should be recorded in our said Court and when you have received her acknowledgment & examined her as aforesaid that You distinctly and openly certify us thereof in our said Court under your hands and seals sending then there this indenture & this writ.

WITNESS WILLIAM MOSS Clerk of the said Court, this sixth day of August 1802.

WM. MOSS Cl.

DISTRICT OF COLUMBIA, County of Alexandria To Wit:

In Obedience to the within Commission we did examine the said SARAH privily & apart from the said JOHN her husband who declared that she executed the said Indenture freely & voluntarily without his persuasions or threats & that she was willing the said indenture together with this Commission should be recorded in the said Court. Given under our Hands & Seals this 13th day of August 1802.   A. FAW   (seal)

JACOB HOFFMAN   (seal)

Page 200. VIRGINIA FAIRFAX To Wit:

Be it remembered that on the 19th day of December in the year Eighteen hundred & three, THOMSON MASON of said County came before me the undersigned justice of the peace for the said County & took before me the following oath in due form of Law to wit: "I THOMSON MASON do swear that I will be faithfull & true to the CommonWealth of Virginia of which I profess to be a citizen and that I will faithfully and justly execute the Office of Brigadier General of the Militia of Virginia according to the best of my skill & judgment so help me God." Given under my hand this day & Year above mentioned.

GEO. SUMMERS

At a Court held for Fairfax County the 15th day of May 1809 GEORGE SUMMERS Gentleman returned a certificate of THOMSON MASONS qualification before as Brigadier General which is ordered to Recorded.   WM. MOSS Cl.

Page 201. KNOW ALL MEN by these presents that we EDWARD W. SIMPSON, WM. SIMPSON and THOMAS GOSSOM are held & firmly bound unto JOHN TYLER Esqr., Governor of the CommonWealth of Virginia and his Successors in the full & just sum of one Thousand Dollars Current Money of the United States to which payment well & truly to be made to the said JOHN TYLER, Governor and his Successors, we bind ourselves and each of us, our and each of our Heirs, executors and Administrators jointly and severally firmly by these presents sealed with our Seals and dated this 15th day of May 1809.

THE CONDITION of the above obligation is such that Whereas the above bound EDWARD W. SIMPSON hath been duly appointed a Constable for that part or section of the County of Fairfax described and Known by District Number 4 in pursuance of two several Acts of Assembly of this CommonWealth passed the twenty first day of January Eighteen hundred & three and the tenth day of January eighteen hundred and seven the first entitled an Act concerning Constables, Now if the said EDWARD W. SIMPSON shall in every respect well & truly Perform and discharge the several duties of his said Office of constable in the District aforesaid agreeable to the several Acts of Asssembly concerning constables defining their duty then the above obligation to be void else to remain in full force, Power and virtue in Law.

Signed & delivered in   EDWARD W. SIMPSON   (seal)
presence of   WILLIAM SIMPSON   (seal)
     The Court   THOS. GOSSOM   (seal)

At a Court held for Fairfax County the 15th day of May 1809 EDWARD W. SIMPSON, WILLIAM SIMPSON & THOMAS GOSSOM acknowledged the within Bond to be their Acts & Deed which is Ordered to be Recorded.   Teste WM. MOSS Cl.

Pages 202-206. THIS INDENTURE made this twelfth day of May in the Year of our Lord one Thousand eight hundred and six between JOHN THOMAS RICKETTS of the County of Fairfax and CommonWealth of Virginia of the one part and DAVID RICKETTS of the County of Loudoun and CommonWealth aforesaid of the other part. WITNESSETH that the said JOHN THOMAS RICKETTS for and in consideration of the sum of nine Thousand Dollars to him in hand paid at or before the Sealing and delivery of these presents by the said DAVID RICKETTS the receipt whereof the said JOHN THOMAS RICKETTS doth hereby acknowledge confessing himself paid & satisfied hath given, granted, bargained, Sold, Aliened & confirmed and by these presents doth give, grant, bargain, sell, alien and confirm unto him the said DAVID RICKETTS his heirs & assigns forever one equal Moiety and undivided half part of the Merchant Mill at Cameron built and erected by STUMP & RICKETTS where the said JOHN THOMAS RICKETTS now lives together with a Moiety and undivided half part of all the Lands, Tenements, buildings, improvements, possessions and Premises, situate in the said County of Fairfax and held in Common by the said JOHN THOMAS RICKETTS with JOHN STUMP JR of Harford County in the State of Maryland lying & being on Great Hunting Creek and the waters and drains leading unto the said creek, being one plantation on which the said Mill stands and on which the said JOHN THOMAS RICKETTS resides containing one Hundred and Thirty acres more or less; also a slip of Land of about two poles wide adjoining to said plantation and extending to the Mill Dams through which slip of Land the Mill Race is Cut which conveys the water from the run and Dams to the Mills in the head race, also a Lot or piece of Land held in common by said JOHN STUMP JR and JOHN THOMAS RICKETTS and the creditors or Trustees of SUTTON & MANDEVILLE or some of them, each Party holding one undivided Moiety of said Lot laying between the said Mill race and Cameron Run and adjoining the Lands of PETER WISE, THOMAS HERBERT, the heirs of SAMUEL HULL and the described plantation of STUMP & RICKETTS the whole Lot containing ten acres more or less, also a Lot of wood Land containing fifty acres more or less adjoining to & bounded by the Lands of JAMES IRVIN, KORN & WISEMILLER & WILKENSON GRIGSBY, all of which Lands and Premises herewith sold, described and conveyed, or intended to be sold, described and conveyed to the said DAVID RICKETTS his heirs & assigns shall be held, enjoyed and Possessed by him, them & all of them, in the same absolute manner in Common with the said JOHN STUMP JR and by the same Meets & bounds the said Moiety or half part of all the said Lands & Premises were and are now held by the said JOHN THOMAS RICKETTS which will more fully and at large appear by the various Deeds, the Dates of them commencing in 1791 and ending this present Year 1806 inclusive, all of Record in the said County of Fairfax, to which Deeds reference is had for more compleatly apertaining the meets & bounds of said Lands & premises, also all the estate right, Title, Property, interest, claim and demand as well in Law as equity of him the said JOHN THOMAS RICKETTS, of, in and to a Moiety or half part of the Mill Lands and premises, containing about four acres and now held and possessed by said JOHN STUMP JR & JOHN THOMAS RICKETTS in common, by certain meet & bounds & known by the name of POWELLS Mills, for which no conveyance is had, also all the right, property, claim, Interest and demand of him the said JOHN THOMAS RICKETTS, of, in and to a moiety or half part of the slaves, livestock, grain & flour in the mills, Farming and Millering tools and utensils, with all the goods, chattle and effects appertaining to him the said JOHN THOMAS RICKETTS, more fully described in the annex'd schedule which is made a part of this Indenture and all the right, title, claim, interest, Property and Demand of him the said JOHN THOMAS RICKETTS, of, in and to the one undivided moiety or half part of the said Lands, premises, Mills, Mill dams, abutments, safe gate, waist gate, Pur heads, Mill race Waters and Water courses, Woods, Trees, Orchards, Buildings and improvements, Profits, commodities, Hereditaments, Rents, Issues, Privileges, advantages, slaves, live stock, with the goods, chattles and effects described in the said annex'd schedule together with the appurtenances of every nature and kind thereunto belonging or in anywise appertaining to him the said DAVID RICKETTS, his heirs executors, administrators and assigns forever. To have and to Hold the Moiety and half part of the said Lands, Hereditaments and all and Singular the premises and improvements, property, goods, chattles and effects hereby granted or intended to be granted to him the said DAVID RICKETTS, his Heirs, executors, administrators & assigns to and for the use & behoof of him the said DAVID RICKETTS, his heirs, executors, Administrators and Assigns forever and for no other intent, use or purpose whatsoever and the said JOHN THOMAS RICKETTS for himself, his heirs and executors, covenants, grants and agrees to and with the said DAVID RICKETTS his heirs and assigns that he or they, any or all of them, without any time hereafter at the request of and at the cost and charges of him the said DAVID RICKETTS his heirs and assigns or any of them, execute and acknowledge any further act and Deed for the more certain conveying & confirming the said undivided Moiety or half part of the said Lands, Mills, premises, goods, chattles and effects, with all & Singular the appurtenances of every Nature and Kind to him the said DAVID RICKETTS, his heirs, executors, administrators and assigns forever as shall or may by him or any of them, or their Council learn'd in the Law, be advised, devised or required & lastly the said JOHN THOMAS RICKETTS further agrees for himself and his heirs the said Lands, buildings, improvements & appurtenances with the goods, chattles and effects to him the said DAVID RICKETTS, his heirs, executors, administrators and assigns and against the claim or claims & demand of him the said JOHN THOMAS RICKETTS and his heirs and all and every person or persons claiming or to claim by, from, or under him, them or any of them, will forever warrant & defend. In testimony whereof the said JOHN THOMAS RICKETTS has hereunto set his hand and affixed his Seal the day & Year first written.

Signed, Sealed & delivered
In presence of   JNO. THOS. RICKETTS   (seal)
WILLIAM SIMMONS
PETER W. LUNGSTRASS
JAMES BLOXHAM
GEORGE HULLS

  Received the day of the date of the above indenture of DAVID RICKETTS the sum of nine Thousand Dollars, the Consideration for the said Mills, Land, premises, goods, chattles & effects. $9000

             JNO. THOS. RICKETTS

Witness present
JAMES BLOXHAM
WILLIAM SIMMONS
PETER W. LUGSTRASS

  The above Deed was acknowledged by JOHN THOMAS RICKETTS & delivered as his Act and deed for the purposes therein mentioned before us the subscribers this twenty ninth day of April one thousand eight hundred & nine.
WITNESSES
JAMES BLOXHAM   JNO. THOS. RICKETTS
WILLIAM SIMMONS
GEORGE HULLS

  A schedule of the Goods, Chattles & effects, the property & right of JOHN STUMP and JOHN THOMAS RICKETTS under the firm of STUMP and RICKETTS attached to & appertaining to the CAMERON estate of said STUMP and RICKETTS to wit: three elderly Negro Men slaves, JERRY, JESSE and NEWTON, eight old horses, seven Milch cows, one young calf, one Bull, a Yoke of Oxen with a Yoak and Ox chain, one Waggon and Gears for a Team of Horses, one Ox Cart, two old Horse carts and Gears for the same; two Bar shear plows and Gears for the same, two sets of swingletrees, one harrow, two old wheel barrows, twenty seven Hogs, the grain, flour, Meal, Bran and Shorts with the empty barrels and casks in the Mills and out Buildings, staves and heading in the Yard, three dozen Mill Picks, three brushing chisels, two Iron bars, ten Pounds cask Nails, ten pounds old spikes, ten branding Irons, six heisting tubs, four sets Scales and weights, a large steel Yard, a crosscut Saw, two other Saws a broad Ax, two Carpenters adds, three gouges, ten chisels, six augers, six plains, a grindstone hung, a small Iron chest now in Alexandria, one hundred old bags, Millers and Negroes beding and covering, one old wheat Fan, two half bushel measures, a tall dish, four bait buckets, eight blend bridles, two old spades, eight old shovels, a garden rake, tine and stakes, six Hay rakes, six pitchforks, six old hoes, four old falling axes, four iron wedges, a pair of Mall rings, three Schythes and one ditto, three sickles, a cutting box, two mattocks, three gravel Picks, one sledge hammer, three other hammers, one thousand Pounds of Salt meat & bacon, thirteen barrels salt fish, five bushels of salt, three fourth parts of a barrel of whiskey and a quarter cask of cheap wine, three dozen poultry old, two dozen young chickens, two boat hooks, a small fishing sein, one cask Vinegar, a firkin of Sugar, thirty pounds of Coffee and loaf Sugar, one pound of Tea.
WITNESS
JAMES BLOXHAM   JNO. THOS. RICKETTS
WILLIAM SIMMONS
PETER W. LUNGSTRASS, GEO. HULLS

The above Schedule was re-acknowledged by JOHN THOMAS RICKETTS and the same delivered as his Act and Deed before us, the subscribers, this twenty Ninth day of April 1809.
WITNESSES
JAMES BLOXHAM   JNO. THOS. RICKETTS
WILLIAM SIMMONS
GEORGE HULLS

    At a Court held for Fairfax County the 15th day of May 1809 this Deed from JOHN THOMAS RICKETTS and a Schedule of property thereto annexed to DAVID RICKETTS and a re-acknowledgment thereon endorsed, were proved by the oaths of JAMES BLOXHAM, WILLIAM SIMMONS and GEORGE HULLS witnesses thereto to be the Act and Deed of the said JOHN THOMAS RICKETTS which together with a receipt thereon endorsed are ordered to be recorded.
Teste WM. MOSS Cl.

PAGES 206 & 207. THIS INDENTURE made and entered into this 17th day of June 1809 between HECTOR KINCHELOE and MARY KINCHELOE his wife and JESSE KINCHELOE and MARY KINCHELOE his wife of the State of Virginia and County of Fairfax of the one part and JOHN H. DYE of the aforesd. State and County of Prince William of the other part. WITNESSETH that the said HECTOR KINCHELOE and MARY KINCHELOE and JESSE KINCHELOE & MARY his wife for and in consideration of the sum of two hundred & thirty pounds, current Money of Virginia to them in hand paid by the said JOHN H. DYE the receipt whereof they the said HECTOR KINCHELOE and MARY his wife and JESSE KINCHELOE and MARY KINCHELOE his wife doth hereby acknowledge have this day granted, bargained, Sold, aliened & Confirmed and do by these presents grant, bargain, Sell, alien & Confirm unto the said JOHN H. DYE his heirs & assigns forever a certain piece or parcel of Land situate, lying & being in the County of Fairfax on Bull Run and Popeshead and bounded as follows Vizt: beginning at a beech on Bull Run near COLO. HOOES old mill ford, thence up Bull Run & binding therewith agreeable to the several meanders thereof to the old Mill Dam, thence South 27° East 39 poles to GIBBS' corner, thence North 85° West 54 poles, thence South 28° West 34 poles to the Meadow Branch, thence South 34° West 42 poles to a poplar on the Spring Branch, thence up the said branch and binding therewith South 4° West 28 poles, thence North 14 1/2° West 19 poles to a poplar stump corner to ROBERT WECKTIFFS tract, thence South 25° West 56 poles to a pile of Stone on a hill near an old Road, thence to the beginning, including Ninety acres as also one acre of Land on the North side of Popeshead opposite DANIEL KINCHELOES old Mill dam which he had condemned for the use of his old Mill together with all Houses, profits, advantages, Hereditaments, Ways, Waters & Watercourses, with the appurtenances of every kind and nature thereunto belonging. To have and to Hold the afsd bargained Premises with their appurtenances of every kind unto the said JOHN H. DYE his heirs & assigns to the only proper use and behoof of him the said JOHN H. DYE his heirs & assigns forever & lastly the afsd. HECTOR KINCHELOE & MARY his wife and JESSE KINCHELOE and MARY his wife for themselves, their heirs, Executors and Adms. do warrant & will forever defend the afsd. bargained premises with their appurtenances (except so much thereof as CORNELIUS KINCELOE has a legal right to which he claims under the Will of NESTOR KINCHELOE decd) unto the said JOHN H. DYE his heirs & assigns forever against the claim of all and every person or persons whatsoever. In WITNESS whereof the said HECTOR KINCHELOE & MARY his wife and JESSE KINCHELOE and MARY his wife have hereunto set their hands & affixed their Seals the day and date first above written.
Signed Sealed & acknowledged   HECTOR KINCHELOE   (seal)
In Presence of [No witnesses listed]   MARY her X mark KINCHELOE   (seal)
                                            JESSE KINCHELOE   (seal)
                                            MARY her X mark KINCHELOE   (seal)
    At a Court held for Fairfax County the 19th day of June 1809 this deed from HECTOR KINCHELOE and MARY his wife and JESSE KINCHELOE and MARY his wife to JOHN H. DYE was acknowledged by the said HECTOR and JESSE to be their Act and Deed and ordered to be recorded and at a court contd. & held for the said County the 20th day of June in the Year aforesaid. This deed was further acknowledged by said Mary, the wife of the said HECTOR and

MARY, the wife of the said JESSE, they being first privately & again in open court examined & thereto consenting to be their acts and deeds are thereupon ordered to be Recorded.
Teste WM. MOSS Cl.

Pages 208 & 209. THIS INDENTURE made this twelfth day of December in the Year eighteen hundred and eight between THOMAS FAIRFAX of the County of Fairfax and State of Virginia on the one part and HENRY GUNNELL SR of the County and State aforesaid on the other part. WITNESSETH that whereas the said FAIRFAX did on the 16th day of November last enter into articles of agreement to convey unto the said GUNNELL a certain Parcel of Land under certain Conditions and Provisos therein specified as by reference thereto will more fully appear, now therefore the said FAIRFAX in compliance with the said engagement and also in consideration of the sum of one dollar the receipt whereof is hereby acknowledged hath bargained and sold and by these presents doth bargain and Sell unto the said GUNNELL and his Heirs the aforesaid Parcel of Land lying & being on both sides of the Run called Wolftrap in the County of Fairfax and bounded as follows Vizt: beginning at a red oak stump, the beginning corner of SAMUEL WILSONS Patent near said run on the side of a hill, thence with a line of said Patent South 40° West 65 poles to the intersection of COLO. BROADWATERS line, thence with the courses of his patent allowing five degrees variation North 41° West 42 poles South 55° West 64 South 15° West 178 poles to a white oak stump on a branch of Difficult run, the beginning corner of said patent, thence North 7° East 212 poles to a bunch of chesnuts, the beginning corner of the land sold by said FAIRFAX to JAMES HUNTER, thence with the line of that Land North 47 1/2° East 80 poles to an ash on Wolf Trap and thence South 62° East 89 Poles to the beginning containing about 594 Acres more or less together with all and Singular the appurtenances. To have and To Hold the fee simple Estate of the said Parcel of Land and its appurtenances unto him the said GUNNELL his heirs and assigns forever & the said FAIRFAX doth hereby covenant and agree with the said GUNNELL his heirs & assigns that he the said FAIRFAX and his heirs, the said Parcel of land with its appurte-nances and all the right, Title and interest hereby granted against the claim of him the said FAIRFAX and his Heirs, shall and will warrant and forever defend by these presents. In WITNESS whereof the said FAIRFAX hath hereunto set his hand & Seal the day & Year above written.
Sealed & delivered in presence of
WM. HERBERT JR, N. HERBERT   THOS. FAIRFAX   (seal)
HUGH W. GUNNELL
     At a Court held for Fairfax County the 19th day of June 1809 this Deed from THOMAS FAIRFAX to HENRY GUNNELL SR was acknowledged by the said THOMAS FAIRFAX to be his act and Deed and ordered to be Recorded.   Teste WM. MOSS Cl.

Pages 209-212. THIS INDENTURE made this 2nd day of December in the Year of our Lord one thousand eight hundred and six between RICHARD WHEELER and MARGARET his wife of the County of Fairfax of the one part and WILLIAM OFFUTT of the aforesaid County of the other part. WITNESSETH that for and in consideration of the sum of four hundred & twenty four dollars Current Money of Virginia, to the said RICHARD WHEELER in hand paid by the sd. WILLIAM OFFUTT at or before the sealing or delivery of these presents the receipt whereof he doth hereby acknowledge and thereof doth acquit and discharge the said WILLIAM OFFUTT his Executors and Administrators by these presents he the said RICHARD WHEELER hath granted, bargained and Sold and by these presents he the said RICHARD WHEELER unto the said WILLIAM OFFUTT and to his Heirs, all that tract or parcel of Land containing one hundred and twelve acres be the same more or less situate, lying and being in the aforesaid County of Fairfax and Parish of Truro and bounded as follows: beginning at a corner white oak to THOMAS SIMPSONS, running thence a straight course to three small chesnut trees and a red oak saplin corner to BOND NEALE now the property of JOHN ARUNDLE, thence with the said JOHN ARUNDLES line to a red oak & chesnut, thence with the said line to WESTS line, thence down the Ox road with the said WEST line to where it intersects with WILLIAM SIMPSONS line, thence with the said SIMPSONS line to a white oak corner of THOMAS SIMPSON, thence with said THOMAS SIMPSON'S to the beginning which tract or parcel of Land is part of a larger tract containing two hundred and thirty five acres which was granted by the right

Honorable, the proprietor of the Northern neck, to JOHN ROBERTSON and by the said JOHN ROBERTSON & MARY his wife sold and conveyed to the [sd.] HENRY ROBERTSON by Deeds of Lease and Release and from the said HENRY ROBERTSON and ELIZABETH his wife sold and conveyed to DRUMMOND WHEELER and recorded in the County Court of Fairfax and by the said DRUMMOND WHEELER devised to the said RICHARD WHEELER by his last Will and Testament and from the said RICHARD WHEELER and MARGARET his wife to the said WILLIAM OFFUTT and all Houses, buildings, orchards, Ways, Waters and Watercourses, profits, commodities, hereditaments and appurtenances whatsoever to the said premises hereby granted or any part thereof belonging or in any wise thereof and the Reversion and Reversions, Remainder and Remainders, Rents, Issues and Profits thereof and also all the estate rights, Title, interest, use, trust, Property, claim and demand whatsoever of him the said RICHARD WHEELER and MARGARET his wife, of, in and to the said Premises and all Deeds, evidences and writings touching the same. To have and To Hold the said Tract or Parcel of Land and all and Singular other the Premises hereby granted and every Part and Parcel thereof with their and every of their appurtenances unto the said WILLIAM OFFUTT his heirs and assigns forever to the only Proper use and behoof of him the said WILLIAM OFFUTT and of his Heirs and assigns forever and the said RICHARD WHEELER and MARGARET his wife for themselves their heirs, Executors and Administrators doth covenant, Promise and grant to and with the said WILLIAM OFFUTT his heirs & assigns by these presents that he the said RICHARD WHEELER and Margaret his wife now at the time of Sealing and delivering these presents are seized of a good, sure and perfect and indefeasible of inheritance in fee simple of and in the Premises hereby granted and conveyed and that they have good Power and lawful and absolute authority to grant and convey the same to the said WILLIAM OFFUTT his heirs and assigns in manner and form aforesaid and that the said Premises now are and so forever shall remain and be free and clear of & from all former and other Gifts, grants, bargains, Sales, dower right and title of dower judgments, executions, titles, troubles, charges & encumbrances whatsoever made, done, committed, or suffered by the said RICHARD WHEELER and MARGARET his wife or any person or persons whatsoever. And lastly that the said RICHARD WHEELER and MARGARET his wife and Heirs all and Singular the Premises hereby granted and conveyed with their appurtenances unto the said WILLIAM OFFUTT his heirs and assigns the aforesaid tract or parcel of Land before mentioned to the said WILLIAM OFFUTT & his Heirs or assigns against them the said RICHARD WHEELER and MARGARET his wife and their Heirs & assigns & from any other Person or persons whatsoever shall & will warrant & defend by these presents. In WITNESS whereof the said RICHARD WHEELER & MARGARET his wife hath hereunto set their hands & Seals the day & Year above written.

Sealed & acknowledged
In Presence of   RICHARD WHEELER   (seal)
W. DENEALE   MARGARET her X mark WHEELER (seal)
JOHN JACKSON
RD. RATCLIFFE
GIDEON M. MOSS

     Received of WILLIAM OFFUTT one hundred and twenty seven Pounds four shillings in full this 2nd day of December 1806.
Teste   RICHD. WHEELER
W. DENEALE
JOHN JACKSON

     At a Court held for Fairfax County the 19th of January 1807 this Deed from RICHD. WHEELER and MARGARET his wife to WILLIAM OFFUTT and a receipt thereon endorsed, were Proved to be the act and Deed of the said RICHD. WHEELER by the oath of WILLM. DENEALE a Witness hereto and ordered to be certified. And at a Court held for the said County the 16th day of May 1808 the same was further proved by the oath of JOHN JACKSON another Witness hereto and ordered to be Certified. And at a Court held for the said County the 19th day of June 1809 the same was further proved by the oath of GIDEON M. MOSS another witness thereto which together with a Commission & return thereto annexed for taking the acknowledgment and privy examination of the said MARGARET and ordered to be Recorded.
                     Teste WM. MOSS Cl.

FAIRFAX COUNTY To Wit:

The CommonWealth of Virginia to JOHN JACKSON, RICHARD RATCLIFFE and WILLIAM DENEALE Gentlemen of the County of Fairfax Greeting: Whereas RICHARD WHEELER and MARGARET WHEELER his wife by their certain indenture of bargain and Sale bearing date the second day of December 1806 have Sold and conveyed unto WILLIAM OFFUTT the fee simple estate of one hundred & twelve acres of Land with the appurtenances situate, lying & being in the County of Fairfax. And whereas the said MARGARET WHEELER cannot conveniently travel to our said County Court of Fairfax to make acknowledgment of the sd. conveyance therefore we do give unto You or any two or more of You Power to receive the acknowledgment which the said MARGARET WHEELER shall be willing to make before You of the conveyances afore-said contained in the said indenture which is hereunto annexed; and we do therefore desire You or any two or more of You personally to go to the said MARGARET WHEELER and receive her acknowledgment of the same and examine her privily and apart from the said RICHARD WHEELER her husband whither she doth the same freely & voluntarily without his persuasions and threats and whither she be willing the said Indenture together with the Commission shall be recorded in our said Court. And when You have received her acknowledgment and examined her as aforesaid that You distinctly and openly Certify us thereof in our said Court under Your hands & seals sending then there the said indenture and this writ. WITNESS WILLIAM MOSS Clerk of the said Court this [left blank] day of [left blank] and in the [left blank] Year of the CommonWealth.

WM. MOSS Cl.

FAIRFAX COUNTY To Wit:

In obedience to the within Commission we did examine the said MARGARET privately and apart from the said RICHARD WHEELER her Husband who declared that she executed the said Indenture freely and Voluntarily without his persuasion or threats and that she was willing the said indenture together with this Commission should be recorded in the said County. Given under our hands & Seals this 2nd day of December 1806.

JOHN JACKSON   (seal)
W. DENEALE   (seal)

Pages 212-215. THIS INDENTURE made this eleventh day of April in the Year of our Lord one thousand eight hundred & nine between JAMES HALLEY and FRANCES his wife of the County of Fairfax in the State of Virginia of the one part and DAVID STUART of the same County and State of the other Part. WITNESSETH that the said JAMES HALLEY and FRANCES his wife for and in consideration of the sum of four hundred & Seventy four Dollars to him the said JAMES HALLEY in hand paid by him the said DAVID STUART at or before the Sealing and delivery of these presents the receipt whereof he doth hereby acknowledge and thereof and of every part thereof doth acquit, release and discharge him the said DAVID STUART, his Heirs, Executors and Administrators by these presents have given, granted, bargained, Sold, aliened and confirmed and by these presents do Give, Grant, bargain, Sell, alien and Confirm unto him the said DAVID STUART his heirs and assigns forever a tract of Land situate, lying and being on the North side of Pohick Run in the said County of Fairfax and bounded as followeth to wit: beginning at two white oaks on said Run side WILLIAM BARKERS Corner, thence North sixty four East fifty four poles to two White oaks said BARKERS corner in the line of WILLIAM FITZHUGHS land, thence North fifty five West thirty nine poles to a dead red oak McKINNYS corner and several white oak saplins, thence leaving the line of FITZHUGH South eighty eight West Ninety nine Poles to a Gum McKENNYS corner, thence South seventy eight, West four-teen Poles to a white oak McKINNYS corner, thence South thirty nine East forty six poles to a stake on the north side of Pohick Run, thence South sixty nine East ten Poles along the several meanders of said run and binding therewith, thence North sixty two and a half east nine Poles, thence North eight east four Poles, thence north twenty nine East ten Poles, thence South sixty one and a half east ten Poles, thence North forty Nine east twelve poles, thence South eighty one east eight Poles, thence North forty eight east nine poles, thence south sixty two East eleven Poles, thence South five east Nineteen poles to the beginning containing twenty three acres two roods thirty two poles which tract of Land was devised to him by his brother WILLIAM HALLY and all Houses, buildings, trees, Woods, Waters,

Watercourses, Profits, Commodities, hereditaments and appurtenances whatsoever, the said Premises belonging or in any wise appertaining and the Reversion and Reversions, Remainder and Remainders, Rents, Issues and Profits thereof and of every part and parcel thereof to Have & To Hold the said Tract of Land, Hereditaments and all and Singular the Premises hereby granted with their appurtenances unto him the said DAVID STUART his heirs and assigns to the only Proper use and behoof (of) him the said DAVID STUART, his Heirs and assigns forever. And the said JAMES HALLEY and FRANCES his wife, for themselves and their Heirs, the said Tract of Land with all and Singular the Premises & appurtenances before mentioned unto the said DAVID STUART his heirs and assigns free from the claim or claims of them the said JAMES HALLEY and FRANCES his wife or either of them, their or either of their heirs and of all and every person or persons whatsoever shall, will & do Warrant and forever defend by these presents. In WITNESS whereof the said JAMES HALLEY and FRANCES his wife have hereunto set their Hands and Seals the day & Year first herein mentioned. Sealed & delivered in

Presence of   JAMES HALLEY   (seal)
EDW. WASHINGTON   FRANCES her X mark HALLEY   (seal)
JAMES BURK
WILLIAM HALLEY
WM. MOSS
JAMES WIGGINTON, W. PAYNE

    Received from DAVID STUART four hundred & Seventy four Dollars the consideration herein mentioned.
WITNESS
EDWD. WASHINGTON   JAMES HALLEY   (seal)
JAMES BURK, WILLM. HALLEY
WM. MOSS, W. PAYNE

    At a Court held for Fairfax County the 19th day of June 1809 this Deed from JAMES HALLEY and FRANCES his wife to DAVID STUART and a receipt thereon endorsed were acknowledged by the said JAMES HALLEY which together with a Commission and return thereto annexed for taking the acknowledgment and Privy examination of the said FRANCES are ordered to be recorded.   Teste WM. MOSS Cl.

    FAIRFAX COUNTY To Wit:
    The CommonWealth of Virginia to WM. PAYNE, WM. DENEALE and HANCOCK LEE, Gentlemen Justices of the County of Fairfax Greeting: Whereas JAMES HALLEY and FRANCES his wife by their certain indenture of Bargain & Sale bearing date the eleventh day of April one thousand eight hundred & nine, have Sold & Conveyed unto DAVID STUART the fee simple estate of a tract of Land in the County of Fairfax with the appurtenances and Whereas the said FRANCES cannot conveniently travel to our said County Court of Fairfax to make acknowledgment of the said conveyance therefore we do give unto you or any two or more of you Power to receive the acknowledgment which the said FRANCES shall be willing to make before You of the conveyance aforesaid contained in the said Indenture which is hereunto annexed and we do therefore desire You or any two or more of You Personally to go to the said FRANCES and receive her acknowledgment of the same and examine her privily and apart from the said JAMES HALLEY her husband whither she doth the same freely and Voluntarily without his persuasions or threats and whither she be willing the said indenture together with this Commission shall be recorded in our said Court and when You have received her acknowledgment and examined her as aforesaid that you distinctly & openly certify us thereof in our said Court under Your hands & Seals sending then there the said indenture and this Writ. WITNESS WILLIAM MOSS Clerk of the said Court at the Court House of the County aforesaid this day of [left blank] 1809 and in the Year [left blank] of the CommonWealth.
                         WM. MOSS Cl.

    FAIRFAX COUNTY:
    Agreeable to the tenor of the Within Commission we have this Day examined FRANCES HALLEY therein designated. She declared that the Execution of the Deed within recited was a Voluntary act and that she freely assents to the record thereof in order to pass her title of

Dower in the Land & appurtenances thereby conveyed. Certified under our hands & Seals as required this 17th day of May 1809.

Truly recorded   W. PAYNE   (seal)
Teste WM. MOSS Cl.   HANCOCK LEE   (seal)

Pages 215 & 216. THIS INDENTURE made this first day of January in the Year 1808 between WILLIAM HERBERT and THOMAS SWANN of the Town of Alexandria in the District of Columbia and RICHARD BLAND LEE of the County of Fairfax, being a Majority of the Trustees of PHILIP RICHARD FENDALL deceased, under a Deed of trust from the said PHILIP R. FENDALL deceased for the use of his creditors dated the twenty seventh day of February one Thousand eight hundred of the one part and JOSEPH SEWELL of the County of Fairfax and State of Virginia of the other part. WITNESSETH that the said WILLIAM HERBERT, THOMAS SWANN and RICHARD BLAND LEE for and in consideration of two hundred and twenty Dollars to them in hand paid the receipt whereof they the said WILLIAM HERBERT, THOMAS and RICHARD BLAND LEE do hereby acknowledge and thereof doth acquit and exonerate him the said JOSEPH SEWELL, his Heirs, Executors and administrators, Have granted, bargained & Sold, aliened, released and confirmed and by these presents do grant, bargain and Sell, Alien, release and confirm unto him the said JOSEPH SEWELL his heirs and assigns the following tract or parcel of Land situate and lying in the County of Alexandria in the District of Columbia beginning at a red oak standing on a high point about 17 Poles from Potomack River a corner of TAYLOR now TURBERVILLES, thence with TURBERVILLES line South 16 1/2° East 140 Poles to a white oak and hickory saplings in or near said line, thence North 56° East 80 poles to a cluster of sycamores standing near the edge of Potomac River, thence up the meanders of said River nearly opposite the beginning containing forty acres more or less which said Parcel of Land is a part of a greater tract, conveyed with other property to the said PHILIP R. FENDALL in the before mentioned, for the purposing of selling the same for the payment of his Debts. To have and To Hold the said forty Acres of Land with their appurtenances as aforesaid unto him the said JOSEPH SEWELL his heirs and assigns to the only proper use and behoof of him the said JOSEPH SEWELL, his Heirs and assigns. And the said WILLIAM HERBERT, THOMAS SWANN and RICHARD BLAND LEE do for themselves, their heirs, Executors & administrators, Covenant, Promise and agree to & with the said JOSEPH SEWELL his heirs & assigns that they will forever warrant and defend the said Premises with all and singular the appurtenances thereto against the claim and demand of all persons or person whomsoever claiming by, through, from, or under them. In WITNESS whereof the said WILLIAM HERBERT, THOMAS SWANN and RICHARD BLAND LEE have herunto set their hands and affixed their seals the Day & Year before Written.

Signed, Sealed and delivered
in Presence of   WM. HERBERT   (seal)
EDM. J. LEE, R.B. LEE, T.S. & W.H.   THO. SWANN   (seal)
N. HERBERT to W.H.   RICHARD BLAND LEE   (seal)
WM. HERBERT JR to W.H.

At a Court held for Fairfax County the 19th day of June 1809 this Deed from WILLIAM HERBERT, THOS. SWANN and RICHARD B. LEE, Trustees of PHILIP R. FENDALL decd, to JOSEPH SEWELL was acknowledged by the said THOMAS SWANN and RICHARD B. LEE to be their Acts & deeds and proved to be the act and Deed of the said WILLIAM HERBERT by the oaths of EDMUND J. LEE, NOBLET HERBERT and WILLIAM HERBERT JR and there upon ordered to be Recorded.
Teste WM. MOSS Cl.

Pages 216-218. THIS INDENTURE made this sixteenth day of January in the Year of our Lord one thousand eight hundred and nine between WILLIAM GARNER of the County of Fairfax of the one part and WILLIAM CHICK of the County of Fairfax of the other part. Whereas the said WILLIAM GARNER is indebted to the said WILLIAM CHICK in the sum of five hundred Dollars by bond bearing even date with even presents & for the further & better securing the Payment of the said Debt hath agreed to convey a certain Lot and Parcel of Land Purchased by him of a certain JOHN WELLS and also a Waggon and team to the persons hereinafter mentioned in trust for the Purpose aforesaid. Now therefore this Indenture WITNESSETH that the

said WILLIAM GARNER in consideration of the Debt aforesaid and for the further consideration of the sum of five Shillings to him paid by the said WILLIAM CHICK the receipt whereof
he doth hereby acknowledge Hath granted, bargained, Sold and Assigned and by these
presents doth grant, bargain, Sell & Assign and confirm to THOMAS SWAN and WILLIAM
COLEMAN and the Survivor of them all that Lot or parcel of Land situate in the County of
Fairfax conveyed by lease to said WILLIAM GARNER by JOHN WELLS and THOMAS FAIRFAX
bearing date the fourth day of March 1807 recorded in the County Court of Fairfax containing
twenty one acres and three quarters of an acre more or less with all and Singular the appurtenances, rents, issues and Profits and all the Right, Title and interest of the said WILLIAM
GARNER in and to the said Lot of Land and also one Waggon and four Horses with their gear
being the same which were lately sold and now delivered to the said WILLIAM GARNER by the
said WILLIAM CHICK To Have and To Hold the said Lot of Land with all messuages, tenements
and Hereditaments thereto belonging or in anywise appertaining together with all Mills, Mill
seats, Woods, Ways, Waters, Watercourses and all right, title, interest, claim and demand at Law
or in equity of the said WILLIAM GARNER his heirs and Executors in and to the said lot of Land
and the appurtenances and the rents, issues and Profits thereof for and during the full term
expressed in the deed aforesaid, that is to say for and during the Natural lives of JOHN DOWDAL
and CHARLES GRIMES his Nephew and JOHN DOWDAL JR his Nephew Yielding and paying
therefore the Rest as stipulated in the said Deed together with the Waggon and team aforesaid
to the said THOMAS SWAN & WILLIAM COLEMAN & the survivor of them, his heirs and assigns
in Trust to and for the several uses, intents and Purposes following that is to say in trust that
they the said THOMAS SWAN and WILLIAM, or either of them or the survivor of them, his
Heirs, Executors or assigns shall and may at any time after the sixteenth Day of October next
sell & dispose of the said Lot of land & appur-tenances together with the Waggon & team in
such manner & form as said trustees may think proper after reasonable Notice or so much
thereof as may be sufficient to pay & discharge what may be then due and owing to the said
WILLIAM CHICK and the Costs attendant on the execution of said trust and after satisfying said
Debt in Trust to and for the proper use and behoof of said WILLIAM GARNER his Heirs and
Assigns. And the said WILLIAM GARNER for himself, his Heirs, executors and Administrators
doth hereby Covenant to and with the said WILLIAM CHICK his heirs and assigns in manner
and form following that is to say that he the said WILLIAM GARNER will well and truly pay to
the said WILLIAM CHICK the sum of five hundred dollars on or before the sixteenth day of
October next and in default thereof that the trustees before named or the survivors of them
his heirs and assigns shall and may peaceably & quietly enter into the said land & premises
and take possession of the same together with the Waggon & team aforesaid for the uses &
purposes herein set forth without the hindrance or denial of the said WILLIAM GARNER &
that he will not do any act or thing to prejudice or defeat the trust aforesaid but will at all
times hereafter make and execute such further and other lawful conveyances as may be
necessary for the better and more perfect conveying and assuring the title to the said Land &
chattles as by the said WILLIAM CHICK and his Counsel shall be lawfully and reasonably
required and that he will warrant and defend the title of the said Land to the said WILLIAM
CHICK his heirs and assigns forever against the lawful claim and demand of all persons
whatever. In WITNESS whereof the parties to these presents have hereunto set their hands
and affixed their Seals the Day and Year first above written.
Sealed & Delivered In
Presence of   WILLIAM GARNER (seal)
JAMES COLEMAN   WILLIAM CHICK   (seal)
JOHN COLEMAN
CHARLES COLEMAN
RICHARD his X mark WELLS
        At a Court held for Fairfax County the 15th day of May 1809 this Deed between WILLIAM
GARNER and WILLIAM CHICK was proved to be the Act and Deed of the Parties by the oaths of
JAMES COLEMAN and JOHN COLEMAN two of the Witnesses thereto and ordered to be Certified.
And at a Court held for the said County the 19th day of June 1809 was further proved to be the

act and deed of the parties by the oath of CHARLES COLEMAN another Witness thereto and ordered to be recorded.   Teste WM. MOSS Cl.

Pages 218-220. In the County Court of Fairfax held the 19th September 1808 On Motion of HECTOR KINCHELOE it is ordered that HUMPREY PEAKE, BERNARD HOOE JR, ALEXANDER WAUGH, ROBERT H. HOOE and MARMADUKE B. BECKWITH or any three be and they are hereby appointed to divide the Lands of which DANIEL KINCHELOE decd died seized among the several Legatees agreeable to the last Will and Testament of the said decedent and make report to this Court.

A Copy from the Minutes.   Teste WM. MOSS Cl.

Laid by a scale 100 poles
to an Inch   [MAP OF THE PLAT]

The 15th of June 1809 at the request of BERNARD HOOE JR, ALEXANDER WAUGH and ROBERT H. HOOE Gentlm. I laid of out of the Tract of Land of which DANIEL KINCHELOE died seized & which the above Plat represents: 20 acres of Land as represented by the small Pat. beginning at "A", the mouth of Meadow Branch, thence South 37° East 18 poles to "B", thence North 28° East 34 poles to "C", thence South 85° 54 poles to "D" GIBBS' Corner, thence North 27° West 39 poles to "E" to the old Mill dam on Popeshead, thence down the sd. Popeshead & binding therewith agreeable to the several Meanders thereof to the beginning. I also laid of 70 Acres out of sd. Plat as represented by Pat. No. 2. Beginning at "F" a Pile of stones, thence South 28 12° East 76 poles to "G" a corner three red oaks saplings & a gum, thence North 44° East 142 poles to "H" a corner on the side of a hill now down a black oak & two Gum saplings marked in its stead, thence North 35° West 48 poles to "I" a red oak on a Hill side near the head of a small branch, thence down the said branch North 40° West 42 poles to "J" a Maple on sd. branch a corner, thence to the beginning. I also laid of 70 acres out of sd. Plat as represented by Plat No. 3 Beg at "K" (on Bull Run) a beach marked as a corner a few poles below the rocky Ford on sd. Run, thence up the sd. Bull Run and binding therewith agreeable to the several meanders thereof to the Mouth of Popeshead, thence up the said Popeshead & bonding there-with to the Mouth of the Meadow Branch, thence South 37° East 16 poles to a stake in sd. branch, thence South 34° West 42 poles to a Poplar marked as a Corner on the Spring branch, thence up the sd. branch and binding therewith South 4° West 28 poles, thence North 14 1/2° West 19 poles, thence to a poplar stump a corner of ROBERT WICKLIFF below the spring thence South 25° West 56 poles to M a pile of Stones on a hill near an old road, thence to the beginning. Given under my hand this 15th day of June 1809.
WM. KINCHELOE

Pursuant to an Order of Fairfax County Court bearing date the 19th day of September 1802 We the undersigned have agreeable to the Will of DANIEL KINCHELOE decd made the following allotments to wit: To the Heirs or Assigns of NESTOR KINCHELOE decd twenty acres of Land as represented in the annexed Plat No. 1 beginning at "A". To HECTOR KINCHELOE we have allotted seventy acres as represented in the annexed Plat No. 2nd beginning at "F" and we have alloted to JESSE KINCHELOE seventy acres as represented in the annexed Plat No. 3rd beginning at "K" the balance of said Land not being devised farther than for and during the life of SUSANNAH KINCHELOE who is now dead and it appearing to us uncertain who is entitled to the same we have declined making any distribution of it until the further [order] of said Court. Given under our hands this 15th day of June 1809.
BERND. HOOE JR
ROBT. H. HOOE
ALEXANDER WAUGH

At a Court Continued & held for Fairfax County the 20th day of June 1809 the within report of Division of the Lands of DANIEL KINCHELOE deceased together with a Plat of Survey annexed was returned which being received by the Court are ordered to be recorded.
Teste WM. MOSS Cl.

Pages 220 & 221. [Marginal Note: Delivered to E. JENKINS 19th February 1816.]

THIS INDENTURE made and entered into the twentieth day of June one thousand eight hundred and nine between JAMES WARDEN and MARGARET his wife of the County of Fairfax and State of Virginia of the one part and ELISHA JENKINS of the County of Prince William State aforesaid of the other Part. WITNESSETH that the said JAMES WARDEN and MARGARET his wife for and in consideration of sixty dollars to them in hand paid the receipt whereof is hereby acknowledged have granted, bargained & sold and by these presents do grant, bargain & sell unto the said ELISHA JENKINS his heirs and assigns all that Messuage, tenement, tract or Parcel of land situate, lying and being in the County of Fairfax being a tract or parcel of land which descended to the said MARGARET upon the death of her father PETER MAUZEY intestate and which was allotted to the said WARDEN and wife by Commissioners appointed by the County Court of Fairfax being Lot number two as by reference to the report of said Commissioners will more at large appear bounded as follows: beginning at [left blank] containing twenty three acres one hundred & twenty eight Poles and also all trees, Woods, under Woods, Ways, Waters, Water courses, advantages and appurtenances whatsoever to the said tract or parcel of Land belonging or in any wise appertaining and the reversion and Reversions, Remainder and Remainders, rents, issues and Profits of the said Premises and all the estate right, title and interest, claim and demand whatsoever of them the said JAMES WARDEN and MARGARET his wife of, in and to the said Tract or Parcel of Land & Premises and every Part thereof. To have and To Hold the said messuage, tenement, tract or Parcel of land and all and Singular the other Premises above mentioned and every Part and Parcel thereof with appurtenances unto the sd. ELISHA JENKINS his heirs and assigns to the only proper use and behoof of him the sd. ELISHA JENKINS his heirs and assigns forever and the said JAMES WARDEN and MARGARET his wife for themselves, their heirs the said Messuage, tenement, tract or Parcel of Land and the Premises and every Part thereof against them & their heirs and against all and every other person or Persons whatever to the said ELISHA JENKINS his heirs and assigns shall and will Warrant and forever defend by these presents. In WITNESS whereof the said JAMES WARDEN and MARGARET his wife have hereunto set their hands and Seals the Day & Year first Written.

Signed Sealed and delivered   JAMES WARDEN   (seal)
In Presence of [No witnesses listed] MARGARET WARDEN (seal)

At a Court Continued and held for Fairfax County the 20th day of June 1809 JAMES WARDEN and MARGARET his wife (she being first privately and again in open Court examined and thereto consenting) acknowledged the within Deed to ELISHA JENKINS to be their act and Deed and ordered to be recorded.   Teste WM. MOSS Cl.

Pages 221 & 222. FAIRFAX COUNTY
JOHN FITZHUGH, son and Heir of NATHANIEL FITZHUGH, by
JOSEPH E. ROWLS his Guardian, LUCY FITZHUGH & GEORGE   IN CHANCERY
MAY and ANN his wife Complainants
      Against
HARRISON FITZHUGH Administrator of SARAH FITZHUGH decd Defendants.

This cause coming on this day to be heard upon the bill and answer and upon hearing the same and by consent of the Parties the Court doth Decree and order that RICHARD COLEMAN, CHARLES TURLY, JOHN COLEMAN, DANIEL KITCHEN and RICHARD B. LEE or any three of them do divide and allot to the parties, Complainants and defendant their respective parts and Proportions of all the Estate of the said SARAH, that is to say one equal fourth Part to the said JOSEPH E. ROWLES for the use of the said JOHN FITZHUGH, one other fourth part to LUCY FITZHUGH and of the Complainants, one other fourth part to GEORGE MAY in right of his wife ANN and one other fourth part to the Defendant HARRISON FITZHUGH and this Court doth further Decree and order that the said JOSEPH E. ROWLES in behalf and as next friend and Guardian of the said JOHN and also that the other Complainants do give bond with security to the said Defendant to pay and refund to him their respective Parts and Proportions of any debts or claims which may appear against the estate of the said SARAH and that the said Defendant do settle his Administration account respecting the said Estate and that the said

Commissioners do make report of their Proceeding herein to the Court in order for a final Decree.

A Copy   Teste WM. MOSS Cl.

In Pursuance of the above Decree we RICHARD B. LEE, CHARLES TURLEY and DANIEL KITCHEN this 29th day of April 1803 Proceeded to make a Division of the Negroes belonging to the estate of SARAH FITZHUGH deceased as hereafter follows: Young DAVID and ALCE valued at one hundred and fifty six Pounds being lott number one We allot to JOHN FITZHUGH the Son of NATHANIEL FITZHUGH deceased; old DAVID, HANNAH and BEN valued at one hundred & twenty six Pounds six shillings being lot number three we allot to LUCY FITZHUGH; FRANK & ANNAKA valued at one hundred & two Pounds being lot number four we allot to GEORGE MAY and ANNA his wife in right of the said ANNA; PETER, COOKE, PHEBE and JUNE valued at one hundred and forty pounds six shillings We allot to HARRISON FITZHUGH it being lot number two. And we do hereby adjudge that when a Division of the other Personal Estate of the said SARAH FITZHUGH takes Place that the aforesaid JOHN FITZHUGH pay unto GEORGE MAY & ANNA his wife in right of the said ANNA the sum of twenty Pounds current Money of Virginia also that the said JOHN FITZHUGH pay unto LUCY FITZHUGH the sum of four Pounds seventeen shillings like Currency and also that HARRISON FITZHUGH pay unto GEORGE MAY and ANNA his wife in right of the said ANNA the sum of nine Pounds three shillings Currency as aforesaid. Given under our Hands the day & Year above mentioned.

RICHARD BLAND LEE
CHARLES TURLEY
DANIEL KITCHEN

At a Court Continued & held for Fairfax County the 20th day of June 1809 this report of the several Persons appointed to divide and allot the Estate of SARAH FITZHUGH deceased among her several representatives was this day returned and received by the Court and thereupon ordered to be Recorded.   Teste WM. MOSS Cl.

Page 223. KNOW ALL MEN by these presents that we BRYAN FOLEY and BENJAMINE DAWSON of Fauquier County and BENJAMIN FARROW of Frederick County are held and firmly bound unto SAMUEL JENKINS and JOHN S. CARTWRIGHT of Fairfax County severally in the sum of two thousand Dollars Money of the United States to the Payment of which we bind ourselves, our Heirs, Executors & administrators jointly and severally firmly by these presents. Sealed with our Seals & dated this 20th day of June 1809. Whereas ELIZABETH FOLEY late ELIZABETH WEST late of Fairfax County deceased was appointed Guardian of MARY and MATILDA WEST daughters of her and of the said JOHN WEST deceased by the Court of Fairfax County on which appointment she entered into bond dated the 16th day of February in the Year 1807 for the faithful discharge of her duty as Guardian of the said Children in the Penalty of two thousand dollars in which bond the said SAMUEL JENKINS and JOHN S. CARTWRIGHT became her securities since which time she has intermarried with the above bound BRYAN FOLEY and at a Court held for Fairfax County in the Month of January last it was ordered on the motion of the said SAMUEL JENKINS that the said BRYAN FOLEY and ELIZABETH his wife should give to the said SAMUEL JENKINS Counter Security or else surrender up the Property and effects of the said Infant Wards; now the condition of this obligation is that if the said BRYAN FOLEY and ELIZABETH his wife shall faithfully account for the Estate and effects of the said infant wards which has or shall come to their hands or the hands of either of them And if the said ELIZABETH shall in all respects fulfil and Perform the Condition of the bond aforesaid by her and the said SAMUEL JENKINS and JOHN S. CARTWRIGHT executed as aforesaid and if she or the said BRYAN FOLEY shall in all respects indemnify and save harmless the said SAMUEL JENKINS and JOHN S. CARTWRIGHT and their legal Representatives from all damages, suits, losses and injuries in any manner to arise from their securityship for the said ELIZABETH as Guardian as aforesaid then this obligation to be Void else to be and remain in full force. acknowledged & Delivered

In Presence of   BRYANT FOLEY JR   (seal)
        The Court   BENJA. DAWSON   (seal)
                Teste WM. MOSS Cl.   B. FARROW   (seal)
[Recorded in Will Book Liber J-1 folio 222]

At a Court Continued and held for Fairfax County the 20th day of June 1809 the within bond from BRYANT FOLEY, BENJAMIN DAWSON and BENJAMIN FARROW to SAMUEL JENKINS and JOHN S. CARTWRIGHT was acknowledged by the said BRYANT FOLEY, BENJA. DAWSON and BENJA. FARROW to be their acts & deeds and ordered to be Recorded.

Teste WM. MOSS Cl.

Pages 224 & 225. THIS INDENTURE made this twentieth day of February eighteen hundred & nine between WILLIAM MACBE OFFUTT of the County of Fairfax and State of Virginia of the one part and WILLIAM OFFUTT of the County and State aforesaid of the other part. WITNESSETH that the said WILLIAM MACBE OFFUTT for and in consideration of his love and Natural affection towards his Son the said WILLIAM OFFUTT and for the sum of one Dollar to him in hand Paid by the said WILLIAM OFFUTT at and before the Sealing and delivering of these presents the right whereof is hereby acknowledged Hath given, granted & sold and by these presents doth give, grant, bargain and sell unto the said WILLIAM OFFUTT his Heirs, Executors, administrators or assigns, a certain tract or Parcel of Land which the said WILLIAM OFFUTT now has in Possession and bounded as followeth: beginning at SIMPSONS corner on Sandy Run, thence up the sd. Run with the meanders to PEYTONS line, thence with the said PEYTONS line to a box oak corner to the said PEYTON and RICHARD WHEELER, thence with the said WHEELERS line to BAXTER SIMPSONS Corner and from thence to the beginning containing one hundred acres of land situate, lying and being in the County of Fairfax & State of Virginia on the North side of Sandy Run which said tract is a Part of a larger tract containing four hundred and twenty three acres and was taken up and Patented by THOMAS SIMPSON deceased and at the time of his Death did among other things Will'd and bequeath'd the said one hundred acres of Land to his daughter MARY WOODWARD who afterwards intermarried with JOHN ROBERTSON and by the deeds of Lease and re-Lease Recorded in the County Court of Fairfax conveyed the same to GEORGE ROBERTSON and by his deed recorded in the said County of Fairfax did convey the same to the said DRUMMOND WHEELER and he conveyed the sd. Land by deed to WILLIAM MACBE OFFUTT and is now deeded by the said WILLIAM MACBE OFFUTT to his Son WILLIAM OFFUTT. To have and To Hold the same his heirs & assigns forever as Witness my hand & Seal this day & date above mentioned.

Signed, Sealed & delivered
in the Presence of   WILLIAM MACBE OFFUTT   (seal)
CHARLES THRIFT
JAMES SANGSTER, THOMAS CARROLL

At a Court held for Fairfax County the 15th day of May 1809 this Deed from WILLIAM M. OFFUTT to WILLIAM OFFUTT was Proved to be the act and deed of the said WILLIAM M. OFFUTT by the oaths of CHARLES THRIFT and THOMAS CARROLL two [of] the Witnesses thereto and ordered to be Certified.

And at Court continued & held for Fairfax County the 21st day of June 1809 this Deed was further proved to be the act and Deed of the said WILLIAM M. OFFUTT by the oath of JAMES SANGSTER another WITNESS thereto and ordered to be Recorded.

Teste WM. MOSS Cl.

Pages 225-228. THIS INDENTURE made this twenty third of June in Year of our Lord one thousand eight hundred and eight between WILLIAM NEWTON and JANE B. his wife and JOHN MUNCASTER & ELIZABETH A. his wife of the Town and County of Alexandria in the District of Columbia of the one part And SAMUEL DUNLAP and JAMES DUNLAP brothers and Legal representatives of JOHN DUNLAP late of the said Town, County and District of the other part. Whereas the said WILLIAM NEWTON, JOHN MUNCASTER, HEZEKIAH SMOOT, JOHN DUNLAP, WILLIAM MITCHELL, JAMES WILSON, ROBERT B. JAMESON, LAWRENCE HOOE, ISAAC GIBSON, PHILIP G. MARSTELLAR and BRYAN HAMPSON became Security for CHARLES TURNERS true and faithfull execution of the Office of Sergeant of the said Town of Alexandria who having executed the said office in an improper manner they were obliged to Pay on account of his Neglect of Duty and mis-application of Money which came to his hands the sum of eleven hundred Pounds current Money and being unable to refund the Money which they were so compelled to pay for him he proposed to convey to them a tract of Land of which he was seized lying upon Occoquan River in the County of Fairfax and State of Virginia said to contain five hundred and twenty six acres in full of the Money by them so advanced which they immediately agreed to take and further agreed to Prevent troublesome embarrassments in the Sale and Conveyance of the said Land which they intended immediately to do to reimburse the Money they were so compelled to Pay for him that the conveyance should be made by the said CHARLES TURNER to the said WILLIAM NEWTON, JOHN MUNCASTER and HEZEKIAH SMOOT and in Pursuance of the said arrangements the sd. CHARLES TURNER and REBECCA his wife by an indenture bearing date the eleventh day of February one thousand eight hundred & two conveyed the said Tract of Land unto the said WILLIAM NEWTON, JOHN MUNCASTER and HEZEKIAH SMOOT their heirs and Assigns forever the same being bounded as followeth to wit: beginning at the Mouth of Sandy Run and running thence North four degrees West two hundred & fifty two Poles to a place shewn by A. MILLS near JOSEPH HAMPTONS fence, thence with a line of Marked trees South eighty six Degrees West two hundred and fifty two Poles to a Place six Poles within an old fallen tree and a fresh marked sapling, thence South eight degrees West one hundred and thirty five Poles to Occoquan River, thence With the meanders of the said River and binding thereupon until it would intersect the aforesaid line if continued, thence from the said Point of intersection continuing the same course one hundred and fifty five Poles more to the sd. Occoquan River, thence with the meanders of the said River and binding thereupon to the beginning which Conveyance is made by the said CHARLES TURNER and REBECCA his wife was for the express Purpose that the said WILLIAM NEWTON, JOHN MUNCASTER, and HEZEKIAH SMOOT should sell the same again for the use and benefit of the said WILLIAM NEWTON, JOHN MUNCASTER, HEZEKIAH SMOOT, JOHN DUNLAP, WILLIAM MITCHELL, JAMES WILSON, ROBERT B. JAMESON, LAWRENCE HOOE, ISAAC GIBSON, PHILIP G. MARSTELLAR and BRYAN HAMPSON to re-imburse them the monies which they had been obliged to Pay on account of the said CHARLES TURNER; but from certain causes no sale has as Yet been made thereof since which the said HEZEKIAH SMOOT hath departed this life intestate leaving infant Heirs and the said JOHN DUNLAP hath also departed this life leaving the said SAMUEL and JAMES his legal representatives who have required to have such part and proportion of the said Land to which the said JOHN DUNLAP had an equitable title conveyed to them. Now this Indenture WITNESSETH that the said WILLIAM NEWTON and JANE B. his wife & JOHN MUNCASTER and ELIZABETH A. his wife in consideration of the Premises and one dollar to them in hand Paid by the said SAMUEL DUNLAP and JAMES DUNLAP at or before the Sealing and delivery of these presents the receipt whereof is hereby acknowledged Have granted, bargain, sold, aliened and confirmed and by these presents do Give, Grant, bargain, Sell, alien & confirm unto them the said SAMUEL DUNLAP and JAMES DUNLAP their heirs and Assigns forever one equal undivided eleventh part of the said Tract of Land so conveyed, by the said CHARLES TURNER and REBECCA his wife unto the said WILLIAM NEWTON, JOHN MUNCASTER and HEZEKIAH SMOOT being the said JOHN DUNLAPS full part and proportion thereof and of all Houses, buildings, trees, Woods, Waters, Water Courses, Profits, Commodities, Hereditaments & appurtenances whatsoever to the said Premises belonging or in anywise appertaining and the Reversion and Reversions, Remainder and Remainders, rents, issues and Profits thereof and of every Part and Parcel thereof. To have and To Hold all and Singular the Premises hereby granted with their appurtenances unto them the said SAMUEL DUNLAP and JAMES DUNLAP their heirs & Assigns to the only Proper use and behoof of them the said SAMUEL DUNLAP and JAMES DUNLAP their heirs and Assigns forever. In WITNESS whereof the said WILLIAM NEWTON and JANE B. his wife and the said JOHN MUNCASTER and ELIZABETH A. his wife have hereunto set their Hands and Seals the day & Year first herein before mentioned.

Sealed and delivered   WM. NEWTON   (seal)
In Presence of [No witnesses listed]   JANE B. NEWTON   (seal)
                                              JOHN MUNCASTER   (seal)
                                              ELIZABETH A. MUNCASTER (seal)

DISTRICT OF COLUMBIA COUNTY OF ALEXANDRIA To Wit:
          I GEORGE DENEALE Clerk of the United States Circuit Court of the District of
(SEAL)   Columbia do hereby certify that at a Court continued and held for the
          County of Alexandria the 12th day of July 1808 this Deed from WILLIAM NEWTON

and JANE B. NEWTON his wife and JOHN MUNCASTER and ELIZABETH MUNCASTER his wife to SAMUEL DUNLAP and JAMES DUNLAP brothers and legal representatives of JOHN DUNLAP late of the Town of Alexandria was acknowledged by the parties to be their Act & Deed and ordered to be Certified to the County Court of Fairfax. In Testimony whereof I have hereunto set my hand & Seal of office this 14th day of December 1808.

G. DENEALE Cl.

At a Court Continued and held for Fairfax County the 20th day of June 1809 this Deed from WILLIAM NEWTON and wife and JNO. MUNCASTER and wife to SAMUEL DUNLAP and JAMES DUNLAP brothers and legal represntatives of JOHN DUNLAP deceased having been duly acknowledged before the United States Circuit Court of the District of Columbia held for the County of Alexandria and certified by GEORGE DENEALE Clerk of the said Court under the Seal of his office is on motion of the said SAMUEL and JAMES DUNLAP together with a Certificate thereon endorsed and a Commission and return thereto annexed for taking the acknowledgment and privy examination of the said JANE B. and ELIZABETH wives of the said WILLIAM NEWTON and JOHN MUNCASTER and ordered to be recorded.

Teste WM. MOSS Cl.

FAIRFAX COUNTY To Wit:

The CommonWealth of Virginia to JOSEPH DEAN, ROBERT YOUNG, AMOS ALEXANDER, JOHN McKENNY & A. FAW Gentlemen Justices of the County of Alexandria Greeting: Whereas WILLIAM NEWTON and JANE his wife and JOHN MUNCASTER and ELIZABETH A. his wife by their certain indenture of Bargain & Sale bearing date the 23rd Day of June 1808 have Sold & Conveyed unto JAMES & SAMUEL DUNLAP the fee simple estate of Piece or Parcel of Ground with the appurtenances situate, lying and being in the said County of Fairfax and Whereas the said JANE B. and ELIZABETH A. cannot conveniently travel to our said County Court of Fairfax to make acknowledgment of the said conveyance therefore we do give unto you or any two or more of you Power to receive the acknowledgment which the said JANE and the said ELIZABETH A. shall be willing to make before You of the conveyance aforesaid contained in the said indenture which is hereunto annexed and we do therefore desire You or any two or more of You Personally to go to the said JANE and ELIZABETH A. and receive their acknowledgment of the same and examine them privily and apart from the said WILLIAM & JOHN their husbands whither they do the same freely and voluntarily without their Persuasions or threats and whither they be willing the said indenture together with this Commission shall be recorded in our said Court. And when you have received their acknowledgment and examined them as aforesaid that You distinctly & openly certify us thereof in our said Court under your hands and seals sending then there the said indenture and this Writ. WITNESS WILLIAM MOSS Clerk of our said Court at the Courthouse of the County aforesaid this 14th day of July 1808 and in the 33rd Year of the CommonWealth.

WM. MOSS Cl.

DISTRICT OF COLUMBIA COUNTY OF ALEXANDRIA:

In obedience to the within writ to us directed we the Subscribers did Personally call on the within named ELIZABETH A. MUNCASTER and examined her privily and apart from the said JOHN MUNCASTER her husband touching her acknowledgment of the said Deed & she declared that she executed the same freely & voluntarily without his persuasions or threats and that she is willing the same together with this Commission shall be recorded in the County Court of the County of Fairfax & State of Virginia. Given under our hands and Seals his 14th day of July 1808.   ROBERT YOUNG   (seal)
JOSEPH DEAN   (seal)

DISTRICT OF COLUMBIA, County of Alexandria:

In obedience to the within Commission to us directed we did Personally call on the said JANE B. NEWTON and examine her privily and apart from her said husband And out of his hearing touching her acknowledgment of the Within mentioned deed when she declared it to be her own free and voluntary act done without either the threats or persuasions of her said Husband and that she was willing the said deed together with this Commission should be admitted to record in the County Court of Fairfax in the CommonWealth of Virginia thereby to

pass away her right of Dower. Given under our hands and Seals in Alexandria the 17th day of August 1808.   AMOS ALEXANDER   (seal)
                                                                JOSEPH DEAN   (seal)

Pages 229-231. THIS INDENTURE made this sixteenth day of June in the Year of our Lord one thousand eight hundred and nine between GEORGE VEALE one of the Legal representatives of ELIJAH VEALE late of the County of Hyde in the State of North Carolina of the one part and GEORGE SLACUM of the Town and County of Alexandria in the District of Columbia of the other Part. Whereas the Proprietor of the Northern Neck did by his Deed Poll bearing date the tenth day of July one thousand seven hundred and forty four grant unto JOHN GOWEN his heirs and assigns forever a tract of Land lying upon the drains of Pohick in the County of Fairfax and State of Virginia bounded as followeth to wit: beginning at a red oak in a Glade Near a branch of the North Run of Pohick and Corner to ROBERT CARTER Esquire, thence with his line north seventy seven Degrees East eighty Poles to a white oak corner to the said CARTER, then with another of his lines North sixty Degrees East ninety four Poles to a red oak in the line of the Widow COFFER, thence with her line South thirty degrees West thirty two Poles, then with another of her lines South ten Degrees West one hundred and thirty Poles to a Chesnut corner to the said COFFER, thence South fifty Poles to the line of RICHARD SIMPSON, thence with this line South seventy five degrees West one hundred & twenty five Poles to a black oak in the said line, thence North one hundred and seventy four Poles to the beginning containing one hundred & forty four acres which tract of Land the said JOHN GOWEN by indentures of Lease & release, sold & Conveyed unto BOND VEALE the said Indentures bearing date the fourteenth & fifteenth days of July one thousand seven hundred & forty six who by his last Will and Testament devised the said tract of Land to his Son JOHN VEALE who by his last will and Testament devised the same unto his Son the said ELIJAH VEALE which said BOND VEALE removing to Carolina the said tract of Land was taken up by THOMAZIN ELLZEY as a piece of vacant Land for which he obtained a Patent from the State of Virginia and upon the said ELIJAH VEALE coming from Carolina he found ELLZEY in the possession of it who refusing to give it up the said ELIJAH VEALE brought his Ejectionment to recover the possession of it which engaged the said GEORGE SLACUM to attend to the Conduct of in his absence and by his Writing obligatory bearing date the twenty third day of March one thousand seven hundred and Ninety seven bound himself to Convey the same to the said GEORGE SLACUM upon his recovery of it which ejectment was determined in his favor and the possession of it obtained by the said GEORGE SLACUM but before a conveyance was made of it by the said ELIJAH VEALE to the said GEORGE SLACUM he departed this life intestate leaving six children to wit: the said GEORGE, SARAH, ELIZABETH, JOHN, THOMAS and ELIPHATE to whom the same descended. Now this Indenture WITNESSETH that the said GEORGE VEALE as well for and in Consideration of the sum of fifty five Pounds current Money of Virginia to the said ELIJAH VEALE in his lifetime paid by the said GEORGE SLACUM as for and in consideration of the further sum of one Dollar to him the said GEORGE VEALE in hand paid by him the said GEORGE SLACUM at or before the Sealing and Delivery of these presents the receipt whereof he doth hereby acknowledge Hath given, granted, bargained, Sold, Aliened and confirmed and by these presents Doth Give, Grant, bargain, Sell, alien and Confirm unto him the said GEORGE SLACUM his heirs and assigns forever one equal undivided sixth Part of the said Tract of Land and all Houses, buildings, Trees, Woods, Waters, Water Courses, Profits, commodities, hereditaments and appurtenances whatsoever to the Premises hereby granted belonging or in anywise apper-taining and the reversion and Reversions, Remainder and Remainders, Rents, issues and Profits thereof and of every Part and Parcel thereof. To have and To Hold all and Singular the Premises hereby granted with their appurtenances unto him the said GEORGE SLACUM his heirs and assigns to the only Proper use and behoof of him the said GEORGE SLACUM his heirs and assigns forever and the said GEORGE VEALE doth for himself, his Heirs, Executors and Administrators, Covenant, Grant and agree to and with the said GEORGE SLACUM his heirs and assigns that he the said GEORGE VEALE hath now good, right, full Power and lawfull authority to sell and convey all and Singular the said Premises with their appurtenances in the manner aforesaid unto him the said GEORGE SLACUM his heirs and assigns and that he the said GEORGE VEALE and his Heirs will at any time hereafter upon the request and at the Costs & charge of him the said GEORGE SLACUM his heirs and assigns execute and acknowledge any further lawful act and Deed for the more certain assuring and conveying all and Singular the Premises hereby granted with their appurtenances unto him the said GEORGE SLACUM his heirs and assigns as by him the said GEORGE SLACUM his heirs and assigns his, their, or any of their council learned in the Law shall or may be advised or required and lastly that he the said GEORGE VEALE and his heirs all and Singular the sd. Premises with their appurtenances unto him the said GEORGE SLACUM his heirs and assigns against the claim & demand of him the said GEORGE VEALE and his Heirs and all and every other Person or Persons whatsoever shall and will warrant and forever defend by these presents. In WITNESS whereof the said GEORGE VEALE hath hereunto set his hand and Seal the Day & Year first herein before mentioned.

Sealed & Delivered
in presence of   GEORGE VEALE   (seal)
WM. HERBERT JR, W. DENEALE
G. DENEALE, GEO. YOUNGS
N. HERBERT

At a Court held for Fairfax County the 19th day of June 1809 this Deed from GEORGE VEALE to GEORGE SLACUM was proved to be the Act and Deed of the said GEORGE VEALE by the oaths of GEORGE DENEALE, GEORGE YOUNGS and NOBLET HERBERT three of the Witnesses thereto and Ordered to be Recorded.   Teste WM. MOSS Cl.

Page 231. THE COMMONWEALTH OF VIRGINIA:

To all Persons to whom these presents shall come Greeting: KNOW YE that our GOVERNOR on recommendation from the Court of the County of Fairfax hath with the advice of our Council of State constituted and appointed WILLIAM H. TERRETT, Coroner of the said County with authority to execute the said duties of the said office Prescribed by Law. In Testimony whereof these our letters are sealed with the Seal of the CommonWealth and made patent.

WITNESS JOHN TYLER Esquire our said Governer at Richmond on the twenty
(SEAL)   ninth day of May in the Year of our Lord 1809 and the CommonWealth the 33rd.
JNO. TYLER

At a Court Continued and held for Fairfax County the 21st day of June 1809 this Commission from the Governor of Virginia to WILLIAM HENRY TERRETT appointing him coroner of this County was Produced to the Court and Ordered to be Recorded.
Teste WM. MOSS Cl.

Pages 231 & 232. KNOW ALL MEN by these presents that we WILLIAM H. TERRETT, GEORGE SUMMERS & JOHN C. HUNTER are held and firmly bound unto JOHN TYLER Esquire Governor of the CommonWealth of Virginia and to his successors in office in the sum of ten thousand Dollars to the payment whereof well and truly to be made we bind ourselves our Heirs exors. and admrs. jointly and severally firmly by these presents sealed with our seals and dated this 21st day of June 1809.

THE CONDITION of this obligation is such that if the above bound WILLIAM H. TERRETT who is appointed a Coroner for the County of Fairfax by Commission from the Governor of this CommonWealth shall well, truly and faithfully execute the office of Coroner for the said County, then this obligation to be void else to remain in full force & virtue.

Signed acknowledged and delivered
in presence of   W. H. TERRETT   (seal)
The Court   GEO. SUMMERS   (seal)
Teste WM. MOSS   JNO. C. HUNTER   (seal)

At a Court Continued and held for Fairfax County the 21st day of June 1809 the within bond from WILLIAM H. TERRETT, GEO. SUMMERS and JOHN C. HUNTER to the Governor of this CommonWealth was acknowledged by the said WILLIAM H. TERRETT, GEO. SUMMERS and JOHN C. HUNTER to be their Acts and deeds and thereupon ordered to be recorded.
Teste WM. MOSS Cl.

Page 232. KNOW ALL MEN by these presents that we EDWARD W. SIMPSON and WILLIAM SIMPSON are held and firmly bound unto JOHN TYLER Esquire Governor of the CommonWealth of Virginia and his Successors in the full and just sum of one thousand Dollars Current Money of the United States to which Payment well and truly to be made to the said JOHN TYLER Governor & his Successors we bind ourselves and each of us, our and each of our Heirs, Executors and Administrators jointly and severally firmly by these presents sealed with our seals and dated this 23rd day of June 1809.

THE CONDITION of the above obligation is such that whereas the above bound EDWARD W. SIMPSON hath been duly appointed a Constable for that part or Section of the County of Fairfax described and known by District number 4 in Pursuance of two several Acts of Assembly of this CommonWealth passed the twenty first day of January eighteen Hundred & three and the tenth Day of January eighteen hundred & seven the first entitled "An Act concerning Constables" the second "an Act to amend the Act concerning Constables;" now if the said EDWARD W. SIMPSON shall well & truly perform and discharge the several duties of his said Office of constable within the District aforesaid agreeable to the several Acts of Assembly concerning Constables defining their duty then the above obligation to be void else to remain in full force, power and virtue in Law.

EDWARD W. SIMPSON   (seal)
WM. SIMPSON   (seal)

At a Court Continued & held for the County of Fairfax the 23rd day of June 1809 this Bond from EDWARD W. SIMPSON and WILLIAM SIMPSON to the Governor of Virginia was acknowledged by the said EDWARD and WILLIAM to be their acts and Deeds and ordered to be Recorded.   Teste WM. MOSS Cl.

Pages 232 & 233. KNOW ALL MEN by these presents that we SAMPSON MARTIN, MORRISS FOX and EDWARD DULIN are held & firmly bound unto JOHN TYLER Esquire Governor of the CommonWealth of Virginia and his Successors in the full and just sum of one thousand Dollars Current Money of the United States to which Payment well and truly to be made to the said JOHN TYLER Governor and his Successors and bind ourselves and each of us, our & each of our heirs, Executors & Admins, jointly and severally firmly by these presents. Sealed with our Seals and dated this 22nd day of June 1809.

THE CONDITION of the above obligation is such that whereas the above bound SAMPSON MARTIN hath been duly appointed a Constable for that part or Section of the County of Fairfax described & known by District number three in pursuance of two several Acts of Assembly of this CommonWealth passed the twenty first day of January eighteen hundred and three and the tenth day of January eighteen hundred & seven the first entitled "An Act Concerning Constables" and the second "An Act to amend the act concerning Constables;" now if the said SAMPSON MARTIN shall in every respect well and truly perform and discharge the several duties of his said office of Constable within the District aforesaid agreeable to the several acts of Assembly concerning Constables Defining their duty then the above obligation to be void else to remain in full force, power & Virtue in Law.

Signed Sealed & acknowledged in   SAMPSON MARTIN (seal)
Presence of   MORRISS FOX   (seal)
                                         EDWD. DULIN   (seal)

At a Court Continued and held for Fairfax County the 23rd June 1809 this Bond from SAMPSON MARTIN, MORRISS FOX and EDWARD DULIN to the Governor of Virginia was acknowledged by the said MARTIN, FOX and DULIN to be their Acts & deeds and ordered to be recorded   Teste WM. MOSS Cl.

Pages 233 & 234. KNOW ALL MEN by these presents that we DANIEL BRADLEY, WILLIAM MILLAN and JAMES BRADLEY are held and firmly bound unto JOHN TYLER Esquire Governor of the CommonWealth of Virginia and his Successors in the full and just sum of one thousand Dollars Current Money of the United States to which payment well and truly to be made to the said JOHN TYLER Governor and his Successors we bind ourselves and each of us, our and each of our Heirs and Executors and Administrators jointly and severally firmly by these presents sealed with our Seals and dated this 22nd day of June 1809.

THE CONDITION of the above obligation is such that whereas the above bound DANL. BRADLEY hath been duly appointed a Constable for that part or section of the County of Fairfax described & known by District number one in pursuance of two several acts of Assembly of the CommonWealth passed the twenty first day of January eighteen hundred and three and the tenth day of January eighteen hundred and seven the first entitled "An act concerning Constables" and the second "An act to amend the act concerning constables" Now if the said DANIEL BRADLEY shall in every respect well & truly perform and discharge the several duties of his said Office of Constable within the District aforesaid agreeable to the several Acts of Assembly concerning Constables defining their duty then the above obligation to be void else to remain in full force power and Virtue in Law.

DANIEL BRADLEY   (seal)
W. MILLAN   (seal)
JAMES BRADLEY   (seal)

At a Court contd. and held for Fairfax County the 22nd day of June 1809 this Bond from DANIEL BRADLEY, WILLIAM MILLAN and JAMES BRADLEY to the Governor of Virginia was acknowledged by the said DANIEL BRADLEY, WILLM. MILLAN and JAMES BRADLEY to be their acts and Deeds and ordered to be Recorded.   Teste WM. MOSS Cl.

Pages 234 & 235. KNOW ALL MEN by these presents that we SPENCER DONALDSON, GEORGE DARNE & ROBERT BOGGESS JR are held and firmly bound unto JOHN TYLER Esquire Governor of the CommonWealth of Virginia and his Successors in the full and just sum of one Thousand Dollars Current Money of the United States to which payment well and truly to be made to the said JOHN TYLER Governor and his Successors, we bind ourselves and each of us, our and each of our Heirs, Executors & Administrators jointly and severally firmly by these presents, Sealed with our Seals and dated the 22nd day of June 1809.

THE CONDITION of the above obligation is such that whereas the above bound SPENCER DONALDSON hath been duly appointed a Constable for that part or Section of the County of Fairfax described and known by District number two, in persuance of two several acts of assembly of the CommonWealth passed the twenty first day of January eighteen hundred & three and the tenth day of January eighteen hundred & seven, the first entitled "An act concerning constables" and the second "An Act to amend the Act concerning Constables" Now if the said SPENCER DONALDSON shall in every respect well and truly perform and discharge the several duties of his said office of Constable within the District aforesaid agreeable to the several Acts of Assembly concerning constables defining their duty then the above obligation to be void else to remain in full force power & virtue In Law.

Signed acknowledged & delivered	SPENCER DONALDSON (seal)
In the presence of	GEO. DARNE (seal)
The Court	ROBERT BOGGESS JR (seal)
WM. MOSS Cl.	

At a Court Continued and held for Fairfax County 22nd June 1809 this Bond from SPENCER DONALDSON, GEO. DARNE and ROBERT BOGGESS JR to the Governor of Virginia was acknowledged by the said SPENCER, GEO. and ROBERT to be their acts and Deeds and Ordered to be Recorded.   Teste WM. MOSS Cl.

Page 235. KNOW ALL MEN by these presents that we WILLIAM PADGETT, GEO. MINOR and JAMES WIGGINTON are held & firmly bound unto JOHN TYLER Esquire Governor of the CommonWealth of Virginia and his Successors in the full and just sum of one Thousand Dollars Current Money of the United States to which payment well and truly to be made to the said JOHN TYLER Governor and his Successors we bind ourselves and each of us, our and each of our, Heirs, Executors and Administrs jointly and severally firmly by these presents Sealed with our Seals and dated this 22nd day June 1809.

THE CONDITION of the above obligation is such that whereas the above bound WILLM. PADGETT hath been duly appointed a Constable for that part or section of the County of Fairfax described and known by District number three in pursuance of two several Acts of Assembly of this CommonWealth passed the twenty first day of January eighteen hundred and three and the tenth Day of January eighteen hundred and seven the first entitled "an Act concerning

Constables" and the second "An Act to amend the act concerning Constables" Now if the said WILLIAM PADGETT shall in every respect well and truly perform and discharge the several duties of his said office of Constable agreeable to the several Acts of Assembly concerning Constables defining their duty then the above obligation to be void else to remain in full force power and Virtue in Law.

Signed, Sealed & acknowledged   WM. PADGETT   (seal)
in presence of   GEO. MINOR   (seal)
     The Court   JAS. WIGGINTON (seal)

At a Court Continued and held for Fairfax County the 23rd June 1809 this Bond from WILLIAM PADGETT, GEO. MINOR and JAMES WIGGINTON to the Governor of Virginia was acknowledged by the said WILLIAM, GEO. and JAMES to be their acts and Deeds and ordered to be Recorded.   Teste WM. MOSS Cl.

Pages 236-238. THIS INDENTURE made this sixteenth Day of April in the Year of our Lord one thousand eight hundred and eight between WILLIAM HERBERT, NICHOLAS FITZHUGH and EDMUND J. LEE of the Town and County of Alexandria in the District of Columbia executors of the last Will and testament of RICHARD CONWAY Deceased of the one part and GEORGE SLACUM of the Town, County and District aforesaid of the other part. WITNESSETH whereas the said RICHARD CONWAY did by his last Will and testament bearing date the fifth day of June in the Year one thousand eight hundred and four order, authorise, empower and direct the said WILLIAM HERBERT, NICHOLAS FITZHUGH and EDMUND J. LEE who by his last Will and testament as aforesaid were appointed his executors to sell certain parts of his real estate therein described and which was not otherwise disposed of by the Codicil attached to the same and bearing date the seventeenth day of November in the Year eighteen hundred and six which together with the said Will has been duly Proven and recorded. Now this Indenture WITNESSETH that the said WILLIAM HERBERT, NICHOLAS FITZHUGH and EDMUND J. LEE, executors as aforesaid for and in consideration of the premises and of the sum of two hundred and eighteen Dollars and five cents to them in hand paid at and before the sealing and delivery of these presents the receipt whereof is hereby acknowledged have granted, bargained and Sold and by these presents do grant, bargain and sell unto the said GEORGE SLACUM his heirs and assigns forever a certain piece or parcel of ground situate, lying and being in the County of Fairfax and State of Virginia near WILLIAM TERRETTS and between the two parcels of land sold by the said executors to GEORGE H. TERRETT and ANDREW BALMAIN and bounded as follows: beginning at a stake in the line of WEST, PEARSON and HARRISON, thence along the same North forty nine and an half West to a stake and blazed saplin being the corner of the patent and corner to the land sold GEORGE H. TERRETT, thence north forty four east seventy five poles to the old Leesburgh road, thence down the same and binding therewith South fifty four east thirty poles South sixty four east twenty two and a half poles to a stake, thence South thirty seven and three quarters West eighty one poles to the beginning containing twenty six acres and sixty nine one hundred & sixtieths of an acre with all and singular the appurtenances thereto belonging or in any manner appertaining. To have and To hold the said premises with the appurtenances as aforesaid to him the said GEORGE SLACUM his heirs and assigns to the only use and behoof of him, his Heirs and assigns forever. And the said WILLIAM HERBERT, NICHOLAS FITZHUGH and EDMUND J. LEE the said executors for themselves and their Heirs covenant, Promise and agree to and with the said GEORGE SLACUM his heirs and assigns that they will forever warrant and defend the hereby granted premises against the claim and demand of all persons and person whomsoever claiming by, through, from or under them or either of them. In Testimony whereof the said WILLIAM HERBERT, NICHOLAS FITZHUGH and EDMUND J. LEE have set their hands and seals the day & Year before Written.

Sealed and Delivered   WM. HERBERT   (seal)
in Presence of   N. FITZHUGH   (seal)
                              EDM. J. LEE   (seal)

Received 29th November 1808 of MR. GEORGE SLACUM Two hundred and eighteen Dollars and five cents in full for the amount of the Within consideration.

WITNESS   WM. HERBERT

DISTRICT OF COLUMBIA To Wit:

(SEAL)

I GEORGE DENEALE Clerk of the United States circuit court of the District of Columbia for the County of Alexandria do hereby Certify that at a Court continued & held for the District and County aforesaid the 5th day of December 1808 this Deed from WILLIAM HERBERT, NICHOLAS FITZHUGH and EDMUND J. LEE Executors of RICHARD CONWAY deceased and a receipt to GEORGE SLACUM was acknowledged by the said WILLIAM HERBERT, NICHOLAS FITZHUGH and EDMUND J. LEE to be their act and deed and ordered to be certified to the County Court of Fairfax in the CommonWealth of Virginia. In Testimony whereof I have hereunto set my hand & affixed the public seal of my office on this 15th day of February in the Year of our Lord 1809.

G. DENEALE Cl.

DISTRICT OF COLUMBIA To Wit:

I, WILLIAM CRANCH Chief Judge of the Circuit Court of the District of Columbia do hereby certify that the above attestation of GEORGE DENEALE Clerk of the said Court for Alexandria County, is in due form. Given under my hand this [left blank] day of July 1809.

At a Court held for Fairfax County the 17th day of July 1809 this Deed from WILLIAM HERBERT, NICHOLAS FITZHUGH and EDMUND J. LEE Executors of RICHARD CONWAY deceased to GEORGE SLACUM with a receipt thereon endorsed having been duly acknowledged before the United States Circuit Court of the Distict of Columbia held for the County of Alexandria and Certified by GEORGE DENEALE Clerk of the said Court under the seal of his office also by WILLIAM CRANCH Chief Judge of the said Court is on Motion of the said GEORGE SLACUM together with the Certificates thereon endorsed are ordered to be Recorded.

Teste WM. MOSS Cl.

Page 238. KNOW ALL MEN by these presents that I AMY SIMONS of the County of Fairfax and CommonWealth of Virginia for and in consideration of the natural love and affection which I have and do bear towards my Grand Children JAMES and JOHN HURST of the County aforesaid as well as for the further consideration of six Shillings current money to me in hand paid by the said JAMES and JOHN HURST at or before the Sealing and delivery of these presents the receipt whereof I do hereby acknowledge have Given, Granted, bargained & Sold and by these presents do Give, Grant, bargain and Sell and unto my said Grand Children JAMES & JOHN HURST the following property to wit: two feather beds and furniture; one cow and calf, one Iron pot and one Dutch Oven, three flag bottomed chairs, one square table and one corner Cupboard. To have and To Hold the said property above mentioned unto my said Grand Children JAMES and JOHN HURST their heirs and Assigns forever and I the said AMY SIMONS do for myself, my Heirs, Executors and Administrators the said property above mentioned unto them the said JAMES and JOHN HURST their heirs, Executors, Administrators and Assigns against the claim of me and my Heirs and against the claim or claims of all and every person or persons whatsoever shall and will warrant and forever defend by these presents. In WITNESS whereof I have hereunto set my hand and affixed my Seal this fourteenth day of April in the Year of our Lord one thousand eight hundred & nine.

Signed and acknowledged
in presence of   AMY her AS mark SIMONS   (seal)
GID. M. MOSS, THO. R. MOTT
THOMPSON PICKETT

At a Court held for Fairfax County the 17th day of July 1809 this Deed of Gift from AMY SIMONS to JAMES & JOHN HURST was acknowledged by the said AMY SIMONS to be her act & deed & thereupon ordered to be recorded.   Teste WM. MOSS Cl.

Pages 239-241. THIS INDENTURE made this fifth day of August in the Year of our Lord one thousand eight hundred and seven between JOHN M. CONWAY and his wife CATHARINE of the County of Stafford of the one part and AMOS ALEXANDER of the County of Alexandria of the other part. WITNESSETH that the said JOHN M. CONWAY and his wife CATHARINE for and in consideration of the sum one Dollar to them in hand paid by the said AMOS ALEXANDER, receipt whereof they do hereby acknowledge have granted, bargained & sold and do by these presents bargain & sell unto the said AMOS ALEXANDER that tract or parcel of Land situate, lying and being in the County of Fairfax containing two hundred seventy three and half acres be the same more or less it being one moiety of a five hundred and forty seven acre tract which was devised by the REVD. JOHN MONCURE late Clerk of the County of Stafford to his two Daughters ANN and JANE MONCURE which will more fully appear reference being had to said Will. To have and To Hold the said equal half or moiety of the aforesaid five hundred and forty seven acres of Land with all and singular the appurtenances thereto belonging unto the sd. AMOS ALEXANDER his heirs and assigns forever and the said JOHN M. CONWAY and CATHARINE his wife for themselves their heirs, Exors and Administrators doth covenant, Grant and agree to and with the said AMOS ALEXANDER his Heirs, Exors, administrators and assigns that he or they shall and may forever hereafter peaceably and quietly have, hold, occupy, possess and enjoy the aforesaid tract or parcel of Land in fee simple forever against the claim or claims of all persons whatsoever as witness our hands and seals the day and date above written.

Signed Sealed & delivered

In the presence of   J. M. CONWAY   (seal)
HUGH W. MINOR   C. S. CONWAY   (seal)
GIDEON M. MOSS
JOHN W. ASHTON

At a Court held for Fairfax County the 18th Day of April 1808 this Deed from JOHN M. CONWAY to AMOS ALEXANDER was proved to be the act and Deed of the said JOHN M. CONWAY by the oaths of HUGH W. MINOR and GIDEON M. MOSS Witnesses hereto and ordered to be certified. And at a Court Contind. & held for the said County the 19th April 1808 the same was further proved by the oath of JOHN W. ASHTON another Witness hereto and ordered to be Recorded.
                                        Teste WM. MOSS Cl.

At a Court held for Fairfax County the 17th Day of July 1809 this Deed from JOHN M. CONWAY and CATHARINE his wife to AMOS ALEXANDER having been heretofore duly proved to be the act and Deed of the said JOHN M. and admitted to Record and the said CATHARINE not having at that time Signed the said Deed. On Motion of the said AMOS ALEXANDER It is ordered that the same be again recorded together with a Commission and return thereto annexed for taking the acknowledgment and privy examination of the said CATHARINE and the order of the proof aforesaid.   Teste WM. MOSS Cl.

FAIRFAX COUNTY To Wit:

The CommonWealth of Virginia to BENJAMIN TOLSON & THOMAS TRISTON Gentlemen of the County of Stafford Greeting: Whereas JOHN M. CONWAY and CATHARINE his wife by their certain indenture of bargain and sale bearing date the fifth day of August one thousand eight hundred and seven have sold and conveyed unto AMOS ALEXANDER the fee simple estate of an undivided Moiety of a tract of land the whole of which supposed to contain five hundred and forty seven acres or the one half thereof two hundred seventy three and a half acres more or less, with the appurtenances situate, lying and being in the County of Fairfax and whereas the said CATHARINE CONWAY cannot conveniently travel to our said County Court of Fairfax to make acknowledgment of the said conveyance therefore we do Give unto You or any two or more Power to receive the acknowledgment which the said CATHARINE shall be willing to make before You of the conveyance aforesaid contained in the said Indenture which is hereunto annexed and we do therefore desire You or any two or more of You personally to go to the said CATHARINE CONWAY and receive her acknowledgment of the same and examine her privily and apart from the said JOHN N. CONWAY her husband whither she doth the same freely and voluntarily without his persuasions or threats and whither she be willing the said Indenture together with this Commission shall be recorded in our said Court and when You have received her acknowledgment and examined her as aforesaid that You distinctly and openly certify us thereof in our said Court under Your hands and seals sending then there the said Indenture and this Writ. WITNESS WILLIAM MOSS Clerk of the said Court this 15th day of February 1809 and in the 33rd Year of the CommonWealth.
                                        WM. MOSS Cl.

COMMONWEALTH OF VIRGINIA County of Stafford:

In Pursuance of the within Commission to us directed we did call on the within named CATHARINE wife of the within named JOHN M. CONWAY and did examine her privily and apart

and out of the hearing of her said husband touching her execution of the within mentioned deed when she acknowledged the Signature thereto to be her own act & Deed done of her own free will and accord without either the threats or persuasions of her said husband and that she was willing the same together with this Commission should be recorded in the County Court of Fairfax or else thereby to pass away her right of Dower. Given under our hands and Seals this 15th day of February 1809.   BENJA. TOLSON   (seal)
                                                                    THOS. TRISTON   (seal)

Pages 241 & 242. THIS INDENTURE made the seventeenth day of July in the Year one thousand eight hundred and Nine between EDWARD BATES SR of the County of Fairfax in the Common-Wealth of Virginia of the one part and JOSEPH BIRCH of the County of Alexandria in the District of Columbia of the other part: Whereas EDWARD BLACKBURN by virtue of a patent from the proprietors office dated the 7th day of June 1777 was seized in fee simple of a tract of Land in the County of Hampshire in the CommonWealth of Virginia lying on the Drains of Maple Run of the North River of the Great Cacapehon and bounded as follows: beginning at a chesnut oak standing on a ridge, running thence South 35° West 104 poles to a black & white oak in JOHN MAUZEYS line, thence with his line crossing red stone road South 48° East 166 Poles to a white oak MAUZEYS corner, thence South 18° West across a Drain of Crooked Run 126 Poles to two pines on a ridge, thence North 76° East 28 poles to a pine MR. MAC CRAYS corner, thence with MAC CRAYS line South 42° East 180 Poles crossing Maple Run to a Double chesnut oak, MAC CRAYS corner, thence South 70° East 60 poles to two locusts on a ridge, thence North 38° East 200 poles to a chesnut and black oak on the North side of a ridge, thence North 30° West 510 poles crossing said Road to the beginning which is by the said patent supposed to contain four hundred and eighteen Acres which said tract of Land was afterwards conveyed to the said EDWARD BATES SR who being seized in fee thereof sold and conveyed one hundred and fifty acres thereof to THOS. BATES and one hundred and twenty five acres to SAMPSON HENDERSON. Now this Indenture WITNESSETH that the said EDWARD BATES SR in consideration of the sum of one hundred & seventy Dollars to him in hand paid by the said JOSEPH BIRCH the receipt whereof is hereby acknowledged hath Granted, bargained and Sold, aliend and confirmed and do by these presents Grant, bargain and sell, alien and confirm unto the said JOSEPH BIRCH all the rest and residue of the said tract of Land not sold as aforesaid to the said THOMAS BATES and SAMPSON HENDERSON together with all the appurte-nances thereto belonging to hold to the said JOSEPH BIRCH his heirs and assigns forever to his and their only proper use. And the said EDWARD BATES SR for himself his heirs, executors & Administrators do hereby covenant & agree with the said JOSEPH BIRCH his heirs and assigns that they will on the request and at the Costs of the said JOSEPH BIRCH his heirs or assigns execute and deliver all such further assurances and conveyances as shall be Necessary more fully and compleatly to transfer the title to the land conveyed to the said JOSEPH BIRCH his heirs and assigns according to the true intent and meaning hereof and that he will warrant and defend the premises hereby conveyed to the said JOSEPH BIRCH his heirs and assigns against the claims and demands of him and his Heirs forever. In Testimony whereof I have hereunto set my hand and Seal the day and Year first before written.
Sealed and Delivered in
presence of [No witnesses listed]   EDWARD BATES (seal)
          At a Court held for Fairfax County the 17th day of July 1809 this Deed from EDWARD BATES to JOSEPH BIRCH was acknowledged by the said EDWARD BATES to be his act and Deed and thereupon ordered to be Recorded.   Teste WM. MOSS Cl.

Pages 242 & 243. KNOW ALL MEN by these presents that we ADAM MITCHELL, JOHN HENNING and THOMAS MILLAN are held and firmly bound unto JOHN TYLER Esquire Governor of the CommonWealth of Virginia in the full and just sum of one thousand Dollars current money of the United States to which payment well and truly to be made to the said JOHN TYLER Governor and his Successors we bind ourselves and each of us, our and each of our Heirs, executors and administrators jointly and severally firmly by these presents. Sealed with our Seals and dated this 17th day of July 1809.

THE CONDITION of the above obligation is such that whereas the above bound ADAM MITCHELL hath been duly appointed a Constable for that part or section of the County of Fairfax described & known by District Number [left blank] in pursuance of two several acts of Assembly of this CommonWealth passed the twenty first day of January one thousand eight hundred & three and the tenth Day of January one thousand eight hundred and seven the first entitled "An act concerning Constables" and the second "An act to amend the act concerning Constables." Now if the said ADAM MITCHELL shall in every respect well And truly perform & discharge the several duties of his said Office of Constable within the District aforesaid agreeable to the several Acts of assembly concerning Constables defining their duty then the above obligation to be void else to remain in full force power and virtue in Law.
Signed, Sealed and
acknowledged in presence of   ADAM MITCHELL   (seal)
           The Court   THOS. MILLAN   (seal)
           WM. MOSS   JOHN HENING   (seal)
          At a Court held for Fairfax County the 17th day of July 1809 this Bond from ADAM MITCHELL, THOMAS MILLAN and JOHN HENNING to the Governor of this CommonWealth was in open Court acknowledged by the said ADAM MITCHELL, THOMAS MILLAN and JOHN HENNING to be their respective acts & deeds and thereupon ordered to be Recorded.
                              Teste WM MOSS Cl.

Page 243. KNOW ALL MEN by these presents that we WILLIAM DEVAUGHN, RICHARD RATCLIFFE, JOSEPH POWELL and GEORGE WILLIAMS are held and firmly bound unto JOHN TYLER Esquire Governor of the CommonWealth of Virginia and his Successors in the full and just sum of one thousand Dollars Current money of the United States to which payment well and truly to be made to the said JOHN TYLER Governor & his Successors we bind ourselves and each of us, our and each of our Heirs, Executors and Administrators jointly and severally firmly by these presents. Sealed with our Seals & dated this 17th Day of July 1809.
          THE CONDITION of the above obligation is such that whereas the above bound WILLIAM DEVAUGHN hath been duly appointed a Constable for that part or Section of the County of Fairfax described and known by District number four in pursuance of two several acts of Assembly of this CommonWealth passed the twenty first day of January one thousand eight hundred and three and the tenth day of January 1807 the first entitled "An Act concerning Constables" and the second "An act to amend the act concerning constables." Now if the said WILLIAM DEVAUGHN shall in every respect well and truly perform & discharge the several duties of his said Office of Constable within the District aforesaid agreeable to the several Acts of Assembly concerning constables defining their duty then the above obligation to be void else to remain in full force power & virtue in Law.
                              WILLIAM DEVAUGHN   (seal)
                              RD. RATCLIFFE   (seal)
                              JOSEPH POWELL   (seal)
                              GEO. WILLIAMS   (seal)
          At a Court held for Fairfax County the 17th day of July 1809 this Bond from WILLIAM DEVAUGHN, JOSEPH POWELL, RICHARD RATCLILFFE and GEORGE WILLIAMS to the Governor of this CommonWealth was in open Court acknowledged by the said WILLIAM, JOSEPH, RICHARD and GEORGE to be their respective acts and Deeds and thereupon ordered to be Recorded.
                              Teste WM. MOSS Cl.

Page 244. KNOW ALL MEN by these presents that we WILLIAM PADGETT, JOSEPH POWELL and JAMES WIGGINTON are held and firmly bound unto JOHN TYLER Esquire Governor of the CommonWealth of Virginia and his Successors in the full and just sum of One Thousand Dollars Current Money of the United States to which payment well and truly to be made to the said JOHN TYLER Governor & his successors we bind ourselves and each of us, our and each of our Heirs, Executors and Administrators jointly and severally firmly by these presents. Sealed with our seals and dated this 17th day of July 1809.
          THE CONDITION of the above obligation is such that whereas the above bound WILLIAM PADGETT hath been duly appointed a Constable for that part or Section of the County of

Fairfax Described & known by District number four in pursuance of two several Acts of Assembly of this CommonWealth passed the twenty first day of January 1803 and the tenth day of January 1807 the first entitled "An Act concerning Constables" and the second "An Act to amend the act concerning Constables." Now if the said WILLIAM PADGETT shall in every respect well and truly perform and discharge the several duties of his said Office of Constable within the District aforesaid agreeable to the several Acts of Assembly concerning Constables defining their duty then the above obligation to be void else to remain in full force, Power and Virtue in Law.

WM. PADGETT	(seal)	
JOSEPH POWELL	(seal)	
JAMES WIGGINTON	(seal)	

At a Court held for Fairfax County the 17th day of July 1809 this Bond from WILLIAM PADGETT, JOSEPH POWELL and JAMES WIGGINTON was in open court acknowledged by the said WM. PADGETT, JOSEPH POWELL and JAMES WIGGINTON to be their respective acts and Deeds and Ordered to be Recorded. Teste WM. MOSS Cl.

Pages 245-254. THIS INDENTURE made this ninth day of January in the Year of our Lord one thousand eight hundred and nine between RICHARD BLAND LEE of Sully in the County of Fairfax and State of Virlginia and ELIZABETH his wife of the one part and BUSHROD WASHINGTON of Mount Vernon in the said County of Fairfax and State of Virginia of the second part and HENRY SMITH TURNER of the County of Jefferson, THOMAS BLACKBURN of the County of Fairfax and BUSHROD WASHINGTON JR of the County of Westmoreland and State of Virginia of the third part: Whereas the said RICHARD BLAND LEE party to these presents stands justly indebted by Bond bearing date the ninth day of January in the year one Thousand eight Hundred & Nine to the first named BUSHROD WASHINGTON in the full sum of Ten thousand thirty four Dollars & twenty eight Cents lawful money of the United States which sum is payable on the first day of March in the Year one Thousand eight Hundred & fourteen with Interest thereon after the Rate of six per centum per Annum from the first day of March next after the date of the presents which Interest is to be annually paid on the first day of March and the first Years' interest to be paid on the first day of March in the Year one Thousand eight hundred & ten. And whereas it is reasonable and just that the said RICHARD BLAND LEE should give to the said BUSHROD WASHINGTON full and ample security for the Payment of the aforesd. principal sum of Ten thousand & thirty four dollars & 28 Cents at the time when Payment shall become due and also for the Punctual annual Payment of interest on the said Principal sum. Now this Indenture WITNESSETH that the said RICHARD BLAND LEE and ELIZABETH his wife for and in consideration of the Premises and also for and in consideration of the sum of five Dollars lawful Money of the United States to them in hand paid by the said HENRY SMITH TURNER, THOMAS BLACKBURN & BUSHROD WASHINGTON JR at or before the sealing & delivery of these presents the receipt whereof the said RICHARD BLAND LEE doth hereby acknowledge and thereof doth acquit and discharge them the said HENRY SMITH TURNER, THOMAS BLACKBURN & BUSHROD WASHINGTON JR their Executors, admors and Assigns and also for and in consideration of the covenents & agreements herein after expressed & contained to be kept, done and Performed on the part of the said BUSHROD WASHINGTON of Mount Vernon and also on the Part of the said HENRY SMITH TURNER, THOMAS BLACKBURN & BUSHROD WASHINGTON JR and on the part of each of them have Granted, bargained & sold, aliened & confirmed and by these presents do Grant, bargain and sell and alien & Confirm unto them the said HENRY SMITH TURNER, THOMAS BLACKBURN & BUSHROD WASHINGTON JR and the Survivor or successor of them and the Heirs of the last survivor of them a certain tract or parcel of land containing by estimation about five hundred & twenty nine acres, known and called by the name of Sully and on which the said RICHARD BLAND LEE now resides which said Tract of land is situate, lying & being in the County of Fairfax & State of Virginia and is described & bound as follows: beginning at a swamp white oak a corner to the lands of the said RICHARD BLAND LEE and of the Heirs of GEORGE RICHARD LEE TURBERVILLE deceased, thence with a line dividing their lands South twenty six and one half Degrees East two hundred and forty poles to the road leading from Frying Pan Meeting House to Centreville, then pursuing the said Road South forty degrees West & South eighteen degrees West to the Road leading from the old mill of SAMUEL LOVE deceased which Mill is now down and was on Cub Run to the Ox Road, thence pursuing the said Road to LOVES Mill South seven & three quarters degrees West an Hundred & thirty six and one half poles to the Little River Turnpike Road to Alexandria, thence with the said Road North sixty four and one half Degrees West one hundred & thirty four poles to a Red oak Saplin, thence due North one hundred & seventy one and an half poles to a pile of Stones, thence due East sixty nine and an half poles to a stake, thence due North one Hundred & forty two poles to the line dividing the land of the said RICHARD BLAND LEE from the land of the Heirs of the said GEORGE RICHARD LEE TURBERVILLE deceased, thence pursuing the said land South seventy five degrees East ninety nine poles South eighty four degrees East sixty four poles to two small persimmon trees, thence South twenty six degrees East to the beginning containing five hundred and twenty nine acres which said tract of land is the same that was conveyed by deed bearing date on the day of [left blank] in the Year one thousand eight hundred & two by the said RICHARD BLAND LEE and ELIZABETH his wife to a certain ZACCHEUS COLLINS of the City of Philadelphia and State of Pennsylvania and reconveyed by the said ZACCHEUS COLLINS to the said ELIZABETH the wife of the said RICHARD BLAND LEE by deed bearing date on the fifth day of October in the Year one Thousand eight Hundred & two as will more fully appear, by the said Deeds now of Record in the Office of the County Court of Fairfax and Also one other tract or parcel of land called Langley Farm situate, lying and being in the County of Fairfax near the Little Falls of the River Potomac which last mentioned Tract of Land is described as follows to wit: containing sixteen hundred acres be the same more or less and being all the land and Estate in the said County of Fairfax which was settled on HENRY LEE JR the son of HENRY LEE SR and MATILDA his wife, of Stratford in the County of Westmoreland and State of Virginia by a deed of settlement bearing date on the tenth day of August in the Year one thousand seven Hundred and Ninety as will more fully appear by refering to the said deed now of Record in the Office of the General Court of the State of Virginia and which said land has been by a good and sufficient deed conveyed to the said RICHARD BLAND LEE in fee simple by the said HENRY LEE SR and the said HENRY LEE JR by their joint deed dated on the fifth Day of June in the Year one thousand eight hundred & eight as will more fully appear by reference thereto now of Record in the Office of the County of Fairfax. To have and To Hold the aforesaid two tracts or parcels of land with their and each of their appurtenances unto them the said HENRY SMITH TURNER, THOMAS BLACKBURN and BUSHROD WASHINGTON JR and the survivors & survivor of them and the heirs of the last Survivor of them in trust for the following purposes and none other that is to say to hold the said two tracts of land in trust & for the use of the said RICHARD BLAND LEE his heirs & assigns until after a sale shall be of the said Tracts of Land or either of them under the authority of this deed and after such sale be made then to and for the use of the purchasers or purchaser thereof until a conveyance shall be made to such purchasers or purchaser their heirs or Assigns and if it shall so happen that the said RICHARD BLAND LEE his Heirs, Executors or Administrators, shall fail to pay the whole of the aforesaid sum of ten thousand & thirty four dollars & twenty eight Cents being the Principal sum on or before the first day of March in the Year one thousand eight hundred & fourteen the day appointed by the Condition of the said bond for the Payment thereof or fail to pay the interest in the said sum of ten thousand & thirty four Dollars and twenty eight cents annually as the same shall become due and shall suffer the said annual interest to remain due and unpaid to the said BUSHROD WASHINGTON of Mount Vernon his Heirs, Executors, Administrators or Assigns for Ninety days after the same shall become due and Payable on either of the above events happening it shall and may be lawful for the said HENRY SMITH TURNER, THOMAS BLACKBURN & BUSHROD WASHINGTON JR or any one of them or the survivors or survivor or either of them if two of them be then living or the Heirs of the last survivor of them on the request of the said BUSHROD WASHINGTON of Mount Vernon or on the request of the Executors, Administrators or assigns of the said BUSHROD WASHINGTON made in writing to sell so much of the said Property as may be sufficient for raising the sum which shall be then due and owing which sale is to be made on the respective tracts of land and at public Auction and upon the said Trustees or such of them as shall be required to make the said sale giving thirty days previous notice of the time and place of sale in one of the Newspapers Published in the Town of Alexandria or City of Washington or in any Newspaper published in the City of Richmond if none be published in the Town of

Alexandria or City of Washington and the said sale to be made for ready Money unless the said BUSHROD WASHINGTON of Mount Vernon his Executors, Administrators or assigns shall in writing direct otherwise and the Money or Proceeds arising from the said sale to be applied in the first place in discharge of costs of the said sale and the residue to be paid over by the said Trustees or such of them as shall act to the said BUSHROD WASHINGTON of Mount Vernon his Executors, Administrators or Assigns in Payment of whatever sum of Money that may be then due under this Deed of Trust as far as the same will go in Payment thereof. But it is hereby understood that the sale for the payment of the principal sum is not to be made unless the same or any part thereof shall remain due and unpaid to the said BUSHROD WASHINGTON of Mount Vernon his Executors, Administrators or Assigns for thirty days after the same shall be due to wit: on the first day of March in the Year one thousand eight hundred & fourteen. And the said RICHARD BLAND LEE doth hereby for himself, his Heirs, Executors and Administrators grant an irrevocable Power and authority to the said HENRY SMITH TURNER, THOS. BLACKBURN and BUSHROD WASHINGTON JR or either of them to receive, collect, distrain and sue for and in his the said RICHARD BLAND LEES name all rents which shall or may become due after the first day of January one thousand eight Hundred and nine from the tenants on the aforesaid sixteen hundred Acres of land called Langley farm and the said Rents when received to pay over to the said BUSHROD WASHINGTON of Mount Vernon his Executors, Admin-istrators or Assigns which are to be applied towards the Payment of the annual interest on the said Principal sum of ten thousand & thirty four Dollars & twenty eight cents; and it is hereby expressly understood between the said RICHARD BLAND LEE and BUSHROD WASHINGTON of Mount Vernon that the Power hereby given to the said Trustees to receive the Rents as aforesaid is not intended to be construed to impair or diminish the Power of the said Trustees to sell any part or the whole of the hereby granted Premises if necessary in case the interest be not paid on the said Principal Sum on the days herein before mentioned as the same becomes due but the said Power of receiving the said Rents by the said Trustees is hereby Declared to be intended as an auxilary and additional security for the Payment of the said Debt and Interest. And the said BUSHROD WASHINGTON of Mount Vernon doth for himself, his Heirs, Executors, Administrators & assigns, Covenant & agree to and with the said RICHARD BLAND LEE, his heirs, Executors, admors or assigns, that in case it should be necessary to sell any part of the hereby granted property that he the said BUSHROD WASHINGTON of Mount Vernon his Heirs, Executors, Administrators or assigns will cause and require the said Trust-ees or such of them as shall act in the sale thereof to sell in the first instance that tract or parcel of land called Langley Farm and also will have the same laid off in convenient parcels for the purpose of selling it for the greatest price, the expense of laying off the same to be paid by the said RICHARD BLAND LEE his heirs or assigns and the said BUSHROD WASHINGTON of Mount Vernon doth for himself, his Heirs, Executors, Administrators or Assigns, Covenant and agree to and with the said RICHARD BLAND LEE his Heirs, executors, Administrators and assigns in manner following: that the said RICHARD BLAND LEE his heirs & assigns shall be at liberty upon receiving the written consent of the said BUSHROD WASHINGTON his Heirs, Executors, Administrators or assigns to sell any part of the said Tract of Land called Langley farm and also upon Condition of the purchaser or purchasers of the same paying over to the said BUSHROD WASHINGTON his Executors, Administrators or Assigns the Money arising from such sale or securing the Payment of the said Money to the said BUSHROD WASHINGTON his Executors, Administrators or Assigns if he or they shall elect to have the same secured to them. And the said HENRY SMITH TURNER, THOS. BLACKBURN and BUSHROD WASHINGTON JR do each of them for themselves severally and not jointly and their several Heirs Covenant & agree to and with the said RICHARD BLAND LEE his Heirs, Executors, administrators or assigns that upon such sale being made as last aforesaid with the assent aforesaid of the said BUSHROD WASHINGTON and on the payment of the Money arising from such sale to the said BUSHROD WASHINGTON his Executors, Administrators or assigns or security accepted by the said BUSHROD WASHINGTON his Executors, Administrators or Assigns that they will make & execute to such purchasers or purchaser good and sufficient Deeds conveying to them all the right & estate they the said HENRY SMITH TURNER, THOMAS BLACKBURN and BUSHROD WASHINGTON JR have in and to the Property aforesaid sold as aforesaid. And further the said BUSHROD WASHINGTON of Mount Vernon doth covenant & agree for himself his heirs & assigns to and with the said RICHARD B. LEE his heirs and assigns that upon the expiration of the present leases of the Tenants on the hereby granted tract of land called Langley the said RICHARD BLAND LEE his heirs or assigns shall be at liberty of renewing the same upon these express Conditions & no others to wit: that the said leases do not exceed the term of five Years & also that the sum of six hundred Dollars Rent at least be reserved and also that the said leases shall contain the usual Covenants and particularly that of authorising the said RICHARD BLAND LEE his heirs or assigns or the said Trustees or the Survivors or Survivor of them and the Heirs of the said Survivor in the name of the said RICHARD BLAND LEE his heirs & assigns for the use of the said BUSHROD WASHINGTON of Mount Vernon his heirs and assigns to re-enter in case there should not be sufficient property to pay the rent reserved on the respective leased Premises. And the said HENRY SMITH TURNER, THOMAS BLACKBURN & BUSHROD WASHINGTON JR doth each for himself and each of his Heirs covenant & agree to and with the sd. RICHARD BLAND LEE his heirs & assigns that in case the said RICHARD BLAND LEE his heirs or assigns should lease again the said tract of land called Langley or any part thereof that they will do all necessary acts to give validity to such new leases. And the said HENRY SMITH TURNER, THOMAS BLACKBURN and BUSHROD WASHINGTON JR doth each for himself & his heirs Covenant & agree to & with the said RICHARD BLAND LEE his heirs & assigns that in case the said RICHARD BLAND LEE his heirs, Executors, administrators or assigns should pay the amount of the aforesaid ten thousand & thirty four Dollars & twenty eight cents with all the interest thereon in the manner and at the times herein before stated that then they the said HENRY SMITH TURNER, THOMAS BLACKBURN and BUSHROD WASHINGTON JR will by good and sufficient Deeds or Deed re-convey the aforesaid hereby granted tracts of land or such parts thereof as shall be unsold under the authority of this Deed unto the said RICHARD BLAND LEE his heirs and assigns or unto the said ELIZABETH LEE her heirs & assigns as the title to such parts shall be found existed in the said RICHARD BLAND LEE or ELIZABETH his wife before the execution of this Deed. And the said RICHARD BLAND LEE and ELIZABETH his wife do for themselves their heirs, Executors & administrators covenant and agree to & with the said BUSHROD WASHINGTON of Mount Vernon that he the said RICHARD BLAND LEE & ELIZABETH his wife and their Heirs shall & will at any time when thereto reasonably required execute such other or further deed as shall be deemed by the Counsel of the said BUSHROD WASHINGTON his heirs or assigns learned in the Law necessary for the better assuring the said hereby granted property unto the said HENRY SMITH TURNER, THOMAS BLACKBURN & BUSHROD WASHINGTON JR for the purposes of the Trust aforesaid and for none other & at the proper Costs and Charges of the said BUSHROD WASHINGTON his Heirs and Assigns. And they the said HENRY SMITH TURNER, THOMAS BLACKBURN & BUSHROD WASHINGTON JR doth each for himself and his Heirs to and with the said BUSHROD WASHINGTON his heirs & assigns and with the said RICHARD BLAND LEE & his heirs & assigns Covenant & agree that they and their Heirs will well & truly execute the trusts hereby vested in them. And the said RICHARD BLAND LEE for himself & his heirs doth agree with the said HENRY SMITH TURNER, THOMAS BLACKBURN & BUSHROD WASHINGTON JR & their Heirs & Assigns that he the said RICHARD BLAND LEE & his Heirs the aforesaid two tracts of Land hereby granted & their & each of their appurtenances unto them & the survivors or Survivor of them and the Heirs of the Survivor will forever warrant and Defend against the claim & demand of all and every person whomsoever except against the Tenants aforesaid on the same claiming their rights as Tenants. In WITNESS whereof the said RICHARD BLAND LEE and ELIZABETH his wife, BUSHROD WASHINGTON of Mount Vernon, HENRY SMITH TURNER, THOS. BLACKBURN & BUSHROD WASHINGTON JR have each of them set their hands & Seals on the day & Year first before written.

Sealed & delivered in the	RICHARD BLAND LEE	(seal)
Presence of	ELIZABETH LEE	(seal)
JOHN COLEMAN	[No other signatures	(seal)
RICHARD COLEMAN	listed]	(seal)
EDM. J. LEE		(seal)
		(seal)
		(seal)

MEMORANDUM - It is hereby understood between the within named BUSHROD WASHINGTON of Mount Vernon & RICHARED BLAND LEE Parties to the within Indenture that the sum for securing the Payment of which the said Deed is given is the amount due to the said BUSHROD WASHINGTON on a Mortgage given by HENRY LEE of Stratford Westmoreland County to him the said BUSHROD WASHINGTON on an Estate in Westmoreland called Cabin Point which farm is the balance of principal and interest due on said Mortgage on the first day of March in the Year one thousand eight hundred & Nine. But if any errors have been committed in calculating said Balance so that in Law more or less is justly due to the said BUSHROD WASHINGTON such errors are to be corrected & the balance so found to be properly due & no other to be considered as principal sum due & secured by this Deed. In WITNESS whereof the said BUSHROD WASHINGTON & RICHARD BLAND LEE have each of them set their hands & seals on the day of the date of this Indenture.   [No signature listed]   (seal)
                                                                RICHARD BLAND LEE   (seal)

At a Court held for Fairfax County the 21st day of August 1809 this Deed from RICHARD BLAND LEE and ELIZABETH his wife and a Memorandum thereon endorsed to HENRY S. TURNER, THOS. BLACKBURN & BUSHROD WASHINGTON JR in trust for the use of BUSHROD WASHINGTON was acknowledged by the said RICHARD BLAND LEE to be his act & Deed which together with a Commission & Return hereto annexed for taking the acknowledgment & privy examination of ELIZABETH wife of the said RICHARD BLAND LEE are ordered to be Recorded.
                                        Teste WM. MOSS Cl.

FAIRFAX COUNTY To Wit:

The CommonWealth of Virginia to DAVID STUART, RICHARD COLEMAN & JOHN COLEMAN Gentlemen of the County of Fairfax Greeting: Whereas RICHARD BLAND LEE and ELIZABETH his wife by their certain indenture of bargain & sale bearing date the ninth day of January in the Year one Thousand eight hundred & nine have sold & conveyed unto HENRY SMITH TURNER, THOS. BLACKBURN & BUSHROD WASHINGTON JR the fee simple estate of two certain tracts of land situate in the said County of Fairfax one called Sully and the other called Langley with the appurtenances situate, lying & being in the County of Fairfax and whereas the said ELIZABETH cannot conveniently travel to our said County Court of Fairfax to make acknowledgment of the said conveyance therefore we do give unto you or any two or more of you power to receive the acknowledgment which the said ELIZABETH shall be willing to make before you of the conveyance aforesaid contained in the said Indenture which is hereunto annexed. And we do therefore desire You or any two or more of you personally to go to the said ELIZABETH and receive her acknowledgment of the same and examine her privily & apart from the said RICHARD BLAND LEE her husband whither she doth the same freely and voluntarily without his persuasions or threats and whither she be willing the said indenture together with this Commission shall be recorded in our said Court. And when You have received her acknowledgment & examined her as aforesaid then You distinctly & openly Certify us thereof in our said Court under Your hands & seals sending then there the said indenture and this Writ. WITNESS WILLIAM MOSS Clerk of the said Court this tenth day of January 1809 and in the 33rd Year of the CommonWealth.
                                        WM. MOSS Cl.

VIRGINIA FAIRFAX COUNTY:

In Pursuance of the within commission to us directed we RICHARD COLEMAN & JNO. COLEMAN have examined the within named ELIZABETH wife of the within named RICHARD BLAND LEE touching her execution of the within mentioned indenture of bargain & Sale to HENRY SMITH TURNER, THOS BLACKBURN & BUSHROD WASHINGTON JR who has acknowledged the execution thereof by her signature to be her act and Deed freely done without the fear, threats or coercion of her said Husband and prays that the same may be duly admitted to record. WITNESS our hands and seals this second day of March in the Year of our Lord one thousand eight hundred & Nine.   RICHARD COLEMAN   (seal)
                                                                JOHN COLEMAN   (seal)

Pages 254 & 255. THIS INDENTURE made the sixteenth day of April in the Year of our Lord eighteen hundred & eight between WILLIAM HERBERT, NICHOLAS FITZHUGH and EDMUND J. LEE of the Town and County of Alexandria in the District of Columbia, (executors of the last

Will and Testament of CAPTAIN RICHARD CONWAY deceased) of the one part and ANDREW
BALMAIN of the County of Fairfax & State of Virginia of the other part. WITNESSETH whereas
the said RICHARD CONWAY did, by his last will & Testament bearing date the fifth day of June
in the Year eighteen hundred & four order, authorise, empower and direct, the said WILLIAM
HERBERT, NICHOLAS FITZHUGH and EDMUND J. LEE (who by his last will & testament as aforesaid were appointed his Executors) to sell certain parts of his real Estate, therein designated
and not otherwise disposed of, by the Codicil attached to the same & bearing date the seventeenth day of November in the Year eighteen hundred and six which together with the said
will was duly proven and Recorded. Now this Indenture WITNESSETH that the said WILLIAM
HERBERT, NICHOLAS FITZHUGH and EDMUND J. LEE, executors as aforesaid for and in consideration of the Premises and of the sum of two hundred & fifty four Dollars & thirteen Cents to
them in hand paid by the said ANDREW BALMAIN at & before the sealing & delivery of these
presents the receipt is hereby acknowledged is granted, bargained & sold and by these
presents do grant, bargain and sell unto the said ANDREW BALMAIN his heirs & assigns a tract
or parcel of land situate, lying & being in the County of Fairfax and State of Virginia &
bounded as follows to wit: beginning at a black jack on the South side of the old Leesburg
road, thence South seventeen and a quarter West ninety nine poles to a Stake in the line of
WEST, PEARSON & HARRISON, thence along said line North 494° West 67 poles to a stake, thence
North 314° East 82 poles to the old road, thence South 64° East 32 34 poles to the beginning
containing twehty six acres & one hundred & twenty poles with all and Singular the
appurtenances thereto belonging or in any manner appertaining. To have and To Hold this
said Premises with all and singular the appurtenances thereto belonging unto him the said
ANDREW BALMAIN his heirs & assigns forever to the only use & behoof of him his heirs &
assigns And the said WILLIAM HERBERT, NICHOLAS FITZHUGH and EDMUND J. LEE Executors as
aforesaid do for themselves, their Executors & Administrators covenant, Promise and agree to
and with the said ANDREW BALMAIN his heirs and assigns that they will forever warrant &
defend the said premises against the claim & demand of all and every person or persons
whatsoever claiming by, through, from or under them or either of them. In Testimony
whereof the said parties have hereunto set their hands and affixed their seals the day & year
before written.

Sealed & Delivered in   WM. HERBERT   (seal)
Presence of   N. FITZHUGH   (seal)
R. J. TAYLOR   EDM J. LEE   (seal)
N. HERBERT
WM. HERBERT JR

    At a Court held for the County of Fairfax the 15th day of May 1809 this Deed from
WILLIAM HERBERT, NICHOLAS FITZHUGH and EDMUND J. LEE, Executors of RICHARD CONWAY
deceased to ANDREW BALMAIN was proved by the oaths of ROBERT J. TAYLOR & WILLIAM
HERBERT to be the act & deed of the said WM. HERBERT, NICHOLAS FITZHUGH & EDMD. J. LEE and
ordered to be certified. And at a Court held for the County aforesd. the 21st day of August 1809
this Deed was further proved by the oath of NOBLET HERBERT, another Witness thereto and
ordered to be Recorded.   Teste WM. MOSS Cl.

Pages 255-258. THIS INDENTURE made this ninth day of January in the Year of Lord one
thousand eight hundred & nine between RICHARD BLAND LEE of the County of Fairfax &
CommonWealth of Virginia of the one part and EDMUND J. LEE of the Town of Alexandria &
District of Columbia, REV. WILLIAM MAFFIT & RICHARD COLEMAN of the said County of Fairfax
and CommonWealth aforesaid of the other part. Whereas ELIZABETH LEE wife of the said
RICHARD BLAND LEE hath on the day of the date of these presents consented to and executed a
Deed to LUDWELL LEE Esqr. of the County of Loudoun, relinquished her right to dower in & to a
certain tract of land lying in the County of Spotsylvania on the River Rappahannock &
CommonWealth aforesaid containing eight thousand Acres be the same more or less to dower
in five undivided eights of the said Tract the said ELIZABETH was entitled. And whereas the
said RICHARD BLAND LEE hath agreed and is desirous of fully indemnifying the said
ELIZABETH for her said dower so relinquished and whereas the said ELIZABETH hath also on
the day of the date of these presents executed a Deed of trust to HENRY SMITH TURNER of

Jefferson County, THOS. BLACKBURN of Fairfax County and BUSHROD WASHINGTON JR of Westmoreland County, jointly with her said Husband RICHARD BLAND LEE, conveying to the said HENRY SMITH TURNER, THOS. BLACKBURN & BUSHROD WASHINGTON JR two certain tracts or parcels of land situate, lying & being in the said County of Fairfax, one situate on the River Potowmack near the Little Falls thereof containing sixteen hundred acres be the same more or less and the other being the Estate whereon the said RICHARD BLAND LEE now resides, containing five hundred & thirty acres be the same more or less which said tracts of land are particularly described in the said deed of Trust and which tracts are conveyed to the said HENRY SMITH TURNER, THOS. BLACKBURN & BUSHROD WASHINGTON JR for the purpose of securing the payment by the said RICHARD BLAND LEE, his heirs, executors or Administrators, the just & full sum of ten thousand thirty five dollars & twenty eight Cents in the manner specified in the said Deed of trust and at the time therein expressed to the Honorable BUSHROD WASHINGTON, one the Judges of the Supreme Court of the United States and whereas the said RICHARD BLAND LEE has agreed and is desirous of indemnifying the said ELIZABETH his wife for joining in the said Deed of trust. Now this Indenture WITNESSETH that for and in consideration of the premises & in further consideration of the sum of five Dollars lawful Money of Virginia to him the said RICHARD BLAND LEE in hand paid by the said EDMUND J LEE, WILLIAM MAFFIT & RICHARD COLEMAN the receipt whereof the said RICHARD BLAND LEE doth hereby acknowledge hath bargained & sold and by these presents doth bargain & sell unto the said EDMUND J. LEE, WILLIAM MAFFITT & RICHD. COLEMAN and to the survivors or survivor of them and to the executors or Administrators of the last survivor of them, all his household & kitchen furniture consisting of beds, bed steads, bed furniture, plate, china ware, glass, tables, chairs, table linen, carpets, side boards, Beaufetts, Wardrobes and every kind & Species of furniture now in the House & kitchen of the said RICHARD BLAND LEE & estimated to be worth sixteen hundred Dollars, also the following slaves namely JOHN and his wife ALICE & their children PATTY, BETTY, HENRY, CHARLES, JOHNNY, MARGARET, MILLY and FRANK; LUDWELL and his wife NANCY and their Children CAROLINE, HARRIET, FREDERICK, LUDWELL & BARBARA; HENNY and her child EALENOR; RACHEL and her child RACHEL; two sisters KITTY & LETTY and their Brothers ALEXANDER and ALFRED and the following Men: GEORGE a Blacksmith, HENRY a carpenter, HENRY BUTLER a Waggoner, TOM a Carter, THORNTON a Cook & SAML. a smith and JACK a plow boy. To have and to hold all the above described furniture and the above named Slaves with their increase unto them the said EDMUND J. LEE, WILLIAM MAFFITT & RICHARD COLEMAN and the survivors or survivor of them, or the Executors or Administrators of the last survivor in Trust for the following uses & upon the following conditions that is to say for the use of the said ELIZABETH LEE during her natural life and after her death to pass to her heirs as the law may direct provided she dies intestate, or to such persons as she may bequeath the same by her last Will & Testament provided she shall make the said property to pass fully & completely & without limitation or condition to her heirs or legatees, provided always the said RICHARD BLAND LEE may at any time during his life sell or otherwise dispose of any part of the above property, furniture or Slaves, with the consent of a majority of the said trustees or of the Survivors or Survivor, or of the Executors or Administrators of the last survivor, other property either real or personal to the full value of the said furniture or slaves so sold or otherwise disposed of. And provided further that whenever the said RICHARD BLAND LEE shall fully pay & discharge the Debt intended to be paid to JUDGE WASHINGTON without selling any part of the property conveyed in Trust to HENRY SMITH TURNER, THOS. BLACKBURN & BUSHROD WASHINGTON JR which is now held by the said ELIZABETH LEE in her own proper right, then this Indenture so far as it relates to the following Slaves, Namely LUDWELL, THORNTON, HENRY BUTLER, TOM, SAMUEL, JACK and EALENOR, shall be null void and of no effect in Law or equity. In testimony of the premises the said RICHARD BLAND LEE and the said EDMUND J LEE, WILLIAM MAFFITT & RICHARD COLEMAN have hereunto affixed their hands & seals the day & Year herein first above written.

Signed Sealed & delivered
in the presence of us   RICHARD BLAND LEE   (seal)
JOHN COLEMAN as R.B.L. & R.C.   EDM. J. LEE   (seal)
STEPHEN DANIEL

THOS. R. MOTT   WM. MAFFITT   (seal)
GID. M. MOSS as R.B.LEE & E.J.LEE   RICHARD COLEMAN   (seal)
SANFORD PAYNE

At a Court held for Fairfax the 17th day of July 1809 this Deed from RICHARD BLAND LEE to EDMUND J. LEE, WILLIAM MAFFITT & RICHARD COLEMAN, in trust for the use of ELIZABETH LEE wife of the said RICHARD BLAND LEE was acknowledged by the said RICHARD BLAND LEE and ordered to be Certified. And at a Court held for the said County of Fairfax the 21st day of August 1809 this Deed was further acknowledged by the said EDMUND J. LEE, WILLIAM MAFFITT & RICHARD COLEMAN and ordered to be Recorded.

Teste WM. MOSS Cl.

Pages 258-260. THIS INDENTURE made this second day of August in the year of our Lord one thousand eight hundred & nine between RICHARD COLEMAN Esqr. of the County of Fairfax & CommonWealth of Virginia & ELIZABETH his wife of the one part and SALLY LANE of the County and CommonWealth aforesaid of the other part. WITNESSETH that the said RICHARD COLEMAN & ELIZABETH his wife for and in consideration of the sum of fourteen hundred & thirty seven dollars & fifty cents to him in hand paid by the said SALLY LANE at and before the ensealing and delivery of these presents the receipt whereof he the said RICHARD COLEMAN doth hereby acknowledge and thereof and of every part thereof doth exonerate & acquit the said SALLY LANE, her executors, Administrators and assigns by these presence have Granted, bargained and Sold, aliened, Released and confirmed and by these presents Do grant, bargain & Sell, alien, Release & Confirm unto the said SALLY LANE her heirs & assigns forever all the Kentucky Lands of which WM. LANE SR her late husband died seized whither in Law or equity & whither he was solely seized of the same or seized as a joint Tenant or Tenant in Common with any other person or persons and which said Lands were lately sold by the said SALLY LANE as executrix of WILLIAM LANE decd to the said RICHARD COLEMAN and conveyed to him by deed bearing date the [left blank] day of July one thousand eight hundred & nine together with all houses, buildings, ways, waters, water-courses, profits, commodities & advantages to the said Lands belonging or in anywise appertaining & the Reversion and Reversions, remainder & Remainders, rents, issues & profits thereof and also all the estate right, title, interest, property claim & demand of them the said RICHARD COLEMAN & ELIZABETH his wife, of, in & to the same & every part & parcel thereof To Have & to Hold the said hereby granted premises with all & singular the appurtenances hereunto belonging unto the said SALLY LANE her heirs & Assigns to the only proper use & behoof of the said SALLY LANE his heirs & assigns forever. In WITNESS whereof the said RICHARD COLEMAN & ELIZABETH his wife have hereunto set their hands & affixed their Seals the day & Year first before written.

Sealed & delivered
In Presence of   RICHARD COLEMAN   (seal)
SALLY ROWLS   ELIZABETH COLEMAN   (seal)
SUSAN W. LANE
MOLLY her X mark KELLY
G. W. LANE

At a Court held for Fairfax County the 21st day of August 1809 this Deed from RICHARD COLEMAN & ELIZABETH his wife to SALLY LANE was acknowledged by the said RICHARD COLEMAN to be his act & Deed which together with a Commission & return hereto annexed for taking the acknowledgment and privy examination of the said ELIZABETH wife of the said RICHARD COLEMAN are ordered to be Recorded.

Teste WM. MOSS Cl.

FAIRFAX COUNTY To Wit:

The CommonWealth of Virginia to FRANCIS ADAMS, RICD. B. LEE & HUMP. PEAKE Gentlemen of the County of Fairfax Greeting: Whereas RICD. COLEMAN & ELIZABETH his wife by their certain indenture of bargain & Sale bearing date the second day of August eighteen hundred & nine, have sold & conveyed unto SALLY LANE the fee simple estate of all the Kentucky lands of which her late husband, WILLIAM LANE SR died in anywise seized with the appurtenances situate, lying & being in the County of [left blank] and whereas the said

ELIZABETH cannot conveniently travel to our said County Court of Fairfax to make acknowledgment of the said conveyance therefore we do give unto You or any two or more of You
power to receive the acknowledgment which the said ELIZABETH shall be willing to make
before You of the Conveyance aforesaid contained in the said Indenture which is hereunto
annexed. And we do therefore desire you or any two or more of you personally to go to the
said ELIZABETH and receive her acknowledgment of the same and examine her privily & apart
from the said RICHARD COLEMAN, her husband whither she doth the same freely and voluntarily without his persuasions & threats and whither she be willing the said Indenture
together with this Commission shall be recorded in our said Court. And when You have
received her acknowledgment & examined her as aforesaid that You distinctly & openly
certify us thereof in our said Court under Your hands & seals sending then there the said
indenture and this Writ. WITNESS WILLIAM MOSS Clerk of our said Court at the Courthouse of
the County aforesaid this nineteenth day of August 1809 and in the 34th Year of the Common-
Wealth.   WM. MOSS Cl.
          FAIRFAX COUNTY:
          In obedience to the within Commission, we the undersigned waited on the within
named ELIZABETH COLEMAN & having examined her privily & apart from her husband
RICHARD COLEMAN touching the conveyance of the within mentioned Kentucky Lands, do
find that she hath done the same freely & of her own accord & without the persuasions or
threats of her said Husband & that she is willing the deed annexed together with the
Commission shall be recorded in the County Court of Fairfax. Given under our hands & seals
this 19th August 1809.   FRANCIS ADAMS   (seal)
                                                 HUMP. PEAKE   (seal)

Pages 260 & 261. THIS INDENTURE made this sixth of July in the Year one thousand eight
hundred & nine between ANTHONY RAINS & ELIZABETH his wife of the County of Fairfax &
State of Virginia of the one part and WILLIAM SIMMS of the County & State aforesaid of the
other part. WITNESSETH that the said ANTHONY RAINS and ELIZABETH his wife for and in
consideration of the sum of sixty dollars Current Money of Virginia to them in hand paid by
the said WILLIAM SIMMS at and before the sealing & delivery of these presents the receipt
whereof is hereby acknowledged hath Granted, bargained, Sold, Aliened, Released &
confirmed & by these presents doth Grant, bargain, sell, alien, Release & Confirm unto him
the said WILLIAM SIMMS his heirs & assigns all his the said ANTHONY RAINS & ELIZABETH his
wifes rights, title, interest & estate of, in & to a certain dividend piece of land situate in the
County of Fairfax and State of Virginia: beginning in the line of JOHN HARPERS land which
was deeded by the said JOHN HARPER to his Son CHARLES HARPER lying on the Northwest side
of the Colchester Road at a small sweet Gum and a white oak, thence along said line North ten
& three quarters East forty poles to a Stake near a box oak, thence South sixty two & half east
twenty five poles unto the middle of said Colchester Road, thence along said Road south forty
seven West forty one poles to the beginning which land was surveyed for six acres by
WILLIAM PAYNE, surveyor of Fairfax County December 24th 1793. To have and to hold the said
land with all the premises & appurtanances thereupon unto the said WM. SIMMS his heirs &
assigns to the use of him the said WM. SIMMS his heirs & assigns forever free & clear of all
restriction, Preservation & the said ANTHONY RAINS & ELIZABETH his wife doth hereby for
themselves their heirs & assigns, covenant, Promise, grant & agree to & with the said WM.
SIMMS, his heirs and to warrant and defend to him the said WM. SIMMS his heirs & assigns
the said piece of dividend land herein before mentioned & described from & against him the
said ANTHONY RAINS & ELIZABETH his wife and their heirs and assigns from & against all &
every other person or persons claiming whatsoever. In WITNESS whereof the said ANTHONY
RAINS & ELIZABETH his wife have set their hands & affixed their seals the date & Year first
above Written.
Signed Sealed & delivered
in the Presence of us   ANTHONY his X mark RAINS
JAMES IRVIN
WILLIAM DEVAUGHN
DENNIS JOHNSTON

Received the day & date above written sixty Dollars in full fore the sale of the above land.
DENNIS JOHNSTON   ANTHONY his X mark RAINS
JAMES IRVIN
At a Court held for Fairfax County the 21st day of August 1809 this Deed from ANTHONY RAINS to WILLIAM SIMMS with a receipt thereon endorsed was acknowledged by the said ANTHONY RAINS to be his act & deed & ordered to be Recorded.
Teste WM. MOSS Cl.

Pages 262. MEMORNADUM of an agreement made this twenty second day of June in the Year one thousand eight hundred & nine between NICHOLAS DARNE one of the children of HENRY DARNE deceased of the one part and GEORGE DARNE & ROBERT DARNE Executors of the said HENRY DARNE: WITNESSETH that the said NICHOLAS DARNE agrees to dismiss the suit which he has now defending in the County Court of Fairfax against the said Executors of the said HENRY DARNE at the Costs of each party and also to give his bond with security to be approved of by the said executors payable to them the said Executors, conditioned to pay to the said GEORGE DARNE & ROBERT DARNE executors of the said HENRY DARNE the sum of thirty seven Pounds without interest after the Death of PENELOPE DARNE the mother of the said NICHOLAS, GEORGE and ROBERT DARNE upon the above conditions being done & performed: the said GEORGE DARNE & ROBERT DARNE do hereby agree on their part to sign such an instrument of writing as shall be prepared by THOMAS SWANN & EDMUND J. LEE binding themselves as two of the Heirs & devisees of the said HENRY DARNE to convey to the said NICHOLAS DARNE their interest in & to a childs Share of the Real & personal estate of the said HENRY DARNE and also do hereby agree to use their influence with the rest of the Heirs & devisees of the said HENRY DARNE to execute the said instrument of writing, releasing their interest in & to one full childs share of the Real & Personal estate of the said HENRY DARNE to the said NICHOLAS DARNE his heirs & assigns. In WITNESS whereof the said parties to this Agreement have hereunto set their hands & seals on the day & Year first above written.
Signed Sealed &
delivered in presence of   GEO. DARNE   (seal)
H. GUNNELL   ROBT. DARNE   (seal)
CHARLES G. BROADWATER   NICHS. DARNE   (seal)
EDM. J. LEE
At a Court held for Fairfax County the 21st day of August 1809 this Agreement between GEORGE DARNE & ROBERT DARNE executors of HENRY DARNE Deceased & NICHOLAS DARNE was acknowledged by the parties and ordered to be Recorded.
Teste WM MOSS Cl.

Page 263. MEMORANDUM of Agreement made & entered into this third day of July 1809 between GEORGE DARNE, ROBT. DARNE, SAMUEL ADAMS & JEMIMA his wife, JOHN SAUNDERS & ELIZABETH his wife, PENELOPE DAVIS, NANCY DARNE, POLLY DARNE & SALLY DARNE, Heirs & devisees of HENRY DARNE deceased of the one part and NICHOLAS DARNE, one of the children of the said HENRY DARNE of the other part. Whereas the said NICHOLAS DARNE hath instituted a suit in County Court of Fairfax against the executors of the said HENRY DARNE decd to recover from them a claim which he the said NICHOLAS DARNE, had set up against the estate of the said HENRY DARNE decd as by reference to the Account filed in the said suit will appear and whereas the said NICHOLAS DARNE hath agreed with the aforesaid heirs & Devisees of the said HENRY DARNE to dismiss the said suit & pass his bond to the exors of the said HENRY DARNE decd for the payment of the sum of thirty seven Pounds at the time of the death of his mother PENELOPE DARNE upon condition that the said Heirs & devisees will admit him the said NICHOLAS DARNE to an equal share of the estate of the said HENRY DARNE decd in the same manner as if the said HENRY DARNE had died intestate and whereas the said Heirs & Devisees have agreed to admit the said NICHOLAS DARNE to a share of the said estate upon the terms & conditions aforesaid and the said NICHOLAS DARNE in consequence thereof hath dismissed his said suit and hath passed his bond for the payment of the aforesaid sum of thirty seven Pounds upon the Death of his Mother as aforesaid. Now this agreement WITNESSETH that the said GEORGE DARNE, ROBERT DARNE, SAMUEL ADAMS & JEMIMA his wife, JOHN SAUNDERS & ELIZABETH his wife, PENELOPE DAVIS, NANCY DARNE, POLLY DARNE & SALLY DARNE, heirs & Devisees of the said HENRY DARNE decd do for themselves their heirs, exors & admns, Covenant, Promise & agree to & with the said NICHOLAS DARNE that he the said NICHOLAS DARNE shall have, take, receive & enjoy the same share, interest & benefit from the estate of the said HENRY DARNE decd as if he the said HENRY DARNE had died intestate & that he the said NICHOLAS DARNE his heirs & assigns shall in all respects be entitled [to] a fair & equal childs part of the said estate in common with the other children of the said HENRY DARNE decd. In WITNESS whereof the parties to these presents have hereunto set their hands & affixed their Seals this third day & Year first before written.

Sealed & Delivered	GEO. DARNE	(seal)
in presence of	ROBT. DARNE	(seal)
ISAAC McLAIN	SAMUEL ADAMS	(seal)
JAMES WIGGINTON	JEMIMA ADAMS	(seal)
	JN. SANDERS	(seal)
	ELIZABETH her + mark SANDERS	(seal)
	PENELOPE her + mark DAVIS	(seal)
	ANN DARNE	(seal)
	POLLY DARNE	(seal)
	SALLY DARNE	(seal)

At a Court held for Fairfax County the 21st day of August 1809 this agreement between GEORGE DARNE, ROBERT DARNE, SAMUEL ADAMS & JEMIMA his wife, JOHN SAUNDERS & ELIZABETH his wife, PENELOPE DAVIS, NANCY DARNE, POLLY DARNE and SALLY DARNE, Heirs & Devisees of HENRY DARNE deceased and NICHOLAS DARNE one of the Children of the said HENRY DARNE was proved to be the Act and deed of the parties by the oath of JAMES WIGGINTON and ordered to be Recorded.   Teste WM MOSS Cl.

Pages 264-266. THIS INDENTURE made this eighth day of August in the Year of our Lord one thousand eight hundred & nine between WILLIAM BARTLEMAN, Trustee of the Town & County of Alexandria in the District of Columbia of the one part & JOHN GREEN of the Town, County & district aforesaid of the other part. Whereas JOHN GREEN & MARY his wife by their Indenture bearing date the Seventeenth day of November eighteen hundred & eight, conveyed to the said WILLIAM BARTLEMAN & HUGH SMITH in trust for HUGH SMITH the herein after described premises to secure the payment of a certain sum of Money therein mentioned and whereas the said HUGH SMITH is secured in the payment of the same by the said JOHN GREEN & has released the said GREEN (reference being had to the said Deed now of record in the Office of Alexandria). Now this indenture WITNESSETH that the said WILLIAM BARTLEMAN, in consideration of the premises and of the sum of one Dollar to him the said BARTLEMAN in hand paid by him the said GREEN before sealing & delivery of these presents by the said WILLIAM BARTLEMAN the receipt whereof by the said BARTLEMAN is acknowledged hath Given, Granted, bargained & Sold, released, transfered and set over and by these presents doth Give, Grant, bargain & sell, release, transfer & set over unto the said JOHN GREEN his heirs & assigns forever a piece or parcel of Ground situate, lying & being in the County of Alexandria and District aforesaid being part of a larger tract commonly called & known by the name of PEARSONS Tract which said tract of land was by the will of JOHN WEST deceased devised to his two sons, JOHN & THOMAS WEST to be equally divided between them & was by them conveyed to the said JOHN GREEN by indenture bearing date the seventeenth day of December eighteen hundred & four & which said Deed is of Record in the Clerks Office of Alexandria County Bounded as follows to wit: beginning at a Dogwood & Hickory standing in or near a line of the Original patent of PEARSON, thence with said line South eighteen degrees West sixty poles at or near the corner of the said Patent, thence South Twenty degrees East ninety three Poles to several small saplins blazed as a Corner to said Piece or Parcel of land, thence North seventy Degrees East thirty eight poles to a stake in or near the line run from the Stone near Hunting Creek where the POHICKORYS corner to HOWSONS Patent is said to have stood, thence with said course North twenty Degrees West one hundred & forty poles to the beginning containing twenty seven and a half acres & nineteen poles. To have and to hold the said Premises with all

Houses, out-Houses and appurtenances whatsoever to the same belonging or in anywise appertaining to the said JOHN GREEN his heirs & assigns to the only Proper use & behoof of the said JOHN GREEN his heirs & assigns forever. And the said WILLIAM BARTLEMAN releases, transfers & sets over all right, Title, interest & property which he may have acquired by virtue of the Trust created to him in the Conveyance from the said Green to him as Trustee for the said HUGH SMITH. And the said BARTLEMAN doth for himself & his heirs Covenant to & with the said GREEN & his Heirs that he has not encumbered the said estate by any convey- ance whatever or in any other manner whereby the title of the said JOHN GREEN or those under him can be affected in any manner whatever. In WITNESS whereof the said WILLIAM BARTLEMAN hath hereunto set his hand & affixed his seal the day & Year first before Written. Signed Sealed & Delivered
in presence of   WM. BARTLEMAN   (seal)
N. HERBERT, J. D. SIMMS
WM. KING
        DISTRICT OF COLUMBIA To Wit:
                I GEORGE DENEALE Clerk of the United States Circuit Court of the District of
(SEAL)   Columbia for the County of Alexandria do hereby certify that at a Court
                continued & held for the County aforesaid the tenth day of August 1809 WILLIAM BARTLEMAN acknowledged this Deed to JOHN GREEN to be his act and deed & ordered to be recorded & certified to the County Court of Fairfax in the CommonWealth of Virginia. In Testimony whereof I have hereunto set my hand & affixed the public seal of my office on this 11th day of August 1809.   G. DENEALE Cl.
        DISTRICT OF COLUMBIA To Wit:
        I WILLIAM CRANCH Chief Judge of the United States Circuit Court of the District of Columbia, do hereby certify that the above attestation of GEORGE DENEALE Clerk of the said Court for Alexandria County is in due form Given under my hand this 11th day of August 1809.
                                        W. CRANCH
        At a Court held for the County of Fairfax the 21st day of August 1809 this Deed from WILLIAM BARTLEMAN to JOHN GREEN having been duly acknowledged before the United States Circuit Court of the District of Columbia held for the County of Alexandria and certified by GEORGE DENEALE Clerk of the said Court under the Seal of his office, also by WILLIAM CRANCH Chief Judge of the said Court, is on motion of the said JOHN GREEN together with the certificates thereon endorsed, ordered to be Recorded.
                                    Teste WM. MOSS Cl.

Pages 266-268. THIS INDENTURE made this twenty eighth day of January in the Year of our Lord one thousand eight hundred & nine between JOHN WINTERBERRY of the Town & County of Alexandria in the District of Columbia of the one part and ROBERT HARTSHORNE of the City of New York of the other part: WITNESSETH that the said JOHN WINTERBERRY for and in consideration of the sum of five hundred Dollars to him in hand paid the receipt whereof he doth hereby acknowledge from the said ROBERT HARTSHORNE & thereof doth exonerate & discharge him his Executors, Administrators & Assigns hath Granted, Bargained & Sold, aliened & confirmed & by these presents doth Grant, bargain & Sell, Alien & Confirm unto the said ROBERT HARTSHORNE his heirs & assigns forever a tract or Parcel of land situate, lying & being upon the Drains of Great Hunting creek in the County of Fairfax & State of Virginia, being a part of that tract of land mortgaged by JOSIAH WATSON to CHARLES HIGBIE & lately sold under a decree of Fairfax County Court for the payment of the claim of the said CHARLES HIGBIE, the tract of land hereby intended to be conveyed being described in the Platt of the said land so Mortgaged to the said CHARLES HIGBIE & the several divisions made thereof by the Commissioners appointed to make sale of & by the number 10, the same being bounded as followeth to wit: beginning at a stake on the edge of the Turnpike Road, sixty seven poles to the westward of the first avenue laid out by the Commissioners through the said land, it being a corner to that other lott of the said tract of land described in the said platt by number 9 & running thence with the line of lott, North fifteen degrees East fifty poles to a stake in the line of that lott described in the platt by number 15, being another corner of the said lott number 9 & running thence with the line of the said lott Number 13 North seventy nine

Degrees West seventeen Poles to a stake in the said line a corner to that other lott described in the said platt number 11, thence with the line of that lott south fifteen Degrees West fifty poles to a stake on the edge of the Turnpike road another corner to number 11, thence with the Turnpike Road south seventy nine degrees east seventeen poles to the beginning containing five Acres fifty poles which Tract of land JAMES KEITH & GEORGE GILPIN two of the Commissioners acting under the Decree of the Court of Fairfax County conveyed unto FRANCIS PEYTON by Indenture bearing date the [left blank] day of [left blank] one thousand eight hundred and [left blank] who by Indenture bearing date the first day of March in the Year 1805 conveyed the same to the said JOHN WINTERBERRY and all the Houses, buildings, trees, Woods, Waters, Water Courses, Roads, Lanes, Avenues, profits, commodities, hereditaments & appurtenances whatsoever to the same belonging or in any wise appertaining and the Reversion and Reversions, Remainder and Remainders, Rents, Issues & Profits thereof and of every Part & parcel thereof To Have & to hold the said tract or parcel of land, Hereditaments & all and Singular the premises with their appurtenances unto him the said ROBERT HARTSHORNE his heirs & assigns to his and their only proper use and behoof forever. And the said JOHN WINTERBERRY doth for himself, his Heirs, Executors & Administrators, covenant & Grant to & with the said ROBERT HARTSHORNE his heirs & assigns that now at the time of sealing and Delivering these presents he the said JOHN WINTERBERRY is seized in his own right of a good, sure, perfect & indefeasible Estate of Inheritance in Fee simple of & in the said Tract of land hereby conveyed, Hereditaments & all & singular the Premises hereby granted with their appurtenances without any manner or Condition, Mortgage, Limitation of use or uses, or any other matter, cause or thing, to alter, change, charge or determine the same. And also that he the said JOHN WINTERBERRY & his heirs, will at any time hereafter upon the request and at the cost & charge of him the said ROBERT HARTSHORN his heirs & assigns execute & acknowledge any further & other lawful act & Deed for the more certain assurance & conveying the said Tract of Land, Hereditaments and all and Singular the Premises hereby granted with their appurtenances unto him the said ROBERT HARTSHORNE his heirs & assigns as by him the said ROBERT HARTSHORNE his heirs & assigns his or their Counsel learned in the Law shall or may be advised or required. And lastly that the said JOHN WINTERBERRY & his heirs the said tract or parcell of land, Hereditaments and all and Singular the Premises thereunto belonging with their appurtenances unto the said ROBERT HARTSHORNE his heirs & assigns against the claim & demand of him the said JOHN WINTERBERRY his heirs & assigns & of all and every other person and persons whatsoever shall & will warrant and forever defend by these presents. In WITNESS whereof the said JOHN WINTERBERRY hath hereunto set his hand & Seal the day & year first herein written.

Sealed & Delivered in
Presence of   JOHN WINTERBERRY   (seal)
CLEON MOORE
HENRY MOORE
ELISHA TALBOTT
DAVID SAUNDERS
      DISTRICT OF COLUMBIA To Wit:
           I GEORGE DENEALE Clerk of the United States Circuit Court of the District of
(SEAL)   Columbia for the County of Alexandria do hereby certify that at a Court
           continued & held the fourteenth day of July 1809 JOHN WINTERBERRY
acknowledged this Deed to ROBERT HARTSHORNE to be his act & Deed and ordered to be certified to the County Court of Fairfax in the CommonWealth of Virginia. In Testimony whereof I have hereunto set my hand & affixed the public seal of my office on the 17th day of July Eighteen hundred & Nine.   G. DENEALE Cl.
      DISTRICT OF COLUMBIA To Wit:
           I WILLIAM CRANCH Chief Judge of the United States Circuit Court of the District of Columbia do hereby certify that the above attestation of GEORGE DENEALE Clerk of the said Court for Alexandria County is in due form. Given under my hand this 17th day of July 1809.
                    W. CRANCH

At a Court held for Fairfax County the 21st day of August 1809 this Deed from JOHN WINTERBERRY to ROBERT HARTSHORNE having been duly acknowledged before the United States Circuit Court of the District of Columbia held for the County of Alexandria & Certified by GEORGE DENEALE Clerk of the said Court under the seal of his office, also by WILLIAM CRANCH Chief Judge of the said Court is on motion of the said ROBERT HARTSHORNE together with the Certificates thereon endorsed Ordered to be Recorded.

Teste WM. MOSS Cl.

Page 269. McINTOSH &c TO GOVERNOR, Bond:

KNOW ALL MEN by these presents that we WALTER McINTOSH, LOYD McINTOSH, STEPHEN DONOHOE & JOHN STANHOPE are held & firmly bound unto JOHN TYLER Esquire Governor of the CommonWealth of Virginia and his Successors in the full & just sum of one Thousand Dollars Current Money of the United States to which Payment well & truly to be made to the said JOHN TYLER Governor &c his successors we bind ourselves and each of us, our and each of our heirs, Executors & Administrators, jointly & severally firmly by these presents sealed with our seals & dated this twenty first day of August 1809.

THE CONDITION of the above obligation is such that whereas the above bound WALTER McINTOSH hath been duly appointed a Constable for that part or section of the County of Fairfax described & known by District number one in Pursuance of two Acts of Assembly of this CommonWealth passed the twenty first day of January 1803 and the tenth day of January one Thousand eight hundred & seven the first entitled "an Act concerning Constables" and the second "An Act to amend the Act concerning Constables." Now if the said WALTER McINTOSH shall in every respect well & truly perform & discharge the several duties of his said office of Constable within the District aforesaid agreeable to the several acts of Assembly concerning Constables defining their duty, then the above obligation to be void else to remain in full force power and Virtue in Law.

WALTER McINTOSH	(seal)
LOYD McINTOSH	(seal)
STEPHEN DONOHOE	(seal)
JOHN STANHOPE	(seal)

At a Court held for Fairfax County the 21st day of August 1809 this Bond from WALTER McINTOSH, LOYD McINTOSH, STEPHEN DONOHOE and JOHN STANHOPE to the Governor of this CommonWealth was acknowledged by the said WALTER, LOYD, STEPHEN & JOHN to be their Act & Deed and thereupon ordered to be Recorded.

Teste WM. MOSS Cl.

Pages 270-272. [Margin Note: Delivered to ELISHA JENKINS, 19th February 1816]

JN. HERIFORD & ux to JENKINS . . . Deed . . B & sale

THIS INDENTURE made & entered into this fourth day of May one thousand eight hundred & nine between JOHN HERIFORD and SARAH HERIFORD his wife of the County of Fairfax & State of Virginia of the one part and ELISHA JENKINS of the County of Prince William & State aforesaid of the other part. WITNESSETH that for and in consideration of the sum of one hundred & Ninety Dollars to them in hand paid at or before the sealing & delivery these receipt whereof they do hereby acknowledge have Granted, bargained & sold and do by these presents Grant, bargain & sell unto the said ELISHA JENKINS his heirs & assigns a certain tract or parcel of land siutate lying & being in the County of Fairfax, being part of a tract late the property of PETER MAUZEY deceased father of said SARAH HERIFORD and which descended to her by his dying intestate and allotted to the said JOHN & SARAH HERIFORD by Commissioners appointed by the County Court of Fairfax, being lot number ten, as by reference to the report of said Commissioners will more fully appear bounded as follows (Viz:) beginning at [left blank] Containing twenty three Acres one hundred & fifty poles. To have and to Hold the said Tract or parcel of land together with all & Singular Houses, buildings, Waters, Water Courses, ways, Profits & the appurtenances in anywise thereto belonging or appertaining unto him the said ELISHA JENKINS his heirs & assigns forever to their own proper use & behoof forever & the said JOHN & SARAH HERIFORD for themselves & their heirs do Covenant, grant & agree to & with the said ELISHA JENKINS his heirs & assigns that they

JOHN & SARAH HERIFORD the said Land & Premises with their appurtenances unto the said ELISHA JENKINS his heirs & assigns will forever warrant & defend not only against the claim of them & their heirs, but also against the claim or claims of all & every person & persons whatever. In Testimony whereof the said JOHN & SARAH HERIFORD have hereunto set their hands & affixed their seals the day & Year first written.

Signed Sealed & Delivered
in the presence of   JOHN HERIFORD   (seal)
TOWNSHEND WAUGH   SARAH HEREFORD   (seal)
TRAVIS PRITCHARTT
WILLIAM P. HEREFORD
JAS. WAUGH, W. DENEALE

At a Court held for Fairfax County the 21st day of August 1809 this Deed from JOHN HEREFORD & SARAH his wife to ELISHA JENKINS was proved by the oaths of TRAVERS PRITCHARTT, JAMES WAUGH & WILLIAM DENEALE to be the act & deed of the said JOHN HEREFORD which together with a Comission & Return thereto annexed for taking the acknowledgment & privy examination of the said SARAH, Ordered to be Recorded.

Teste WM MOSS Cl.

FAIRFAX COUNTY To Wit:

The CommonWealth of Virginia to CHARLES LITTLE, JAMES WAUGH and WILLIAM DENEALE Gentlement Trustees of the County of Fairfax Greeting: Whereas JOHN HERIFORD and SARAH HERIFORD his wife by their certain Indenture of bargain & sale bearing date the fourth day of May 1809 have sold & conveyed unto ELISHA JENKINS the fee simple estate of twenty three acres one hundred & fifty poles of land with the appurtenances situate, lying & being in the said County of Fairfax and whereas the said SARAH HERIFORD cannot conveniently travel to our said County Court of Fairfax to make acknowledgment of the said conveyance therefore we do give unto you or any two or more of you power to the acknowledgment which the said SARAH shall be willing to make before you of the conveyance aforesaid contained in the said Indenture which is hereunto annexed. And we do therefore desire You or any two or more of you personally to go to the said SARAH and receive her acknowledegment of the same and examine her privily and apart from the said JOHN HERIFORD her husband whither she doth the same freely & voluntarily without his persuasions or threats and whither she be willing the said Indenture together with the Commission shall be recorded in our said Court. And when You have received her acknowledgment & examined her as aforesaid that You distinctly & openly certify us thereof in our said Court under Your hands & seals sending then there the said Indenture & this Writ. WITNESS WILLIAM MOSS Clerk of the said Court at the Courthouse of the County aforesaid this 4th day of May 1809 and in the 33rd Year of the CommonWealth.

WM. MOSS Cl.

FAIRFAX COUNTY:

In obedience to the within Dedimus, we the subscriber did on the Nineteenth day of August one thousand eight hundred & nine go to the House of the within named JOHN HERIFORD & did then & there examine the within named SARAH the wife of the said JOHN HERIFORD privately & apart from her said husband whither she was willing to execute the same freely without the threat or persuasion of her said husband; she the said SARAH did then & there in our presents execute the said Indenture & did freely & voluntarily acknowledge and Convey all her right of Dower in the Lands & inheritance therein mentioned to the said ELISHA JENKINS and his Heirs forever. Certified under our hand & Seals the day & Year aforesaid.   W. DENEALE   (seal)
                                                                 JAS. WAUGH   (seal)

Pages 272-274. THIS INDENTURE made this fourteenth Day of April in the Year of our Lord Christ one thousand eight hundred & nine between JOHN MOSS of the County of Fairfax in the CommonWealth of Virginia of the one part and WILLIAM MOSS of the County & CommonWealth aforesaid of the other part. Whereas the said JOHN MOSS as well to advance the interest of his Son ROBERT MOSS as for the consideration therein mentioned, did by his certain Deed of Gift bearing date the [left blank] day of [left blank] in the Year [left blank]

Give, Grant and convey unto him the said ROBERT MOSS his heirs & assigns forever a certain piece or parcel of land situate, lying & being in the County & CommonWealth aforesaid supposed to contain one hundred & seventy acres be the same more or less it being one full third part of the two tracts of Land Purchased by him the said JOHN MOSS, the one of a certain DANIEL SUMMERS & REBECCA his wife by Deed dated the eleventh day of September 1777, the other of a certain BALDWIN DADE & CATHARINE his wife by deed dated the twentieth day of October 1788 reference being had unto the said three several Deeds now on record in the County Court of Fairfax will more fully & at large appear. And Whereas the said JOHN MOSS is desirous of advancing the interest of his Son the said WILLIAM MOSS in like manner. Now this indenture WITNESSETH that as well to effect the purposes aforesaid as for and in consideration of the sum of one Dollar Money of the United States to him the said JOHN MOSS by him the said WILLIAM MOSS in hand paid the receipt whereof he the said JOHN MOSS doth hereby acknowledge. He the said JOHN MOSS hath Given, Granted & Conveyed and by these presents doth give, Grant & Convey unto him the said WILLIAM MOSS his heirs and assigns forever one full third part of the aforesaid two tracts of land purchased by him as aforesaid, it being one undivided moiety of the residue of the same as now held by him the said JOHN MOSS, To Have & to hold unto him the said WILLIAM MOSS his heirs & assigns forever the aforesaid Moiety of the residue of the said two tracts of Land together with all and Singular its appurtenances to the only proper use & behoof of him the said WILLIAM MOSS his heirs & assigns forever. And he the said JOHN MOSS doth for himself and his heirs by these presents warrant & forever defend the said Lands and premises hereby conveyed unto him the said WILLIAM MOSS his heirs & assigns against the claim of him the said JOHN MOSS and his heirs & all & every other person or persons claiming by, from or under him, them or any of them. In WITNESS whereof he the said JOHN MOSS hath hereunto set his hand & affixed his Seal the day Month & Year first within mentioned.

Acknowledged & delivered
In the presence of   JOHN MOSS   (seal)
HUGH W. MINOR
THO. MOSS
CHAS. J. CATLETT

    At a Court continued & held for Fairfax County the 17th day of April 1809 this Deed of Gift from JOHN MOSS to WILLIAM MOSS was proved to be the Act & deed of the said JOHN MOSS by the oaths HUGH W. MINOR & CHAS. J. CATLETT and ordered to be Certified. And at a Court contd. & held for the said County the 22nd day of August 1809 this Deed of Gift was further proved to be the Act and Deed of the said JOHN MOSS by the oath of THOS. MOSS another Witness thereto & Ordered to be recorded. Teste WM. MOSS Cl.

Page 274. WHEREAS IGNATIUS WHEELER was appointed by the County Court of Fairfax my Guardian & I having received the Amount of all the Estate or effects that has come into his hands and he being desirous of having a general discharge from the same, I Do hereby acquit & discharge him the said IGNATIUS WHEELER from all claims & demands as my Guardian aforesaid & declare to have received full satisfaction from the same. WITNESS my hand this 27th day of January 1808.
Teste   WM. STANHOPE
THOS. MOSS
SPENCER JACKSON

    At a Court held for Fairfax County the 19th day of September 1808 this Instrument of writing between WILLIAM STANHOPE & IGNATIUS WHEELER was proved to be the Act & deed of the said WM. STANHOPE by the oath of SPENCER JACKSON a Witness hereto & ordered to be Certified. And at a Court contd. & held for the said County the 22nd day of August 1809 the same was further proved by the oath of THOS. MOSS, another Witness thereto & ordered to be Recorded.   Teste WM. MOSS Cl.

Pages 274-278 THIS INDENTURE made this 26th day of June in the Year one thousand eight hundred & five between JOHN GREEN & MARY his wife of the Town of Alexandria in the District of Columbia of the one part and CUTHBERT POWELL & GEORGE SLACUM of the same

Town of the other part. Whereas the said JOHN GREEN, from losses and misfortunes in trade has become unable to satisfy the full amount of the several debts for which he is responsible, but with a desire to do justice to his Creditors, has already surrendered to the said CUTHBERT POWELL & GEORGE SLACUM Trustees by his said Creditors appointed all his personal Estate as contained in a Schedule thereof to them delivered, to be appropriated towards the payment of his Debts so far as it will go in equal proportions & has also agreed to convey to the said trustees for the same purposes the tract of land herein after described. Now this Indenture WITNESSETH that the said JOHN GREEN & MARY his wife in consideration of the premises and of the sum of one dollar to him in hand paid by the said CUTHBERT POWELL & GEORGE SALCUM the receipt whereof he doth hereby acknowledge have Granted, bargained & sold and do by these presents Grant, Bargain & sell to the said CUTHBERT POWELL & GEORGE SLACUM a certain piece of land situate in the County of Alexandria being part of a larger tract known by the name of PEARSONS tract and bounded as follows: beginning at a Dog Wood & Hiccory standing in or near the line of the Original Patent of PEARSON, thence with the said line South eighteen Degrees West sixty poles at or near the Corner of the said patent, thence South twenty Degrees East Ninety three poles to several small saplings blazed as a corner, thence North seventy degrees east thirty eight poles to a stake in or near the line run from the Stone near Hunting Creek where the pohiccory corner to HOWSONS patent is said to have stood, thence with the said course north twenty degrees West one hundred & forty poles to the beginning except eight acres & twelve poles thereof where the House stands, designated as Lot Number 8 in the division made by SIMON SUMMERS which is hereto annexed which said Reservation is made for the purpose of satisfying the Balance of Purchase Money for the whole Tract containing twenty seven & a half acres & nineteen poles due to LUDWELL LEE, by whose directions the said tract was conveyed to the said JOHN GREEN by THOS. WEST & JN. WEST by Deed dated the seventeenth day of December eighteen hundred & four, recorded in the Court of Alexandria County. To have and to hold the said tract of Land hereby conveyed with the exception aforesaid to the said CUTHBERT POWELL & GEORGE SLACUM & the Survivor and the Heirs of such Survivors forever In Trust however to sell & dispose of the same in such manner as the Majority in number & Value of the Creditors of the said JOHN GREEN shall desire & to apply the proceeds thereof to the payment of the said Creditors in equal proportions & the said JOHN GREEN for himself and his heirs doth hereby Covenant & agree with the said CUTHBERT POWELL & GEORGE SLACUM their heirs & assigns to warrant and defend the premises hereby conveyed to them their heirs & assigns, against the claims & demands of all persons whatsoever. And the said CUTHBERT POWELL & GEORGE SLACUM do for themselves severally and for their several heirs covenant and agree with the said JOHN GREEN his Heirs, Executors & Administrators, faithfully to execute & fulfil the trust in them reposed. In Testimony whereof the parties to these presents have hereunto set their hands & seals the day & Year first before written.
Signed, Sealed & Delivered

In presence of		
RICHD. WALSH	JOHN GREEN	(seal)
JAS. HARPER	MARY her X mark GREEN	(seal)
JOHN MacLEOD (as it respects JOHN GREEN)	CUTHBERT POWELL	(seal)
	GEORGE SLACUM	(seal)

[MAP OF THE PLAT]

When MR. JOHN GREEN determines in what way he will have the remaining part of his tract laid off a platt with explanatory notes will be returned to said GREEN.
SAML. SOMMERS

DISTRICT OF COLUMBIA To Wit:

(SEAL)   I GEORGE DENEALE Clerk of the United States Circuit Court of the District of Columbia for the County of Alexandria do hereby certify that at a Court continued & held the Nineteenth day of July 1805. This Deed from JOHN GREEN to CUTHBERT POWELL & GEORGE SLACUM was acknowledged by the said JOHN GREEN & CUTHBERT POWELL to be their act & deed and ordered to be certified. And at another Court contd. & held for the District & County aforesaid the sixth day of July 1809 this Deed was further acknowledged by the said GEORGE SLACUM to be his Act & deed which together with a Commission & Return for the privy examination of MARY GREEN wife of the said JOHN are ordered to be recorded and Certified to the County Court of Fairfax in the CommonWealth of Virginia. In Testimony whereof I have hereunto set my hand & affixed the public Seal of my office on this tenth day of August 1809.   G. DENEALE Cl.

DISTRICT OF COLUMBIA To Wit:

I WILLIAM CRANCH Chief Judge of the United States Circuit Court of the District of Columbia, do hereby certify that the above attestation of GEORGE DENEALE Clerk of the said Court for Alexandria County is in due form. Given under my hand this 10th day of August 1809.   W. CRANCH

At a Court Continued & held for Fairfax County the 22nd day of August 1809 this Deed from JOHN GREEN & MARY his wife to CUTHBERT POWELL & GEORGE SLACUM having been duly acknowledged by the parties before the United States Circuit Court of the District of Columbia for the County of Alexa. & admitted to record and certified by GEORGE DENEALE Clerk of the said Court under the Seal of his Office also by WILLIAM CRANCH Chief Judge of the said Court is on motion of the said CUTHBERT POWELL & GEORGE SLACUM together with the Certificates thereon endorsed and a Commission and return for taking the acknowledgment & privy examination of the said MARY & a platt & Survey hereto annexed, Ordered to be Recorded.
                    Teste WM. MOSS Cl.

DISTRICT OF COLUMBIA, COUNTY OF ALEXANDRIA:

The United States of America to ABRAHAM FAW, JONAH THOMPSON & JACOB HOFFMAN Gentlemen justices of the said County of Alexandria Greeting: Whereas JOHN GREEN & MARY his wife by their certain indenture of bargain & sale bearing date the twenty sixth day of June 1805 have sold & conveyed unto CUTHBERT POWELL & GEORGE SLACUM of the Town of Alexa. the fee simple estate of a certain messuage or tract or parcel of land it being a part of a tract of land commonly known by PEARSON tract in trust for the Creditors of the said JOHN GREEN with the appurtenances situate, lying & being in the said County of Alexandria and whereas the said MARY wife of the said JOHN cannot conveniently travel to our United States Circuit Court of the District of Columbia for the County of Alexandria to make acknowledgment of the said conveyance therefore we do give unto you or any two or more of you Power to receive the acknowledgment which the said MARY shall be willing to make before You of the conveyance aforesaid contained in the said Indenture which is herewith annexed. And we do therefore desire You or any two or more of You personally to go to the said MARY & receive her acknowledgment of the same and examine her privily & apart from the said JOHN GREEN her husband wither she doth the same freely & Voluntarily without his persuasions or threats and whither she be willing the said Indenture together with this Commission shall be recorded in our said Court. And when You have received her acknowledgment & examined her as aforesaid that You distinctly & openly certify us thereof in our said Court under Your hands & seals sending then there the said Indenture & this writ. WITNESS the Hon. WILLIAM KILTY, Chief Judge of our said Court, this twenty sixth day of June 1805.
                    G. DENEALE Cl.

DISTRICT OF COLUMBIA, ALEXANDRIA COUNTY:

In pursuance of the within Commission to us directed we examined MARY GREEN wife of JOHN GREEN within named who acknowledged her signature to the Deed hereto annexed, the same being explained to her and said she was willing the said Deed together with this Commission might be recorded and that she made this acknowledgment freely & Voluntarily, that she was not induced thereto by the persuasions of her said husband or thro fear of his displeasure. Certified under our hands & Seals this 26th day of June 1805.
                    A. FAW   (seal)
                    JONAH THOMPSON   (seal)

Pages 278-283. THIS INDENTURE made this second day of May eighteen hundred & nine between WILLIAM BARTLEMAN Trustee of the one part JOHN GREEN & MARY his wife of the second part and CUTHBERT POWELL & GEORGE SLACUM of the third part all of the Town & County of Alexandria in the District of Columbia. Whereas JOHN GREEN & MARY his wife, by deed recorded in the clerks office of Alexandria County conveyed to WILLIAM BARTLEMAN in

trust for HUGH SMITH certain lots in the County aforesaid for the purposes mentioned in the sd. deed reference being thereto had will more fully appear. And whereas the said SMITH & BARTLEMAN are desirous of releasing their lien on the two lots herein after described, to satisfy a previous one created on the same by the said GREEN & wife to said POWELL & SLACUM for the benefit of his creditors and the said GREEN being anxious to secure their title & Confirm their interest in the same. Now this Indenture WITNESSETH that the said WILLIAM BARTLEMAN & JOHN GREEN for and in consideration of the sum of one dollar to them in hand paid by the said POWELL & SLACUM the receipt whereof they do hereby acknowledge have Given, Granted, Bargained & Sold, aliened, released, transferred & confirmed and by these Do Give, Grant, bargain & sell, alien, release, transfer and confirm two lots situate in the County aforesaid and bounded as followeth to wit: Lots No. 1 and 2 beginning at a Stone standing at the South East corner of Lot No. 3 in the Western boundary of HOWSONS Patent, running thence South 20° East with the line of said patent reversed forty eight poles to a Stone, thence south 70° West thirty eight Poles, thence North 20° West forty eight poles to the corner of lot number 3, thence North 10° East thirty eight poles with the line of lot No. 3 to the beginning containing eleven acres sixty four poles. Lot No. 4, beginning at a stake standing in or near a Dogwood & Hickory in the line of the Patent of PEARSON & the Western boundary of HOWSONS Patent and now called ALEXANDERS back line at "A" running thence South 98° West 60 poles to a stake at "B" thence South 20° East ten poles & twenty links to the Corner of Lot No. 3, thence South 70° East with the line of Lot No. 3 thirty eight poles to the Western boundary of HOWSONS patent, thence North 20 West with the line of HOWSON fifty seven poles twenty links to the beginning at "A" containing eight acres & twenty three poles, Reference being had to the annexed platt of a Survey made by GEORGE GILPIN of the said premises being part of a larger Tract of Land known by the name of PEARSONS tract given by him to his Daughter MARGARET who intermarried with a certain WILLIAM H. TERRETT who together with his said wife conveyed it by deed now of record in the office of the General Court of Virginia, to HUGH WEST who devised it to JOHN WEST who devised it to his two Sons JOHN & THOMAS WEST who conveyed it to JOHN GREEN by Deed bearing date [left blank] day of [left blank] eighteen hundred and [left blank] now of Record in the Clerks Office of Alexandria County, the said lots having been previously conveyed to the said POWELL & SLACUM, for the purposes contained in the deed to them from the said GREEN & MARY his wife bearing date the twenty sixth day of [left blank] in the Year eighteen hundred & five and recorded in the Clerks Office of Alexandria County & conveyed a second time by the said GREEN & wife to WILLIAM BARTLEMAN in trust for HUGH SMITH through mistake, To Have & To Hold the said Premises with their appurtenances unto the said POWELL & SLACUM their heirs & assigns to the only Proper use & behoof of the said POWELL & SLACUM their heirs & assigns forever and the said WILLIAM BARTLEMAN for himself & his heirs, the said Lots or parcells of Ground and every part thereof with their appurtenances, against him & his heirs & against all and every person & persons whatsoever claiming by, from & under him and them or any of them to the said POWELL & SLACUM & their Heirs shall & will warrant & forever defend by these presents & the said JOHN GREEN & MARY his wife for themselves & their Heirs the said Lots or parcels of Ground before described & every part thereof with their appurtenances, against them & their heirs and against all & every person or persons whatssoever to the said POWELL & SLACUM and their heirs & assigns, shall and will warrant & forever defend by these presents. In WITNESS whereof the parties to these presents have hereunto set their hands & affixed their seals the Day & Year first before written.
Signed Sealed & Delivered
In presence of
A. FAW to J.G., J. McKENNY to J.G.
N. HERBERT to J.G. & W.B.
W. HERBERT JR to W.B.
JAS. CAMPBELL to W.B.

WM. BARTLEMAN	(seal)
JOHN GREEN	(seal)
MARY GREEN	(seal)

    MR. WILLIAM BARTLEMAN Trustee for my benefit in a certain deed of Conveyance from JOHN GREEN & MARY his wife to him will please Convey the within described Lots of land to CUTHBERT POWELL & GEORGE SLACUM, trustees for the benefit of the Creditors of the said

GREEN, the said lots having been conveyed to You for my benefit in mistake. Given under my hand & Seal this first day of May 1809.
Witness
WILLIAM ALLISON   HUGH SMITH   (seal)
      DISTRICT OF COLUMBIA To Wit:
              I GEORGE DENEALE Clerk of the United States Circuit Court of the District of
(SEAL)   Columbia for the County of Alexandria do hereby certify that at a Court
              continued & held for the District & County aforesaid the 29th day of July 1809
this deed from WILLIAM BARTLEMAN & JOHN GREEN & MARY his wife to CUTHBERT POWELL & GEORGE SLACUM was proved by the oath of NOBLET HERBERT, WILLIAM HERBERT JR & JAS. CAMPBELL to be the act & deed of the said WM. BARTLEMAN & the said JOHN GREEN acknowledged the same to be his act & Deed and a Memorandum hereon endorsed from HUGH SMITH was acknowledged by the said HUGH SMITH to be his act & Deed which together with a Commission & Return for the privy examination of MARY GREEN wife of the said JOHN are ordered to be recorded & Certified to the County Court of Fairfax in the CommonWealth of Virginia. In Testimony whereof I have hereunto set my hand & affixed the public Seal of my Office this 9th day of August 1809.   G. DENEALE Cl.
      DISTRICT OF COLUMBIA To Wit:
      I WILLIAM CRANCH Chief Judge of the United States Circuit Court of the District of Columbia do hereby Certify that the above attestation of GEORGE DENEALE Clerk of the said Court for Alexandria County is in due form. Given under my hand this 9th day of August 1809.
                     W. CRANCH
      At a Court contd. & held for Fairfax County the 22nd day of August 1809 this Deed between WM. BARTLEMAN of the one part And JOHN GREEN & MARY his wife of the second part to CUTHBERT POWELL & GEORGE SLACUM and a Memorandum thereon endorsed from HUGH SMITH having been duly proved & acknowledged before the United States Circuit Court of the District of Columbia held for the County of Alexandria and admitted to record and certified by GEORGE DENEALE Clerk of the said Court under the Seal of his office also by WILLIAM CRANCH Chief Judge of the said Court is on Motion of the said CUTHBERT POWELL & GEORGE SLACUM together with the Certificates thereon endorsed & the Commissions & Returns thereto annexed for taking the acknowledgment & privy examination of the said MARY, Ordered to be recorded.   Teste WM. MOSS Cl.
      DISTRICT OF COLUMBIA, COUNTY OF ALEXANDRIA:
      The United States of America to ABRAHAM FAW, JOHN McKINNEY and GEORGE GILPIN Gentlemen Justices of the said County of Alexandria Greeting: Whereas JOHN GREEN and MARY his wife by their certain indenture of Bargain & Sale bearing date the second day of May 1809 have sold & conveyed unto CUTHBERT POWELL & GEORGE SLACUM the fee simple estate of certain Lots of land in the County of Alexandria, being part of a larger tract called PEARSONS tract with the appurtenances situate, lying & being in the County aforesaid and whereas the said MARY cannot conveniently travel to our United States Circuit Court of the District of Columbia for the County of Alexandria to make acknowledgment of the said Conveyance therefore we do give unto you or any two or more of you power to receive the acknowledgment which the said MARY shall be willing to make before You of the Conveyance aforesaid contained in the said Indenture which is hereunto annexed. And we do therefore desire You or any two or more of You personally to go to the said MARY and receive her acknowledgment of the same and examine her privily and apart from the said JOHN GREEN her husband whither she doth the same freely & voluntarily without his persuasions or threats and whither she be willing the said indenture together with this Commission shall be recorded in our said Court & when You have received her acknowledgment & examined her as aforesaid that You distinctly & openly certify us thereof in our said Court under Your hands & seals sending then there the said indenture & this writ. WITNESS the Hon. WILLIAM CRANCH Chief Judge of our said Court this 2nd day of May 1809.
                     G. DENEALE Cl.
      COUNTY OF ALEXANDRIA, DISTRICT OF COLUMBIA:
      In obedience to the within Commission to us directed we waited on the within named MARY wife of JOHN GREEN & examined her privily & apart from her said husband when she

acknowledged the said Deed without the threats or persuasions of her said husband and is willing that the same together with this Commission shall be Recorded. Given under our hands this 2nd May 1809.   A. FAW   (seal)
                                                        J. McKINNEY   (seal)

FAIRFAX COUNTY To Wit:

The CommonWealth of Virginia to ABRAHAM FAW, JOHN McKINNEY and GEORGE GILPIN Gentlemen of the County of Alexandria Greeting: Whereas JOHN GREEN & MARY his wife by their certain indenture of Bargain & Sale bearing date the second day of May 1809 have sold & conveyed unto CUTHBERT POWELL & GEORGE SLACUM the fee simple estate of certain Lots in the County aforesaid being part of a larger tract called PEARSONS Tract situate, lying & being in the said County of Fairfax and whereas the said MARY cannot conveniently travel to our said County Court of Fairfax to make acknowledgment of the said conveyance therefore we do give unto you or any two or more of you Power to receive the acknowledgment which the said MARY shall be willing to make before You of the Conveyance aforesaid contained in the said indenture which is hereunto annexed and we do therefore desire you or any two or more of You personally to go to the said MARY & receive her acknowledgment of the same and examine her privily & apart from the said JOHN GREEN her husband whither she doth the same freely & Voluntarily without his Persuasions or threats and whither she be willing the said Indenture together with this Commission shall be recorded in our said Court. And when You have received her acknowledgment & examined her as aforesaid that You distinctly & openly Certify us thereof in our said Court under Your hands & seals sending then there the said indenture & this Writ. WITNESS WILLIAM MOSS Clerk of our said Court at the CourtHouse of the County aforesaid this 2nd day of May 1809 and in the 33rd Year of the CommonWealth.
                                        WM. MOSS Cl.

COUNTY OF ALEXANDRIA DISTRICT OF COLUMBIA To Wit:

In Obedience to the Within Commission to us directed we waited on the within named MARY wife of the within named JOHN GREEN and examined her privily & apart from her said husband when she acknowledged the said Deed and is willing that it shall be together with this Commission recorded without the threats or persuasions of her said husband. Given under our hand this 2nd day of May 1809.   A. FAW   (seal)
                                                        J. McKINNEY   (seal)

Pages 284-286. THIS INDENTURE made this first day of July in the Year of our Lord one thousand eight hundred and nine between CUTHBERT POWELL and GEORGE SLACUM of the Town & County of Alexandria in the Dictrict of Columbia Trustees for the Creditors of JOHN GREEN of the one part and TIMOTHY MOUNTFORD JR of the Town, County & District aforesaid of the other part. Whereas JOHN GREEN, by deed bearing date the twenty sixth day of June eighteen hundred & five conveyed in Trust for the benefit of his creditors the herein after described Premises for the purposes therein mentioned as by a reference to the said deed now of record in the Clerks office of Alexandria County and whereas in execution of the said Trust the said POWELL & SLACUM did expose to sale at Public auction the said Property at which said Sale the said TIMOTHY MOUNTFORD JR became the purchaser thereof. Now this Indenture WITNESSETH that the said POWELL & SLACUM for and in consideration of the sum of two hundred & ninety seven Dollars & seventy Cents to them in hand paid by the said T. MOUNTFORD JR before the sealing & delivery of these presents the receipt whereof the said POWELL & SLACUM do hereby acknowledge have Given, Granted, bargained and sold & by these presents do Give & Grant, bargain & sell two Lotts of Land situate in the County aforesaid being part of a larger tract of Land known by the name of PEARSONS Tract given by the said PEARSON the patentee to his daughter & WILLIAM H. TERRETT who intermarried with her and by the said WILLIAM H. TERRETT & MARGARETT his wife conveyed to HUGH WEST, by him devised to JOHN WEST and by him devised to his two Sons JOHN & THOMAS WEST & by them conveyed to JOHN GREEN which said Lots are bounded as followeth to wit: beginning Lots No. 1, 2 at a Stone standing at the South East corner of Lot No. 3 in the Western boundary of HOWSONS patent, running thence South 20° East with the line of said patent reversed forty eight Poles to a Stone, thence South 70° West thirty eight poles, thence North 20° West forty eight poles to the Corner of Lot No. 3, thence North 70° East thirty eight poles with the line of

Lot No. 3 to the beginning containing eleven acres sixty four poles; a part of the above described Lots lies in the County of Fairfax and State of Virginia. Lot No. 4 beginning at a stake standing in or near to a dogwood & Hickory in the line of the patent of PEARSON & the Western boundary of HOWSONS patent and now called ALEXANDERS back line, marked on the Plat at "A," running thence South 18° West sixty poles to a stake at "B," thence South 20° East ten poles twenty links to the corner of lot No. 3, thence South 70° East with the line of lot No. 3 thirty eight poles to the Western boundary of HOWSON'S Patent, thence North 20° West with the line of HOWSONS patent fifty seven poles twenty links to the beginning at "A," containing eight acres twenty three poles as described in the plat of a survey made by GEORGE GILPIN Esqr. of the above described premises. To have and To Hold the premises aforesaid unto the said TIMOTHY MOUNTFORD JR his heirs & assigns to the only proper use & behoof of the said TIMOTHY MOUNTFORD JR his heirs & assigns forever and the said CUTHBERT POWELL & GEORGE SLACUM, for themselves and their heirs, the said two Lots or parcels of ground & every part thereof with their appurtenances, against them & their Heirs and against all & every person or persons claiming by, from, through or under them, either or any of them, to the said TIMOTHY MOUNTFORD JR his heirs & assigns shall & will warrant & forever defend by these presents. In WITNESS whereof the parties to these presents have hereunto set their hands & affixed their Seals the day & Year first before written.
Signed, Sealed & Delivered
in Presence of   CUTHBERT POWELL (seal)
N. HERBERT   GEORGE SLACUM   (seal)
WM. HERBERT JR
GEO. YOUNGS
        DISTRICT OF COLUMBIA to wit:
                I GEORGE DENEALE Clerk of the United States Circuit Court of the District of
(SEAL)   Columbia for the County of Alexandria do hereby Certify that at a Court
                contd. & held the 29th day of July 1809 this Deed from CUTHBERT POWELL and
GEORGE SLACUM to TIMOTHY MOUNTFORD JR was proved by the oath of NOBLET HERBERT, WILLIAM HERBERT JR and GEORGE YOUNGS to be the act and deed of the said CUTHBERT POWELL & GEORGE SLACUM and ordered to be recorded & Certified to the County Court of Fairfax in the CommonWealth of Virginia. In Testimony whereof I have hereunto set my hand & affixed the public Seal of my office on this 9th day of August 1809.
                                        G. DENEALE Cl.
        DISTRICT OF COLUMBIA to wit:
                I WILLIAM CRANCH Chief Judge of the United States Circuit Court of the District of Columbia, do hereby certify that the above attestation of GEORGE DENEALE Clerk of the said Court forAlexandria County is in due form. Given under my hand this 9th day of August 1809.
                                        W. CRANCH
        At a Court contd. & held for Fairfax County the 22nd day of August 1809 this Deed from CUTHBERT POWELL & GEORGE SLACUM to TIMOTHY MOUNTFORD JR having been duly proved before the United States Circuit Court of the District of Columbia held for the County of Alexandria and Certified by GEORGE DENEALE clerk of said Court under the Seal of his Office, also by WILLIAM CRANCH Chief Judge of the said Court, is on Motion of the said TIMOTHY MOUNTFORD together with the certificates thereon endorsed Ordered to be recorded.
                                        Teste WM. MOSS Cl.

Pages 286-291. THIS INDENTURE made this ninth day of August in the year of our Lord one thousand eight hundred & Nine between JOHN GREEN and MARY his wife of the Town & County of Alexandria in the District of Columbia of the one part and TIMOTHY MOUNTFORD JR of the Town, County & District aforesaid of the other part. Whereas JOHN and THOMAS WEST, devisees of JOHN WEST deceased conveyed to the said JOHN GREEN by their indenture bearing date the seventeenth day of December eighteen hundred & four a parcel of land situate in the Town & County aforesaid being part of a tract of land known by the name of PEARSONS patent. Now this Indenture WITNESSETH that the said JOHN GREEN in consideration of the sum of four hundred Dollars to him in hand paid by TIMOTHY MOUNTFORD JR before the Sealing & delivery of these presents the receipt whereof is acknowledged by the said GREEN, the said

JOHN GREEN & MARY his wife Have Given, Granted, bargained & Sold and by these presents do Give, Grant, Bargain & sell unto the said TIMOTHY MOUNTFORD JR his heirs and assigns forever a part of that tract of land conveyed to the said JOHN GREEN by the said JOHN and THOMAS WEST, the rest having been conveyed to CUTHBERT POWELL and GEORGE SLACUM by the said GREEN & MARY his wife in trust for the benefit of his Creditors and by them conveyed to TIMOTHY MOUNTFORD JR as will appear, the several Deeds now of record in the Clerks office of Alexandria County bounded as follows to wit: beginning at a Stake standing in the line of HOWSON patent at the north east corner of Lot No. 3, running thence South twenty Degrees East with the Western boundary of HOWSONS patent reversed thirty four poles five links, thence South seventy degrees West thirty eight poles, thence North twenty degrees, West thirty four poles five links to the Corner of Lot No. 4, thence North seventy Degrees East to the beginning containing eight acres and twelve poles, as by a reference to a plat annexed to the Deed from CUTHBERT POWELL & GEORGE SLACUM to TIMOTHY MOUNTFORD JR bearing date the [left blank] day of [left blank] eighteen hundred & Nine and of record in the Clerks of Alexandria County will appear pursuant to a survey made by GEORGE GILPIN Esqr. together with all houses & buildings and all and every appurtenances to the same belonging or in anywise appertaining and the reversion & reversions, Remainder and Remainders, Rents, issues and profits thereof & every part & parcel thereof. To have and To hold the said piece or parcel of ground unto the said TIMOTHY MOUNTFORD JR his heirs and assigns to the only proper use and behoof of the said TIMOTHY MOUNTFORD JR his heirs and assigns forever. And the said JOHN GREEN & MARY his wife do for themselves & their heirs covenant & agree to and with the said TIMOTHY MOUNTFORD JR that they are now seized in their own right of a good, sure & perfect title in fee simple and that they will make any further conveyance that may be deemed neecessary in Law for the more perfect assurance of the title of the said TIMOTHY MOUNTFORD JR by the Counsil of the said TIMOTHY MOUNTFORD JR And the said JOHN GREEN & MARY his wife, for themselves & their heirs, the said piece or parcel of ground to the sd. TIMOTHY MOUNTFORD JR and his heirs, shall & will warrant against the claim & demand of the said JOHN GREEN & MARY his wife & of all and every person and persons whatsoever by these presents. In WITNESS whereof the parties to these presents have hereunto set their hands and affixed their Seals the day & Year first before written.
Signed, Sealed & Delivered
in presence of   JOHN GREEN   (seal)
N. HERBERT   MARY her + mark GREEN (seal)
CUTHBERT POWELL
A. FAW
          Received Alexandria August 9th 1809 of TIMOTHY MOUNTFORD JR four hundred dollars the consideration within mentioned.
Witness   JOHN GREEN
J. D. SIMMS
          DISTRICT OF COLUMBIA To Wit:
                    I GEORGE DENEALE Clerk of the United States Circuit Court of the District of
(SEAL)   Columbia for the County of Alexandria do hereby Certify that at a Court
                    contd. & held the 10th day of August 1809 JOHN GREEN acknowledged this Deed
and receipt to TIMOTHY MOUNTFORD to be his act and Deed which together with a Commission & return for the privy examination of MARY GREEN wife of the said JOHN are ordered to be recorded & certified to the County Court of Fairfax in the CommonWealth of Virginia. In Testimony whereof I have hereunto set my hand & affixed the public Seal of my office on this 11th day of August 1809.   G. DENEALE Cl.
          DISTRICT OF COLUMBIA To Wit:
                    I WILLIAM CRANCH Chief Judge of the United States Circuit Court of the District of Columbia do hereby certify that the above attestation of GEORGE DENEALE Clerk of the said Court for Alexandria County is in due form. Given under my hand this 11th day of August 1809.   W. CRANCH
          At a Court contd. & held for Fairfax County the 22nd day of August 1809 this Deed from JOHN GREEN & MARY his wife to TIMOTHY MOUNTFORD JR having been duly acknowledged before the United States Circuit Court of the District of Columbia held for the County of

Alexandria & admitted to Record & Certified by GEORGE DENEALE Clerk of the said Court under the Seal of his office, also by WILLIAM CRANCH Chief Judge of said Court, is on motion of the said TIMOTHY MOUNTFORD JR together with the Certificates thereon endorsed and the Commissions & returns thereto annexed for taking the acknowledgment and privy examination of the said MARY, Ordered to be Recorded.

Teste WM. MOSS Cl.

DISTRICT OF COLUMBIA, COUNTY OF ALEXANDRIA:

The United States of America To CUTHBERT POWELL, A. FAW & JOHN McKINNEY, Gentleman justices of the said County of Alexandria Greeting: Whereas JOHN GREEN & MARY his wife by their certain indenture of Bargain & sale bearing date the ninth day of August 1809 have sold & Conveyed unto TIMOTHY MOUNTFORD JR the fee simple estate of a certain tract of Land situate in the Town & County of Alexandria in the District of Columbia, being part of the tract conveyed to the said GREEN by JOHN and THOMAS WEST as devisees of JOHN WEST their father with the appurtenances situate, lying & being in the said County of Alexandria and whereas the said MARY cannot conveniently travel to our United States Circuit Court of the District of Columbia for the County of Alexandria to make acknowledgment of the said conveyance therefore we do give unto you or any two or more of you power to receive the acknowledgment which the said MARY shall be willing to make before you, of the conveyance aforesaid contained in the said indenture which is hereunto annexed. And we do therefore desire You or any two or more of you personally to go to the said MARY and Receive her acknowledgment of the same and examine her privily & apart from the said JOHN GREEN her husband whither she doth the same freely & voluntarily without his persuasions or threats and whither she be willing the said Indenture together with this Commission shall be recorded in our said Court. And when You have received her acknowledgment & examined her as aforesaid that You distinctly & openly certify us thereof in our said Court under your hands & seals sending then there the said indenture & this Writ. WITNESS the Hon WILLIAM CRANCH Chief Judge of our said Court, this Ninth day of August 1809.

G. DENEALE Cl.

DISTRICT OF COLUMBIA, COUNTY OF ALEXANDRIA To Wit:

In obedience to the within Commission to us directed we the undersigned justices of the peace for the County aforesaid certify that we personally went to the said MARY GREEN and examined her privily & apart from her said husband JOHN GREEN, that she declared she executed & signed the annexed deed freely & voluntarily without the persuasion or threats of her said husband and was willing that the same together with this Commission might be recorded as her act & deed. Given under our hands & Seals this ninth day of August 1809.

A. FAW   (seal)
CUTHBERT POWELL (seal)

FAIRFAX COUNTY To Wit:

The CommonWealth of Virginia to A. FAW, C. POWELL & JOHN McKINNEY Gentlemen Justices of the County of Alexandria Greeting: Whereas JOHN GREEN & MARY his wife by their certain indenture of bargain & Sale bearing date the Ninth day of August 1809 have sold and conveyed unto TIMOTHY MOUNTFORD JR the fee simple estate of a certain tract of Land in the County of Alexandria & Fairfax, being part of a tract called & known by the name of PEARSONS tract, with the appurtenances situate, lying & being in the said County of Fairfax and whereas the said MARY cannot conveniently travel to our said county Court of Fairfax to make acknowledgment of the said conveyance therefore we do give unto you or any two or more of you power to receive the acknowledgment which the said MARY shall be willing to make before You of the conveyance aforesaid contained in the said indenture which is hereunto annexed and we do therefore desire You or any two or more of you personally to go to the said MARY and receive her acknowledgment of the same and examine her privily and apart from the said JOHN GREEN her husband whether she doth the same freely and voluntary without his persuasions or threats and whither she be willing the said indenture together with this Commission shall be recorded in our said Court and when you have received her acknowledgment and examined her as aforesaid that You distinctly and openly certify us thereof in our said Court under your hands and seals sending then there the said indenture & this Writ.

WITNESS WILLIAM MOSS Clerk of our said Court at the Courthouse of the County aforesd this 11th day of August 1809 and in the 34th Year of the CommonWealth.
                                                            WM. MOSS Cl.
        DISTRICT OF COLUMBIA, COUNTY OF ALEXANDRIA:
        In obedience to the within Commission to us directed we the undersigned justices of the County aforesaid certify that we personally went to the said MARY GREEN and examined her privily and a part from her said husband JOHN GREEN, that she declared she executed & signed the annexed deed freely & Voluntarily without the persuasion or threats of her said husband and was willing that the same together with this commission might be recorded as her act and Deed. Given under our hands & Seals this eleventh day of August 1809.
                                            CUTHBERT POWELL   (seal)
                                            A. FAW   (seal)
        DISTRICT OF COLUMBIA To Wit:
                I GEORGE DENEALE Clerk of the United States Circuit Court of the District of
(SEAL)   Columbia for the County of Alexandria do hereby Certify that CUTHBERT
                POWELL & ABRAHAM FAW Gentlemen, before whom the above acknowledgment appears to have been made was at the time of making the same and now are two justices of the peace in & for the sd. County of Alexandria duly commissioned & sworn and that to all certificates & other acts by them so given due faith & credit is and ought to be followed. In Testimony whereof I have hereunto set my hand & affixed the public Seal of my office on this 11th day of August 1809.   G. DENEALE Cl.
        DISTRICT OF COLUMBIA To Wit:
        I WILLIAM CRANCH Chief Judge of the United States Circuit Court of the District of Columbia do hereby Certify that the above attestation of GEORGE DENEALE Clerk of the said Court for Alexandria County is in due form. Given under my hand this 11th day of August 1809.   W. CRANCH

Pages 291-293. THIS INDENTURE made this twenty sixth day of May in the Year one thousand eight hundred & nine between ROBERT J. TAYLOR of Alexandria in the District of Columbia Executor of the last will & testament of CHRISTOPHER NOLAND deceased of the one part & ALEXANDER BAGGETT of the same Town of the other part. Whereas the said CHRISTOPHER NOLAND was in his lifetime seized & possessed of a lot of ground in the County of Fairfax in the CommonWealth of Virginia, being part of a Tract of Land known by the name of Stump Hill and designated in the Platt thereof by No. 27 which said lot No. 27 is bounded as follows: beginning on the North side of the Turnpike road at a stake and extending thence North six Degrees West fifty poles to a stake, thence North seventy seven Degrees West sixteen poles to a Stake, thence South six degrees East [left blank] poles to an avenue three poles wide, thence South fifty one degrees East with the line of said avenue [left blank] poles to the Turnpike road, thence North seventy seven degrees East [left blank] poles to the beginning containing four acres & one hundred & twenty two poles which said Lot was conveyed to the said CHRISTOPHER NOLAND by FRANCIS PEYTON by Deed dated the fifth day of August in the Year 1805 and recorded in the Office of the said County of Fairfax on the 22nd day of April 1806 and whereas the said CRISTOPHER NOLAND by his last will and Testament dated the 25th day of the same Month in the Year last mentioned did amongst other things direct that his Executor should make sale of all his estate, real & personal and appointed the said ROBERT J. TAYLOR Executor of his said Will by whom the same was duly proved & Administration granted to him by the Court of the County aforesaid on the 15th day of September in the Year last mentioned and the said Executor having exposed the said Lot to public sale on the day of the date hereof, due notice of the time & place having been previously given by advertizement, the same was struck off to the said ALEXANDER BAGGETT at the sum of Ninety two Dollars it being the highest bid made for it. Now this indenture WITNESSETH that the said ROBERT J. TAYLOR Executor of the said CHRISTOPHER NOLAND in execution of the said Will & in consideration of the sd. sum of Ninety two dollars to him in hand paid by the said ALEXANDER BAGGETT the receipt whereof he does hereby acknowledge, has granted, bargained & sold & does by these presents grant, bargain & sell unto him the said ALEXANDER BAGGETT the said Lot No. 27 herein before described, to hold to him his heirs & assigns to his & their only use forever and the said ROBERT J. TAYLOR, as executor of CHRISTOPHER NOLAND, does hereby covenant & agree for himself and his heirs to warrant & defend the said Lot to the said ALEXANDER BAGGETT his heirs & assigns against all claims & demands from him the said ROBERT J. TAYLOR his heirs and assigns & from all persons whatsoever claiming or to claim in any manner from or under him, as Executor of the said CHRISTOPHER NOLAND. IN TESTIMONY whereof the said ROBERT J. TAYLOR has hereto set his hand & affixed his Seal the day & Year first before written.

Sealed & delivered   R. J. TAYLOR executor   (seal)
in the presence of [No witnesses listed]   of CHRISTOPHER NOLAND

    At a Court Continued & held for Fairfax County the 22nd day of August 1809 ROBERT J. TAYLOR, executor of CHRISTOPHER NOLAND, acknowledged this deed to ALEXANDER BAGGETT to be his act & deed and ordered to be recorded.
                              Teste WM. MOSS Cl.

Page 293. WHEREAS BENJAMIN DULANY did by an instrument of writing under his hand dated the 15th day of December 1805 for the consideration therein named convey unto me a female Negroe called AGREEABLE which said Girl was purchased by me with the Money provided by GEORGE WEBSTER her father with intent that she should be emancipated and whereas no Deed of emancipation has as Yet been executed, now know all Men by these presents that I BENJAMIN BURTON of Fairfax to carry into effect the intent with which the said Negroe was Conveyed to me, Do hereby emancipate & forever set free the said Girl from all claims & right to her service which I hold under the conveyance aforesaid. Given under my hand & Seal this 23rd day of August 1809.

Witness
R. J. TAYLOR   BENJN. BURTTON   (seal)
ROBT. RATCLIFFE

    At a Court contd. & held for Fairfax County the 22nd August 1809 BENJAMIN BURTTON acknowledged this deed of manumission to female negroe AGREEEABLE to be his act & deed and ordered to be Recorded.   Teste WM. MOSS Cl.

Page 294. KNOW ALL MEN by these presents that I CHARLES J. LOVE of the County of Fairfax and CommonWealth of Virginia for and in Consideration of one Dollar to me in hand paid at or before the Sealing and delivery hereof the receipt whereof I do hereby acknowledge and for various other considerations me thereunto moving have given, Granted, bargained & sold and do hereby give, grant, bargain & Sell unto CHARLES WIGHMAN FORREST, Son of HENRY FORREST now of the County & CommonWealth aforesaid One Negroe Man named LEWIS, aged about twenty two years. To Have & to hold the said Negro LEWIS unto the said CHARLES WIGHMAN FORREST his Executors, Administrators and Assigns and to his & their only use & behoof. In Testimony whereof I have hereto set my hand & Seal this 21st day of January 1807.

Signed Sealed and delivered
in the Presence of   CH. J. LOVE   (seal)
SARAH JENKINS
THOMAS DIXON
HUMPHREY GWYNN

    At a Court Continued & held for Fairfax County the 22nd day of August 1809 CHARLES J. LOVE acknowledged this Bill of Sale of HENRY W. FORREST to be his Act and Deed and Ordered to be recorded.

Pages 295-297. THIS INDENTURE made & entered into this 1st November 1808 between CHARLES J. LOVE & FRANCES his wife of the County of Fairfax & State of Virginia of the one part And CHARLES TYLER JR of the County of Prince William and State aforesaid of the other part. WITNESSETH that the said CHARLES J. LOVE & FRANCES his wife for and in consideration of the sum of one hundred & eight Dollars lawful money of Virginia to him in hand paid by the said CHARLES TYLER JR at and before the ensealing & delivery of these presents the receipt whereof he doth hereby acknowledge HATH bargained & sold and by these presents doth bargain & sell unto the said CHARLES TYLER JR his heirs & assigns forever one half of all the woodland containing 9 Acres belonging or in anywise appertaining to Lott No. [left blank] as described and Given to JOHN NEALE decd Son of THOMAS NEALE decd for his share in the tract of land belonging to his father as aforesaid reference being had to the platt and division of said Estate now on record in the County Court of Loudoun will more fully appear. To have and to hold the said Piece parcel or Tract of Land with the tenements & hereditaments and all and Singular other the Premises herein before mentioned & Sold and every part & parcel thereof unto the said CHARLES TYLER JR his heirs & assigns forever. And the said CHARLES J. LOVE and FRANCES his wife for themselves & their heirs the aforesaid piece or parcel of land as before mentioned & described unto the said CHARLES TYLER JR his heirs & assigns forever free from the claim or claims of them the said CHARLES J. LOVE & FRANCES his wife their heirs, Exors or Admors & from the claim or claims of all and every other person or persons whatsoever shall, will and doth Warrant & forever defend by these presents. In WITNESS whereof the said CHARLES J. LOVE & FRANCES his wife hath hereunto set their hands & affixed their Seals the day & Year above Written.

Signed Sealed and acknowledged

in presence of	CH. J. LOVE (seal)
CHR. NEALE	FRANCES P. LOVE (seal)
GUSTO. H. SCOTT	
ELIZA D. SCOTT	

At a Court held for Fairfax County the 15th day of May 1809 this Deed from CHARLES J. LOVE & FRANCES his wife to CHARLES TYLER JR was proved to be the act and deed of the said CHARLES J. LOVE by the oath of CHRISTOPHER NEALE, a Witness thereto & ordered to be certified and at a Court contd. & held for Fairfax County the 22nd day of August in the Year aforesaid the same was acknowledged by the said CHARLES J. LOVE to be his act and deed which together with a Commission and return thereto annexed for taking the acknowledgment & privy examination of said FRANCES are ordered to be Recorded.

Teste WM. MOSS Cl.

FAIRFAX COUNTY To Wit:

The CommonWealth of Virginia to FRANCIS ADAMS, RICD. B. LEE & HUMPH. PEAKE, Gentleman justices of the County of Fairfax Greeting: Whereas CHARLES JONES LOVE and FRANCES P. LOVE his wife by their certain indenture of bargain & Sale bearing date the 1st day of November 1808 have sold & conveyed unto CHARLES TYLER JR the fee simple estate of nine acres of Wood land the same being one moiety of all the Wood Land belonging to Lott No. [left blank] which was assigned to JOHN NEALE decd out of the tract of his father THOMAS NEALE decd with the appurtenances situate, lying & being in the said County of Fairfax and whereas the said FRANCES P. cannot conveniently travel to our said County Court of Fairfax to make acknowledgment of the said conveyance therefore we do give unto You or any two or more of You power to receive the acknowledgment which the said FRANCES P. shall be willing to make before You of the conveyance aforesaid contained in the said indenture which is hereunto annexed and we do therefore desire You or any two or more of You personally to go to the said FRANCES P. and receive her acknowledgment of the same and examine her privily and apart from the said CHARLES JONES LOVE her husband whither she doth the same freely & voluntarily without his persuasions or threats and whither she be willing the said Indenture together with this Commission shall be recorded in our said Court. And when You have received her acknowledgment and examined her as aforesaid that You distinctly & openly Certify us thereof in our said Court under your hands & seals sending then there the said indenture & this Writ. WITNESS WILLIAM MOSS Clerk of the said Court at the Court-House of the County aforesaid this 7th day of January 1809 and in the 33rd Year of the CommonWealth.   WM. MOSS Cl.

FAIRFAX:

In obedience to the within Commission we the undersigned justices of the peace for this County waited on the within named FRANCES P. LOVE and examined her privily & apart from her husband touching the Conveyance within mentioned and do find that she hath done the same freely & of own accord without being persuaded or threatened thereto by her sd.

husband and that she is willing the deed together with this Commission shall be recorded in the County Court of Fairfax. Given under our hands & seals the 7th January 1809.

HUMPH. PEAKE   (seal)
FRANCIS ADAMS

Pages 297-300. THIS INDENTURE made the first day of April in the Year one thousand eight hundred & Eight between NEWMAN BECKWITH & JUDITH his wife of the County of Fairfax and State of Virginia of the one part and MARY COFFER of County & State aforesaid of the other part. WITNESSETH that the said NEWMAN BECKWITH and JUDITH his wife for and in consideration of the sum of five hundred Dollars to them in hand paid at or before the Sealing & delivery of these presents the receipt of which is hereby acknowledged and thereof they do release the said MARY COFFER her heirs, Executors, Administrators & assigns forever they the said NEWMAN BECKWITH & JUDITH his wife have granted, bargained & sold, aliened, enfeoffed and confirmed and by these presents do Grant, bargain & sell, alien, enfeoff and confirm unto the said MARY COFFER her heirs & assigns forever a certain messuage, tenement, tract or parcel of land lying & being in the County of Fairfax containing eighty five acres and twenty five poles it being part of a tract of Land known by the Name of the Wolf Run tract which descended to PEGGY BRONAUGH by the death of her Father MARMADUKE BECKWITH intestate which was allotted to the said PEGGY by Commissioners appointed by the Court of Fairfax County reference being had to their report will more fully appear & conveyed by JOHN BRONAUGH & PEGGY his wife to said NEWMAN BECKWITH by Deed bearing date the 20th day of February eighteen hundred & two as by reference to said Deed will more at large appear and is bounded as follows: beginning at red [oak] "B" a pile of stones corner to Lotts No. 5 and 6, thence with a line of lott No. 5 South 89° 45' east 89 poles to figure 4, three black oaks in or near a line of the tract., thence with said line North 56° East 44 1/2 poles to figure 7 two red oaks, thence North 25° 15' West 129 1/2 poles to figure 6, a pile of Stones in or near a line of the tract, thence with said line South 73° 45' West 77 poles to figure 5 corner to Lott No. 6, thence with a line of said Lott South 1° 30' East 120 poles to the beginning containing eighty five acres & twenty five poles together with all and Singular the Houses, buildings, trees, Woods, under Woods, Ways & hereditaments whatsoever to the said land and premises hereby bargained & sold, belonging or in anywise appertaining and the Reversion & reversions, Remainder & remainders, rents, Issues & profits thereof. To have and To hold the said Messuage, tenement, tract or parcel of land and all and Singular the other premises hereby bargained & Sold with their and every of their appurtenances unto the said MARY COFFER her heirs & assigns forever to the only proper use & behoof of the said MARY COFFER her heirs & assigns forever and the said NEWMAN BECKWITH & JUDITH his wife now at the time of sealing and delivering these presents do covenant, Promise & agree to and with the said MARY COFFER her heirs & assigns forever that they have good, right, lawful and absolute authority to grant & convey the said land and premises hereby bargained & sold with their and every of their appurtenances in manner & for aforesaid and that the same is & so forever shall be free and clear of all former & other gifts, grants, bargains & Sales, Dower right & title of Dower or encumbrance whatever committed or suffered by said NEWMAN BECKWITH and JUDITH his wife or any other person or persons for them. And lastly that they the said NEWMAN BECKWITH & JUDITH his wife for themselves their heirs, Executors & Administrators the aforesaid land and Premises with their & every of their appurtenances to the said MARY COFFER her heirs & assigns forever shall and will warrant and forever defend against the claim of all and every person & persons Whatsoever. In WITNESS whereof the said NEWMAN BECKWITH & JUDITH his wife have hereunto set their hands & Seals the day & Year first written.

Signed Sealed and delivered
in Presence of   NEWMAN BECKWITH   (seal)
TOWNSHEND WAUGH   JUDITH BECKWITH   (seal)
JAMES TURLEY
SAMPSON TURLEY

       At a Court held for Fairfax County the 21st day of November 1808 this Deed from NEWMAN BECKWITH & JUDITH his wife to MARY COFFER was proved to be the act and deed of the said NEWMAN BECKWITH by the oath of TOWNSHEND WAUGH a witness thereto and ordered to be Certified. And at a Court held for the said County the 16th day of January 1809 the same was further proved by the oath of JAMES TURLEY another witness thereto and ordered to be Certified. And at a Court contd. & held for the said County the 22nd day of August 1809 the same was further proved by the oath of SAMPSON TURLEY another witness thereto & ordered to be recorded.   Teste WM. MOSS Cl.

FAIRFAX COUNTY To Wit:

The CommonWealth of Virginia to WILLIAM LANE, HUMPHREY PEAKE & FRANCIS ADAMS Gentlemen justices of the County of Fairfax Greeting: Whereas NEWMAN BECKWITH & JUDITH his wife by their certain indenture of bargain & sale bearing date the first day of April 1808 have sold & conveyed unto MARY COFFER the fee simple estate of a certain tract or parcel of land situate, lying & being on Wolf Run in the County of Fairfax, it being that part of the said tract which was allotted to PEGGY BRONAUGH in the division of her fathers estate & containing Eighty five acres with the appurtenances situate, lying and being in the said County of Fairfax. And whereas the said JUDITH cannot conveniently travel to our said County Court of Fairfax to make acknowledgment of the said conveyance therefore we do give unto you or any two or more of you power to receive the acknowledgment which the said JUDITH shall be willing to make before [you] of the conveyance aforesaid contained in the said indenture which is hereunto annexed. And we do therefore desire You or any two or more of You personally to go to the said JUDITH and receive her acknowledgment of the same and examine her privily and apart from the said NEWMAN her husband whither she doth the same freely & voluntarily without his persuasions or threats and whither she be willing the said indenture together with this Commission shall be recorded in our said Court. And when You have received her acknowledgment & examined her as aforesd that You distinctly & openly certify us thereof in our said Court under your hand & seals sending then there the said indenture and this Writ. WITNESS WILLIAM MOSS Clerk of the said Court at the Courthouse of the County aforesd this first day of April 1808 and in the 32nd Year of the CommonWealth.
WM. MOSS Cl.

FAIRFAX COUNTY:

In obedience to the within Commission, we the subscribed waited on the within named JUDITH BECKWITH & having examined her privily & apart from her husband touching the conveyance of the tract of land within named we find that she hath done the same freely & voluntarily without the persuasions or threats of her sd. husband & that she is willing that the Deed for the same together with this Commission shall be recorded in the County Court of Fairfax. Given under our hands & seals this 1st April 1808.
FRANCIS ADAMS   (seal)
HUMPH. PEAKE   (seal)

Pages 300-303. THIS INDENTURE made this fourth day of March in the Year one thousand eight hundred and Nine between RICHARD A. HUNTER and MARY ANN GOLDSMITH his wife of Alexandria in the District of Columbia of the first part and DENNIS MacCARTY JOHNSTON of the same place of the second part. WITNESSETH that the said RICHARD A. HUNTER & MARY ANN his wife, in consideration of the sum of five hundred dollars to him the said RICHARD in hand paid by the said DENNIS MacCARTY JOHNSTON the receipt of which is hereby acknowledged have Granted, Bargained & sold, aliened, released & confirmed and do by these presents Grant, bargain & sell, alien, release & confirm unto him the said DENNIS MacCARTY JOHNSTON all that parcel of land situate in the County of Fairfax and CommonWealth of Virginia adjoining the lands of MAJOR WILLIAM JOHNSTON contained within the following boundaries: beginning at two white oaks corner to LEWIS' patent & also a corner on the dividing line between the said MAJOR JOHNSTON and the lands belonging to the Estate of WILLIAM HUNTER deceased of which the land hereby conveyed is a part, thence North thirty two degrees thirty five minutes West two hundred & fifty nine poles to a Stone in the line of MILE ASHFORDS patent, thence along a line of said patent North fifty one degrees ten minutes East sixty six poles twenty links to a Stake on a hill side [left blank] from ASHFORDS corner red oak, thence running across the land South thirty two degrees thirty five minutes East two hundred & twenty nine poles to a stake and several marked bushes in the cut line, thence along said line

South twenty seven degrees West 75 poles five links to the beginning containing one hundred acres being part of a larger tract of land granted to JOHN LEWIS by patent from the Proprietors Office dated the [left blank] day of March 1730 One half of which tract by divers minor conveyances became vested in WILLIAM HUNTER late of Alexandria deceased the father of the said RICHARD and on a Division of his estate amongst his children by December of the Circuit Court of the District of Columbia held at Alexandria at November term last past, the land conveyed was amongst other things allotted to the said RICHARD and the said suit in which the said Decemberee was made was instituted in the name of CATHARINE A. BAILEY against the Heirs of the said WILLIAM HUNTER. To Hold all & Singular the premises hereby granted to him the said DENNIS McCARTY JOHNSTON his heirs & assigns to his & their only proper use forever. And the said RICHARD A. HUNTER for himself his heirs, executors & Administrators does hereby covenant with the said DENNIS McCARTY JOHNSTON his heirs & assigns in manner following that is to say, that he the said RICHARD is at the time of sealing this indenture seized in fee simple in his own right of a good & sufficient estate in the premises conveyed free from any mortgage, condition, limitation, or encumbrance what- soever & that he and his heirs will at all times hereafter on request execute & deliver all further assurances & conveyances which may be necessary, More fully and compleatly to transfer the Premises before described to the said DENNIS MacCARTY JOHNSTON his heirs & assigns. And Lastly that he the said RICHARD and his heirs all And Singular the premises conveyed will forever warrant and Defend to the said DENNIS MacCARTY JOHNSTON his heirs and assigns against the claims of all persons whatever. In Testimony of which the said RICHARD A. HUNTER And MARY ANN his wife have hereto set their hands & seals the day & Year first before written.

Sealed & delivered   RICD A. HUNTER   (seal)
in the presence of [No witnesses listed]   MARY ANN G. HUNTER   (seal)
        CORPORATION OF ALEXANDRIA:

        This day Personally appeared RICHARD ARRELL HUNTER before me CUTHBERT POWELL Mayor of the Corporation aforesaid of which the said RICHARD is an inhabitant and acknowledged the foregoing Deed of bargain & Sale to DENNIS MacCARTY JOHNSTON & that he has sealed & delivered the same as his act and Deed.
        In Testimony of which I have hereto set my hand & affixed my
(SEAL)   Seal of Office this 4th day of March 1809.
                        CUTHBERT POWELL
                        MAYOR

        At a Court contd. & held for Fairfax County the 22nd day of August 1809 this Deed from RICHARD A. HUNTER & MARY ANN GOLDSMITH his wife to DENNIS MacCARTY JOHNSTON having been duly acknowledged before CUTHBERT POWELL Mayor of the corporation of Alexandria & certified by him under the Seal of his Office is on motion of the said DENNIS McCARTY JOHNSTON together with a certificate thereon endorsed & a commission & return hereto annexed for taking the acknowledgment & privy examination of the said MARY ANN GOLDSMITH are Ordered to be recorded.   Teste WM. MOSS Cl.
        FAIRFAX COUNTY To Wit:

        The CommonWealth of Virginia to JOSEPH DEAN & RICHD. LIBBY Gentlemen justices of the County of Alexandria in the District of Columbia Greeting: Whereas RICHD. A. HUNTER & MARY ANN GOLDSMITH his wife by their certain indenture of bargain & sale bearing date the fourth day of March 1809 have sold & conveyed unto DENNIS MacCARTY JOHNSTON the fee simple estate of one hundred acres of Land part of a larger tract granted to JOHN LEWIS by patent dated the [left blank] day of March 1730 with the appurtenances situate, lying & being in the said County of Fairfax adjoining the lands of MAJOR WILLIAM JOHNSTON and whereas the said MARY ANN cannot conveniently travel to our said county Court of Fairfax to make acknowledgment of the said conveyances therefore we do give unto you or any two or more of you power to receive the acknowledgment which the said MARY ANN shall be willing to make before You of the conveyance aforesaid contained in the said indenture which is hereunto annexed and we do therefore desire You or any two or more of You personally to go to the said MARY ANN & receive her acknowledgment of the same & examine her privily & apart from the said RICHD. A. HUNTER her husband whither she doth the same freely & voluntarily without his persuasions or threats and whither she be willing the said indenture together with this Commission shall be recorded in our said Court. And when You have received her acknowledgment & examined her as aforesaid that You distinctly and openly certify us thereof in our said court, under your hands & seals sending then there the said indenture & this Writ WITNESS WILLIAM MOSS Clerk of the said Court at the Court House of the County aforesaid the tenth day of June and in the 33rd Year of the CommonWealth.

WM. MOSS Cl.

DISTRICT OF COLUMBIA, County of Alexandria:

To the Worshipful Justices of Court of the County of Fairfax the subscribers, justices of the peace of the County of Alexandria do respectfully certify that under the authority of the within Commission they have examined the said MARY ANN GOLDSMITH therein mentioned, privily & apart from her said husband RICHARD A. HUNTER, respecting her execution of the indenture hereto annexed and on the commission described which we shewed & explained to her; on examination she acknowledged that she had willingly signed & Sealed the same & consented to its being duly recorded with the Commission & return, all which is Certified under our hands & Seals this 15th day of June 1809.

JOSEPH DEAN   (seal)
RICHD. LIBBY   (seal)

Pages 303 & 304. THIS INDENTURE made the 19th day of August in the Year one thousand eight hundred & nine between DODDRIDGE PITT CHICHESTER & FANNY his wife of the County of Fairfax & State of Virginia of the one part and BENEDICT JONES of the County & State aforesaid of the other part. WITNESSETH that the said DODDRIDGE PITT CHICHESTER & FANNY his wife for and in consideration of the sum of one dollar current money to them in hand paid by the said BENEDICT JONES at or before the ensealing & delivery of these presents, (the receipt whereof is hereby acknowledged) have bargained & sold and by these presents do and each of them doth bargain & sell unto the said BENEDICT JONES his heirs & assigns a certain tract or parcel of land lying & being in the County aforesaid & bounded as follows to wit: beginning at a black oak standing in the Pohick road & in the line of Division between ALEXANDER HENDERSON & SAMUEL BAILEY, now CHICHESTERS, JONES & others, thence along said line North 40° East 123 poles to two hiccory saplings in the line of MERCERS patent, thence along said line South 17° 30' East 114 poles to several marked saplings near the edge of an old field, thence North 86° 30' West 44 1/2 poles to a white oak on the N.E. side of the Pohick road where an old path enters said Road, thence along the said road with the several courses thereof to the beginning containing thirty six acres Ninety poles together with all & Singular the appurtenances to the same belonging or in anywise appertaining and the reversion & reversions, remainder & remainders, Yearly and other rents, Issues & profits thereof and of every part and parcel thereof. To have and To hold the said tract or parcel of Land with the tenements, hereditaments & all & singular other the premises herein before mentioned or intended to be bargained & sold and every part & parcel thereof with every of their rights, members & appurtenances to the said BENEDICT JONES his heirs & assigns forever to & for the only proper use & behoof of him the said BENEDICT JONES his heirs & assigns forever and the said DODDRIDGE PITT CHICHESTER and FANNY his wife for themselves & their heirs, the said tract or parcel of land with all and Singular the premises & appurtenances before mentioned unto the said BENEDICT JONES, his heirs assigns, free from the claim or claims of them the said DODDRIDGE PITT CHICHESTER and FANNY his wife, or either of them, their or either of their heirs and all and every person or persons or whatsoever shall, will & do warrant & forever defend by their presents. In WITNESS hereof the said DODDRIDGE PITT CHICHESTER and FANNY his wife have hereunto set their hands & seals the day & Year first above written.

Signed Sealed & delivered
in the presence of   DODDRIDGE P. CHICHESTER (seal)
HENRY NOBEL JONES, JUDSON JONES   FANNY CHICHESTER   (seal)
EDWARD his X mark STONE

Received of BENEDICT JONES the sum of one Dollar in full for the consideration within mentioned. Witness my hand this 19 day of August 1809.

D. P. CHICHESTER

At a Court held for Fairfax County the 18th day of September 1809 this deed from DODDRIDGE P. CHICHESTER and FANNY his wife to BENEDICT JONES was proved by the oaths of HENRY N. JONES, JUDSON JONES & EDWARD STONE which together with a receipt thereon endorsed are Ordered to be Recorded.   Teste WM. MOSS Cl.

Pages 305 & 306. THIS INDENTURE made on the 19th day of August in the Year of our Lord one thousand eight hundred & nine between BENEDICT JONES of the County of Fairfax and State of Virginia of the one part and DODDRIDGE PITT CHICHESTER of the County & State aforesaid of the other part. WITNESSETH that the said BENEDICT JONES for and in consideration of the sum of twenty one Dollars sixty six cents current money of the United States to him in hand paid by the said DODDRIDGE PITT CHICHESTER at or before the ensealing & delivery of these presents (the receipt whereof is hereby acknowledged) have bargained & sold and by these presents doth bargain & sell unto the said DODDRIGE PITT CHICHESTER his heirs and assigns a certain lot or parcel of land lying & being in the county aforesaid containing four acres fifty three poles and bounded as follows to wit: beginning at a black oak standing in the Pohick road and in the line of division between ALEXANDER HENDERSON and SAMUEL BAILEY now CHICHESTERS, JONES & others, thence along said line South 40° West 47 poles to near a small Gum sapling on the east of a drain in the line of BAILEYS sale to JONES, thence with sd. line North 14° West 34 poles to the said Pohick Road, thence along said road North 80° East 26 1/2 poles South 81° 30' East 12 poles to the beginning together with all and singular the appurtenances to the same belonging or in anywise appertaining and the reversion & reversions, remainder & remainders, Yearly & other rents, issues & profits thereof and of every part and parcel thereof to Have & to hold the said lot or parcel of land with the tenements, hereditaments & all & singular other the premises herein before mentioned or intended to be bargained & sold and every part & parcel thereof with every of their rights, numbers & appurtenances unto the said DODDRIDGE PITT CHICHESTER his heirs & assigns forever to and for the only proper use and behoof of him the said DODDRIDGE PITT CHICHESTER his heirs & assigns forever and the said BENEDICT JONES for himself his heirs, the said Lott or parcel of land with all and singular the Premises and appurtenances before mentioned unto the said DODDRIDGE PITT CHICHESTER his heirs & assigns free from the claim or claims of him the said BENEDICT JONES or his heirs and of all and every person or persons whatsoever shall, will and do warrant & forever defend by their presents. In WITNESS whereof the said BENEDICT JONES hath hereunto set his hand & seal this day & Year first above written.
Signed Sealed & delivered
in the presence of   BENEDICK JONES   (seal)
HENRY NOBLE JONES
JUDSON JONES, EDWARD his X mark STONE
        Received of DODDRIDGE PITT CHICHESTER the sum of twenty one dollars sixty six Cents in full the consideration within mentioned. Witness my hand this 19th day of August 1809.
Teste   BENEDICK JONES
        At a Court held for Fairfax County the 18th day of September 1809 this Deed from BENEDICK JONES to DODDRIDGE PITT CHICHESTER was acknowledged by the said BENEDICT JONES to be his act and deed and ordered to be recorded
                           Teste WM. MOSS Cl.

Pages 306 & 307. THIS INDENTURE made the twenty fifth of February in the Year of our Lord one thousand eight hundred & Nine between JENNINGS BECKWITH of the County of Fairfax & State of Virginia of the one part and EDWARD FORD of County & State aforesaid of the other part. WITNESSETH that the said JENNINGS BECKWITH for and in consideration of the sum of one thousand dollars to him in hand paid at or before the sealing and delivery of these presents the receipt whereof is hereby acknowledged and thereof he doth release the said EDWARD FORD, his heirs, executors, Administrators and Assigns forever, he the said JENNINGS BECKWITH hath granted, bargained & Sold, aliened, enfeoffed & confirmed & doth by these presents grant, bargain & sell, alien, enfeoff & confirm unto the said EDWARD FORD his heirs and assigns forever a certain messuage, tenement, tract or parcel of land lying & being in the County of Fairfax containing eighty five acres and [left blank] Poles, it being part of a tract

known by the name of Wolf Run tract which descended to the said JENNINGS BECKWITH by the death of his father MARMADUKE BECKWITH intestate which was allotted to the said JENNINGS BECKWITH by Commissioners appointed by the Court of Fairfax County as by reference to their report will more fully appear & bounded as follows: beginning at red "A" two red oaks corner to lot number two, thence South twenty seven degrees ten minutes East one hundred & twelve poles to figure three near two small white oaks, on or near a line of the tract, thence with said line South fifty six degrees West forty three and an half poles to "F" a poplar, thence South nine degrees West seventy five poles to "E" thence North forty six Degrees West one hundred & forty one poles to figure two, a red oak sapling corner to Lot number two, thence with a line of said Lot North forty three degrees fifteen minutes East one hundred & forty poles to the beginning containing eighty five acres [left blank] poles more or less together with all & Singular the houses & buildings, trees, woods, underwoods, ways, waters, Water-Courses & hereditaments belonging to the said land and premises hereby bargained & sold, belonging or in anywise appertaining and the Reversion & Reversions, Remainder & Remainders, Rents, Issues & profits thereof to have & to Hold the said messuage, tenement, tract or parcel of Land & all and Singular the other Premises hereby bargained & Sold with their and every of their appurtenances unto the said EDWARD FORD his heirs & assigns forever to the only proper use & behoof of him the said EDWARD FORD his heirs & assigns forever. And the said JENNINGS BECKWITH now at the time of Sealing & delivering of these presents doth covenant & agree to & with the said EDWARD FORD his heirs & assigns forever that hath good, right, lawful and absolute authority to grant & convey the said land & premises hereby bargained & sold, with their & every of their appurtenances in manner and form aforesaid and that the same is & forever shall be free and clear of all former & other gifts, grants, bargains & sales, Dower right & title to Dower or encumbrance whatsoever committed or suffered by said JENNINGS BECKWITH or any other person or persons for him. And Lastly the said JENNINGS BECKWITH for himself his heirs, Executors & administrators the aforesaid land & premises with their and every of their appurtenances to the said EDWARD FORD his heirs & assigns forever shall and will warrant & forever defend against the claim or demand of all and every person & persons whatsoever. In Testimony whereof the said JENNINGS BECKWITH hath hereunto set his hand & Seal the day & Year first written.
Signed Sealed & delivered
in the presence of   JENNINGS BECKWITH   (seal)
TOWNSHEND WAUGH
WILLIAM L. WILKERSON
SAPLEY BECKWITH
        At a Court held for Fairfax County the 18th day of September 1809 JENNINGS BECKWITH acknowledged the within Deed to EDWARD FORD to be his act and deed which is ordered to be recorded.   Teste WM. MOSS Cl.

Pages 308 & 309. TO ALL PEOPLE whom these presents shall come Greeting: Know ye that we JOSEPH ASBURY And HANNAH NEAL TALBOTT now HANNAH ASBURY both of the County of Prince William & CommonWealth of Virginia for and in consideration of the sum of one hundred & twenty Dollars to us in hand before the ensealing hereof well and truly paid by WILLIAM SMITH TALBOTT of the County of Fairfax & CommonWealth aforesaid the receipt whereof we do hereby acknowledge and we ourselves therewith fully satisfied & contented and thereof & of every part & parcel thereof do exonerate & acquit & discharge him the said WILLIAM S. TALBOTT, his heirs, Executors & administrators forever by these presents Have Given, Granted, bargained, Sold, aliened, conveyed & confirmed & by these presents do freely, fully and absolutely Give, Grant, Bargain, Sell, alien, convey & Confirm unto the said WILLIAM S. TALBOTT his heirs & assigns forever all our right and interest in and of the land purchased by BENJAMIN TALBOTT from REID BROWN lying & being in the County of Fairfax & CommonWealth aforesaid on the Waters of Piney branch, Rocky Run and Difficult. To Have & to hold the said granted & bargained premises with all the appurtenances, priviledges & commodities [to] the same belonging or in anywise appertaining to him the said WILLIAM S. TALBOTT his heirs & assigns forever to his and their own proper use, benefit & behoof forever and we the sd. JOSEPH ASBURY & HANNAH N. ASBURY for ourselves, our heirs, executors & administrators do covenant, promise & grant to and with the said WILLIAM S. TALBOTT his heirs & assigns that before the ensealing hereof we are the true, sole, lawfull owners of the above bargained Premises and are lawfully seized and possessed of the same in our own proper right as a good and perfect and absolute estate of inheritance in fee simple and have in ourselves good, right, full power and lawful authority to grant, bargain, sell, convey & confirm said bargained premises in manner as aforesaid and that the said WILLIAM S. TALBOTT his heirs & assigns shall & may from time to time and all times forever hereafter by force & virtue of these presents lawfully, peaceably & quietly have, hold, occupy, possess and enjoy the said demised, bargained premises with the appurtenances, free & clear & freely & clearly acquited, exonerated & discharged of, from and all manner of former or other gifts, grants, bargains, sales, leases, mortgages, will entails, jointures, dowers, judgments, executions or encumbrances of what name or nature soever that might in any measure or degree obstruct or make void this present deed, furthermore we the said JOSEPH ASBURY & HANNAH ASBURY for ourselves, our heirs, executors & administrators do covenant and engage the above demised premises to him the said WILLIAM S. TALBOTT his heirs & assigns against the lawfull claims or demands of any other person or persons whatsoever forever hereafter to warrant and secure & defend by these presents. In WITNESS whereof we have hereunto set our hands & Seals the sixth day of September 1809.

Signed Sealed & delivered
in presence of   JOSEPH ASBURY   (seal)
REUBIN CALBERT   HANNAH N. ASBURY   (seal)
JOHN his + mark CALBERT
PATRICK his + mark McWIN

At a Court held for the County of Fairfax the 18th day of September 1809 JOSEPH ASBURY & HANNAH his wife she being first privately & again in open Court examined and thereto consenting acknowledged this deed to WILLIAM S. TALBOTT and ordered to be recorded.   Teste WM. MOSS Cl.

Pages 309 & 310. THIS INDENTURE made this twenty eighth day of August one thousand eight hundred & nine between CHARLES L. BROADWATER of the County of Fairfax & State of Virginia of the one part and WILLIAM E. BROADWATER of the same County & State of the other part. WITNESSETH that the said CHARLES L. BROADWATER for and in consideration of the good will & affection which [he] has & bears to his Son, the said WILLIAM E. BROADWATER as well as for the further consideration of five dollars to him the said CHARLES L. BROADWATER in hand paid by the said WILLIAM at or before the Sealing & delivery of these presents the receipt whereof is hereby acknowledged has given & granted to the said WILLIAM E. BROADWATER his heirs & assigns all that tract or parcel of land situate & being in the County & State aforesaid & bounded as follows to wit: beginning at a red oak standing on the East side of Ellzeys Church Road in the first hollow below the ford of [left blank] branch & the North side of the hill extending thence North 170° West 294 poles to WALLS & HOWSONS line, thence with the line South 18 1/2° East 192 poles to a hickory the corner of HARRIS, on thence with another of their lines South 1° West 61 poles to the sd. CHARLES BROADWATERS line, thence with his line North 87° East 80 poles then North 31° 50' East 118 to the beginning, being the same tract of land which CHARLES BRAODWATER deceased conveyed to the said CHARLES L. BROADWATER by deed dated the [left blank] day of [left blank] in the Year [left blank] and is recorded in the County Court of Fairfax. To have and To hold the said tract or part of land and every part thereof and all its appurtenances unto the said WILLIAM E. BROADWATER his heirs & assigns forever to & for the only proper use & behoof of him the said WILLIAM E. BROADWATER forever. And the said CHAS. L. BROADWATER for himself & his heirs the said Tract of Land & all the appurtenances thereto belonging unto the said WILLIAM E. BRODWATER his heirs & assigns free from the claim of him the said CHARLES L. BROADWATER and his Heirs & all & every person or persons whatsoever shall, will & do warrant & forever defend by these presents provided nevertheless that the said CHARLES L. BROADWATER reserves & claims the free use & occupancy of the said tract of land herein before mentioned to be conveyed, given, or granted, with all its appurtenances during the Natural life of him

the said CHARLES L. BROADWATER. In WITNESS whereof the said CHARLES L. BROADWATER hath hereunto set his hand & affixed his seal the day & date first above written.
Signed Sealed & delivered
in presence of   CHARS. L. BROADWATER   (seal)
SAMPSON MARTIN
JOHN FOUSHEE
THOMAS FLOOD JR, ELKANAH NALLEY
    At a Court held for Fairfax County the 18th day of September 1809 this Deed of Gift from CHARLES L. BROADWATER to WILLIAM E. BROADWATER was acknowledged by the said CHARLES to be his act and deed and ordered to be recorded.
                                    Teste WM. MOSS Cl.

Pages 310 & 311. KNOW ALL MEN by these presents that I CHARLES L. BROADWATER of the County of Fairfax & State of Virginia for and in consideration of the good will & affection which I bear to my Son WILLIAM E. BROADWATER as well as for the consideration of five Dollars to me in hand paid by the said WILLIAM E. BROADWATER the receipt whereof I do hereby acknowledge have given, granted & confirmed unto the said WILLIAM E. BROADWATER two certain Negroes to wit: SPENCER & MARIA which said Negroes are at this time in the possession of MRS. BROADWATER. To have and to hold the said Negroes SPENCER & MARIA & all their increase forever. In WITNESS whereof I have hereunto set my hand & seal this eighth day of August in the Year of our Lord eighteen hundred & Nine.
Signed Sealed & delivered
in presence of   CHARS. L. BROADWATER   (seal)
JOHN MOORE
THOMAS FLOOD JR
    Recd. August 8th 1809 from WILLIAM E. BROADWATER Five Dollars, the consideration above mentioned.
Teste
JOHN MOORE   CHARS. L. BROADWATER
THOMAS FLOOD JR
    At a Court held for Fairfax County the 18th day of September 1809 this Deed of Gift from CHARLES L BROADWATER to WILLIAM E. BROADWATER was acknowledged by the said CHARLES L. BROADWATER to be his act & deed which together with a receipt thereon endorsed are ordered to be recorded.   Teste WM. MOSS Cl.

Pages 311 & 312. KNOW ALL MEN by these presents that I SIBITH HURST of the County of Fairfax & State of Virginia do for myself and in my own right give, grant and by these presents make over, give, grant & confirm unto my Daughter SUSANNAH FENLEY one Negro man FRANK & one negro woman named CHLOE for the valuable consideration of the natural love & affection which [I] bear to my sd. daughter & also the valuable consideration of one dollar to me in hand paid which sd. Negroes FRANK & CHLOE I give, grant & Confirm unto the said SUSANNAH FENLEY for her own proper use & benefit forever and do by these presents warrant & forever defend the sd. Negros to her use forever against the claim of my heirs, Executors &c & all and every person claiming in or under me. I also Give, Grant & confirm unto my grand-daughter NANCY FENLEY one negro Boy named PETER, also I give grant & confirm unto my Grand daughter JARNET S. FENLEY one Negro boy named HIRAM, also I give grant & confirm unto my Grandson JOHN W. FENLEY one Negro boy named SIMON and to my Grandson JAMES H. FENLEY one Negro boy the name of MICHAEL. I also give to my Grandson WILLIAM MICHAEL FENLEY, at my death one Negro man by the name of ISAAC which several Negroes is by these presents given, granted & confirmed unto my several Grand children respectively named above & their respective heirs forever and for the natural love & affection which I bear to respective Grandchildren & the value of one Dollar each to me in hand paid by SUSANNAH FENLEY their mother do by these presents confirm the aforesaid Gift unto them & their respective Heirs forever against the claim of me, my heirs & all other persons claiming in or under me & will forever warrant & defend the same as Witness my hand & Seal this 18th day of September 1809.

SYBITH her + mark HURST(seal)

At a Court held for Fairfax County the 18th day of September 1809 this Deed of Gift from SYBITH HURST to her daughter SUSANNAH FENLEY & her Grandchildren NANCY FENLEY & others was acknowledged by the said SYBITH HURST and ordered to be recorded.

Teste WM. MOSS Cl.

Page 312. [left blank] 1809 I am willing that MR. DANIEL LEWIS shall have a road thro my land on the condition of paying all charges of the motion which he has made at Fairfax Court: beginning at Difficult Run at the old pond, thence thro my land at the back of my field between said field & run, thence thro my old field to a small branch that leads out of the field to the edge of my woods, thence along said woods some distance in a direction to the land of said HENRY GUNNELL & THOMAS FAIRFAX; thence with their lines to a chesnut & white oak corner of said HENRY GUNNELL, THOS. FAIRFAX & JNO. HUNTER, where this road will fall in DOCTR. GANTTS mill road which leads to Fairfax old Court House.

H. GUNNELL

At a Court held for Fairfax County the 18th day of September 1809 this instrument of writing from HENRY GUNNELL to DANIEL LEWIS was acknowledeged by the said HENRY GUNNELL & Ordered to be recorded.   Teste WM. MOSS Cl.

Pages 313-315. THIS INDENTURE made this thirtieth day of August in the Year one thousand eight hundred & Nine between GEORGE HUGUELY of the County of Fairfax & CommonWealth of Virginia of the first part & EDWARD LANHAM of the same county of the second part. Whereas from domestic considerations it has been judged expedient by the said GEORGE HUGUELY & SARAH his wife that a provision should be made out of the said GEORGE'S estate for the support & maintanance of the said SARAH and of her three children: ELISHABO, MATILDA LEE & GEORGE FENDALL and the said GEORGE being willing to make such a provision & to place the same on a permanent establishment. Now this indenture WITNESSETH that the said GEORGE to effect the object proposed & in consideration of one Dollar to him by the said EDWARD LANHAM in hand paid of which the receipt is hereby acknowledged has Given, Granted, bargained & sold and does by these presents Give, Grant, bargain & sell unto the said EDWARD LANHAM all and Singular the articles of personal property in the annexed schedule described & enumerated, to have to the said EDWARD LANHAM his heirs, Executors & Administrators forever in trust however for the following issues & none other that is to say for the sole and separate use of the said SARAH as to all the said property and the increase of the stock & Slaves during her natural life free from the interruption & controul of her said husband & from and after her death then for the use of the said three children, or of such of them & in such proportions as she shall by her last will & testament or her letter of appointment under her hand in the nature of her last will, order & direct and in default of such appointment then to the use of the said three children, their Executors & administrators equally to be divided; and should any of the said children die during the lifetime of the said SARAH leaving issue alive at the time of such death then the issue of such child is to stand in the same situation as the father or mother of such child as to all the purposes of this instrument, but if any of the said Children should die without leaving issue as aforesaid then all the rights of the child so dying in the property conveyed shall be & remain to the survivor or survivors subject to the power of disposal to the said SARAH so as aforesaid given and if all the said children should die during the life of the said SARAH without leaving issue, then the property hereby conveyed shall, after the death of the said SARAH be and inure to the use of the said GEORGE his Executors, administrators & Assigns provided always and on the condition that if the same SARAH shall survive the said GEORGE and shall make any claim to distribution of his personal estate except under a devise to her made by his will then this Indenture shall be void and all the estate & interest hereby vested in the said EDWARD LANHAM for her use shall cease & determine & the property conveyed shall revert to the Executors or Adminis- trators of the said GEORGE HUGUELY unless the said GEORGE shall have made a will & made no provision therein for the said three children in which case the same EDWARD & his Executors

& Administrators shall immediately on such claim being made by the said SARAH hold the property hereby conveyed & its increase for the use of the said three children & their representatives equally to be divided amongst them. And the said GEORGE HUGUELY for himself his heirs, Executors & Administrators does hereby covenant & agree with the said EDWARD LANHAM, his executors & administrators to warrant & defend the property conveyed against the claims & demands of all persons whatever. And the said EDWARD on his part covenants faithfully to execute the Trusts hereby reposed in him. In WITNESS whereof the parties to these presents have hereto set their hands & seals the day & Year above written.
Sealed & delivered
in the presence of   GEORGE HUGUELY   (seal)
R. J. TAYLOR, JAS. WIGGINTON   EDWARD LANHAM   (seal)
LEWIN JONES
          Schedule of property conveyed to EDWARD LANHAM in trust for SARAH HUGUELY by deed dated the thirtieth of August 1809 by GEORGE HUGUELY: a Negro Man LAWRENCE aged 27 Years, Negro Woman ANN 25 Years, Negro boy JUDSON 11 and girl SARAH three Years old, a dark bay mare called FANCY, two good feather beds, two sheets, two blankets, two coverlets, one bed quilt, one beaureau, one table, one large looking Glass, tester & bedstead, half dozen windsor chairs, six pewter plates, two pewter basons, six green edged plates, a tea pot, six pewter tea spoons, one waiter, iron pot and dutch oven, a wool spinning wheel, a chest, a cow commonly called the bell cow & calf, a red heifer, a red steer, a young black sow, five shoats, three pigs & two big hogs.
WITNESS
R. J. TAYLOR   GEORGE HUGUELY
JAMES WIGGINTON
LEWIN JONES
          At a Court held for Fairfax County the 18th day of September 1809 this Deed from GEORGE HUGUELY to EDWARD LANHAM, in trust for the use of SARAH HUGUELY & a Schedule of property thereto annexed was proved by the oaths of ROBERT J. TAYLOR, JAMES WIGGINTON & LEWIN JONES to be the act & deed of the said GEORGE HUGUELY and ordered to be recorded.
                              Teste WM. MOSS Cl.

Pages 315 & 316. THIS INDENTURE made this first day of August one thousand eight hundred & nine between THOMAS FLOOD of the County of Fairfax & state of Virginia of the one part & LEWIS SCISSON of the County & State aforesaid of the other part. WITNESSETH that the said THOMAS FLOOD for and in consideration of the rents, conditions & covenants herein after mentioned on the part of the said LEWIS SCISSON to be paid, kept & performed hath Granted, demised, leased, set and to farm let & by these presents doth grant, demise, lease, set & to farm let unto the said LEWIS SCISSON, his Heirs, Executors or Administrators all that tract or parcel of land whereon sd. FLOOD now lives containing two hundred acres more or less & bounded by the outside fencing around said farm, to have & to hold the said tract or parcel of land with all and singular its appurtenances to the said LEWIS SCISSON his heirs &c for and during the Natural lives of him the said THOS. FLOOD and his wife CATHE. FLOOD, or the longest liver of them said FLOOD is to give said SISSON immediate possession of the field he cultivated this Year in corn with the liberty of seeding it in small grain and on or before the first day of January next give him possession of the ballance of said farm; the said SCISSON on his part doth covenant to and with the said FLOOD to pay him his heirs or assigns the sum of forty pounds Virginia Currency per annum, the first Rent to become due the first day of January 1811; the said SCISSON further agrees to reserve two small pieces of wood land, the one lying next to JEREMIAH MOORES, the other near where JN. WRENNS old buildings stood, the balance of the wood land which is included in said boundary is to be cleared by said SISSON (as soon as he may choose so to do) and after taking of the rales & using them for the benefit of the farm, he is to dispose of the balance of the wood as he may think proper; said FLOOD further agrees to & with said SCISSON that if after clearing what land he is allowed to clear (he should want rales or firewood) that he is to go on said FLOODS wood land for the same provided he commits no unnecessary waste; said SISSON further agrees to Let the said FLOOD occupy the fresh field (which is at this time in Tobacco) the ensuing Year and during the term of said lease allow sd.

FLOOD the liberty of pasturage for two Cows & 2 horses; said SISSON is not to cultivate the land more than once in three Years except the manured parts; the said SISSON further agrees that if said FLOOD should sell to AMOS ALEXANDER the part of said farm as pointed out in presence of THOS. FLOOD JR that he will relinquish his right thereto and will at all times during his said lease keep said farm in tenantable repair and commit no waste of wood or timber except on the part where he is permitted to clear; said FLOOD further agrees to let said SISSON extend the fence, enclosing the field last cleared across the branch to JAMES DOVE'S lot & allow him to clear & cultivate the land which will be enclosed thereby; said SISSON is not to sell or dispose of his lease without the consent of the said FLOOD; it is understood between the parties that the wood which said SISSON is allowed to sell is not to exceed six Waggon loads per Year. In WITNESS whereof the parties have hereunto set their hands & seals the day & date above mentioned.

Signed & acknowledged
in presence of us   THOS. FLOOD   (seal)
JOSEPH POWELL, HENRY TAYLOR   LEWIS his X mark SISSON   (seal)
BENJAMIN SEBASTIAN

    At a Court held for Fairfax County the 18th day of September 1809 this Deed between THOMAS FLOOD & LEWIS SCISSON was proved by the oaths of JOSEPH POWELL, HENRY TAYLOR & BENJAMIN SEBASTIAN & ordered to be recorded.

Teste WM. MOSS Cl.

Page 317. KNOW ALL MEN by these presents that we IGNATIUS WHEELER, STEPHEN DONOHOE, JOHN STANHOPE, JOHN MOSS and WILLIAM WALTER WILLIAMS all of Fairfax County are held and firmly bound unto SPENCER JACKSON of the same County in the sum of six thousand Dollars to the payment of which we bind ourselves, our heirs, Executors & Administrators, jointly & severally firmly by these presents. Sealed with our Seals & dated this 18th day of September 1809. Whereas the said SPENCER JACKSON became bound as one of the securities of the said INGNATIUS WHEELER as Executor of IGNATIUS WHEELER deceased and the above bound IGNATIUS WHEELER has agreed to give the said SPENCER JACKSON security to indemnify him against all damage & loss in any manner to arise from the responsibility by him as aforesaid undertaken, now the Condition of this obligation is such that if the said IGNATIUS WHEELER herein before named shall in all respects faithfully administer the estate of the said decedent and shall account for & pay over the same to the several creditors, Devisees, Distributees & others entitled to receive the same and shall fully & completely indemnify & save harmless the said SPENCER, his heirs, Executors & administrators, from all suits motions, prosecutions, damages & loss in any manner arising or to arise from or in consequence of the suretyship aforesaid then this obligation to be void.

WITNESS   IGNAS. WHEELER   (seal)
R. J. TAYLOR   STEPHEN DONOHOE   (seal)
WM. MOSS   JOHN STANHOPE   (seal)
                                                            W. W. WILLIAMS   (seal)
                                                            JOHN MOSS   (seal)

    At a Court held for Fairfax County the 18th day of September 1809 this Bond from IGNATIUS WHEELER, STEPHEN DONOHOE, JOHN STANHOPE, WILLIAM W. WILLIAMS & JOHN MOSS to SPENCER JACKSON was acknowledged by the said INGNATIUS, STEPHEN, JOHN, WILLIAM & JOHN MOSS to be their act and deed & ordered to be recorded.

Teste WM. MOSS Cl.

Page 318. KNOW ALL MEN by these presents that I WILLIAM HENDERSON of the CommonWealth of Virginia & County of Fairfax for and in consideration of the natural love & affection which I bear to my Son CHARLES WILLIAM HENDERSON of the County aforesaid as well as for the further consideration of one Dollar to me in hand paid by the said CHARLES WILLIAM HENDERSON at or before the ensealing & delivery of these presents the receipt is hereby acknowledged Have Given & Granted & by these presents do give & grant unto the said CHARLES WILLIAM HENDERSON his Executors, Administrators or Assigns, one Negro Girl named PENNY (being the Daughter of LUCINDA), also a Negro boy named LEWIS (the Son of

SARAH). To have and to Hold the said two Negroes PENNY & LEWIS unto him the said CHARLES W. HENDERSON his Executors, Administrators & Assigns forever. And the said WILLIAM HENDERSON for himself, his executors & administrators, the said WILLIAM HENDERSON unto the said CHARLES WILLIAM HENDERSON his Executors, Administrators & assigns against the claim of him the said WILLIAM HENDERSON his Executors & administrators & against the claim or claims of all and every person or persons whatsoever shall and will warrant & forever defend by them these presents. In WITNESS whereof I have hereunto set my hand & affixed my seal this 14th day of August 1805.

Signed, Sealed & delivered
in presence of   WILLIAM his X mark HENDERSON (seal)
W. PAYNE, GEORGE WILLIAMS
THEOPHELUS BOWIE
THOMAS MOSS

At a Court held for Fairfax County the 18th day of September 1809 This Deed of Gift from WILLIAM HENDERSON to CHARLES WILLIAM HENDERSON was proved to be the act & deed of the said WILLIAM HENDERSON by the oaths of GEORGE WILLIAMS & THOMAS MOSS and ordered to be recorded.   Teste WM. MOSS Cl.

Pages 318 & 319. Whereas GEORGE MASON of Pohic. some Years ago leased to a certain RICHARD PARROTT, JAMES H. BLAKE & ANTHONY BANNING a mill seat on Pohic creek for a term of Years & which term is not expired as will appear by said lease duly recorded in the Clerks office of Fairfax County which lease was afterwards sold by RICHARD PARROTT one of said firm, to ROBERT SMYTHEY & ROBERT SMOCK as pr. contract under their hands & seals and which Contract was afterwards assigned over by ROBERT SMOCK to JAMES H. BLAKE so as compleatly to vest in said BLAKE the Lease aforesaid and whereas it was agreed by said BLAKE and AMINTA MASON & MARY MASON heirs of sd. GEORGE MASON decd that said lease should be null & void and of no effect and said BLAKE declined exercising ownership over the same & permitted them to take possession thereof and as these parties have neglected to enter into any instrument of writing which might be made a record of concerning the premises, it is now agreed on by the subscribers that said lease shall be of no avail & that the Heir or Heirs of GEORGE MASON may exercise ownership over the same as if no such instrument had ever been been executed & said PARROTT, BLAKE & BANNING are hereby released from all engagements on their part concerning the same. In WITNESS whereof we have hereunto subscribed our names & affixed our Seals this 23rd day of November 1809.

Signed & Sealed in
the presence of   JAMES H. BLAKE   (seal)
JOHN his + mark HAMBLETON   ELIJAH GRAHAM   (seal)
WILLIAM his + mark HARLEY   AMINTA GRAHAM   (seal)

At a Court held for Fairfax County the 20th July 1807 this instrument of writing between JAMES H. BLAKE, ELIJAH GRAHAM & AMINTA GRAHAM was proved to be the act & deed of the parties by the oath of WILLIAM HARLEY, a Witness hereto and ordered to be certified; and at a Court held for the said County the 16th day of May 1808 the same was further proved by the oath of JOHN HAMBLETON, another witness hereto and ordered to be certified; and at a Court contd. & held for the sd. County the 19th September 1809 the same having been heretofore duly proved by two Witnesses being the only subscribing Witnesses to the said instrument is on motion of the said JAMES H. BLAKE admitted to Record for safe keeping.   Teste WM. MOSS Cl.

Pages 320 & 321. THIS INDENTURE made this 25th April 1809 between MOSES THOMAS of the County of Fairfax & state of Virginia of the one part & MORRISS FOX of the County & State aforesaid of the other part. WITNESSETH that the said MOSES THOMAS, to secure to the said MORRISS FOX to secure the sd. FOX from suffering on account of his being security for the said MOSES THOMAS in several cases to a considerable amount and in consideration of the sum of one Dollar to him in hand paid by the said MORRISS FOX at or before the sealing of these presents the receipt whereof is hereby acknowledged he the said MOSES THOMAS has Granted, bargained & sold & by these presents doth Grant, bargain & sell unto the said MORRISS FOX a certain parcel or Lot of land situate, lying & being at West-end in the County of Fairfax, beginning at the old Turnpike Gatepost & containing about 1/4 of an Acre being the same that was purchased by said MOSES THOMAS of JAMES LOCKINGS and also the following personal property to wit: one negro man named HARRY, one bay mare, one black mare, two sorrel Horses, three Bay Horses, one Waggon & Gear, four feather beds, fourteen sheep, ten head cattle, twenty five hogs, one black Horse, one Sorrel Colt, the wheat now Growing, also Tobacco, Corn & Hay, one Dutch Pan, one Cupbourd, 1 Desk, 2 Chests, six chairs, three tables, three Bedsteads, two Mattoxes, two axes, two pots & three ovens & five ploughs &c, To have & to hold the said parcel or lot of land with all and singular the appurtenances thereto belonging and also all & Singular the aforesaid articles of personal property unto the said MORRISS FOX, his heirs, Executors & Administrators or Assigns forever to secure to the said MORRISS FOX, on account of his being security in several cases against I, the said MOSES, to have & To hold the aforesaid property real & personal until the said MORRISS FOX shall be relieved from being security for me, the aforesaid MOSES THOMAS. In Testimony whereof the aforesaid MOSES THOMAS has hereunto set his hand & Seal the day & Year first written.

MOSES THOMAS   (seal)

At a Court contd. & held for Fairfax County the 19th day of September 1809 MOSES THOMAS acknowledged this Deed to MORRISS FOX to be his act & deed & ordered to be recorded.

Teste WM. MOSS Cl.

Pages 321-324. THIS INDENTURE made this 28th day of February in the Year of our Lord one thousand eight hundred and nine between WILLIAM SIMPSON & JANE his wife of the parish of TRURO & County of Fairfax of the one part & EDWARD WASHINGTON of the Parish & County aforesaid of the other part. WITNESSETH that the said WILLIAM SIMPSON & JANE his wife for and in consideration of the sum of eighty seven pounds Current money of Virginia to them in hand paid by the said EDWARD WASHINGTON at or before the sealing & delivery of these presents the receipt Whereof the said WILLIAM SIMPSON doth hereby acknowledge and thereof doth acquit & discharge the said EDWD. WASHINGTON, his Heirs, Exors & Administrators & every of them; & by these presents the said WILLIAM SIMPSON & JANE his wife hath Granted, Bargained, Sold, Aliened, enfeoffed & confirmed unto the said EDWARD WASHINGTON & to his heirs & assigns forever all that parcel or tract of land situated lying & being in the parish & County aforesaid containing eighty three & a half acres, being one half of a certain tract of land sold to WM. SIMPSON by ELIZABETH WEST and being part of one third of a tract of land by estimation taken up by ANDREW SMARR, BURDITT HARRISON & THOS. HARRISON & Granted by Deed to them from the Proprietors Office of the Northern Neck of Virginia bearing date the twenty second day of February seventeen hundred & twenty nine, it being the land & inheritance fallen to JOHN SMARR by the death of his father ANDREW SMARR & afterwards sold & conveyed by JOHN SMARR, SYLVESTER GARNER & MARY his wife to WILLIAM WEST of the County of Loudoun as will more fully appear by Deed from JOHN SMARR, SYLVESTER GARNER & MARY his wife to the before mentioned WILLIAM WEST bearing date the twenty Ninth of January seventeen hundred fifty & by the last will & Testament of WILLIAM WEST deceased bearing date the twenty sixth of June seventeen hundred & sixty Nine was devised by the said WILLIAM WEST to ELIZABETH WEST & her heirs forever, the said ELIZABETH WEST being Grand daughter to WILLIAM WEST decd & daughter to CHARLES WEST & ANN his wife, the above eighty three & a half acres of land bounded as follows: beginning at a box & red oak standing on the North East side of the Ox road, running thence with a line dividing this land between WILLIAM SIMPSON & EDWARD WASHINGTON North 31° East 147 poles to South Run (a branch of Pohick) at several Young Chestnuts & a Dog Wood, thence down the said South Run & binding therewith to a beach corner of WILLIAM GODFREYS 105 Acre Tract, thence with said GODFREYS line South 11° West 72 poles a hicory another corner of GODFREY & still with his line South 29° East 46 poles to a white oak corner to GODFREY & CARTER, thence with the line of the Patent South 37° West 100 poles to the Ox road at a Box oak in the line of CARTER and standing on the SW side thereof thence up and binding on the said Ox road North 59° West 35 poles, thence North 43° West 50 poles to the beginning together with all houses, Ways, Water, Water courses, emoluments & hereditaments thereunto belonging & the Reversion & Reversions, Rents, issues & profits thereof To Have & To Hold the said

parcel of land hereby granted & the appurtenances unto him the said EDW. WASHINGTON his heirs & assigns forever to the only use & behoof of him the said EDW. WASHINGTON his heirs & assigns forever & the said WM. SIMPSON for himself & his heirs unto the said EDWARD WASHINGTON his heirs & assigns the said tract & parcel of land hereby granted & the appurtenances warrant & defend against him the said WILLIAM SIMPSON & his heirs & all persons whatsoever claiming the same by, from, through or under him or his heirs or any of them & forever defend by these presents. In WITNESS whereof the parties hereunto have to these presents severally set their hands & Seals the day & Year first written.
Signed Sealed &delivered
in the presence of   WILLIAM SIMPSON (seal)
W. PAYNE, W. DENEALE, RD. SIMPSON   JANE SIMPSON   (seal)
EDWARD W. SIMPSON, THOMAS COFFER

Recd. of EDWARD WASHINGTON the sum of eighty seven pounds Virginia currency, being the consideration within mentioned in full. Witness my hand this 28th day of February 1809.
Teste
W. PAYNE, W. DENEALE   WILLIAM SIMPSON
RD. SIMPSON, EDW. W. SIMPSON

At a Court contd. & held for the County of Fairfax the 19th day of September 1809 This deed from WILLIAM SIMPSON & JANE his wife to EDWARD WASHINGTON was proved by the oaths of WILLIAM DENEALE, EDWARD W. SIMPSON & RICHARD SIMPSON to be the act and deed of WILLIAM SIMPSON which together with a Commission & return thereto annexed for taking the acknowledgment & privy examination of the said JANE wife of the said WILLIAM SIMPSON are ordered to be Recorded.   Teste WM. MOSS Cl.

FAIRFAX COUNTY To Wit:
The CommonWealth of Virginia to CHARLES LITTLE, WILLIAM PAYNE & WILLIAM DENEALE Gentleman justices of the County of Fairfax Greeting: Whereas WILLIAM SIMPSON & JANE his wife by their certain indenture of bargain & Sale bearing date the 28th day of February 1809 have sold & conveyed unto EDWARD WASHINGTON the fee simple Estate of Eighty three & an half acres of Land with the appurtenances situate, lying & being in the said County of Fairfax and whereas the said JANE cannot conveniently travel to our said County Court of Fairfax to make acknowledgment of the said conveyance therefore we do give unto you or any two or more of you Power to receive the acknowledgment which the said JANE shall be willing to make before You of the conveyance aforesaid contained in the said indenture which is hereunto annexed. And we do therefore desire You or any two or more of You Personally to go to the said JANE & receive her acknowledgment of the same & examine her privily & apart from the said WM. SIMPSON her husband whither she doth the same freely & voluntarily without his persuasions or threats & whither she be willing the said indenture together with this commission shall be recorded in our said Court and when You have received her acknowledgment & examined her as aforesaid that You distinctly & openly certify us thereof in our said Court under your hands & seals sending then there the said indenture & this Writ. Witness WILLIAM MOSS Clerk of the said Court at the Courthouse of the County aforesaid this 28th day of February 1809 and in the 33rd Year of the CommonWealth.
                                        WM. MOSS Cl.

FAIRFAX COUNTY:
Pursuant to the within Commission to us directed we the subscribers have waited on JANE SIMPSON & proceeded to take her privy examination separate & a part from her said husband when the said JANE voluntarily & freely relinquished all her right of Dower in and to a certain tract of land which is this day conveyed by the said WILLIAM SIMPSON which Deed is hereunto annexed and also the said JANE consented that the same may be recorded as Given under our hands & Seals this 28th day of February 1809.
                                        W. PAYNE   (seal)
                                        W. DENEALE (seal)

Delivered BUSHROD WASHINGTON

Pages 324-328. THIS INDENTURE made the seventh day of April in the Year of our Lord eighteen hundred & Nine between AUGUSTIN J. SMITH of Alexandria of the first part, BUSHROD WASHINGTON JR now of Westmoreland County & EDMUND J. LEE of Alexandria in the District of Columbia of the second part & BUSHROD WASHINGTON of Mount Vernon in the County of Fairfax of the third part. Whereas the said AUGUSTIN J. SMITH of the first part stands justly indebted to the said BUSHROD WASHINGTON of the third part in the sum of four thousand two hundred Dollars Principal debt which became due & payable to the said BUSHROD WASHINGTON on the twentieth day of February last past besides one Years interest for securing the payment whereof the said AUGUSTIN J. SMITH did on the 27th day of March in the Year eighteen hundred & five by indenture bearing date on the same day & Year, Mortgage to the said BUSHROD WASHINGTON a certain tract or parcel of land lying & being in the County of Fairfax whereon the said SMITH then resided containing eight hundred & fifty seven acres which the said SMITH purchased from BATTAILE FITZHUGH & bounded as by a survey thereof made by WILLIAM PAYNE surveyor of Fairfax County & by the deed of the said FITZHUGH to the said SMITH together with all buildings, improvements, commodities, heredi-taments & appurtenances to the same belonging or in anywise appertaining & the Reversion & Reversions, Remainder & Remainders, Rents, issues and profits thereof as by the said deed which was duly acknowledged by the said SMITH & recorded in the County of Fairfax will more fully & at large appear; and whereas the said principal debt became due & payable on the said twentieth day of February last & the said WASHINGTON of the third part is willing & has agreed to extend the Credit for the said Debt until the twentieth day of February in the year Eighteen hundred & twelve in consideration of the said SMITH giving to the said WASHINGTON of the third part additional security for the said debt & also a deed of trust of the equity of redemtion of the said SMITH in the above mentioned mortgaged premises for securing the punctual payment of the interest of the said Debt annually as the same shall become due & a speedy remedy for enforcing payment of the principal debt when the same shall become due. Now this indenture WITNESSETH that the said AUGUSTINE J. SMITH for and in consideration of the premises & also in consideration of one Dollar to him in hand paid by the said BUSHROD WASHINGTON JR & EDMUND J. LEE at & before the ensealing and delivery of these presents the receipt whereof the sd. AUGUSTINE J. SMITH doth hereby acknowledge & of & from the same doth release and discharge the said parties of the second part hath Given, Granted, bargained & sold, aliened, released, assigned & set over & doth by these presents Give, Grant, bargain & sell, alien, release, assign & set over unto the said BUSHROD WASHINGTON JR & EDMUND J. LEE parties of the second part & the survivor of them & the heirs of the survivor all & singular the estate right, title, interest, equity of redemption, claim & demand whatso-ever of him the said AUGUSTINE J. SMITH, his heirs, Exors & Admors of, in and to the above mentioned tract and parcel before described & all & singular the commodities, hereditaments & appurtenances to the Same belonging or in any wise appertaining & also the following Negro slaves together with their future increase: that is to say SYPHAX & ESTHER with their five children; BILLY, RACHEL & their five children; SALLY & MARY with three children; NELSON; BILL 30 years old; MENSON 28 Years old; JEFFERY 26 Years old. To have and to Hold the hereby Granted premises & Slaves with their future increase unto the said BUSHROD WASHINGTON JR & EDMUND J. LEE & the survivor of them & the heirs of the Survivor in trust for the following purposes & none other, that is to say to hold the sd. hereby Granted premises & Slaves in trust for the said AUGUSTINE J. SMITH his heirs & assigns until after a sale shall be of the same or any part thereof under the authority of this Deed and after such Sale be made, then to & for the use of the Purchaser or purchasers thereof until a conveyance thereof shall be made to such Purchaser or purchasers their heirs or Assigns and if it shall so happen that the said AUGUSTINE J. SMITH, his Heirs, Executors or Administrators, shall fail to pay the whole of the aforesd. sum of four thousand two hundred Dollars, being the principal sum, on or before the twentieth day of February in the Year Eighteen hundred & twelve, or shall fail to pay the interest on the said sum of four thousand two hundred dollars annually at the rate of six per centum by the Year as the same shall become due on either or any of the above events happening it shall and may be lawful for the said BUSHROD WASHINGTON JR & EDMUND J. LEE or either of them or the Survivor of them or the Heirs of the survivor on the request of the said BUSHROD WASHINGTON of the third part, or on the request of his Executors,

Administrators or Assigns, made in writing, to sell so much of the Premises & property hereby Granted as may be sufficient for raising the sum which shall be then due & owing which sale is to be made at public Auction the said Trustees or either of them who may be required to make the said sale giving thirty days Previous Notice of the time and place of Sale in one of the News Papers published in the Town of Alexandria, Georgetown, or City of Washington and the said Sale or sales to be made for ready money & the same to be applied in the first place in discharge of the costs of the said sale and the residue to be paid over by the said Trustees, or the one who shall act, to the said BUSHROD WASHINGTON of the third part his Executors, Administrators or assigns in payment of whatever sum of money that may be then due under the Deed of trust as far as the same will go in payment thereof. And the said AUGUSTINE J. SMITH for himself, his Heirs, Executors & Administrators doth Grant an irrevocable power & authority to the said BUSHROD WASHINGTON JR & EDMUND J. LEE or either of them to receive, collect, destrain & sue for in his the said AUGUSTINE J. SMITHS name the rents which shall or may become due from the tenants on the aforementioned Land and the said Rents when received to pay over to the said BUSHROD WASHINGTON of the third part his Executors, Administrators or assigns in discharge of the interest on the aforesd. principal sum which may be then due & owing and the residue of the said rents to pay over to the said AUGUSTINE J. SMITH, his Heirs, Executors, Administrators or Assigns; but it is hereby expressly understood between the parties hereto that the power hereby given to the said Trustees to receive the rents as aforesd. is not intended, nor is it to be so construed as to impair or diminish the power of the said Trustees to sell any part or the whole of the property hereby Granted if necessary in case the interest be not punctually paid on the days when the same shall become due, but the said power of receiving the said Rents by the said Trustees is hereby declared to be intended as an auxilary & additional security for the payment of the said principal Debt & interest and the said AUGUSTINE J. SMITH doth for himself, his heirs, Executors & Adminis-trators convenant & agree to and with the said BUSHROD WASHINGTON of the third part his Executors, Administrators & assigns that he the said AUGUSTINE J. SMITH his Executors & Administrators, will well & truly pay or cause to be paid to the said BUSHROD WASHINGTON his Executors, Administrators or Assigns, the aforesd. principal sum of four thousand two hund-red Dollars on or before the twentieth day of February Eighteen hundred & twelve together with legal interest thereon after the rate of six per centum by the Year, the first payment of interest to be made at the expiration of one Year from and after the twentieth day of February last past & so at the expiration of each succeeding year until the principal sum is paid and the said parties of the second part do each for himself and not jointly covenant with the said party of the first part and with the sd. party of the third part that they & their heirs will well & truly execute the trust hereby vested in them & further that after the purposes of this trust are fully complied with that they will by proper Deed reconvey the property hereby granted & which may not have been sold to the said AUGUSTINE J. SMITH his heirs, Executors, Administrators & assigns, as they may be entitled thereto. In WITNESS whereof the parties to these presents have set their hands and affixed their Seals the day & Year first above written.

Signed Sealed & delivered
in presence of us
R. J. TAYLOR
JESSE T. RAMSAY
RICHARD H. WASHINGTON
HUMPH PEAKE (as to B.W. JR)
WM. MOSS to B.W. JR

AUG. J. SMITH	(seal)
BUSHD. WASHINGTON JR	(seal)
EDM. J. LEE	(seal)
BUSHD. WASHINGTON	(seal)

     MEMO: It is agreed that the Power herein given to the Trustees to receive, Collect, sue for & distrain for the rents which may accrue is hereby revoked and whereas the said AUGUSTINE J. SMITH is indebted to the said WASHINGTON of the third part two hundred & fifty two Dollars for interest due on the 20th of February last and the said WASHINGTON having subscribed for ten shares in the Bridge to be errected over Little Hunting Creek which subscription the sd. SMITH hath agreed to pay when the calls are made in discharge of the above interest due & so much of the interest to become due as the same will now discharge. The sd. SMITH hereby covenants & agrees that if the calls when made are not punctually paid by him, his Exors & adminors, that the Trustees may on ten days Notice to be given in any Newspaper in Alexandria dispose of any of the within property for satislfying the same & the Costs & Charges of Sale.

WITNESS   AUG. J. SMITH   (seal)
R. J. TAYLOR   [No signature]   (seal)
JESSE T. RAMSAY   [No signature]   (seal)
RICHARD H. WASHINGTON   BUSH. WASHINGTON   (seal)

    At a Court contd. & held for Fairfax County the 22nd day of August 1809 this Deed between AUGUSTINE J. SMITH of the first part & BUSHROD WASHINGTON JR and EDMUND J. LEE of the second part & BUSHROD WASHINGTON of the third part and a memorandum thereon endorsed was proved to be the act and Deed of the sd. AUGUSTINE J. SMITH and BUSHROD WASHINGTON by the oaths of ROBERT J. TAYLOR & RICHARD WASHINGTON and acknowledged by the said EDMUND J. LEE and ordered to be Certified. And at a Court held for the said County the 18th day of September 1809 the same was further acknowledged by the said AUGUSTINE J. SMITH to be his act and deed and ordered to be Recorded.

                          Teste WM. MOSS Cl.

Pages.328-332. THIS INDENTURE made this eighth day of September in the Year of our Lord Eighteen hundred & Nine between BENJAMIN DULANY SR and ELIZABETH his wife of the County of Alexandria in the District of Columbia of the first part, DANIEL DULANY of the County of Fairfax and State of Virginia, Son to the said BENJAMIN of the second part and the Wife and several children of the said BENJAMIN DULANY SR now unmarried of the third Part. WITNESSETH that whereas the said BENJAMIN DULANY SR has a great variety of Valuable Property lying in Various directions which for the want of more active attention produces little or no profit, Whereas it might be made very productive and useful to his family if properly managed and Whereas the said BENJAMIN DULANY SR feels himself very infirm & incapable of those active exertions in the management of his various scattered property which his interest and that of his family requires and being desirous to promote the interest, welfare & happiness of his family by all the means in his power and believing he can in no wise better secure their interest than transferring the whole of his property, Real, personal and mixed to the management of his Son the said DANIEL DULANY (in whom he has the utmost confidence) whose Youth & activity will render it more productive, he the said BENJAMIN DULANY SR has therefore after mature reflection determined upon the transfer of all his property, Real, personal & mixed to the said DANIEL DULANY in trust, to manage & direct the same & receive the rents & profits thereof and apply the proceeds in such manner as shall herein & after be directed under the Conditions and stipulations also herein after mentioned and Whereas there was some time back an agreement entered into between the said BENJAMIN DULANY SR & ELIZABETH his wife in which it was stipulated and so covenanted that the said BENJAMIN DULANY SR should pay unto his said Wife a certain sum of money therein mentioned at the times & in the manner in the said agreement set forth as well as to do & perform sundrie other things all of which will more fully at large appear by reference to the said agreement or contract bearing date the day of [left blank] in the Year [left blank] and considered as a part of this instrument & whereas it has been believed by all the parties concerned that the foregoing arrangement of Tranferring the property of the said BENJAMIN DULANY SR in trust as aforesaid would be much more beneficial to the family than as it now is, the said BENJAMIN DULANY SR & ELIZABETH his wife have agreed thereto and the said ELIZABETH Wife to the said BENJAMIN has also agreed upon this Conveyance being so executed to release & acquit the said BENJAMIN DULANY SR from all further & other obligation arising out of or under the said agreement or contract aforesaid. And whereas it is as necessary for the said BENJAMIN DULANY SR to provide a future support & provision for himself as for his family, it is & has been agreed that the said BENJAMIN DULANY SR shall retain as accepted out of the General conveyance of all his estate, real, personal & mixed, all his the said BENJAMIN DULANY'S, Bank shares now standing in his name as well as all the Cash on hand and in deposit in the name of the said BENJAMIN DULANY and in addition to the above, the said DANIEL DULANY is to pay to the said BENJAMIN DULANY SR Yearly & every Year during his the said BENJAMIN DULANY'S natural life Five hundred Dollars, the first payment to become due on the eighth day of September in the Year Eighteen hundred & ten and afterwards on the same day in each succeeding Year during the Natural life of the said BENJAMIN DULANY SR and moreover the said DANIEL DULANY shall & is to Give ample & satisfactory security for the payment of the annual sum of five hundred Dollars during the Natural life of the said BENJAMIN DULANY SR. And it is also understood that this consequence in Trust aforesaid is only for and during the Natural life of the said BENJAMIN DULANY SR & no longer and that the said BENJAMIN DULANY SR has the full & absolute right to dispose by Will or otherwise of the Reversion of all and Singular the hereby conveyed premises as though this Instrument had never been made or executed, but nothing further and whereas also it is annexed as an express condition that after paying the five hundred dollars aforesaid to the said BENJAMIN DULANY SR in manner aforesaid deducting the same always out of the Rents & profits of the hereby granted premises, the balance of the proceeds of the Estate & premises hereby conveyed after deducting the necessary expenses attending the same shall be given and applied by the said DANIEL DULANY, his Heirs, Executors and Administrators, to the said ELIZABETH DULANY (his Mother) and the other Children of the said BENJAMIN DULANY SR which are now unmarried for their mutual and General support and advantage and in no other way whatsoever & for the purpose of carrying the aforesaid intentions into effect according to the spirit & meaning of the parties. Now this indenture WITNESSETH that the said BENJAMIN DULANY SR and ELIZABETH his wife for and in consideration of the premises and of the further sum of five Dollars to the said BENJAMIN DULANY SR & ELIZABETH his wife in hand paid by the said DANIEL DULANY at & before the sealing & delivery of these presents the receipt whereof is hereby acknowledged have Granted, bargained, sold, Assigned, transfered, set over and confirmed and by these presents do give, grant, bargain, sell, assign, transfer, set over & confirm unto the sd. DANIEL DULANY, his Heirs, Executors & Administrators for and during the natural life of the said BENJAMIN DULANY SR all and singular the Estate, real, personal and mixed of him the said BENJAMIN DULANY SR or of which the said BENJAMIN DULANY SR has any right, title or claim to whither the same be in possession, remainder or reversion whensoever the same may be or be Except the Bank shares standing in the name of the said BENJAMIN DULANY and the Cash on hand and in deposit in the name of the said BENJAMIN DULANY SR all of which is to remain at the said BENJAMIN DULANY'S SR's own disposal at pleasure. To have and to hold all & singular the premises and all & singular the estate, Real, personal & mixed of the said BENJAMIN DULANY SR whither the same be in possession, remainder or Reversion and wheresoever the same may be unto the said DANIEL DULANY, his Heirs, Executors and Administrators during the natural life of the said BENJAMIN DULANY SR except the Bank stock standing in the name of the said BENJAMIN DULANY SR and the Cash on hand and in deposit in the name of the said BENJAMIN DULANY SR all of which to be at his disposal & not herein included in trust however for the following purposes, uses and intents and none other to wit: In the first place out of the Rents & profits of the hereby Granted premises to pay to the said BENJAMIN DULANY SR five hundred dollars per Annum at the expiration of each Year from the date of these presents that is to say on the eighth day of September in each & every year hereafter during the natural life of the said BENJAMIN DULANY SR; Secondly after deducting the necessary expenses attending the same & management of the premises to pay over to the said ELIZABETH DULANY wife of the said BENJAMIN DULANY SR & the children of the said BENJAMIN DULANY SR now unmarried for their mutual support, benefit & advantage, all and singular the balance of the proceeds of the Rents & profits of the hereby granted premises during the natural life of the said BENJAMIN DULANY SR the time for which the same is Conveyed &c and the said BENJAMIN DULANY SR for the purposes of carrying fully into effect his instrument doth hereby constitute, nominate & appoint the said DANL. DULANY his Attorney in fact and as such to do all things necessary to the fulfilment of the true spirit & meaning of this instrument Either in the name of the said BENJAMIN DULANY SR or otherwise as may be most proper for the fulfilment of these presents, ratifying and confirming all my said Attorney shall Lawfully do in the premises as fully as tho I, the said BENJAMIN DULANY SR was present & personally consenting thereto. And the said ELIZABETH DULANY wife of the said BENJAMIN DULANY SR for and in consideration of the premises and of the Execution of these presents of Trust by the said BENJAMIN DULANY SR Doth release & hereafter acquit the said BENJAMIN

DULANY SR and all others bound for him from all further other payment of all & every allowance, annuity & other duty or obligation whatsoever arising from or under an agreement or covenant made by the said BENJAMIN DULANY SR for her benefit and in this instrument before refered to, the same having by mutual agreement been merged in this present transaction & conveyance and the said DANIEL DULANY for himself, his Heirs, Executors & Administrators Grants, Covenants & agrees to & with the said BENJAMIN DULANY SR his Executors, Administrators & assigns to pay to him the said BENJAMIN DULANY SR or his Assigns on the eighth day of September in the Year Eighteen hundred & Ten and on that Day in every Year afterwards during his the said BENJAMIN DULANY SR natural life the sum of five hundred dollars as is herein before stipulated. And the said DANIEL DULANY for himself, his Heirs, Executors & Administrators grants, covenants & agrees to & with all & every of the parties to these presents their heirs, Executors, Administrators or Assigns as well jointly & severally To faithfully & truly execute & perform all & singular the duties, Trusts and Confidences herein & hereby reposed & confided in & to him. In WITNESS whereof the parties have hereunto set their hands & seals the day & Year first above written.
Signed Sealed & delivered
In presence of   B. DULANY   (seal)
W. H. FOOTE, HENRY P. DAINGERFIELD   [no signature]   (seal)
THOS. J. HERBERT, N. HERBERT   DANL. DULANY   (seal)
WM. HERBERT JR

At a Court held for Fairfax County the 18th day of September 1809 this Deed from BENJAMIN DULANY & ELIZABETH his wife to DANIEL DULANY son of the said BENJAMIN in trust for the use of the Wife & several children of the said BENJAMIN DULANY now unmarried was proved by the oaths of NOBLET HERBERT and WILLIAM HERBERT JR & ordered to be certified. And at a Court held for the said County the 20th day of November 1809 the same was further proved by the oath of WILLIAM H. FOOTE & ordered to be recorded.
Teste WM. MOSS Cl.

Page 333. KNOW ALL MEN by these presents that I ANTHONY THORNTON of the Town of Centreville in the County of Fairfax for and in consideration of the sum of thirty six pounds to me in hand paid by CHARLES TYLER JR at & before the sealing & delivery of these presents the receipt whereof I do hereby acknowledge have Granted, bargained & sold and by these presents do Grant, bargain & sell unto the said CHARLES TYLER JR his Executors, Administrators & Assigns, one slave, a female named BECK, a Yellow Woman now in the possession of MRS. CATY COCKERILL. To Have & To Hold all and singular the said slave above bargained and sold, or mentioned or intended so to be to the said CHARLES TYLER JR his Executors, Administrators & Assigns forever. And I, the said ANTHONY THORNTON for myself, my Heirs, Executors & Administrators, all & singular the said slave Unto the said CHARLES TYLER JR his Executors, Administrators & Assigns against me the said ANTHONY THORNTON, my Executors & Administrators and against all & every other person & persons whatsoever shall & will warrant & forever defend by these presents. In WITNESS whereof I have hereunto set my hand & affixed my seal this 16th day of September 1809.
Witnes
ALEXN. WAUGH, SAML. SMITH   ANTHONY THORNTON   (seal)
THOS. PEAKE. HUMPH. PEAKE

At a Court held for Fairfax County the 20th day of November 1809 this Bill of Sale from ANTHONY THORNTON to CHARLES TYLER JR was proved to be the Act & deed of the said ANTHONY THORNTON by the oaths of ALEXANDER WAUGH, THOMAS PEAKE & HUMPHREY PEAKE witnesses hereto and ordered to be Recorded.
Teste WM. MOSS Cl.

Pages 333 & 334. THIS INDENTURE made this seventh day of September One thousand eight hundred & nine between JOHN JOHNSON of the County of Fairfax and State of Virginia of the one part and ABEL BLAKENY of the same County and State of the other part. WITNESSETH that the said JOHN JOHNSON hath put, placed & bound his son WILLIAM JOHNSON and the said WILLIAM JOHNSON doth by these presents Put, place & bind himself in apprentice to him the said ABEL BLAKENY for the term of four Years and six Months from the date hereof. And it is further understood by and between the parties to these presents that the said WM. JOHNSON shall serve the said ABEL BLAKENY anywhere within the limits of the United States, where-soever the said BLAKENY shall choose to remove himself during all which time he the said apprentice his master faithfully shall serve, his secrets keep, his lawful commands obey and in every respect behave himself as a good & faithful apprentice ought to do during the term aforesaid. And the said ABEL BLAKENY doth obligate & oblige himself to cause the said WILLIAM JOHNSON to be taught the art & mystery of House Carpenter & Joiner and also furnish him with good & sufficient meat, drink, washing, lodging & apparel and give him nine Months schooling during the said Term. In WITNESS whereof the parties to these presents have hereunto set their hands & Seals the day & Year above Written.

Sealed & Delivered	JOHN JOHNSON	(seal)
In presence of	ABEL BLAKENY	(seal)
TR. C. NASH	WILLIAM his + mark JOHNSON	(seal)

At a Court held for Fairfax County the 21st day of November 1809 this indenture between JOHN JOHNSON, ABEL BLAKENY and WILLIAM JOHNSON was proved by the oath of TRAVERS COULSTON NASH a Witness thereto and ordered to be Recorded.
Teste WM. MOSS Cl.

Page 334 & 335. THIS INDENTURE made this tenth day of May in the Year of our Lord one thousand eight hundred and Nine between JOHN THOMAS RICKETTS of the County of Fairfax and CommonWealth of Virginia and WILLIAM NEWTON of the Town of Alexandria and District of Columbia of the one part and RICHARD BLAND LEE of the County of Fairfax & Common-Wealth aforesaid of the other part. Whereas the said RICHARD BLAND LEE did on the twentieth day of July in the Year of our Lord one thousand eight hundred and three execute a certain deed of Mortgage to the said JOHN THOMAS RICKETTS and WILLIAM NEWTON and a certain FRANCIS DEAKINS of the town of George Town and District of Columbia for three hundred and seventy five acres of Land situate in the sd. County of Fairfax and being part of the tract of land on which the said RICHARD BLAND LEE now resides to secure the payment of certain bonds thereon mentioned and whereas the bonds due to said JOHN THOMAS RICKETTS and WILLIAM NEWTON have been fully discharged and paid. Now this indenture WITNESSETH that the said JOHN THOMAS RICKETTS and WILLIAM NEWTON for and in consideration of the premises and in further consideration of one Dollar to them in hand paid by the said RICHARD BLAND LEE the receipt whereof they do hereby acknowledge Have Granted, bargained & sold, released and confirmed and by these presents do Grant, bargain & sell, release & confirm unto the said RICHARD BLAND LEE his heirs & assigns all the right, title and interest conveyed to them the said JOHN THOMAS RICKETTS & WILLIAM NEWTON by the said RICHARD BLAND LEE by the herein before mentioned deed of Mortgage for the said tract or parcel of three hundred and seventy five acres of land in the said deed of mortgage more particularly described. In Testimony whereof the said JOHN THOMAS RICKETTS and the said WILLIAM NEWTON have hereunto set their hands & Seals the day & Year first above Written.

Signed Sealed & delivered		
in the Presence of us	JNO. THOS. RICKETTS	(seal)
EDM. J. LEE W. N. & J. T. R.	WM. NEWTON	(seal)
THO. SWANN		
WM. MOSS to WM. N.		
GEO. YOUNGS to J. T. R.		

At a Court continued and held for Fairfax County the 21st day of November 1809 this Deed from JOHN THOMAS RICKETTS and WILLIAM NEWTON to RICHARD BLAND LEE was proved to be the act and deed of the said JOHN THOMAS RICKETTS by the oaths of EDMUND J. LEE, THOMAS SWANN and GEORGE YOUNGS and to be the act and deed of the said WILLIAM NEWTON by the oaths of EDMUND J. LEE, THOMAS SWANN and WILLIAM MOSS and ordered to be recorded.
Teste WM. MOSS Cl.

Pages 336-339. THIS INDENTURE made this nineteenth day of September in the Year of our Lord one thousand eight hundred and nine between ANTHONY CHARLES CAZENOVE and ANN

his wife of the Town & County of Alexandria in the District of Columbia of the one part and
DAVID WATKINS of the County of Fairfax in the State of Virginia of the other part.
WITNESSETH that the said ANTHONY CHARLES CAZENOVE and ANN his wife for and in consider-
ation of the sum of one hundred seventy three dollars & seventy one cents to him the said
ANTHONY CHARLES CAZENOVE in hand paid by him the said DAVID WATKINS at or before the
Sealing and delivery of these presents the receipt whereof he the said ANTHONY CHARLES
CAZENOVE doth hereby acknowledge and thereof and of every part and parcel thereof doth
acquit, release and dishcarge him the said DAVID WATKINS his Heirs, Executors and Aminis-
trators, by these presents Have Given, Granted, bargained & sold, aliened and confirmed and
by these presents do Give, Grant, bargain, sell, alien & confirm unto him the said DAVID
WATKINS his heirs & assigns forever a tract or parcel of land situate, lying and being upon
the drains of Great Hunting creek in the said County of Fairfax and State of Virginia, being
one of those Lotts into which that tract of Land called & known by the name of Stump Hill was
divided and by JAMES KEITH, GEORGE GILPIN and FRANCIS PEYTON sold and conveyed unto him
the said ANTHONY CHARLES CAZENOVE his heirs and assigns by an indenture bearing date the
twenty third day of April one thousand Eight hundred and four and in the platt of the said
Tract of Land and the division thereof is described by number 8 the same being bounded as
followeth to wit: beginning at a stake on the Turnpike road corner to that other dividend of
the said tract described by the number 7, thirty three poles to the Westward of the first
avenue laid out through the said Tract and running thence North fifteen degrees East fifty
poles to a stake in the line of the Lott number 14, thence with the line of that Lot North
seventy Nine degrees West seventeen poles another stake in the said line corner to the Lott
number 9, thence with the line of that lott south fifteen degrees West fifty poles to a stake on
the side of the turnpike road another corner to Lott number 9, thence with the Turnpike road
south seventy nine degrees East seventeen poles to the beginning containing five acres and
fifty poles and all Houses, buildings, Trees, Woods, Waters, Roads & Lanes, avenues, profits,
commodities, Hereditaments & apputenances whatsoever to the premises belonging or in
anywise appertaining and the Reversion & reversions, remainder & Remainders, Rents,
issues & profits thereof and of every part and parcel thereof. To have and to hold the said
tract or parcel of land, hereditaments and all and singular the premises hereby granted with
their appurtenances unto him the said DAVID WATKINS his heirs & assigns to the only proper
use and behoof of him the said DAVID WATKINS his heirs and assigns forever. And the said
ANTHONY CHARLES CAZENOVE doth for himself, his heirs, Executors and Administrators,
covenant, grant and agree to and with the said DAVID WATKINS his heirs & assigns that he
the said ANTHONY CHARLES CAZENOVE is now at the time of the sealing and delivery of these
presents seized in his own right of a good, sure, perfect, absolute and indefeasible estate of
inheritance, in fee simple in the said tract or parcel of Land, Hereditaments and all and
singular the said premises with their appurtenances without any manner of condition,
Mortgage, Limitation of use or uses, or any other matter, cause or thing to alter, change,
charge or determine the same and also that he the said ANTHONY CHARLES CAZENOVE and his
heirs will at any time hereafter upon the request and at the cost and charge of him the said
DAVID WATKINS his heirs & assigns execute & acknowledge any further lawful act and deed
for the more certain assuring & conveying the said tract or parcel of Land, Hereditaments &
all and singular the Premises with their appurtenances unto him the said DAVID WATKINS his
heirs and assigns as by him the said DAVID WATKINS his heirs and assigns his, their or any of
their Counsil learned in the Law shall or may be advised or required and Lastly that he the
said ANTHONY CHARLES CAZENOVE and his heirs, all & singular, the same premises with their
appurtenances unto him to the said DAVID WATKINS his heirs and assigns against the claim
and demand of him the said ANTHONY CHARLES CAZANOVE and his heirs & every other person
or persons whatsoever shall and will warrant and forever defend by these presents. In
WITNESS whereof the said ANTHONY CHARLES CAZANOVE and ANN his wife have hereunto set
their hands & Seals the day & Year first herein before mentioned.
Sealed & delivered
in presence of   ANT. CHS. CAZENOVE   (seal)
GEO. YOUNGS   ANNE CAZENOVE   (seal)
R. J. TAYLOR

N. HERBERT
THOMAS WATKINS
        Received of DAVID WATKINS the sum of one hundred seventy three dollars & seventy
one cents the consideration herein mentioned.
WITNESS   ANT. CHS. CAZENOVE
GEO. YOUNGS, R. J. TAYLOR
N. HERBERT, THOS. WATKINS
        At a Court continued and held for Fairfax County the 21st day of November 1809 this
Deed from ANTHONY C. CAZENOVE and ANNE his wife to DAVID WATKINS and a receipt thereon
Endorsed were proved by the oaths of GEORGE YOUNGS, ROBERT J, TAYLOR and NOBLET
HERBERT which together with a Commission and Return thererto annexed for taking the
acknowledgment & privy Examination of the said ANNE wife of the said ANTHONY C. CAZENOVE
are Ordered to be Recorded.   Teste WM. MOSS Cl.
        FAIRFAX COUNTY To Wit:
        The CommonWealth of Virginia to JACOB HOFFMAN, CUTHBERT POWELL & GEO. GILPIN
Gentlemen Justices of the County of Alexandria in the District of Columbia Greeting: Whereas
ANTHONY CHARLES CAZENOVE and ANNE his wife by their certain indenture of Bargain & sale
bearing date the nineteenth day of September 1809 have sold and conveyed unto DAVID
WATKINS the fee simple estate of a tract of Land with the appurtenances situate, lying and
being upon the drains of Great Hunting creek in the said County of Fairfax and whereas the
said ANNE cannot conveniently travel to our said County Court of Fairfax to make acknowledgment of the said conveyance therefore we do give unto you or any two or more of you
power to receive the acknowledgment which the said ANN shall be willing to make before you
of the conveyance aforesaid contained in the said indenture which is hereunto annexed and
we do therefore desire You or any two or more of you personally to go to the said ANNE and
receive her acknowledgment of the same and examine her privily and apart from the said
ANTHONY CHARLES her husband whither she doth the same freely & voluntarily without his
persuasions or threats and whither she be willing the said Indenture together with this
Commission shall be recorded in our said Court. And when you have received her acknowledgment and examined her as aforesaid that you distinctly and openly Certify us thereof in
our said court under Your hands & seals sending then there the said Indenture & this Writ.
WITNESS WILLIAM MOSS Clerk of our said Court at the Courthouse of the County aforesaid this
19th day of September 1809 and in the 34th Year of the CommonWealth.
                                          WM. MOSS Cl.
        DISTRICT OF COLUMBIA, COUNTY OF ALEXANDRIA To Wit:
        In obedience to the within commission we did examine the said ANN privily and apart
from the said ANTHONY CHARLES her husband who declared that she Executed the said
indenture freely and Voluntarily without his persuasions or threats and that she was willing
the same together with this commission should be recorded in the said Court. Given under our
hands & seals this 7th day of October one thousand Eight hundred & nine.
Truly Recorded   JACOB HOFFMAN   (seal)
        Teste WM. MOSS Cl.   CUTHBERT POWELL   (seal)

Pages 340 & 341. THIS INDENTURE made and entered into this fifteenth day of March in the
Year of our Lord one thousand eight hundred & Nine between ANN SUMMERS of the County of
Christian and State of Kentucky of the one part and REZIN WILCOXEN of the County of Fairfax
and State of Virginia of the other part. WITNESSETH that the said ANN SUMMERS for and in
consideration of the sum of five shillings to her in hand paid by the said WILCOXEN the
receipt whereof she by these presents does acknowledge and of the same does acquit &
Exonerate the said WILCOXEN, his heirs, Executors and Administrators have bargained, sold,
Aliened, released, confirmed and made over unto the said WILCOXEN and by these presents do
bargain, sell, alien, release, confirm and make over unto the said WILCOXEN his heirs and
assigns forever all her right, title, interest & claim in & to all that tract of land situate in
Fairfax County aforesaid which the father of said ANN SUMMERS, COLO. GEORGE SUMMERS
owned at the time of his death supposed to contain three hundred & eighty Acres or thereabouts be the same more or less and which land adjoins the land of RICHARD RATCLIFFE, JOHN

MASON, the Widow of the late JOHN O'DANIEL, the lands of the said WILCOXEN and perhaps the lands of some others whose names are not now recollected together with all appurtenances of every kind and Nature in anywise appertaining to the aforesaid Lands owned as aforesaid by the said COL. GEORGE SUMMERS. To have and to hold the said Lands be the same more or less with the said Appurtenances unto the said WILCOXEN his heirs & assigns forever for the only proper use and behoof of him the said WILCOXEN his heirs & assigns forever. And the said ANN SUMMERS for herself, her Heirs, Executors & Administrators do covenant and agree with the said WILCOXEN, his heirs, Executors, Administrators & Assigns to warrant and forever defend the aforesaid lands & appurtenances unto the said WILCOXEN his heirs and assigns forever against all persons claiming by, from or under the said ANN SUMMERS. In Testimony whereof the said ANN SUMMERS has hereunto subscribed her name and affixed her seal the day & Year first within written.   ANN SUMMERS   (seal)
          CHRISTIAN COUNTY:
          Clerks Office 15th March 1809 this day came before me, JOHN CLARK clerk of said County Court the within named ANN SUMMERS and acknowledged the foregoing indenture of Bargain and Sale unto REZIN WILCOXEN as her proper Act and deed, hand & Seal and requested that the same might be Recorded and I do thereby certify that the same has been duly Recorded in my said Office in deed Book B Page 171.
          In Testimony whereof I have hereunto set my hand & affixed
(SEAL)   the Seal of our said County Court the day & date above Written.
                              JNO. CLARK
          STATE OF KENTUCKY, CHRISTIAN COUNTY To Wit:
          I JAMES THOMPSON, Presiding Justice of the Peace in & for the County aforesaid do hereby certify that the aforesaid JNO. CLARK (whose signature is affixed to the within Indenture) is Clerk to our said County Court and that his certificate aforesaid is in due form of law and that he is entitled to due faith & credit when acting in his Official Capacity. In WITNESS whereof I have hereunto set my hand & Seal this 15th day of March 1809.
                              J. THOMPSON (seal)
          At a Court continued & held for Fairfax County the 25th day of November 1809 This Deed from ANNE SUMMERS to REZIN WILCOXEN having been duly acknowledged before JOHN CLARK clerk of Christian County in the State of Kentucky and admitted to Record & Certified by him under the Seal of his Office also by JAMES THOMPSON Presiding Justice of the peace for said County is on motion of the said REZIN WILCOXEN together with the Certificates thereon Endorsed Ordered to be Recorded.   Teste WM. MOSS Cl.

Pages 342-345. THIS INDENTURE made this eighteenth day of May in the Year of our Lord one thousand eight hundred and Eight between JOHN WISE and ELIZABETH his wife of the Town and County of Alexandria in the District of Columbia of the one part and JANE MONROE of the County of Fairfax and State of Virginia of the other part. WITNESSETH that the said JOHN WISE and ELIZABETH his wife for and in consideration of the sum of thirty Dollars to him in hand paid by the said JANE MONROE the receipt whereof he doth hereby acknowledge and thereof doth acquit, exonerate & discharge the said JANE MONROE, her Executors, Administrators and Assigns forever by these presents have Granted, bargained and sold, aliened and confirmed and by these presents do Grant, bargain & sell, alien & confirm unto the said JANE MONROE her heirs and assigns forever a piece or parcell of land situate in the county of Fairfax, adjoining the lands of WILLIAM HENRY TERRETT and lands of MARY FENDALL formerly held by WILLIAM BIRD & bounded as followeth to wit: beginning on the North side of the Turnpike road a stake corner of a piece of land conveyed as a mill seat by ENOCH FRANCIS to said WILLIAM BIRD containing about two and quarter acres and by sundry conveyances is now in the tenure & seizure of WILLIAM DOUGLASS of the said Town and County, thence Northwardly with the lines of the said mill Lot to the corner of the dividing line of the said TERRETT and land sold by JOHN HAWKINS to JOHN WISE, thence with TERRETTS line southwestwardly to the land of MRS. FENDALL near the Turnpike road, thence Eastwardly with the turnpike road and MRS. FENDALLS line to the beginning containing one acre & one half more or less and all the Houses, out Houses, woods, underwoods, Ways, Waters, Watercourses, profits, commodities, hereditaments and appurtenances whatsoever to the same belonging or in anywise appertaining (the same being a part of the said Land conveyed by the said HAWKINS to the said WISE) and the Reversion & Reversions, Remainder & Remainders, rents, Issues & profits thereof. To have and To hold the said piece or parcell of land and premises with all and singular the appurtenances unto the said JANE MONROE her heirs & assigns, to her and their only proper use and behoof forever. And the said JOHN WISE for himself his heirs, Executors & Administrators doth hereby covenant and Grant to and with the said JANE MUNROE her heirs & assigns that now at the time of sealing and delivering these presents he is seized in his own right in Fee simple of and in the said hereby granted & conveyed piece or parcell of land & premises with the appurtenances and that the same is clear of and free from all & all manner [of] former and other Gifts, Grants, bargains, sales, mortgages, uses, limitation of uses, titles, troubles, charges & incumbrances whatsoever had made, committed, done or suffered, by the said JOHN WISE or any other person or persons whatsoever. And the said JOHN WISE the said hereby granted and conveyed piece or parcel of land & premises with the appurtenances unto the said JANE MONROE her heirs & Assigns doth hereby warrant and forever defend against the claim & demand of them the said JOHN WISE and ELIZABETH his wife and of all and every other person and persons whatsoever. In WITNESS whereof the said JOHN WISE and ELIZABETH his wife have hereunto set their hands & seals the day & Year first within Written. Sealed & delivered in presence of

JOHN McLAUGHLIN   JOHN WISE   (seal)
THOMAS TRIPLETT, D. MINOR   [No signature]   (seal)
     Alexandria May 18th 1808 Recd. of JANE MONROE thirty dollars the consideration within mentioned.
Witness   JOHN WISE
JOHN McLAUGHLIN
     DISTRICT OF COLUMBIA To Wit:
          I GEORGE DENEALE Clerk of the United States circuit Court of the District of
(SEAL)   Columbia for the County of Alexandria do hereby certify that at a court
          continued & held for the District and County aforesaid the fifteenth day of
December 1808 JOHN WISE acknowledged this Deed & receipt to JANE MONROE to be his act and deed & ordered to be certified to the County Court of Fairfax in the CommonWealth of Virginia. In Testimony whereof I have hereunto set my hand & affixed the public seal of my Office on this ninth day of February 1809.   G. DENEALE Cl.
     DISTRICT OF COLUMBIA To Wit:
     I WILLIAM CRANCH Chief Judge of the United States circuit Court of the District of Columbia do hereby certify that the above attestation of GEORGE DENEALE Clerk of the said Court for Alexandria County is in due form. Given under my hand this 23rd day of October 1809.   W. CRANCH
     At a court held for Fairfax County the 18th day of December 1809 this Deed from JNO. WISE and ELIZABETH his wife to JANE MUNROE having been duly acknowledged by the said JNO. WISE before the United States circuit court of the District of Columbia held for the County of Alexandria and certified by GEORGE DENEALE Clerk of the said Court under the seal of his office, also by WILLIAM CRANCH Chief Judge of the said court, is on motion of the said JANE MONROE together with a receipt & certificates thereon endorsed ordered to be Recorded.
                         Teste WM. MOSS Cl.

Pages 345-347. MEMORANDUM of agreement entered into the twentieth day of February eighteen hundred & Eight between BENJAMIN DULANY & ROBERT MOSS both of the County of Alexandria in the District of Columbia. WITNESSETH that whereas the said ROBERT MOSS did in the Year of our lord one thousand eight hundred & six obtain from the Registers Office in the State of Virginia a pattent or Grant for one hundred & sixty four acres of Land lying in the County of Fairfax adjoining the lands of the said BENJAMIN DULANY which said one hundred & sixty four acres was untill then supposed to be vacant. But the said BENJAMIN DULANY having since found a patent in the name of DANIEL FRENCH dated the nineteenth day of February seventeen hundred & thirty for one hundred & twenty seven acres which he supposes to cover a part of the said one hundred & sixty four acres and which he claims in right of his wife she being the Daughter & devisee of the said DANIEL FRENCH. Therefore in

order to settle every difficulty that may arise between the Parties and their representatives, they have mutually agreed to survey agreeable to the courses & distances mentioned in their respective pattents; And the said ROBERT MOSS for himself & his Heirs doth agree that if it shall be found on running the courses & distances in the pattent granted to the said FRENCH that any part of the land contained in his Pattent should be covered by the aforesaid Pattent Granted to the said DANIEL FRENCH that he will and doth hereby relinquish all claim to the same and the said BENJAMIN DULANY doth for himself and his Heirs agree to relinquish and doth hereby relinquish all claim to the Land included in the said MOSS's Pattent except so much (if any) as shall be included within the courses & distances mentioned in the Pattent granted to the before mentioned DANIEL FRENCH. In WITNESS whereof the parties have here-unto set their hands and seals the day & date aforesaid.
Signed and Sealed
In Presence of us   BENJ. DULANY   (seal)
RICHD. M. SCOTT, SIM. SOMMERS   R. MOSS   (seal)
P. TRIPLETT, RICHARD LEWIS
          DISTRICT OF COLUMBIA To Wit:
          I GEORGE DENEALE Clerk of the United States circuit court of the District of
(SEAL)   Columbia for the County of Alexandria do hereby certify that at a court
          continued & held for the District & County aforesaid the tenth day of December
1808 This Agreement between BENJ. DULANY and ROBERT MOSS was proved by the oath of SIMON SOMMERS and RICHARD LEWIS to be the act and deed of the said BENJAMIN DULANY and ordered to be certified. And at the same court contd. & held the twenty third day of December 1808: This Agreement was further proved by the oath of PHILIP TRIPLETT to be the act and deed of the said BENJAMIN DULANY & ROBERT MOSS acknowledged the same to be his act and deed & ordered to be certified to the county court of Fairfax in the CommonWealth of Virginia. In Testimony whereof I have hereunto set my hand & affixed the public seal of my office on this 16th day of February in the Year of our Lord 1809.
                              G. DENEALE Cl.
          DISTRICT OF COLUMBIA To Wit:
          I WILLIAM CRANCH Chief Judge of the United States circuit court of the District of Columbia do hereby certify that the above attestation of GEORGE DENEALE Clerk of the said Court for Alexandria county is in due form. Given under my hand this 23rd day of October 1809.   W. CRANCH
          At a court held for Fairfax County the 18th day of December 1809 This Memorandum of Agreement between BENJAMIN DULANY and ROBERT MOSS having been duly proved to be the act and deed of the said BENJAMIN DULANY and acknowledged by the said ROBERT MOSS,before the United States circuit court of the District of Columbia held for the county of Alexandria and certified by GEORGE DENEALE Clerk of the said court under the seal of his Office, also by WILLIAM CRANCH Chief Judge of the said court, is on motion of the said ROBERT MOSS together with the certificates thereon endorsed Ordered to be Recorded.
                              Teste WM. MOSS Cl.

Pages 347 & 348. KNOW ALL MEN by these presents that I JAMES WILEY of the County of Fairfax & CommonWealth of Virginia for and in consideration of the sum of five hundred & sixty one dollars to him in hand paid by HENRY GANTT of the County of Jefferson and CommonWealth aforesaid hath Granted, Bargained & sold and by these presents Doth Grant, bargain & sell unto the said HENRY GANTT the following negro slaves to wit: SUMMERSET, TUBMAN and ISAIAH which said Negro slaves were conveyed to the said JAMES WILEY by EDWARD GANTT by deed Bearing date the 15th day of October 1807 in trust to secure the payment of a sum of money due from the said EDWARD GANTT to the said HENRY GANTT and were sold by the said JAMES WILEY at pulic sale on the 13th day of October 1809 at which said sale the said HENRY GANTT became the purchaser at the price of five hundred & sixty one dollars. To Have & To Hold the said Negro slaves to the said HENRY GANTT his heirs and assigns to the only proper use and behoof of the said HENRY GANTT his heirs & assigns forever. And the sd. JAMES WILEY doth hereby warrant & defend the said Negro slaves to the said HENRY GANTT and his heirs against the claim and demand of him the said JAMES WILEY & those claiming under him, but against no other persons nor against any claim which the said slaves or either of them may set up to their freedom. In WITNESS whereof the said JAMES WILEY hath hereunto set his hand & affixed his seal this first day of December one thousand Eight hundred & nine.   JAMES WILEY   (seal)

At a court held for Fairfax County the 18th day of December 1809 JAMES WILEY acknowledged this Bill of sale to HENRY GANTT to be his act and deed & ordered to be recorded.

Teste WM. MOSS Cl.

Pages 348-350. THIS INDENTURE made this 29th day of October 1808 between JOSEPH SIMPSON and ANN SIMPSON his wife, formerly ANN NEALE, widow and relict of THOMAS NEALE decd, of the one part and CHARLES TYLER JR all of the County of Fairfax and State of Virginia of the other part. WITNESSETH that the said JOSEPH SIMPSON and ANN his wife as aforesaid hath this day leased to the said CHARLES TYLER JR all his Dower right in the tract of land formerly owned by the said THOS. NEALE decd lying & being in the county of Fairfax & bounded by the waters of Great Rockey Cedar Run on the south west and by WILLIAM LANE JR, CHARLES J. LOVE and COLEMAN BROWNS Lands on the South west & north west containing 250 acres be the same more or less (reserving to STEPHEN DANIEL a Lease on the same Dower for all the land on the left hand side of the Road leading from Centreville to Little River) with all & singular the appurtenances thereunto belonging or in any wise appertaining for and during the natural life of her the said ANN SIMPSON and no longer, he the said CHARLES TYLER JR paying for the same the annual rent of seventy dollars current money of Virginia to them the said JOSEPH SIMPSON & ANN his wife or to their Assigns, during the natural life of the said ANN SIMPSON the Rent to commence of the first day of January next and payable every twelve months afterwards. It is understood between the parties that the said CHARLES TYLER JR is to pay the tax on the said Land during the Term of this lease. In Testimony whereof the said parties have hereunto set their hands & affixed their seals the day & date above written.
Signed Sealed & acknowledged
in presence of   JOSEPH SIMPSON   (seal)
GUSTAVUS H. SCOTT   ANN SIMPSON   (seal)
CHR. NEALE   CHARLES TYLER JR   (seal)
ANTHONY THORNTON

At a court held for Fairfax County the nineteenth day of December 1808 this Deed of Lease from JOSEPH SIMPSON & ANN his wife to CHARLES TYLER JR was proved to be the act and deed of the said JOSEPH SIMPSON by the oath of ANTHONY THORNTON as Witness hereto and ordered to be certified and at a court held for Fairfax County the 15th day of May 1809. This Deed of Lease was further proved by the oath of CHRISTOPHER NEALE another Witness hereto & ordered to be certified. And At a Court held for the said County the 18th day of December 1809 the same was further proved by the oath of GUSTAVUS H. SCOTT & ordered to be Recorded.

Teste WM. MOSS Cl.

Pages 350 & 351. KNOW ALL MEN by these presents that I GUSTAVUS HALL SCOTT of the County of Fairfax and CommonWealth of Virginia for & in consideration of the sum of one dollar to me in hand paid by CHARLES J. LOVE of the county & CommonWealth aforesaid the receipt whereof I do hereby acknowledge hath bargained, sold & delivered & by these presents doth bargain, sell and deliver unto the said CHARLES J. LOVE the following negro slaves to wit: CHARLES, HENRY, JIM, PEGGY & her two children MATILDA & JOHN and also all my Household furniture, my stock of Horses, cattle, sheep, hogs and farming utensils, a schedule of all which is hereunto annexed. To have and To Hold the said hereby Granted premises unto the said CHARLES J. LOVE, his executors and Administrators forever. And the said GUSTAVUS HALL SCOTT, for himself and his Heirs, the said hereby Granted premises unto the said CHARLES J. LOVE his Executors and Administrators, against the claim and demand of all & every person and persons whatsoever shall & will warrant & forever defend by these presents, AS WITNESS my hand & seal this 6th day of December one thousand eight hundred & nine.
Sealed & delivd in presence of

CHARLES TYLER JR.   GUSTS. H. SCOTT   (seal)
PETER JETT
HUMPH. PEAKE
    Schedule referred to in the within deed: houshold & kitchen furniture, consisting of
beds & beding, Tables, Chairs &c &c and all the Horses, cattle, sheep, Hogs & farming utensils
of every kind.
    At a Court held for Fairfax County the 18th day of December 1809 this Bill of sale from
GUSTAVUS H. SCOTT to CHARLES J. LOVE was acknowledged by the said GUSTAVUS H. SCOTT to be
his act and deed which is ordered to be recorded with the schedule thereto annexed.
                          Teste WM. MOSS Cl.

Pages 351-353. THIS INDENTURE made this 20th day of June in the Year one thousand eight
hundred & nine between EDWARD DULIN of Fairfax County and State of Virginia of the one
part And JOHN DULIN of aforesaid county & state of the other part. WITNESSETH that the said
EDWARD DULIN in consideration of the sum of two thousand five hundred Dollars lawfull
money to him in hand paid by the said JOHN DULIN at or before the ensealing & delivery of
these presents the receipt whereof is hereby acknowledged have bargained & sold and by
these presents do bargain & sell unto the said JOHN DULIN his heirs & assigns all that tract or
parcell of land lying & being in the county of Fairfax & CommonWealth of Virginia, whereon
the said EDWARD DULIN doth at present reside and which he holds in right of his fathers will,
also all that tract or parcel of land lying & being as before on which the said EDWARD DULIN
resides which he owns by deed of Bargain and sale made on the 21st day of October 1793 by
WILLIAM DULIN & MARY his wife to EDWARD & JOHN DULIN reference thereunto being had
will more fully be made to appear situate and adjoining (a tract or parcel of land now owned
by the above mentioned JOHN DULIN on which he resides, of which said land he the said JOHN
DULIN became possessed by the before mentioned will of his father E. DULIN deceased and the
before mentioned deed of bargain and sale of WILLIAM DULIN and MARY his wife to the said
EDWD. & JOHN DULIN) the same being a moiety of two tracts or parcels of land purchased by
EDWARD DULIN the father of EDWD. & JOHN the one of JOHN FITZHUGH and the other of SIMON
PEARSON and MILKEY his wife which sd. deeds will make the same more fully appear
containing four hundred & seventy acres or thereabouts be the same more or less together
with all & singular the Houses, Barnes, stables, Yards, Gardens, orchards, lands, fences, woods,
waters & water courses, priviledges, profits, commodities, advantages, emoluments, hereditaments & appurtenances whatsoever to the tract or parcel of land belonging, or to the same in
any wise appertaining or known as part or member thereof and the Reversion or Reversions,
Remainder or Remainders, Yearly & other Rents, Issues & profits thereof and of every part or
parcel thereof. To have and to Hold the sd. tract or parcel of land with the tenements, hereditaments & all & singular other the premises herein before mentioned, or intended to be
bargained and sold and every land part and parcell thereof to the said JOHN DULIN his heirs &
assigns forever to and for the only proper use & behoof of him the said JOHN DULIN his heirs
and assigns forever and the said EDWARD DULIN for himself and his heirs the said tract or
parcel of with all & singular the premises & appurtenances before mentioned unto the said
JOHN DULIN his heirs & assigns free from the claim or claims of him the sd. EDWD. DULIN &
his heirs & of all & every person or persons whatsoever do warrant and defend by these
presents. In WITNESS whereof the said EDWD. DULIN have hereunto set his hand & seal the
day & Year first above witten.
Signed, Sealed & delivered
in presence of   EDWD. DULIN   (seal)
DANIEL McCARTY CHICHESTER
RB. DARNE
ELIZABETH CHICHESTER
    At a court held for Fairfax County the 18th day of December 1809 EDWARD DULIN
acknowledged this deed to JOHN DULIN to be his act & deed and ordered to be Recorded.
                          Teste WM. MOSS Cl.

Pages 353-355. KNOW ALL MEN by these presents that I CHARLES JONES LOVE of Salisbury in the County of Fairfax & CommonWealth of Virginia as well to effect the objects herein after mentioned as for and in consideration of the sum of one dollar to him the said CHARLES J. LOVE in hand paid by CHARLES TYLER JR of the county of Prince William and CommonWealth aforesaid the receipt whereof the said CHARLES J, LOVE doth hereby acknowledge hath Bargained, sold & delivered and by these presents doth bargain, sell & deliver unto the said CHARLES TYLER JR the following negro slaves to wit: CHARLES, JIM, HENRY, PEGGY and her two children MATILDA & JOHN and also all the Houshold furniture & stock of Horses, Cows, cattle, sheep, Hogs and Farming utensils purchased by the said CHARLES J. LOVE of GUSTAVUS HALL SCOTT by deed bearing date the sixth day of this present Month reference being thereunto had the same will more fully appear. To have and To Hold the said hereby granted premises unto the said CHARLES TYLER JR his Executors & Administrators forever. In Trust however for the uses, intents & purposes following that is to say for the joint use & benefit of the said GUSTAVUS HALL SCOTT and ELIZABETH DOUGLASS his wife during their joint lives and afterwards to the use of the survivor of them during the life of such survivor. But if the said ELIZABETH DOUGLASS should survive the said GUSTAVUS H. SCOTT then the whole premises are to remain & inure to her only during her widowhood, her thirds during her life whither single or married and from and after the death of the said GUSTAVUS H. SCOTT & ELIZABETH DOUGLASS his wife to & for the use & benefit of the children of the said GUSTAVUS H. SCOTT & ELIZABETH DOUGLASS his wife living at the time of the death of the survivor of them their heirs & Assigns forever. And also upon this further trust that the said CHARLES TYLER JR shall & may at any time & at all times when he in his desiration shall think proper sell & dispose of the property hereby conveyed, or any part thereof to any person or persons he may think proper provided he invests the Moneys arising from the sd. sales in other personal property and shall settle the said property to the same uses as are expressed & contained in this present deed. And the said CHARLES J. LOVE, for himself & his heirs the said hereby Granted premises unto the said CHARLES TYLER JR his Executors and administrators, against the claim & demand of all & every person & persons whatsoever shall & will warrant & forever defend by these presents. Given under my hand & seal this ninth day of December 1809.
Sealed & delivered in
presence of   CH. J. LOVE   (seal)
JNO. LOVE
JAMES A. BALL, JOHN DIXON
        At a Court held for Fairfax County the 18th day of December 1809 this deed from CHARLES J. LOVE to CHARLES TYLER JR in Trust for the use of ELIZABETH DOUGLASS SCOTT and others was acknowledged by the said CHARLES J. LOVE to be his act and deed & ordered to be recorded.   Teste WM. MOSS Cl.

Pages 355-362. THIS INDENTURE made this first day of June in the Year eighteen hundred & nine between HAZLEWOOD FARISH of Fredericksburgh, Virginia of the first part, THOMAS TRIPLETT of the town & County of Alexandria in the District of Columbia of the second part and NATHANIEL ELLICOTT of the third part. Whereas the said NATHANIEL ELLICOTT has sold to the said HAZLEWOOD FARISH his line of stages as well the accomodation as mail line of stages running between Alexandria and Dumfries consisting of two large stages and two mail stages, including also the stable and Lott on which it stands as now owned & used by the said ELLICOTT in Dumfries. Also twenty two horses such as the said FARISH may choose from those now running upon the said line; and whereas the said HAZLEWOOD FARISH has given for the same his several notes payable at different times in all amounting the sum of four thousand three hundred dollars dated all on the first of June 1809 one payable on the first day of November 1809 for $566, one due the 1st February 1810 for $425, one due the 1st May 1810 for $425, one due 1st August 1810 for $425, one due 1st November 1810 for $425 making $2266 payable in all the Year 1809 and 1810 up to 1st November. Also five other notes dated on the first day of June 1809 falling due as follows: one note due 1st June 1810 for $406.80, one due 1st September 1810 for $406.80, one due 1st December 1810 for $406.80, one due 1st March 1811 for $406.80 and one due 1st June 1811 for $406.80 making the sum of two thousand thirty four dollars which with the before recited notes of $2266 makes the sum of $4300 to which is to be added the sum of two hundred dollars which the said FARISH is to settle with BENJAMIN BOTTS Esqr. for account of the said ELLICOTT, in all $4500 the sum agreed to be given & paid for the said lines of stages, Horses & Lott & stable aforesaid. And whereas the said HAZLEWOOD FARISH with a view and intention of securing to the said NATHANIEL ELLICOTT a punctual payment of the several sums of money as they become due by the several notes of hand aforesaid has agreed & hereby intends to convey in trust to the said THOMAS TRIPLETT all & Singular the aforesaid property to be sold as hereafter directed in case of the nonpayment of the said notes or any of them as they become due. Now this indenture WITNESSETH that the said HAZLEWOOD FARISH for and in consideration of the premises and of the further sum of five dollars to him in hand paid by the said THOMAS TRIPLETT at and before the sealing and delivery of these presents the receipt whereof is hereby acknowledged hath Granted, bargained, sold, assigned, sett over & confirmed and by these presents doth grant, bargain, sell, assign, sett over & confirm unto the said THOS. TRIPLETT, his heirs, Executors, Administrators or Assigns, all & singular the lines of stages between Alexandria & Dumfries commonly called the accomodation & mail lines of stages consisting of two large stages & two mail stages together with twenty two horses & one Lott & Stable thereupon in Dumfries herein before described to have been sold & conveyed by NATHANIEL ELLICOTT to the said HAZLEWOOD FARISH together with all the right, priviledges & advantages whatsoever thereto belonging. To have and To Hold all and singular the premises and all & singular the two lines of stages, Horses and Lott & stable in Dumfries, described in the premises and all and singular the rights, priviledges & advantages thereto in any manner belonging or appertaining unto the said THOMAS TRIPLETT, his heirs, Executors, Administrators or Assigns forever to the following uses & purposes however and none other: That is to say to hold all & singular the hereby property conveyed in trust in the 1st instance to permit the said HAZLEWOOD FARISH to hold, use & enjoy the hereby conveyed premises & every part thereof by running the said stages between Alexandria and Dumfries as is usual for them now to run untill the falling due of the several notes aforesaid. And in case the said HAZLEWOOD FARISH, his heirs, Executors, Administrators or Assigns shall fail to pay & regularly take up the said notes aforesaid as they respectively become due, then and in that case and in case of failure to take up & pay any one of the said notes as they become due & payable, To Hold and possess the said hereby granted premises from the time of such failure to pay all or any one of the said notes when due, To the use of the said NATHANIEL ELLICOTT, his heirs, Executors, Administrators & Assigns, in the first place to expose to public sale for cash (whenever the said NATHANIEL ELLICOTT or his proper Representative shall request the same in writing under his hand & seal), after giving ten days notice of the time & place of sale in the public newspaper printed in Alexandria all & singular the hereby granted premises, stages, horses & Lot & stable, or so much thereof as shall be sufficient to pay & satisfy such note or notes herein before described as may or shall have been suffered to fall due and remain unpaid together with all costs & charges thereupon and out of the monies arising from such sale first to pay the expences thereof secondly to pay the amount of such note or notes or part thereof as may have not been paid by the sd. FARISH aforesaid with interest costs & charges if any due thereupon and the surplus if any remaining to hold towards the discharge of any of the remaining notes then not due. And so often as any of the said notes aforesaid shall fall due and be suffered to remain unpaid as often as the same shall so happen then in every such case the said THOMAS TRIPLETT, his heirs, Executors or Administrators, whenever he or they shall be so requested by the said NATHANIEL ELLICOTT, his heirs, Execut- ors, Administrators or Assigns shall expose to sale for cash as aforesaid in manner and form aforesaid as much of the hereby conveyed premises at each and every time as may be necessary to pay up and discharge the amount of all such notes, interest, costs and charges as shall have been suffered to fall due and are not paid, in all such cases after paying the expences attending such sale to pay the respective amount or amounts due holding any surplus towards discharging those of the said notes not due. And when the whole shall have become due and are paid if any sum or sums of money shall be in the hands of the sd. trustee in case sale may or shall have been made such surplus or sum or sums of money after deducting any charge or expence incurred out of the same to be paid over to the said HAZLEWOOD FARISH or his proper Representative together with a release of all incumbrance upon such and the whole of such of the premises as shall remain & in case the said HAZLEWOOD FARISH shall not within a reasonable time from the present pay unto the said BENJAMIN BOTTS Esqr., for account of the said N. ELLICOTT the said two hundred dollars & procure the sd. B. BOTTS receipt & discharge for that sum on account of the sd. N. ELLICOTT, then the said THOMAS TRIPLETT to sell so much of the hereby granted premises under the same rules and restriction as is thereby directed in case of the notes as will pay & satisfy the amount with interest &c. And the said HAZLEWOOD FARISH for himself, his heirs, Executors and Administrators doth covenant and agree to & with the said NATHANIEL ELLICOTT, his heirs, executors, Administrators & assigns that he will well and truly pay and take up the said several notes aforesaid described when & as they become due and payable. And the said HAZLEWOOD FARISH for himself, his heirs, exors and admrs further grants, covenants & agrees to and with the said NATHANIEL ELLICOTT, his heirs, Executors, Admins & Assigns that so long as he owns the line of stages they shall run by & through the Town of Occoquan and in case the sd. FARISH &c shall dispose of the same it shall be an annexed condition to such sale: that the said line of stages shall continue to run by & through the Town of Occoquan. And the said NATHANIEL ELLICOTT for himself his heirs, Exors, admins & assigns Grants, covenants & agrees to & with the said HAZLEWOOD FARISH, his heirs, Exrs, admr & Assigns that so long as the said FARISH &c continues to run the stages through Occoquan, or as long as N. ELLICOTT owns the Bridge at Occoquan the stages shall pass free of tole. And the said THOMAS TRIPLETT for himself his heirs, executors & Administrators grants, covenants and agrees as well with the said HAZLEWOOD FARISH, his heirs, executors & Administrators, as with the said NATHANIEL ELLICOTT, his heirs, executors, Admins & Assigns to well, truly and faith-fully execute & perform the several duties & trusts herein imposed on him. In WITNESS whereof the said parties have hereunto set their hands & Seals the day & Year first above written.

Signed Sealed and
delivered in presence of   HAZLEWOOD FARISH   (seal)
JOHN WISE   N. ELLICOTT   (seal)
JOHN CURSON SETON   THOMAS TRIPLETT   (seal)
JOSEPH RIDDLE, JACOB HOFFMAN
HENRY ROSE (for H. FARISH only), FLEMING BATES (ditto), JOHN ELLICOTT JR (ditto)
ALFRED P. GILPIN (for H. F.), ZACHL. WARD
          DISTRICT OF COLUMBIA To Wit:
              I GEORGE DENEALE Clerk of the United States circuit court of the District of
(SEAL)   Columbia for the county of Alexandria do hereby certify that [at] a court
          continued & held for the district and County aforesaid the 27th day of July 1809:
This deed from HAZLEWOOD FARISH to THOMAS TRIPLETT in trust for NATHANIEL ELLICOTT was proved by the oath of JOHN WISE, JOSEPH RIDDLE & JACOB HOFFMAN to be the act and deed of the parties which is ordered to be recorded and certified to the County Courts of Fairfax & Prince William in the CommonWealth of Virginia. In Testimony whereof I have hereunto set my hand and affixed the public seal of my Office on this sixth day of September in the Year of our Lord 1809.   G. DENEALE Cl.
          At a Court held for Prince William County the 2nd day of October 1809 this Deed in Trust from HAZLEWOOD FARISH to THOMAS TRIPLETT was proved as to the execution thereof by HAZLEWOOD FARISH by the oath of ALFRED P. GILPIN and by the affirmation of FLEMING BATES and JOHN ELLICOTT JR and ordered to be recorded.
                    Teste JOHN WILLIAMS Co. Cur.
          At a court held for Fairfax County the 18th day of December 1809 this Deed from HAZLEWOOD FARISH to THOMAS TRIPLETT in trust for the use of NATHANIEL ELLICOTT was proved to be the act and deed of the said HAZLEWOOD FARISH by the oaths of ALFRED P. GILPIN and affirmation of FLEMING BATES & JOHN ELLICOTT JR and the same having been duly proved to be the act and deed of the parties before the United States circuit court of the District of Columbia held for the County of Alexandria and certified by GEORGE DENEALE Clerk of the said court under the seal of his office on motion of the said NATHANIEL ELLICOTT together with the certificates thereon endorsed, ordered to be Recorded.
                    Teste WM. MOSS Cl.

Page 362-365. THIS INDENTURE made this twenty sixth day of January in the year eighteen hundred & Nine between DANIEL HARRINGTON of the County of Fairfax & state of Virginia of the one part and CHARLES TYLER JR of the county of Prince William & State aforesaid & CHRISTOPHER NEALE of the county of Fairfax and state aforesaid of the other part. WITNESSETH that for and in consideration of the sum of one cent to the said HARRINGTON paid the receipt whereof is hereby acknowledged he the said DANIEL HARRINGTON hath granted, bargained & sold & by these presents doth grant, bargain & sell unto the said CHARLES TYLER JR and CHRISTOPHER NEALE the mill formerly in the occupancy of sd. TYLER and known by the name of the Rockey Run Mill together with land to it as follows Viz: beginning at the sd. Rockey Run & running with a straight line parallel to the southwardly end (so as to include a space between said end of the mill & sd. line of forty five feet in breadth), thence to intersect another line & forming a right angle which last said line is to run parallel with the eastwardly side of said mill until it strikes the mill trunk which conveys the water from the race to the wheel between said last line and said eastwardly side of the mill is to be a space of forty five feet, thence to run with the mill race to the mill pond, thence with the eastwardly side of the pond & crossing the run to COLEMAN BROWNES line, thence with said BROWNS line to the bed of the run below the dam, thence with said bed of the run and with sd. BROWNS line quite round to the beginning of the first mentioned line which begins at the run & runs parallel to the southwardly end of the mill. This mortgage is intended to include forty five feet of ground at the south end of the mill, forty five on the east side of the mill and all the land to the northward of the Mill and Race together with all and singular their appurtenances, Remainders and waters and every part and parcel thereof unto the said TYLER and said NEALE to Have and To Hold for themselves & their Heirs & Assigns. Nevertheless if the sum of thirty one hundred & eighty Dollars is paid the sd. TYLER and sd. NEALE Viz: to the sd. TYLER the sum of fifteen hundred dollars, in three payments, agreeable to the tenure of three Bonds for five hundred dollars each the said TYLER holds and also to the sd. NEALE the sum of sixteen hundred & eighty dollars in four payments, agreeable to the tenure of four bonds executed by the said HARRINGTON to the said NEALE which bonds to sd. TYLER & sd. NEALE makes the aforementioned sum of thirty one hundred and eighty dollars, then this mortgage & every clause of it to be void & of no effect but otherwise to remain in force untill sd. bonds to said TYLER & sd. NEALE are fully discharged sd. DANL. HARRINGTON reserves to himself this priviledge to wit: to build a dam on his land which probably will force the water back and raise it within six inches of the under side of the present water wheel and in case of a fresh might stop the running of the mill for a short time untill the water subsised. It is also to be understood that the road from Centreville to Frying pan runs through a corner of this aforementioned ground near to the South West corner of the mill. In WITNESS hereof I DANIEL HARRINGTON have hereunto set my hand & seal the day and Year first above written in presence of
BENNETT WALKER
THOMAS BERKLEY, COLEMAN BROWN   DANIEL HARRINGTON   (seal)

[MAP OF THE PLATT]

At a court held for Fairfax County the 18th day of December 1809 DANIEL HARRINGTON acknowledged this Deed of Mortgage to CHARLES TYLER JR and CHRISTOPHER NEALE to be his act and Deed which together with a platt thereto annexed are ordered to be Recorded.
Teste WM. MOSS Cl.

Pages 365-368. THIS INDENTURE made this 22nd day of June in the Year eighteen hundred & Nine between DANIEL HARRINGTON & MARY his wife of the one part and LUCINDA J. NORRIS of the other part, all of the county of Fairfax & State of Virginia. WITNESSETH that the said DANIEL HARRINGTON and MARY his wife for and in consideration of the sum of seven hundred dollars to them the said DANIEL HARRINGTON and MARY his wife well and truly paid by the said LUCINDA J. NORRIS the receipt whereof is hereby acknowledged they the said DANIEL HARRINGTON and MARY his wife hath Granted, bargained and sold and by these presents doth Grant, bargain and sell unto the said LUCINDA J. NORRIS her heirs & assigns all that Lot of land adjoining the Town of Centreville in the County and State aforesaid. Beginning on the north side of the main street of said Town at the corner of Keens street and running eastwardly with said main street to said LUCINDA J. NORRISS' line one hundred & forty one feet, thence running with the line of sd. LUCINDA J. NORRISS back from sd. main street and with the line of EDMUND DENNY or fence on the back of the ditch four hundred & sixty three feet, thence running a westwardly course with sd. DENNY'S line and forming nearly a right angle to Keens street one hundred and twenty five feet, thence with sd. Keenes street four hundred & sixty four feet, to the beginning at the main street together with all the Buildings, Ways, Waters, Priviledges, Hereditaments & appurtenances whatsoever to the sd. Lot of land belonging or in anywise appertaining & the Reversion & Reversions, Rents & profits of the said Lot of Land and of every part and parcell thereof. And all the estate right, title, interest, claim & demand of them the said DANIEL HARRINGTON & MARY his wife in & to the said Lot of Land & every part thereof To Have & To Hold the said Lot of land and all & singular other the premises above mentioned & every part and parcel thereof with the appurtenances unto the sd. LUCINDA J. NORRIS her heirs & Assigns to the only proper use and behoof of the said LUCINDA J. NORRIS her heirs and Assigns forever. And the said DANIEL HARRINGTON and MARY his wife for themselves & their heirs, the said Lot of land and every part & parcel thereof against themselves and their Heirs & against all and every other persons or person whatsoever to the said LUCINDA J. NORRISS her heirs & Assigns shall & will forever warrant and defend by these presents. In WITNESS whereof the said DANIEL HARRINGTON & MARY his wife have hereunto set their hands & Seals the day & Year first above written.

Signed Sealed & delivered
in presence of   DANIEL HARRINGTON   (seal)
GEO. N. BERKLEY   MARY HARRINGTON   (seal)

The CommonWealth of Virginia to FRANCIS ADAMS, RO. B. LEE and HUMPH. PEAKE Gentlemen Justices of the County of Fairfax Greeting: Whereas DANIEL HARRINGTON and MARY his wife by their certain indenture of Bargain & sale bearing date the 22nd day of June 1809 have sold and conveyed unto LUCINDA J. NORRISS the fee simple estate of a Lot of land being as described in the annexed deed: beginning on the main street at the corner of Keen street and running to LUCINDA J. NORRISS line one hundred & forty one feet, thence back with her line and with EDMUND DENNY'S line four hundred & sixty three feet, thence again with sd. DENNY'S line a Westwardly course to Keens street one hundred & twenty five feet, thence with Keene street to the beginning at the main Street of Centreville with the appurtenances situate, lying & being adjoining to the Town of Centreville in the County of Fairfax. And whereas the said MARY cannot conveniently travel to our said county court of Fairfax to make acknowledgement of the said conveyance therefore we do give unto you or any two or more of you power to receive the acknowledgment which the said MARY shall be willing to make before you of the conveyance aforesaid contained in the said indenture which is hereunto annexed. And we do therefore desire you or any two or more of you personally to go to the said MARY and receive her acknowledgment of the same and examine her privily and apart from the said DANIEL HARRINGTON her husband whither she doth the same freely & voluntarily without his persuasions or threats and whither she be willing the said Indenture together with this Commission shall be recorded in our said Court. And when you have received her acknowledgment & examined her as aforesaid that you distinctly & openly certify us thereof in our said Court under your hands & Seals sending then there the said Indenture and this Writ WITNESS WILLIAM MOSS Clerk of the said Court at the Court House of the County aforesaid this twenty second day of June 1809 and in the 34th Year of the CommonWealth.   WM. MOSS Cl.

FAIRFAX COUNTY:
In obedience to the within Commission to us directed we waited on the within named MARY HARRINGTON and having examined her privily and apart from her husband DANIEL HARRINGTON touching the conveyance of the Lot of Land mentioned in the annexed deed do find that she hath done the same freely & of her own account without the persuasions or threats of her said husband & that she is willing the same may be recorded in the County Court of Fairfax. Given under our hands & Seals this 22nd of June 1809.

FRANCIS ADAMS   (seal)
HUMPH. PEAKE   (seal)

At a Court held for Fairfax County the 18th day of December 1809 this deed from DANIEL HARRINGTON & MARY his wife to LUCINDA J. NORRISS was acknowledged by the said DANIEL HARRINGTON to be his act and deed which together with a commission & return thereto annexed for taking the acknowledgment & privy examintaion of the said MARY are ordered to be recorded.   Teste WM. MOSS Cl.

Pages 369 & 370. THIS INDENTURE made this eighteenth day of November in the year of our lord one thousand eight hundred & nine between GUSTAVUS HALL SCOTT of the County of Fairfax and CommonWealth of Virginia of the one part and CHARLES J. LOVE of the County & CommonWealth aforesaid of the other part. Whereas the said GUSTAVUS HALL SCOTT hath sold to the said CHARLES J. LOVE a tract of land situated in the County of Stafford called Dipple and supposed to contain about seven hundred acres which said tract of land was devised to the said GUSTAVUS HALL SCOTT by GUSTAVUS SCOTT Esqr. of Rock Hill in the county of Washington and District of Columbia and Whereas doubts have been entertained whither the said GUSTAVUS HALL SCOTT could legally sell & convey the aforesaid tract of land under the Will of his father GUSTAVUS SCOTT as aforesaid untill he attained the age of twenty five Years. Now this indenture WITNESSETH that the said GUSTAVUS HALL SCOTT as well to save harmless and indemnify the said CHARLES J. LOVE from all damage, loss or injury which may arise or in any manner accrue to him from the said GUSTAVUS HALL SCOTT not being able to sell and convey the aforesaid tract of land untill he shall have attained the age of twenty five Years as aforesaid as also for & in consideration of the sum of one Dollar to him the said GUSTAVUS HALL SCOTT in hand paid by the said CHARLES J. LOVE at & before the ensealing & delivery of these presents the receipt whereof he doth hereby acknowledge hath Granted, bargained & sold, aliened, released & confirmed and by these presents doth Grant, bargain & sell, alien, release & confirm unto the said CHARLES J. LOVE the following negro slaves to wit: CHARLES, PEG and her youngest child, a boy about eighteen months old; MATILDA, JIM, GRIGSBY & HENRY, also all the Horses, cattle and other stocks of him the said GUSTAVUS HALL SCOTT & all his household furniture, a schedule of which said stock & houshold furniture is hereunto annexed. To have and To hold the said hereby Granted premises with all & singular the appurtenances thereunto belonging unto the said CHARLES J. LOVE his Executors, Administrators and Assigns forever provided nevertheless and upon this express condition that if the said GUSTAVUS HALL SCOTT should attain his age of twenty five and should by a good and sufficient deed convey & Confirm to the said CHARLES J. LOVE his heirs & assigns forever the aforesaid tract of land sold by the said GUSTAVUS H. SCOTT to the said CHARLES J. LOVE as aforesaid with the appurtenances thereunto belonging, that then & in that case these presents shall cease, determine & be void, anything herein contained to the contract thereof in any wise notwithstanding. In WITNESS whereof the said GUSTAVUS HALL SCOTT hath hereunto set his hand & affixed his seal the day & year first before written.
Sealed & delivered
in Presence of   GUSTS. H. SCOTT   (seal)
JAMES WATSON
HUMPHRY GUYNN, JOHN DIXON

At a Court held for Fairfax County the 18th day of December 1809 this Deed of trust from GUSTAVUS H. SCOTT to CHARLES J. LOVE was acknowledged by the said GUSTAVUS H. SCOTT to be his act and deed & ordered to be recorded.   Teste WM. MOSS Cl.

Pages 370-374. THIS INDENTURE made this tenth day of November in the year of our Lord eighteen hundred and eight between CHARLES LITTLE Executor of the last Will & testament of JOHN WEST late of the County of Fairfax & State of Virginia of the one part and ANTHONY BROWN of the County & State aforesaid of the other part. WITNESSETH whereas JOHN WEST late of the County aforesaid by his last will and Testament bearing date the first day of June in the year eighteen hundred and six did for the payment of his debts devise his moiety of a tract of land of two hundred and thirteen acres in the county aforesaid which was devised to him and his brother THOMAS WEST by their father JOHN WEST as will appear by his last will &

Testament bearing date the twenty sixth day of April seventeen hundred and seventy five one half to each & which has been laid off and divided since the death of the said JOHN & THOMAS WEST by & between the said CHARLES LITTLE Executor of the said JOHN WEST & THOMAS WEST, son and devisee of THOMAS WEST as will appear by their Indenture of partition bearing date the 1st day of November Eighteen hundred & eight and whereas the said CHARLES LITTLE having in pursuance of the authority given by the will of his testator and for the payment of his debts caused the said moiety to be laid of in Lotts and sold at public Auction when and where the Lotts Nos 1, 2, 3 and four (as laid down in the Platt of the same made by ROBERT RATCLIFFE Deputy surveyor of the County of Fairfax and which is now of record) were struck off to ANTHONY BROWN as aforesaid as the highest bidder; Now this indenture WITNESSETH that the said CHARLES LITTLE Executor as aforesaid for & in consideration of the premises and of the sum of six hundred & twelve dollars and seventy nine cents to him in hand paid by the said ANTHONY BROWN at and before ensealing and delivery of these presents the receipt whereof is hereby acknowledged have granted, bargained & sold and by these presents do Grant, bargain & sell unto the said ANTHONY BROWN his heirs and assigns the aforesaid Lotts numbered One, Two, Three and Four which lie within the following boundaries to wit: No. One, beginning at several marked bushes corner of GREENE'S lot, thence with his line south twenty East ninety three poles to a stake, thence south seventy west twenty six and one quarter poles to a stake in the division line, thence with said line north twenty six 20' west sixty three and a half poles to a stake in the out line, thence with said line north twenty seven and a half east forty five poles to the beginning containing fourteen acres and one hundred and twenty poles; No. Two, beginning at a red oak bush in ALEXANDERS recovered line, thence South seventy West to & along GREENS line and lott No. One sixty six and one quarter poles to a stake in the division line, thence with said line south twenty six twenty East twenty three and one quarter poles to a stake, thence north seventy East sixty three & three quarter poles to a stake in the said ALEXANDERS recovered line, thence with said line North twenty West twenty three poles to the beginning containing nine acres and forty poles. No. Three, beginning at a stake in ALEXANDERS recovered line a corner of Lott No. Two, thence with a line of said lott south seventy West sixty three and three quarter poles to a stake in the division line, thence with the said line South twenty six degrees twenty minutes East twenty five and three quarter poles to a stake, thence North seventy East sixty and one quarter poles to stake in the said ALEXANDERS line, thence with the said line north twenty Eight west twenty five and one quarter poles to the beginning containing nine acres and one hundred & ten poles; No. Four, beginning at a stake corner of lott No. Three, thence with the line of the said lott, South seventy west sixty and one quarter poles to a stake in the division line, thence with said line South 26° 20' East twenty seven and three quarter poles to a white oak saplin, thence North seventy East fifty one and a half poles to a stake in the out line, thence with said line North eight and a half degrees West twenty eight poles to the beginning containing nine acres & ninety poles with all and singular the appurtenances to the said Lotts belonging or in any manner appurtaining, the said lotts being part of the aforesaid moiety of two hundred and thirteen acres so devised as aforesaid by JOHN WEST to his two sons THOMAS & JOHN one half to each being a tract of land that was patented in the name of CAPTAIN SIMON PEARSON by deed from the proprietor dated the seventeenth day of February seventeen hundred and twenty nine and was devised by the said PEARSON to his daughter MARGARET (who intermarried with W. H. TERRETT) by his last will & Testament bearing date the seventh day of December A.D. seventeen hundred & thirty one and recorded in Stafford Court Lib M folio 101 and the said tract was afterwards conveyed by WILLIAM H. TERRETT & MARGARET his wife to HUGH WEST by indenture bearing date the twentieth day of August seventeen hundred and forty five in consideration of the sum of fifty pounds which indenture recites the courses & distances of the original patent. To have and to hold the said lotts with all & singular the appurtenances thereto unto him the said ANTHONY BROWN his heirs and assigns to the only use and behoof of him his heirs & assigns forever. And the sd. CHARLES LITTLE doth for himself his Executors & Administrators covenant to & with the said ANTHONY BROWN that he will forever warrant & defend the hereby granted premises with their appurtenances against the claim & demand of all persons or person whomsoever claiming by, through, from or under him in any way

...ver. In Testimony whereof the said CHARLES LITTLE Executor as aforesaid hath ...ereunto set his hand & seal the day & Year before written.
Sealed & delivered in presence of
WM. HERBERT JR, JNO. P. DULANY   CHARLES LITTLE   (seal)
MICHL. O'MEARA
     At a Court held for Fairfax County the 18th day of December 1809 CHARLES LITTLE, Executor of JOHN WEST deceased, acknowledged this Deed to ANTHONY BROWN to be his act and deed and ordered to be recorded.   Teste WM. MOSS Cl.

Pages 374-376. THIS INDENTURE made this twenty ninth day of June in the year of our Lord one thousand Eight hundred and seven between JOHN C. SCOTT of the county of Fairfax of the one part; and HENRY GUNNELL of the same county of the other part. Whereas the said JOHN C. SCOTT by sundry conveyances duly proved and recorded in the county court of Fairfax sold and conveyed to the said HENRY GUNNELL his heirs and assigns the following tracts or parcells of land situate, lying & being in the County of Fairfax, Viz: one tract or parcel of land containing four hundred and eight acres on the waters of Pimitts run whereon GERRARD TRAMMELL BLUNDLE and CHARLES SIMMS now lives, one other tract of about one hundred & forty eight acres whereon GEORGE SMITH formerly lived on the waters of Rocky Branch of Difficult Run, one other tract containing 75 acres on the waters of Scotts run and adjoins the land that SAMUEL JENKINS now lives on that I bought of ELIAS B. CALDWELL and R. RANKINS & wife about 200 acres, one other tract of twenty two acres on the waters of Scotts Run which adjoins the above 75 acres and one other parcel of land containing about nine acres on the waters of Rocky branch, this land adjoins the land the said SAMUEL JENKINS lives on as will more fully & at large appear by the aforesaid several deeds of conveyance. Now this indenture WITNESSETH that the said JOHN C. SCOTT as well to satisfy and confirm the title of the said several tracts or parcels of land to the said HENRY GUNNELL as, for and in consideration of the sum of one dollar to him in hand paid by the said HENRY GUNNELL at & before the ensealing and delivery of these presents the receipt whereof he doth hereby acknowledge hath Granted & confirmed and by these presents doth Grant & confirm unto the said HENRY GUNNELL his heirs & assigns the aforesaid several tracts or parcels of land with all & singular the appurtenances thereunto belonging. To have and To Hold the said several tracts or parcels of land with all and singular the appurtenances thereunto belonging unto the said HENRY GUNNELL his heirs & assigns forever to the only proper use and behoof of the said HENRY GUNNELL, his heirs and assigns forever. And the said JOHN C. SCOTT for himself, his heirs, executors & administrators doth covenant, promise and grant to & with the said HENRY GUNNELL his heirs and assigns that the said JOHN C. SCOTT and his heirs and all & every person or persons claiming by, from or under him shall and will from time to time and at all times forever hereafter upon the request & at the cost & charges of the said HENRY GUNNELL his heirs or assigns make, do & execute or cause or procure to be made, done & executed all and every such further and other lawfull & reasonable act & acts, deed or deeds, conveyances or assurances in law as by the said HENRY GUNNELL his heirs or assigns or his or their counsel learned in the law shall be reasonably advised, devised or required. In WITNESS whereof the said JOHN C. SCOTT hath hereunto set his hand & affixed his seal the day & year first before written.
Signed Sealed and
delivered in presence of   JOHN C. SCOTT   (seal)
GUSTAVUS H. SCOTT
HUGH W, GUNNELL, THOMAS GLOVER
     At a court held for Fairfax County the 21st day of December 1807 this Deed of Confirmation from JOHN C. SCOTT to HENRY GUNNELL was proved to be the act and deed of the said JOHN C. SCOTT by the oath of THOMAS GLOVER a Witness hereto and ordered to be certified. And at a Court contd. and held for the said County the19th of April 1808 the same was further proved by the oath of HUGH W. GUNNELL another Witness hereto and ordered to be certified. And at a court held for the said County the 15th day of January 1810 the same was further proved by the oath of GUSTAVUS H. SCOTT and ordered to be recorded.
                         Teste WM. MOSS Cl.

Pages 376-380. THIS INDENTURE made this first day of September in the Year of our Lord one thousand Eight hundred & Nine between GUSTAVUS H. SCOTT and ELIZABETH D. his wife of the County of Fairfax in the State of Virginia of the one part and JAMES KEITH of the Town & County of Alexandria in the District of Columbia of the other part. WITNESSETH that the said GUSTAVUS H. SCOTT and ELIZABETH D. his wife for and in consideration of the sum of thirteen hundred & twenty Eight Dollars & 25/100 to him the said GUSTAVUS H. SCOTT in hand paid by him the said JAMES KEITH at or before the sealing & delivery of these presents the receipt whereof he the said GUSTAVUS H. SCOTT doth hereby acknowledge and thereof and of every part and parcel thereof doth acquit, Release and discharge him the said JAMES KEITH, his heirs, Executors and Administrators, by these presents Have Given, Granted, bargained, sold, aliened & confirmed and by these presents do Give, Grant, bargain, sell, alien & Confirm unto him the sd. JAS. KEITH his heirs & assigns forever a tract of land situate, lying & being upon Wolf Run in the county of Fairfax and state of Virginia, being a part of that tract of one thousand & twenty five acres granted by the proprietor of the Northern Neck to JOHN WAUGH by deed poll bearing date the twenty fifth day of February one thousand seven hundred and nine which had come into the seizen of him the said GUSTAVUS H. SCOTT the same being bounded as followeth to wit: beginning at "A" a dogwood and maple near a stump corner of said KEITHS land standing on the west side of wolf run, thence down the Run with the meanders thereof to "B" at the corner of JOHN CHAPPLE'S fence on said run, thence with said CHAPPLE'S line North 73° 30' West 211 3/4 poles to "C" a post and several marked saplins, said CHAPPLE'S corner, thence North 28° East 179 poles to "D" a pile of stones near JOHN READS spring, thence North 66° 21' West 164 1/2 poles to "E" a spanish oak in the out line of SCOTTS patent, thence with the lines of said patent North 30° 39' East 72 1/2 poles to "F" a large white oak, thence South 80° East 80 poles to "G" a stone and several marked saplings corner of the aforesd. KEITHS land, thence with his line South 64° 19' East 250 3/4 poles to the beginning containing three hundred & seventy nine acres 80 poles and his houses, Buildings, Trees, Woods, Waters, Watercourses, profits, commodities, hereditaments and appurtenances to the same belonging or in anywise appurtaining & the Reversion & Reversions, Remainder & Remainders, Rents, Issues & profits thereof and of every part & parcell thereof. To Have & To hold the said tract of land, hereditaments & all & singular the premises hereby granted with the appurtenances unto him the said JAMES KEITH his heirs & assigns to the only proper use & behoof of him the said JAMES KEITH, his heirs & assigns forever; and the said GUSTAVUS H. SCOTT doth for himself his heirs, Executors and Administrators, covenant, Grant and agree to & with the said JAMES KEITH his heirs & assigns that he the said GUSTAVUS H. SCOTT is now at the time of the sealing & delivery of these presents seized in his own Right of a good, sure, perfect, absolute & indefeasible estate of inheritance in fee simple of and in the said tract of lands, Hereditaments & all singular the premises hereby granted with their appurtenances without any manner of condition, mortgage, limitation of use or uses, or any other matter, cause or thing except the claim of JNO. REED to alter, change, charge or determine the same and also that he the said GUSTAVUS H. SCOTT and his heirs will at any time hereafter upon the request and at the cost & charge of him the sd. JAMES KEITH his heirs & assigns execute & acknowledge any further & other lawfull act and deed for the more certain assuring & conveying the sd. tract of land, hereditaments and all & singular the premises hereby granted with their appurtenances unto him the said JAMES KEITH his heirs & assigns as by him the said JAMES KEITH his heirs & assigns his, their or any of their counsel learned in the law shall or may be advised or required. And Lastly that he the said GUSTAVUS H. SCOTT & his heirs, the said tract of land, hereditaments & all & singular the premises, will their and every of their appurtenances unto him the said JAMES KEITH his heirs and assigns against the claim & demand of him the said GUSTAVUS H. SCOTT & his heirs & all and every other person or persons whatsoever shall and will warrant & forever defend by these presents. In WITNESS whereof the said GUSTAVUS H. SCOTT and ELIZABETH D. his wife have hereunto set their hands & seals the day & Year first herein before mentioned.

Sealed & delivered
in presence of   GUSTS. H. SCOTT   (seal)
JAS. S. TRIPLETT   ELIZABETH D. SCOTT   (seal)
HUMPH. PEAKE
CHARLES TYLER JR.
    Received of JAMES KEITH thirteen hundred & twenty Eight Dollars 25 Cents the
consideration herein mentioned.
Witness
CHARLES TYLER JR   GUSTS. H. SCOTT
    At a court held for Fairfax County the 15th day of January 1810 this Deed from
GUSTAVUS H. SCOTT & ELIZABETH his wife to JAMES KEITH and a receipt thereon endorsed was
acknowledged by the said GUSTAVUS H. SCOTT to be his act and deed which together with a
Commission and return thereto annexed for taking the acknowledgment & privy examination
of the said ELIZABETH D. are ordered to be Recorded.
                              Teste WM. MOSS Cl.
    FAIRFAX COUNTY To Wit:
    The CommonWealth of Virginia to FRANCIS ADAMS, JAMES S. TRIPLETT and HUMPH.
PEAKE Gentlemen Justices of the County of Fairfax Greeting: Whereas GUSTAVUS HALL SCOTT
and ELIZABETH DOUGLASS his wife by their certain indenture of bargain & sale bearing date
the first day of September 1809 have sold & conveyed unto JAMES KEITH the fee simple estate
of a tract of Land situate on Wolf Run in the County of Fairfax containing three hundred and
seventy nine acres & 80 poles with the appurtanances situate, lying & being in the said
County of Fairfax and whereas the said ELIZABETH DOUGLASS cannot conveniently travel to
our said county court of Fairfax to make acknowledgment of the said conveyance therefore
we do give unto you or any two or more of you power to receive the acknowledgment which
the said ELIZABETH DOUGLASS shall be willing to make before you of the conveyance
aforesaid contained in the said Indenture which is hereunto annexed; and we do therefore
desire you or any two or more of you personally to go to the said ELIZABETH DOUGLASS and
receive her acknowledgment of the same & examine her privily and apart from the said
GUSTAVUS HALL her husband whither she doth the same freely & voluntarily without his
persuasions or threats and whether she be willing the said Indenture together with this
Commission shall be recorded in our said Court. And when you have received her acknowledgment & examined her as aforesaid that you distinctly & openly certify us thereof in our
said court under your hands & seals sending then there the said Indenture & this writ.
WITNESS WILLIAM MOSS Clerk of the said court at the Courthouse of the County aforesaid this
second day of October 1809 and in the 34th Year of the CommonWealth.
                              WM. MOSS Cl.
    FAIRFAX COUNTY:
    In obedience to the within comn. to us directed we waited on the within named
ELIZABETH DOUGLASS SCOTT and having examined her privily & apart from GUSTAVUS H.
SCOTT her husband touching the conveyance of the within named tract of land & do find that
she hath done the same freely & voluntarily without the persuasions or threats of her said
husband & that she is willing that the deed for the same together with this commission shall
be recorded in the County court of Fairfax, WITNESS our hands & seals this 2nd October 1809.
                       HUMPH. PEAKE   (seal)
                       JAS. S. TRIPLETT   (seal)

Pages 381-386. THIS INDENTURE TRIPARTITE made this twenty third day of November in the
year one thousand Eight hundred and Nine between ELIZA. PARK LAW of the County of
Fairfax in the state of Virginia of the first part, THOMAS LAW late of the city of Washington
District of Columbia now of the City of Philadelphia CommonWealth of Pennsylvania of the
second part and WILLIAM ROBINSON of the county of Westmoreland state of Virginia of the
third part. WITNESSETH that whereas the said ELIZA. P. LAW and her husband the said
THOMAS LAW have for a long time past and still do live separate and apart from each other by
mutual consent & agreement duly made and executed and she being so separated from her sd.
husband and having a separate maintenance allowed & secured to her & being duly

authorized and priviledged to act for herself as a single woman did on or about the Eighteenth day of July in the year one thousand eight hundred & five out of her own separate funds, property & effects & without any expence or charge whatsoever to her said husband, purchase of a certain FRANCIS PEYTON for and in consideration of the sum of five thousand five hundred dollars to him in hand paid out of her own separate funds, property & effects as aforesaid a certain tract or parcel of land situate, lying and being in the County of Fairfax and state of Virginia and set down and described to be bounded as followeth to wit: beginning upon the south side of the road leading from Alexandria to Leesburgh at the intersection of another road laid off at right angles by ROBERT ALLISSON through certain parcels of land sold by him to different persons and extending with the line of the last mentioned road South 4 degrees West 98 poles 11 links to a stake corner of the land of JONAH THOMPSON, thence north 86 degrees West 98 poles 6 links to another stake, another corner of the said THOMPSONS land, thence south 12 degrees East 11 poles to a white oak claimed by THOMAS WEST at the corner of CARR & SIMPSONS' patent, thence south 40 degrees West 38 poles to a stake on the north side of the old Leesburgh road, thence North 64 degrees West with the said Road 64 poles 11 1/2 links to a stake, thence north 4 degrees East 61 and an half poles to several chesnut oaks in the line of JOSEPH RIDDLE, thence South 86° East 64 3/4 poles to a stake, a corner of the said JOSEPH RIDDLE, thence North 12 degrees West 54 poles to a stake on the south side of the aforesaid road leading from Alexandria to Leesburgh, thence with the line of the said road south 86 degrees East 126 poles 20 links to the beginning containing one hundred & three acres which said tract of land bounded & described as aforesaid was duly & regularly conveyed for the consideration aforesaid by the said FRANCIS PEYTON and SARAH his wife to the said ELIZA. P. LAW by the name and description of ELIZABETH LAW, of the County of Prince George's in the state of Maryland her heirs and assigns forever by a certain Indenture of Bargain & sale made & dated the Eighteenth day of July in the Year one thousand eight hundred and five & recorded among the land records of the said County of Fairfax, all which will more partiularly and at large appear reference being had to the said Deed. Now This indenture WITNESSETH that the said ELIZABETH P. LAW for and in consider-ation of the sum of ten thousand dollars to her in hand paid by the said WILLIAM ROBINSON the receipt whereof is hereby acknowledged hath Given, Granted, bargained & sold and by these presents Doth Give, Grant, bargain & sell unto the said WILLIAM ROBINSON his heirs & assigns forever all the aforesaid tract or parcel of land, described & bounded as aforesaid and conveyed to her as aforesaid situate, lying & being in the County of Fairfax aforesaid & containing one hundred & one acres be the same more or less and all & singular the premises with their appurtenances to the same belonging or in any manner appertaining and the Rents, Issues & profits of the same and all & every right, Title, interest & estate, claim, demand, action and right of action whatsoever of her the said ELIZA. P. LAW in, to or about the same and that the said THOMAS LAW for and in consider-ation of the premises and of the further sum of one cent to him in hand paid by the said WILLIAM ROBINSON the receipt of which is hereby acknowledged hath authorized, approved, consented to and confirmed and by these presents doth authorize, approve, consent to and confirm the said Grant, bargain & sale, assignment & transferance so made as aforesaid by the said ELIZA. P. LAW & doth by these presents Grant, remise, release, confirm & forever renounce & quit claim unto the said WILLIAM ROBINSON his heirs and assigns forever all the said tract or parcel of land with all & singular the appurtenances & advantages thereto in anywise belonging and all & every the right, title, interest & estate claim, demand, action & right of action, power & authority whatsoever of him the said THOMAS LAW in right of the said ELIZA. P. LAW or otherwise or of her the said ELIZA. P. LAW in her own right into concerning or over the same. To have and To Hold all the said tract or parcel of land together with all & singular the appurtenances whatsoever to the same belonging or in anywise appertaining unto the said WILLIAM ROBINSON his heirs & assigns forever to his and their only proper use & behoof. And the said ELIZA. P. LAW doth for herself, her heirs, Executors & administrators hereby covenant & agree with the said WILLIAM ROBINSON his heirs & assigns that she the said ELIZA. P. LAW will forever warrant & defend the hereby conveyed premises to the said WILLIAM ROBINSON his heirs & assigns against the claims and demands of all persons whatsoever. In Testimony of which the parties to these presents have hereto set their hands & seals the day & year first herein written.

Sealed & delivered in
the presence of   ELIZA. P. LAW   (seal)
JOHN BARKER   THOMAS LAW   (seal)
WM. PAYNE, D. STUART
ROBERT RANDOLPH [all] witnesses as to MRS. LAW
W. WEDDERBURN, W. S. STUART
          CITY OF PHILADELPHIA:
          This day, the twenty third of November in the Year of our Lord Eighteen hundred &
nine the within named THOMAS LAW late of the City of Washington District of Columbia now
of the City of Philadelphia State of Pennsylvania, one of the parties in the within & afore-
going Deed or indenture mentioned whose hand and seal are thereunto subscribed & affixed
personally appeared before me JOHN BARKER Mayor of said City & freely & openly acknowledged the same deed or indenture to be his act & deed & declared his consent & desire that the
same may be recorded as his act & deed according to the laws of the CommonWealth of
Virginia in this case made & provided.
          In Testimony whereof I have set my hand & caused the seal of
(SEAL)   the City to be affixed.
                              JOHN BARKER, Mayor
          At a court held for Fairfax County the 18th day of December 1809 this deed from ELIZA.
PARK LAW and THOMAS LAW to WILLIAM ROBINSON was proved to be the act and deed of the
said ELIZA. PARK LAW by the oaths of DAVID STUART and W. S. STUART Witnesses thereto and
ordered to be certified. And at a court held for the said county the 15th day of January 1810
the same was further proved to be the act and deed of the said ELIZA by the oaths of ROBERT
RANDOLPH and WILLIAM WEDDERBURN and the same having been duly acknowledged by the
said THOMAS LAW before JOHN BARKER Mayor of the city of Philadelphia and certified by him
under the seal of his Office is on motion of the said WILLIAM ROBINSON together with the
certificates thereon endorsed & the Commission and return thereto annexed for taking the
acknowledgment & privy examination of the said ELIZA. P. LAW are ordered to be Recorded.
                    Teste WM. MOSS Cl.
          FAIRFAX COUNTY To Wit:
          The CommonWealth of Virginia to CHARLES SETTLE, DD. STUART and WILLIAM PAYNE or
any two of them Gentlemen Justices of the county of Fairfax Greeting: Whereas THOMAS LAW
and ELIZA. PARK LAW his wife by their certain indenture of bargain & sale bearing date the
twenty third day of November in the year one thousand Eight hundred & nine have sold &
conveyed unto WILLIAM ROBINSON the fee simple estate of a certain tract or parcel of land
with the appurtenances situate, lying & being in the said County of Fairfax and whereas the
said ELIZA. PARK LAW cannot conveniently travel to our said county court of Fairfax to make
acknowledgment of the said conveyance therefore we do Give unto you or any two or more of
you power to receive the acknowledgment which the said ELIZA. PARK LAW shall be willing
to make before you of the conveyance aforesaid contained in the said indenture which is
hereunto annexed. And we do therefore desire you or any two or more of you personally to go
to the said ELIZA. P. LAW & receive her acknowledgment of the same and examine her privily
and apart from the said THOMAS LAW her husband whither she doth the same freely &
voluntarily without his persuasions or threats; and whither she be willing the said indenture
together with this Commission shall be recorded in our said court; and when you have
received her acknowledgment & examined her as aforesaid that you distinctly & openly
certify us thereof in our said court under your hands and seals sending then there the said
indenture & this writ. WITNESS WILLIAM MOSS Clerk of the said court at the Courthouse of the
county aforesaid this 11th day of December 1809 and in the 34th Year of the CommonWealth.
                              WM. MOSS Cl.
          FAIRFAX COUNTY To Wit:
          In obedience to the within Commission We did examine the said ELIZA. PARKE LAW
privily & apart from the said THOMAS LAW her husband who declared that she executed the
said indenture freely & voluntarily without his persuasions or threats & that she was willing
the same together with this commission should be recorded in the said court. Given under our
hands & seals this 11th day of December in the year 1809.

DD. STUART   (seal)
W. PAYNE   (seal)

Pages 386-388. THIS INDENTURE made this sixth day of December in the Year of our Lord one thousand Eight hundred & Nine between CHARLES TYLER JR of the County of Prince William and CommonWealth of Virginia of the one part and CHARLES J. LOVE of the County of Fairfax & CommonWealth aforesaid of the other part. Whereas the said CHARLES J. LOVE & FANNY his wife by their indenture bearing the same date with these presents did convey unto the said CHARLES TYLER a tract of land situated upon Cub Run in the said county of Fairfax upon certain trusts in the said deed expressed and among other things upon trust that the said CHARLES TYLER should make and execute to him the said CHARLES J, LOVE mortgage upon the premises in the said deed, conveyed to save harmless and indemnify the said CHARLES J. LOVE from all damage, loss or injury that might arise to him in consequence of GUSTAVUS HALL SCOTT not attaining the age of twenty five years and in case he should attain that age in consequence of his not confirming to the said CHARLES J. LOVE a title to the four tracts of land conveyed to him the said CHARLES J. LOVE by the said GUSTAVUS HALL SCOTT and ELIZABETH DOUGLASS his wife by their indenture bearing date the 18th day of November 1809. Now this indenture WITNESSETH that the said CHARLES TYLER as well in compliance with the Trust aforesaid as for and in consideration of the sum of one dollar to him in hand paid by the said CHARLES J. LOVE at and before the ensealing and delivery of these presents the receipt whereof he doth hereby acknowledge hath Granted, bargained & sold, aliened, Released & Confirmed & by these presents Doth Grant, Bargain & Sell, Alien, Release & confirm unto the said CHARLES J. LOVE his heirs and assigns all that tract or parcel of land situated upon Cub Run in the county of Fairfax aforesaid conveyed by the said CHARLES J. LOVE and FANNY his wife to the said CHARLES TYLER by deed bearing the same date with these presents together with all houses, buildings, ways, waters, watercourses, profits, commodities & advantages to the said tract or parcel of land belonging or in anywise appertaining and the Reversion & Reversions, Remainder and Remainders, Rents, Issues & profits thereof; also all the Estate right, title, interest, property claim & demand of him the sd. CHARLES TYLER of, in and to the same and every part & parcell thereof. To have and To Hold the said hereby Granted Premises with the appurtenances thereunto belonging unto the said CHARLES J. LOVE his heirs & assigns to the only proper use & behoof of the said CHARLES J. LOVE his heirs and assigns forever. Provided Nevertheless and upon this express condition that if the said CHARLES TYLER as trustee under the deed made to him as herein before mentioned his heirs & assigns shall save harmless and indemnify the said CHARLES J. LOVE from all damage, loss or injury that may arise or in any manner accrue to him in consequence of GUSTAVUS HALL SCOTT not attaining the age of twenty five Years and in case he should attain to that age in consequence to his not confirming to the said CHARLES J. LOVE a good & valid title to the four tracts of land conveyed to him by the said GUSTAVUS HALL SCOTT and ELIZABETH DOUGLASS his wife by their indenture bearing date the 18th of November 1809 then & in that case these presents shall cease, determine & be void any thing herein contained in any wise notwithstanding. In WITNESS whereof the said CHARLES TYLER hath hereunto set his hand and affixed his seal the day & year first before written.
Sealed & delivered in presence of
PETER JETT, HUMPH. PEAKE   CHARLES TYLER JR (seal)
ANTHONY THORNTON

      At a court held for Fairfax County the 15th day of January 1810 CHARLES TYLER JR acknowledged this deed of mortgage to CHARLES J. LOVE to be his act & deed which is ordered to be recorded.   Teste WM. MOSS Cl.

Pages 389-394. THIS INDENTURE made this fifth day of January in the Year Eighteen hundred & Ten between EDWARD S. GANTT of the county of Fairfax in the State of Virginia and MARY his wife of the one part and STUART BROWN of the city of Baltimore in the State of Maryland trustee as herein after mentioned of the other part. WITNESSETH that the said EDWARD S. GANTT and MARY his wife for and in consideration of the sum of one dollar to him the said EDWARD S. GANTT in hand paid by the said STUART BROWN Trustee as herein after mentioned and for & in consideration of the covenants herein after reserved & expressed on the part of him the said STUART BROWN trustee as herein after mentioned have Granted, Bargained and sold, Aliened, Released & confirmed and by these presents do Grant, bargain and sell, Alien, Release & confirm unto the said STUART BROWN his heirs & assigns in trust as hereinafter mentioned that is to say in trust for SARAH BROWN wife of the said START BROWN late SARAH HARMAN, JACOB HARMAN, WILLIAM N. HARMAN and GEORGE BROWN CUMMING son & heir of MARIA CUMMING late MARIA HARMAN and the heirs of the said SARAH, JACOB, WILLIAM and GEORGE as tenants in common in fee all that tract or parcel of land situate, lying and being in the County of Fairfax aforesaid known by the name of Mount Salus containing by estimation six hundred & sixty three acres which had been conveyed to the said EDWARD S. GANTT and his heirs by the deed of CHARLES LITTLE, JAMES WILEY and JAMES DOUGLASS commissioners appointed to carry into effect a decree of the circuit court of the United States for the district of Virginia which deed bears date the ninth day of October in the year eighteen hundred and four the aforesaid tract of land being bounded and described as follows: beginning at the remainder of a stump where there is a large Stone planted representing the beginning of this tract and a corner to CAPT. WILEY & WILLIAM SHEPHERDS tract of land, thence South 29 3/4° West 180 poles to a spanish oak stump around which there are several saplings marked standing on the East side of Difficult Run above the mouth of a small branch emptying in on the opposite side of a different Run, thence south twenty five degrees West one hundred and four poles to a box white oak in a valley, thence South forty four and a half degrees East forty four poles to a pile of stones on a hill, thence South four and one half degrees east along some mark'd line trees one hundred twenty two poles to the edge of a glade, thence South fifty and one half degrees east passing line trees 23 poles to a hiccory standing near GUNNELS fence, thence north 87 degrees east ninety poles to a stone in DYERS field, thence north thirty six degrees West one hundred fourteen poles to a place in the field formerly shewn as a corner by THOMAS GUNNELL deceased, thence north twenty and a half degrees East passing two line trees one hundred sixteen and a half poles to a pile of stones near the head of a ditch and a white oak saplin, thence south eighty three and a half degrees east eighty five poles to an old spanish oak on the west side of a branch marked "WX" shewn as a corner, thence north thirty seven and a half degrees East one hundred ten poles to a point in the Road leading from Alexandria to Leesburgh, this course corrected to a corner tree being a red oak marked "WX" the corner of CAPT. WILEYS and REZIN OFFUTTS tracts of land which is part of the land Patented by LEWIS, thence from this point along the road north sixty four degrees West sixteen poles, north 75 degrees west sixty six poles, north fifty three degrees West thirty two poles, north forty two degrees West fifty two poles, north forty eight degrees west two hundred eighty seven poles, north twenty six and a half degrees west twenty two poles to a stump shewn as the dividing corner between this land and the land of CAPT. WILEYS, thence north 89 1/2 degrees west twenty poles, thence north seventy nine and one quarter West thirty poles, north eighty seven and one quarter West ninety poles to a large spanish oak on the East side of Wolf Trap run, thence down the meanders of said Run north ten degrees West nine poles, north seventeen degrees East eleven poles, north eighteen degrees West thirteen poles north twenty two degrees east twelve poles to the confluence of Difficult Run, thence down the same north eleven degrees east twenty one poles, north 45 degrees West twenty one poles north fifteen degrees West twenty one poles north thirty five degrees west thirty six and a half poles to the beginning and all Houses, advantages, Waters & Water-courses and hereditaments to the same belonging and appertaining and all the Right, claim, interest and demand, legal & equitable of them the said EDWARD S. GANTT and MARY his wife and of each of them of, in & to the said tract of land & the appurtenances and the Rents, issues and profits thereof & of every parcel thereof. To have and to Hold the tract of land hereby Granted and the appurtenances as aforesaid unto him the said STUART BROWN his heirs and assigns forever in trust and for the use of the said SARAH, JACOB, WILLIAM & GEORGE and their respective heirs as tenants in common in fee as aforesaid and their respective assigns and the said EDWARD S. GANTT for himself and his heirs doth covenant with the said STUART BROWN and his heirs and Assigns, trustee as aforesaid that he the said EDWARD S. GANTT at the time of sealing and delivery of these presents hath good, Right & lawful title to sell and convey the said Tract of land and the appurtenances unto the said STUART BROWN and his heirs and

Assigns as aforesaid free & clear of all & every incumbrance & charge by him done or suffered except the Dower of his said wife and that he the said EDWARD S. GANTT for himself and his heirs will forever defend and warrant the said tract of land and the appurtenances unto him the said STUART BROWN his heirs and assigns in trust as aforesaid against him the said EDWARD S. GANTT and his heirs and against all & every person claiming or to claim by, from, or under him. And the said STUART BROWN for himself his heirs, Executors and Administrators, trustee as aforesaid doth hereby release, acquit and discharge the said EDWARD S. GANTT, his heirs, executors and administrators and all other Persons whomsoever bound heretofore with the said EDWARD S. GANTT of and from the payment of the sum of nine thousand dollars secured by his eight several bonds dated the ninth day of October in the Year eighteen hundred and four and of and from all interest thereupon accrued and of & from all & every part of the said debt. In WITNESS whereof the parties hereunto have severally the day & year first above mentioned set their hands & Seals to these presents.

Sealed & delivered & signed   EDWD. S. GANTT   (seal)
in the presence of   MARY GANTT   (seal)
WM. GUNNELL JR, JAMES WILEY   (seal)

 At a Court held for Fairfax County the 15th day of January 1810 this deed from EDWARD S. GANTT to STEWART BROWNE was acknowledged by the said EDWARD S. GANTT to be his act & deed which together with a commission & return thereto annexed for taking the acknowledgment & privy examination of the said MARY are ordered to be recorded.
Teste WM. MOSS Cl.

FAIRFAX COUNTY To Wit:
 The CommonWealth of Virginia to JAMES WILEY, WILLIAM GUNNELL and SPENCER JACKSON Gentlemen Justices of the County of Fairfax Greeting: Whereas EDWD. S. GANTT and MARY GANTT his wife by their certain indenture of bargain and sale bearing date the fifth day of January eighteen hundred and ten, have sold and conveyed unto STEWART BROWN of the City of Baltimore the fee simple estate of a tract of land known by the name of Mount Salus, containing 663 acres as conveyed to the said EDWD. S. GANTT by CHARLES LITTLE, JAMES WILEY and JAMES DOUGLASS with the appurtenances situate, lying & being in the said County of Fairfax and Whereas the said MARY GANTT cannot conveniently travel to our said County Court of Fairfax to make acknowledgment of the said conveyance therefore we do give unto you or any two or more of you Power to receive the acknowledgment which the said MARY GANTT shall be willing to make before you of the conveyance aforesaid contained in the said indenture which is hereunto annexed. And we do therefore desire you or any two or more of you personally to go to the said MARY GANTT and receive her acknowledgment of the same and examine her privily & apart from the said EDW. S. GANTT her husband whither she doth the same freely & voluntarily without his persuasions or threats and whither she be willing the said Indenture together with this commission, shall be recorded in our said Court and when you have received her acknowledgment & examined her as aforesaid that you distinctly and openly certify us thereof in our said Court under your hands & seals sending then there the said Writ & this indenture. WITNESS WILLIAM MOSS Clerk of the said court at the Court House of the County aforesaid this ninth day of January 1810 and in the 34th Year of the CommonWealth.   WM. MOSS Cl.

 In obedience to the within commission to us directed from the within named county of Fairfax, We the subscribers have called on the within named MARY GANTT & did examine her separately and apart from her husband EDWARD S, GANTT on which examination she the said MARY GANTT did acknowledge that the conveyance contained in the hereunto annexed indenture of bargain & sale was her voluntary act free from the influence of the persuasions and threats of her said husband and that she is willing that the said Indenture together with this Commission shall be admitted to record in our said Court of Fairfax. Given under our hands & seals this ninth day of January 1810.
Truly Recorded   WM. GUNNELL JR.   (seal)
 Teste WM. MOSS Cl.   JAMES WILEY   (seal)

Pages 394-397. THIS INDENTURE made this first day of November in the year 1809 between JOHN HERIFORD, THOMAS P. HERIFORD and ELIZABETH his wife of the one part and RICHARD S.

WINDSOR of the other part. WITNESSETH that the said JOHN HERIFORD, THOMAS P. HERRIFORD and ELIZABETH his wife for and in consideration of the sum of one thousand dollars lawful money of Virginia to us in hand paid by the said RICHARD S. WINDSOR the receipt whereof is hereby acknowledged we the said JOHN HERIFORD, THOMAS P. HERRIFORD and ELIZABETH his wife hath Granted, Bargained & sold and by these presents doth Grant, Bargain and sell one tract or parcel of land, lying & being in the County of Fairfax on the head waters of Pohick run, beginning as follows Viz: South 61° East 73 poles to a white oak standing on a knowl, thence South 8° East 180 poles to a white oak standing in the bent of middle run, thence South 80° West 64 poles, thence North 57° West 212 poles up the south branch of the said Middle run, thence North 22° West [left blank] poles, thence North 58° East 188 poles, thence along the line of JOHN WILKENSON South 40° East 188 poles to the beginning containing [left blank] (be there more or less) with all the houses, Gardens and Orchards & also all trees, woods, under-woods, Ways, Waters, Water-courses, profits, commodities, advantages, hereditaments and appurtenances whatsoever to the said messuages &c above mentioned belonging, or in any-wise appertaining and the Reversion & Reversions, Remainder and Remainders, Rents, issues and profits of the said premises and of every part and parcel thereof and all the estate right, title, interest, claim and demand whatsoever of them the said JOHN HERRIFORD, THOMAS P. HERRIFORD and ELIZABETH his wife of, in and to the said Messuages &c and premises and every part thereof. To have and To Hold the said messuages and all and singular the premises above mentioned and every part and parcel thereof with the appurtenances unto the said RICHARD S. WINDSOR his heirs & assigns to the only proper use and behoof of the said RICHD. S. WINDSOR his heirs and assigns forever And the said JOHN HERRIFORD, THOMAS P. HERRIFORD and ELIZABETH his wife for themselves and their heirs the said messuages and premises and every part thereof against them & their heirs and against all & every other person and persons whatsoever to the said RICHARD S. WINDSOR his heirs and assigns shall and will warrant & forever defend by these presents. In WITNESS whereof we set our hands and Seals.
Teste

RICHD. CROAKE to THO. S. H.	JNO. HERIFORD	(seal)
WILLIAM S. WILKINSON to ditto	THOS. P. HERIFORD	(seal)
LANE P. RIGG to ditto	ELIZABETH HEREFORD	(seal)

November 1st 1809 Recd. of RICHARD S. WINDSOR, one thousand dollars in full of all debts for the price of the within tract of land. Given under my hand dated as above.
Teste

WILLIAM S. WILKERSON   THOS. P. HEREFORD
RICHD. CROAKE
LANE P. RIGG

At a court held for Fairfax County the 18th day of December 1809 this deed from JOHN HERIFORD, THOMAS P HERIFORD and ELIZABETH his wife to RICHARD S. WINDSOR and a receipt thereon endorsed were proved to be the act and deed of the said THOMAS P. HERIFORD by the oaths of RICHARD CROAKE and LANE P. RIGG and ordered to be certified. And at a court held for the said County the 15th day of January 1810 this deed was acknowledged by the said JOHN HERIFORD and the same together with a receipt thereon endorsed was further proved to be the act and deed of the said THOMAS P. HERIFORD by the oath of WILLIAM S. WILKINSON which together with a Commission and return hereto annexed for taking the acknowledgment & privy examination of the said ELIZABETH are ordered to be Recorded.
Teste WM. MOSS Cl.

FAIRFAX COUNTY To Wit:

The CommonWealth of Virginia to LEVEN POWELL, BURR POWELL & LEVEN LUCKETT Gentlemen Justices of the County of Loudoun Greeting: Whereas JOHN HERIFORD, THOMAS P. HERIFORD and ELIZABETH his wife by their certain indenture of bargain and sale bearing date the 1st day of November 1809 have sold and conveyed unto RICHARD S. WINDSOR the fee simple estate of a tract of land in Fairfax County on the head waters of Pohick run be the same more or less (said to contain three hundred and twenty four acres) with the appurtances situate, lying and being in the said County of Fairfax and Whereas the said ELIZABETH, the wife of the said THOS. P. HERIFORD cannot conveniently travel to our said County court of

Fairfax to make ackowledgment of the said conveyance therefore we do give unto you or any two or more of you power to receive the acknowledgment which the said ELIZABETH shall be willing to make before you of the conveyance aforesaid contained in the said indenture which is hereunto annexed and we do therefore desire you or any two or more of you person- ally to go to the said ELIZABETH and receive her acknowledgment of the same and examine her privily and a part from the said THOMAS P. HERIFORD her husband whither she doth the same freely and voluntarily without his persuasions or threats and whither she be willing the said indenture together with this commission shall be recorded in our said Court and when you have received her acknowledgment and examined her as aforesaid that you distinctly & openly certify us thereof in our said court under your hands & seals sending then there the said indenture & this Writ. WITNESS WILLIAM MOSS Clerk of our said court at the CourtHouse of the County aforesaid this 13th day of December 1809 and in the 34th year of the CommonWealth.   WM. MOSS Cl.

LOUDON COUNTY To Wit:

In Obedience to the within, We the subscribers did this day go to ELIZABETH HERIFORD within named & examine her separately & a part from her husband THOMAS P. HERIFORD, touching the execution of the annexed deed, she acknowledged that she had executed the same, that she had done it freely and voluntarily without the threats or persuasions of her husband and was willing that it should be recorded in the court of Fairfax County. Certified under our hands & seals this 13th day of December 1809.

Truly Recorded   LEVEN POWELL   (seal)
Teste WM. MOSS Cl.   BURR POWELL   (seal)

Page 398. KNOW ALL MEN by these presence that I ELIZA. WASHINGTON of Hayfield in the county of Fairfax being moved by considerations of Religious duty & a desire to promote human happiness (having first made ample provision for them in food and clothing) do hereby Emansipate, set free & discharge from all further duty or service the following Negroes Viz: DAVID, SHANKLIN, DIRHAM, JUDY, PETER, DAVID, FENIX, JACK, GEORGE, SYPHAX, OGMAN, JONATHAN, HELEN & her six children Viz: SUSAN, BILL, HARRIETT, MARIA, GEORGE & JONATHAN. Given under my hand & seal this 17th November One Thousand Eight hundred and nine.
Teste
R. J. TAYLOR   ELIZABETH WASHINGTON (seal)
WM. H. FOOTE

At a Court contd. and held for Fairfax County the 21st day of November 1809 this deed of manumission from ELIZABETH WASHINGTON to negroes DAVID, SHANKLIN, DIRHAM, JUDY, PETER, DAVID, FENIX, JACK, GEORGE, SYPHAX, OGMAN, JONATHAN, HELEN and her six children Viz: SUSAN, BILL, HARRIETT, MARIA, GEORGE & JONATHAN was proved by the oaths of ROBERT J. TAYLOR and WILLIAM H. FOOTE Witnesses thereto and ordered to be recorded. And on the same day, to wit the 21st day of November 1809 Order that the Order made this day receiving the proof and admitting to record this deed of manumission from ELIZABETH WASHINGTON to certain negro slaves be rescinded for reasons appearing to the court. And at a court held for the said County the 15th day of January 1810 this deed was again proved by the oaths of ROBERT J. TAYLOR and WILLIAM H. FOOTE, Witness thereto and ordered to be Recorded.
                              Teste WM. MOSS Cl.

Page 399. BE IT KNOWN unto all men that I CALEB STONE of Fairfax County and State of Virginia do this day give and convey unto my Son FRANCIS STONE two negroes known by the name of JUDE and NANCY her daughter which said negroes I do warrant and defend all right, title, claim or interest unto the said FRANCIS STONE my Son forever, further I agree to keep the sd. negroes and their increase for the said FRANCIS STONE or his heirs &c untill he thinks proper to call for them. Given under my hand & seal this twenty seventh of September Eighteen hundred and nine.
Teste
THOMAS ATHEY   CALEB STONE (seal)
THOMPSON SIMPSON, GEORGE ATHEY

At a Court held for Fairfax County the 19th day of February 1810 this deed of Gift from CALEB STONE to his son FRANCIS STONE was proved to be the act and deed of the said CALEB STONE by the oaths of THOMAS ATHEY and GEORGE ATHEY, Witnesses thereto and Ordered to be recorded.   Teste WM. MOSS Cl.

Pages 399-403. THIS INDENTURE made this 22nd day of December in the Year of our Lord one thousand Eight hundred & Nine between JOHN PHILLPOT GARROTT & ELIZABETH his wife of the County of Fairfax in Virginia of the one part and LESLIE STEWART and THOMAS MONTGOMERY, Merchants [of] Baltimore of the other part. WITNESSETH that the said JOHN PHILPOTT GARROTT for and in consideration of the sum of three thousand one hundred and twenty five dollars Current money of the United States to him the said JNO. P. GARROTT in hand paid by them the said STEWART & MONTGOMERY at or before the sealing and delivery of these presents the receipt whereof is hereby acknowledged and thereof & of every part and parcel thereof doth acquit, release and discharge them the sd. STUART and MONTGOMERY their heirs, Exchs, admors and assigns by these presents Have Given, Granted, bargained, sold, aliened & confirmed & by these presents do Give, Grant, bargain, sell, alien & confirm unto them the said STEWART & MONTGOMERY their heirs & Assigns forever a certain piece or parcel of land situated in Fairfax County in the CommonWealth of Virginia containing two hundred and fifty acres being part of a larger tract of land conveyed by BALDWIN DADE to the said JOHN P. GARROTT as reference to the deed of conveyance recorded in Fairfax County Court will more fully appear and Bounded as followeth to wit: beginning at "O" a stake in the line of the patent and corner to JOHN PHILPOTTS purchase, thence with PHILPOTTS line South 84° 45' East 257 poles to "X" his corner in another supposed line reversed North 27° 30' East 174 poles to "2" a stake in said line, thence North 84° 45' West 45 poles to the line of LOVELESS lease lott, thence with his line South 15° West 37 poles to his corner, thence with another of his lines reversed North 84° 45' West 9 3/4 poles to a small gum bush his corner, thence his line reversed North 15° East 37 poles, thence North 84° 45' West 199 poles to "3" a stake in the line of the patent, thence to the beginning and all houses, out houses, Water, Watercourses, profits, commodities, hereditaments & appurtenances whatsoever to the said piece or parcel of land belonging or in anywise belonging or in anywise appurtaining and the Reversion & reversions, Remainder and remainders, Rents, issues & profits thereof and of every part & parcel thereof. To have and to hold the said hereby granted premises, piece or parcel of land, hereditaments and all and singular the premises hereby Granted with their and every of their appurtenances unto them the said STUART & MONTGOMERY their heirs and assigns forever and the sd. JOHN P. GARROTT doth for himself, his heirs, Exors and Admors grant & agree to and with the said STUART & MONTGOMERY their heirs and assigns that he the said JOHN P. GARROTT is now at the time of sealing & delivering of these presents seized of a good, sure, perfect and indefeasible Estate of Inheritance in fee simple of, in and to the said piece or parcel of land, hereditaments and all and singular the premises hereby granted, with their and every of their appurtenances, without any manner of condition, mortgage, limitation of use or uses, or any other matter, cause or thing to alter, charge or determine the same. And also that he the said JOHN P. GARROTT and his heirs, will at any time hereafter at the request and at the cost & charge of them the said STUART & MONTGOMERY their heirs and Assigns execute and acknowledge any further act and deed for the more certain assuring & convey-ing the said piece, parcel or tract of land, hereditaments and all & singular the premises hereby granted with their and every of their appurtenances unto them the said STUART and MONTGOMERY their heirs and Assigns as by them the said STUART & MONTGOMERY their heirs and Assigns, their or any of their counsel learned in the Law, shall or may be advised or required. And Lastly that he the said JOHN P. GARROTT and his heirs the said piece, parcel or tract of land and all and singular the premises hereby Granted with their and every of their appurtenances unto them the said STUART & MONTGOMERY their heirs and assigns against the claim and demand of him the said JOHN P. GARROTT & his heirs and assigns and against the claim and demand of him the sd. JOHN P GARROTT & his heirs and all & every other person or persons whatsoever shall & will warrant and forever defend by these presents. In WITNESS whereof the said JOHN P. GARROTT have hereunto set his hand and seal the day month and Year first before written.

Sealed and delivered in presence of
TR. C. NASH   JOHN P. GARROTT   (seal)
DANIEL BRADLEY   [No signature listed]   (seal)
THOS. R. MOTT
HUMPH. PEAKE
    At a Court held for Fairfax County the 19th day of February 1810 this deed from JOHN
PHILPOTT GARROTT and ELIZABETH his wife to STUART & MONTGOMERY Merchants in
Baltimore was proved to be the act and deed of the said JNO. P. GARROTT by the oaths of
TRAVERS C. NASH, THOMAS R. MOTT and HUMPHREY PEAKE, Witnesses thereto and ordered to
be recorded.   Teste WM. MOSS Cl.

Pages 402 & 403. KNOW ALL MEN by these presents that I JOHN PHILPOTT GARROTT am held
firmly bound unto LESLIE STEWART and THOMAS MONTGOMERY Merchants of Baltimore in the
Just & full sum of twelve hundred Dollars Current money of the United States to which
payment well and truly to be made to the said STEWART & MONTGOMERY I bind myself, my
Heirs, Exors and admors, jointly & severally firmly by these presents; Sealed with my seal and
dated this 22nd day of December 1809.
    THE CONDITION of the above obligation is such that Whereas the said STUART &
MONTGOMERY hath purchased from the said JOHN P. GARROTT two hundred & fifty acres of
land lying in Fairfax County in the State of Virginia being part of a larger tract purchased by
the said JOHN P. GARROTT from BALDWIN DADE containing seven hundred and twenty acres
and upon which tract of seven hundred and twenty acres the said JOHN P. GARROTT executed a
deed of trust to JAMES WILEY to secure the payment of twelve hundred and forty dollars, now
if the said JNO. P. GARROTT shall in every respect exonerate the said STUART & MONTGOMERY
from the operation of the aforesaid deed of trust by obtaining from the said BALDWIN DADE
his heirs and assigns all legal acquittances on or before the first day of February next, then
the above obligation to be void else to remain in full force & virtue in Law.
Sealed & delivered in presence of
T. C. NASH   JOHN P. GARROTT   (seal)
THOS. R. MOTT
WILLIAM G. WIGGINTON
    I promise & oblige myself and my heirs to transfer and assign over to ZACHARIAH
CLAGET a deed of trust given me by JNO. P. GARROTT to secure the punctual payment of two
bonds as follows: JACOB HACKNEYS bond for $818 dated 18th December 1806, JOHN & ENOS
GARROTS bond 24th November 1806 for $350 which said bonds I have assigned to said CLAGET.
Given under my hand this 24th May 1807.
Teste THOS. BATELER   B. DADE
    This is to certify that I have received full satisfaction for the contents of the within
instrument of writing. Given from under my hand this 29th day of December 1809.
                                    ZACHH. CLAGETT
    Recd: from JNO. P. GARROTT this releasment from ZACH. CLAGETT and B. DADE to him
this 30th day of January 1810.   TR. C. NASH
    At a court held for Fairfax County the 19th day of February 1810 this bond from JOHN P.
GARROTT to STEWART & MONTGOMERY was proved by the oaths of TRAVERS C. NASH, THOMAS R.
MOTT and WILLIAM G. WIGGENTON which together with a receipt thereon endorsed and
Instrument of writing thereto annexed and a receipt thereon endorsed are ordered to be
recorded.   Teste WM. MOSS Cl.

Pages 403-406. THIS INDENTURE made this thirteenth day of October in the Year one thousand
eight hundred and Nine between THOMAS FLOOD JR, THOMAS FLOOD SR & CATHARINE his wife
of the County of Fairfax and State of Virginia of the one part and JOHN MOORE of the County &
State aforesd. of the other part. WITNESSETH that the said THOMAS FLOOD JR, THOMAS SR &
CATHARINE his wife in consideration of eight hundred Dollars lawful money of the state
aforesd. to them in hand paid by the said JOHN MOORE at or before the enseling and delivery
of these presents, the rect. whereof is hereby acknowledged have bargained & sold and by
these presents do and each of them doth bargain & sell unto the said JOHN MOORE his heirs &

assigns all that certain tract or parcel of land lying in the County & State aforesaid being a part of that land lately purchased by said THOMAS FLOOD from JAS. HURST and which is included in a larger tract or parcel of land granted unto TRAMMELL & HARLE by patent bearing date the [left blank] day of [left blank] in the Year [left blank] and bounded as follows (to wit): beginning at a small black oak on the south side of Elzeys Church road supposed to be where the West line of JEREMIAH MOORE'S land crosses the said road, thence South six degrees East one hundred & forty one poles, thence South 32 degrees West fifty six & 1/5 poles to a marked sapling (supposed to be beach) on the upper side of that marked branch & near where the said branch empties into Accotink, thence north three & 1/2 degrees West seventy seven poles to a marked white oak near a stone Quarry which has lately been worked, thence north 36 degrees West eighteen & 4/5 poles to a marked Gum sapling, thence North forty degrees East twenty poles to a stone & stake, thence North thirty six degrees West forty poles to Ellzeys church road before mentioned, thence Easterly along the meanders of said Road & binding therewith to the beginning containing thirty two acres, two roods & four poles with all and singular the appurtenances & the Reversion & Reversions, Remainder & Remainders, Yearly and other Rents, issues & profits thereof & every part & parcel thereof. To have and to Hold the said tract or parcel of land with the tenements, hereditaments and all & singular other the premises herein before mentioned and every part & parcel thereof with every of their Rights, members & appurtenances unto the said JOHN MOORE his heirs & assigns forever. And the said THOMAS FLOOD JR ,THOMAS FLOOD SR & CATHARINE his wife for themselves & their Heirs the said Tract or parcel of Land with all & singular the premises & appurtenances before mentioned unto the said JOHN MOORE his heirs & assigns free from the claim or claims of them the said THOMAS FLOOD JR, THOMAS FLOOD SR & CATHARINE his wife or either of them, their or either of their heirs & of all & every person or persons Whatsoever shall, will & do warrant & forever defend by these presents. And this Indenture further WITNESSETH that the said THOMAS FLOOD JR, THOMAS FLOOD SR and CATHARINE his wife in consideration of the further sum of twelve dollars & fifty cents to them in hand paid by JOHN MOORE at or before the ensealing and delivery of these presents, the rect. whereof is hereby acknowledged have bargained & sold and do & each of them doth bargain & sell unto JOHN MOORE all that tract or parcel of land lying on the south side of Ellzeys Church road (before mentioned between the lines of JEREMIAH MOORE and JOHN MASON except the land included in the following boundaries) to wit: beginning at a large White oak standing on the south side of Ellzeys church road aforesd. and near where the said road crosses hat maked branch (*sic*) and on the East side of said branch, thence South thirty six degrees East 40 poles to a marked Gum sapling a corner of the said JOHN MOORES General Warrantry deed, thence with one of the said JOHN MOORES lines North 40 degrees East twenty poles to a stake and stone, thence North thirty six degrees West 40 poles to Ellzeys church road aforesd, thence Westwardly along the said road & binding thereon to the beginning. To have and Hold the said last mentioned tract or parcel of land except as before excepted with all and singular the premises and appurtenances thereunto belonging or in anywise appertaining unto the said JOHN MOORE his heirs and assigns forever and the said THOMAS FLOOD JR, THOMAS FLOOD SR & CATHARINE his wife for themselves and each of them for their Heirs the said tract or parcel of land last mentioned (except as before excepted) with all and singular the premises & appurtenances thereunto belonging or in anywise appertaining unto the said JOHN MOORE his heirs & assigns free from the claim or claims of them the said THOMAS FLOOD JR and THOMAS FLOOD SR & CATHARINE his wife or either of them, their, either of their [illegible] shall, will & do warrant & forever defend by these presents. In WITNESS whereof and for a full & faithful performance of all the covenants in this indenture the sd. THOMAS FLOOD JR, THOMAS FLOOD SR and CATHARINE his wife have hereunto set their hands & affixed their Seals the day & Year first above written.
Signed Sealed & delivered
In Presence of   THOS. FLOOD   (seal)
JOHN ALLEN, LEWIS SCISSON   THOS. FLOOD JR   (seal)
EDWARD WOOD   CATHARINE her X mark FLOOD   (seal)
    Recd. October 30 from JOHN MOORE Eight hundred & twelve Dollars and fifty cents, the consideration monies within mentioned.

Witness
EDWARD WOOD   THOS. WOOD JR.
LEWIS SCISSON
JOHN ALLEN
     At a court held for Fairfax County the 19th day of March 1810 this deed from THOMAS
FLOOD SR, THOMAS FLOOD & CATHARINE his wife to JOHN MOORE was proved to be the act and
deed of the said THOMAS FLOOD SR and THOMAS FLOOD by the oaths of JOHN ALLEN, LEWIS
SCISSON and EDWARD WOOD which together with a receipt thereon endorsed are ordered to be
recorded.   Teste WM. MOSS Cl.

Pages 406 & 407. [Marginal Note: JAMES COCKERILL]
     KNOW ALL MEN by these presents that I BENJAMIN COCKERILL of the County of Fairfax
& CommonWealth of Virginia do by these presents for and in consideration of the uses,
interest and purposes herein after mentioned, as also for the further consideration of One
Thousand dollars to me in hand paid by HENRY BUTLER, GEORGE COCKERILL and JAMES
COCKERILL at or before the ensealing of these presents the receipt whereof I do for myself,
my heirs hereby acknowledge, Give, bargain & sell and by these presents do Give, bargain
and sell unto the said HENRY BUTLER, GEORGE COCKERILL & JAMES COCKERILL their heirs,
Executors & Administrators forever the following property to wit: negro WILL & MIMA & two
horses, five head of horned cattle, one Waggon & Geer, all my farming utensils, household &
kitchen furniture, twenty hogs & six sheep with all other property that is now in my possession. To Have and To hold the said Negroes WILL & MIMA, Two horses, cattle, Sheep, hogs,
Waggon & Geer, Furniture &c &c &c together with their future increase unto the said HENRY
BUTLER, GEORGE COCKERILL & JAMES COCKERILL their heirs, Exors, Admors forever, In Trust
for the use & purposes following that is to say first the use & maintenance & support of my
wife SARAH COCKERILL during the Term of her natural life and at her death for the use &
equal benefit of all my children except my son JOHN COCKERILL and my daughter SUSANNA
BENNETT whom I have heretofore otherwise provided for and my daughter SARAH COCKERILL
who I wish to have one bed more than her equal part of my personal estate & my Grand sons
JESSE COCKERILL & NATHAN COCKERILL who are to take equally between them one part equal
to one of my children part of such surplus or residue which may remain and is now in the
possession of the said HENRY BUTLER, GEORGE COCKELL & JAMES COCKERILL, Trustees for the
purposes before directed & intended after the death of wife aforesaid the possessions hereby
vested in the said HENRY, GEORGE & JAMES for the benefit and support of my wife SARAH for
the term aforesaid it is intended she shall have her support thereby & thereof and no other
estate therein. And I do for myself, my Heirs, Exors, Admors &c the aforementioned enumerated property & every part & parcel thereof unto the said HENRY BUTLER, GEORGE COCKERILL
& JAMES COCKERILL their heirs, Executors & Admors in trust for the uses, purposes & disposition before mentioned against the future claim, title or demand either in Law or equity of all
persons whatsoever warrant & defend thereby & hereby renouncing & disclaiming all right
Estate in title thereto or to any part thereof and vesting the same & every part thereof in the
said HENRY BUTLER, GEORGE COCKERILL & JAMES COCKERILL Trustees aforesaid as witness my
hand & seal this 26th day of January in the Year 1810.
Signed Sealed & delivered In Presence of us
DANL. KITCHEN   BENJA. COCKERILL   (seal)
CHAS. LANE
DANL. SANDERS
     At a court contd. & held for Fairfax County the 20th day of March 1810 this Deed from
BENJA. COCKERILL to HENRY BUTLER, GEORGE COCKERILL & JAMES COCKERILL in trust for the
use and benefit of SARAH COCKERILL & others was proved to be the act and deed of the said
BENJAMIN COCKERILL by the oaths of DANIEL KITCHEN, CHARLES LANE and DANIEL SANDERS
witnesses thereto & Ordered to be Recorded.   Teste WM, MOSS Cl.

Pages 407 & 408. THIS INDENTURE made this 2nd December 1809 between CHRISTOPHER NEALE
of the Town of Alexa. District of Columbia of the one part & CHARLES J. LOVE of the County of
Fairfax & State of Virginia of the other part. WITNESSETH that the said CHRISTOPHER NEALE

for and in consideration of eight hundred and fifty dollars to him in hand paid at & before the enseating and delivery of these presents the receipt whereof he doth hereby acknowledge have bargained & sold & by these presents doth bargain and sell, alien & confirm all his right, title, Jnt. property and claim in & to Lott No: [left blank] as laid off to his share in the estate of the late THOS. NEALE decd, lying and being in the County of Fairfax & binding on the waters of Flat lick & Great Rockey Cedar Run and for a more minute description reference to the platt & division of said Estate now on Record in the County Court of Loudoun will more fully appear to him the said CHARLES J. LOVE his heirs and assigns forever free from the claim or claims of him the sd. CHRISTR. NEALE his heirs & assigns as WITNESS my hand & seal the day & Year above written.
Witness
RICHD. H. HENDERSON   CHRISTR. NEALE   (seal)
EDWD. SUMMERS
TR. C. NASH

    At a court held for Fairfax County the 19th dayof March 1810 this deed from CHRISTOPHER NEALE to CHARLES J. LOVE was proved to be the act & deed of the said CHRISTOPHER NEALE by the oaths of RICHD. H. HENDERSON and TRAVIS C. NASH and ordered to be certified. And at a court contd. & held for the said County the 21st day of March 1810 the same was further proved to be the act & deed of the said CHRISTOPHER NEALE by the oath of EDWARD SUMMERS and ordered to be Recorded.
Teste WM. MOSS Cl.

Pages 408-411. THIS INDENTURE made this first day of February in the Year of our Lord one thousand eight hundred & Ten between WILLIAM HARTSHORNE of the County of Fairfax, Merchant, of the first part, JAMES KEITH of the Town of Alexandria & JOHN CARLYLE HERBERT of Prince Georges County in the State of Maryland of the second part and the President, Directors & Company of the Bank of Alexandria of the third part. Whereas the said WILLIAM HARTSHORNE & SUSANNA his wife by their certain deed bearing date the fourth day of February eighteen hundred and recorded in the County Court of Fairfax eighteen hundred & two as well to secure the Payment of twenty five thousand dollars which the said WILLIAM HARTSHORNE stood justly indebted to the said President, Directors & Company of the Bank of Alexandria as well on his own account as on account of WILLIAM HARTSHORNE & Son and JEREMIAH YELLOTT, with the interest which should accrue thereon, as also all and every other sum or sums of money which should thereafter become due to the said President, Directors and Company of the Bank of Alexandria from the said WILLIAM HARTSHORNE or WILLIAM HARTSHORNE & Son or JEREMIAH YELLOTT as for and in consideration of the sum of the sum of one dollar to the said WILLIAM HARTSHORNE in hand paid by the said JAMES KEITH & JOHN CARLYLE HERBERT did Grant, bargain & sell, Alien and confirm unto the said JAMES KEITH and JOHN CARLYLE HERBERT their heirs & assigns the following Tracts or parcels of land that is to say one piece or parcel of land situate, lying & being on Holmes Run in the County of Fairfax and bounded as followeth: beginning at the Original beginning of that tract of land taken up, surveyed and patented by WEST, PEARSON & HARRISON and running thence North 75 degrees West allowing two degrees variation 62 poles to Holmes run, thence up the Run with the several meanders thereof and binding thereupon, South 19 poles south 74 degrees West 20 poles, thence North 75° West 132 poles, thence north 16 poles, thence North 55° West 16 poles, thence North 75° West 14 poles, thence North 63 1/2° West 5 poles, thence North 8 poles, thence North 4 poles, thence South 75° East 38 poles with DALTONS line, thence with the mill race North 75° East 7 poles, thence north 65° East 34 poles, thence South 84° East 30 poles, thence South 62° East 4 poles, thence North 37° East 80 poles to the great road, thence with the road South 71° East 40 poles to a stake in a valley, thence North 11 1/2° East 91 poles with SIMPSONS line, thence with SIMPSONS line South 46° East 221 poles to a box oak corner to BRENT with an allowance of 4 degrees variation, thence with BRENTS line North 52° West 258 poles to MRS COX'S spring & thence North 75° East 103 poles to the beginning containing two hundred & seventy two acres be the same more or less, also one acre of Land on the opposite side of Holmes run condemned to accomodate the mill on said Lands bounded as followeth: beginning at a small white hicory on the South West side of Holme's Run and running thence up the Run North 55° West 28 poles to a beach on the side of the Run, thence South 35° West 5 3/4 poles to a stake, thence North 35° East 5 3/4 poles to the beginning; also one other tract or parcel of Land situate, lying & being on the drains of Great Hunting creek in the said County of Fairfax and bounded as followeth: beginning at a red oak marked as a corner and blazed above the chops and running thence North 88° East 143 poles to a white oak on a hill side near a branch, thence South 23 1/2° East 152 poles to an ancient marked red oak on a hill side near a small marshy branch on the Western side of Holmes Run, thence South 53 1/2° West 122 poles to an ancient marked red or black oak on the Western side of a small branch, thence South 21 1/2° West 100 poles to an ancient marked spanish oak standing on the Eastern side of the main road from Alexandria to Rocky Run, thence North 1° 45' West 285 poles to the beginning containing one hundred & eighty four acres, three roods & ten perches and also two lotts or parcels of Ground lying and being upon the East side of Water Street and South side of Wilkes street in the Town of Alexandria distinguished in a plan of the lotts in the Town of Alexandria by numbers (161,162) and bounded as followeth to wit: beginning at the intersection of said Streets, thence Southerly with Water Street one hundred & twenty six feet six inches, thence Eastwardly with a line parallel to Wilkes Street into the river Potowmack, thence Northwardly up the River with the meanders thereof to Wilkes Street, thence Westwardly with Wilkes street to the beginning. To have and To Hold the said several tracts & parcels of land with all and singular the appurtenances thereunto belonging unto the said JAMES KEITH & JOHN CARLYLE HERBERT their heirs & assigns in trust for the uses, intents & purposes set forth, expressed in the aforesd. deed. Now this indenture WITNESSETH that the said WILLIAM HARTSHORNE to give full effect to the aforesaid deed according to the true intent & meaning thereof & to ratify & confirm the same & for and in consideration of one dollar to him in hand paid by the said JAMES KEITH & JOHN CARLYLE HERBERT at & before the sealing & delivery of these presents the receipt whereof he doth hereby acknowledge doth by these presents Grant, demise, bargain, sell, notify & confirm unto the said JAMES KEITH & JOHN CARLYLE HERBERT the aforesd. pieces or parcels of land with all & singular the appurtenances thereunto belonging. To have and To Hold the said several pieces or parcels of land with all & singular the appurtenances thereunto belonging unto the said JAMES KEITH & JNO. CARLYLE HERBERT their heirs & assigns, In Trust to & for the uses, intents & purposes set forth, expressed & declared in the aforesaid deed. In WITNESS whereof the said WILLIAM HARTSHORNE hath hereunto set his hand & affixed his seal the day & Year first before written.

Signed Sealed & delivered In Presence of
JOSEPH RIDDLE   WM. HARTSHORNE   (seal)
WM. HERBERT JR, GEO. YOUNGS
N. HERBERT
R. J. TAYLOR
       At a court contd. & held for Fairfax County the 20th day of March 1810 This deed from WILLIAM HARTSHORNE to JAMES KEITH and JOHN C. HERBERT in Trust for the use of the President, Directors & Company of the Bank of Alexa. was proved to be the act & deed of the said WILLIAM HARTSHORNE by the oaths of WILLM. HERBERT JR, GEO. YOUNGS & NOBLET HERBERT Witnesses thereto and ordered to be Recorded & Certified to the Circuit Court of the District of Columbia held for the County of Alexandria.
                         Teste WM. MOSS Cl.

Pages 412 & 413. THIS INDENTURE made this first day of February in the Year of our Lord one thousand eight hundred and Ten between WILLIAM HARTSHORNE of the County of Fairfax, Merchant, of the first part, JAMES KEITH of the Town of Alexandria and JOHN CARLYLE HERBERT of Prince Georges County in the State of Maryland of the second part and the President, Directors and Company of the Bank of Alexandria of the third part. Whereas the said WILLIAM HARTSHORNE and SUSANNA his wife by their certain deed bearing date the fourth day of February in the Year of our Lord Eighteen hundred and recorded in the General Court of the CommonWealth of Virginia the 9th day of November 1809 as well to secure the Payment of twenty five thousand dollars which the said WILLIAM HARTSHORNE stood justly indebted to the said President, Directors & Company of the Bank of Alexandria as well on his

own account as on account of WILLIAM HARTSHORNE & Son and JEREMIAH YELLOTT, with the interest which should accrue thereon, as also all & every other sum or sums of money which should thereafter become due from the sd. WILLIAM HARTSHORNE or WILLIAM HARTSHORNE & Son or JEREMIAH YELLOTT as for & in consideration of the sum of one dollar to the said WM. HARTSHORNE in hand paid by the said JAMES KEITH & JOHN CARLYLE HERBERT did Grant, bargain & sell, alien & confirm unto the said JAMES KEITH & JOHN CARLYLE HERBERT their heirs & assigns twelve thousand acres of land situate, lying & being on Hughes's River in the County of Wood formerly Monongalia County which sd. twelve thousand acres of land was Granted by the CommonWealth of Virginia to DORSEY PENTICOST, SAMUEL PURVIANCE and ROBERT PURVIANCE by ten several patents each of them bearing date the fifteenth day of October one thousand seven hundred and eighty four and to which said lands JOSEPH TITBALD of the Town of Winchester became entitled & conveyed the same to the said WILLIAM HARTSHORNE by deed bearing date the eighteenth day of July 1795. To have and To Hold the said twelve thousand acres of land with all & singular the appurtenances thereunto belonging unto the said JAMES KEITH & JOHN CARLYLE HERBERT their heirs & assigns to & for the uses, intents & purposes set forth, expressed And declared in the aforesaid deed. Now this indenture WITNESSETH that the said WILLIAM HARTSHORNE to give full effect to the aforesaid deed according to the true intent and meaning thereof & to ratify & confirm the same & for and in consideration of the sum of one dollar to him in hand paid by the said JAMES KEITH & JOHN CARLYLE HERBERT at & before the sealing & delivery of these presents the receipt whereof he doth hereby acknowledge doth by these presents Grant, demise, bargain, sell, ratify & confirm unto the said JAMES KEITH and JOHN CARLYLE HERBERT their heirs & assigns the aforesaid twelve thousand acres of land with all & singular the appurtenances thereunto belonging. To have and To Hold the said JAMES KEITH & JOHN CARLYLE HERBERT their heirs and assigns the aforesaid twelve thousand acres of land with all & singular the appurtenances thereunto belonging, In Trust to & for the uses, intents and purposes set forth, expressed & declared in the aforesaid deed. In WITNESS whereof the said WILLIAM HARTSHORNE hath hereunto set his hand & affixed his seal the day & Year first before written.
Signed Sealed & delivered In presence of
JOSEPH RIDDLE   WM. HARTSHORNE   (seal)
WM. HERBERT JR, GEO. YOUNGS
N. HERBERT, R. J. TAYLOR
       At a court contd. & held for County of Fairfax the 20th day of March 1810 This deed from WILLIAM HARTSHORNE to JAMES KEITH & JOHN C. HERBERT in Trust for the use of the President, Directors & Company of the Bank of Alexandria was proved to be the act & deed of the said WILLIAM HARTSHORNE by the oaths of WILLM. HERBERT JR, GEORGE YOUNGS & NOBLET HERBERT, Witnesses thereto and ordered to be recorded & Certified to the Cirtuit Court of the District of Columbia held for the County of Alexandria.
                              Teste WM. MOSS Cl.

Pages 414-418. [Del. JOHN DUNDAS]
       THIS INDENTURE TRIPARTITE made this twenty second day of April in the Year of our Lord one Thousand eight hundred & nine between ROBERT PATTON JR and ANN CLIFTON his wife of the County of Fairfax in the State of Virginia of the first part, JOHN DUNDAS & THOMAS SWANN of the Town and County of Alexandria in the District of Columbia of the second part and WILLIAM HEPBURN of the same Town, County and District of the third part. Whereas the said ROBERT PATTON JR stands justly indebted to him the said WILLIAM HEPBURN by a writing obligatory bearing date with these presents in the sum of seven hundred thirty three dollars and thirty 3 cents which will become payable on the first day of April next ensuing the date of these presents, also by a writing obligatory bearing date with these presents in the further sum of seven hundred and thiry three dollars and thirty three cents which will become payable on the first day of April one thousand Eight hundred & eleven and by a writing obligatory bearing date with these presents in the further sum of seven hundred thirty three dollars & thirty four cents which will become payable on the first day of April one thousand Eight hundred & twelve, the payment of which several sums of money unto the said WILLIAM HEPBURN his Executors, Administrators and assigns as they severally become due, he the said

ROBERT PATTON JR is willing to secure therefore this indenture WITNESSETH that the said ROBERT PATTON JR and ANN CLIFTON his wife as well to secure the payment of the said several sums of money as for and in consideration of the Trusts herein after contained & expressed on the part and behalf of them the said JOHN DUNDAS and THOMAS SWANN their Executors & Administrators to be executed, fulfilled and performed and one dollar to him the said ROBERT PATTON JR in hand paid by them the said JOHN DUNDAS & THOS SWANN at or before the sealing and delivery of these presents the receipt whereof he doth hereby acknowledge Have Given, Granted, bargained, sold, aliened and confirmed and by these presents do Give, Grant, bargain, sell, alien and confirm unto him the said JOHN DUNDAS & THOS. SWANN their heirs, Executors, administrators & assigns forever a tract or parcel of land situate, lying and being upon the drains of Great Hunting creek in the said County of Fairfax and State of Virginia and bounded as followeth to wit: beginning at a white oak stake one hundred & ninety one poles from COLO. COLVILLS Corner Gum by his old brew house and running thence South West by South 127 poles approaching near to a spanish oak corner to COLO. WEST, thence South East by East 126 poles to a small white oak by the ridge road, thence North East by North 127 poles to a white oak stake, then north East by East 126 poles to the beginning containing one hundred acres which tract of land lies on the top of Cameron hill and the lower road leading to Colchester and was sold & conveyed by the said WILLIAM HEPBURN and AGNESS his wife unto him the said ROBERT PATTEN JR his heirs and assigns by an indenture bearing date the day next before the date of these presents and all Houses, trees, Buildings, Woods, Waters, Water courses, Profits, commodities, hereditaments and appurtenances whatsoever to the said Premises belonging or in anywise appurtaining and the Reversion & Reversions, Remainder & Remainders, Rents, Issues & profits thereof and of every part & parcel thereof. To have and To Hold the said tract or parcel of land, hereditaments & all & singlular the premises hereby Granted with their appurtenances unto them the said JOHN DUNDAS & THOMAS SWANN their heirs, Executors, administrators & assigns forever In Trust to & for the uses & purposes herein after mentioned and to & for no other use or purpose whatever that is to say, in case that he the said ROBERT PATTON JR his heirs, Executors, Admors, or Assigns shall fail to pay unto the said WILLIAM HEPBURN, his Exors, Administrators or Assigns, the said sums of money as they severally become payable, or any one of them or any part of any one of them when payable, then upon this Trust that they the said JOHN DUNDAS & THOMAS SWANN, their Executors or Administrators, do (whenever after any & each failure to pay the sd. sums of money when payable, he or they shall be requested) expose so much of the premises to sale at public auction for ready money (giving one months notice of the time & place of such sale in a newspaper printed in the Town of Alexandria) as will be sufficient to pay the sum of money which had become payable and was not discharged and that he or they do, with the money arising therefrom, pay the costs attending such sale and then the money which had become payable and any interest which had accrued upon it after it became payable and until such sale or sales made, that he the said ROBERT PATTON JR do occupy & possess all & singular the said premises without molestation or interruption and in case that the said ROBERT PATTON JR shall & do well & truly pay the said several sums of money and thereby prevent a sale or in case that a sale or sales be made and only a part of them be disposed, then upon this further trust that they the said JOHN DUNDAS and THOMAS SWANN, their Executors or Administrators, do when properly assured that the said sums of money have been paid and upon the request & at the cost and charge of him the said ROBERT PATTON JR his heirs & assigns convey unto him & them the said premises or such part of them as may not be made sale of, free from any encumberance had or made thereupon by him of them and the said JOHN DUNDAS & THOMAS SWANN do for himself, their heirs, Executors & Administrators covenant, grant & agree to & with the said WILLIAM HEPBURN his Exors, Administrators & assigns & to & with the said ROBERT PATTON JR & his heirs, Executors, Administrators & assigns that they the said JOHN DUNDAS and THOMAS SWANN their Executors and Administrators will well & truly execute, fulfil and perform the several trusts hereby vested in them. In WITNESS whereof the said ROBERT PATTON JR and ANN CLIFTON his wife & the said JOHN DUNDAS & THOMAS SWANN have hereunto set their hands & seals the day & Year first before mentioned.
Sealed & delivered In Presence of

DANL. T. DULANY	ROB. PATTON JR	(seal)
GEO. YOUNGS R.P.	ANN CLIFTON PATTON	(seal)
N. HERBERT	JOHN DUNDAS	(seal)
EDM. J. LEE R.P.	THO. SWANN	(seal)

At a court contd. & held for Fairfax County the 23rd day of November 1809 this Deed from ROB. PATTON JR and ANN CLIFTON his wife to JOHN DUNDAS & THOMAS SWANN in Trust for the use of WILLIAM HEPBURN was proved to be the act & deed of the said ROB. PATTON JR by the oaths of GEO. YOUNGS & EDMUND J. LEE & acknowledged by the said THOMAS SWANN to be his act and deed & ordered to be certified. And at a Court held for the said County the 18th day of December 1809 the same was further acknowledged by the said JOHN DUNDAS to be [his] act & deed & ordered to be certified & at a court contd. & held for the sd. County the 20th day of March 1810 the same was further proved to be the act and deed of the said ROB. PATTON JR by the oath of NOBLET HERBERT which together with a Commission & Reutrn thereto annexed for taking the acknowledgment and privy examination of the said ANNE CLIFTON are Ordered to be Recorded.   Teste WM. MOSS Cl.

FAIRFAX COUNTY To Wit:

The CommonWealth of Virginia to THOMPSON MASON, RICHARD MARSHALL SCOTT and JOHN THOMAS RICKETTS Gentlemen Justices of the County of Fairfax Greeting: Whereas ROBERT PATTON JR & ANN CLIFTON his wife by their certain indenture of Bargain & sale bearing date the twenty second day of April 1809 have sold and conveyed unto JOHN DUNDAS And THOMAS SWANN the fee simple Estate of a tract of land containing one hundred acres with the appurtenances situate, lying & being in the said County of Fairfax and whereas the said ANN CLIFTON cannot conveniently travel to our said county court of Fairfax to make acknowledgment of the said conveyance therefore we do Give unto you or any two or more of you power to receive the acknowledgment which the said ANN CLIFTON shall be willing to make before You of the conveyance aforesaid contained in the said Indenture which is here-unto annexed. And we do therefore desire You or any two or more of you personally to go to the said ANN CLIFTON and receive her acknowledgment of the same and examine her privily and apart from the said ROBERT her husband whither she doth the same freely & voluntarily without his Persuasions or threats and whither she be willing the said Indenture together with this commission shall be recorded in our said Court and when You have received her acknowledgment & examined her as aforesaid that You distinctly & openly certify us thereof in our said Court under Your hands & seals sending then there the said Indenture and this Writ. WITNESS WILLIAM MOSS Clerk of our said Court at the Courthouse of the said County, this 22nd day of July 1809 and in the 34th Year of the CommonWealth.

WM. MOSS Cl.

STATE OF VIRGINIA, FAIRFAX COUNTY To Wit:

In Obedience to the within Commission we did examine the said ANN CLIFTON privily and apart from the said ROBERT her husband who declared that she executed the said Indenture freely & voluntarily without his persuasions or threats and that she was willing the same together with this Commission should be recorded in the said Court. Given under our hands & seals this fifteenth day of November 1809.

| | THOMSON MASON | (seal) |
| | JNO. THOS. RICKETTS | (seal) |

Page 419.   [MAP OF THE PLAT]

Plat of part of ROBERT MOSS vacancy clear of the course & distance of a patent of land granted DANIEL FRENCH for 127 acres dated the 19th February 1730 now claimed by BENJAMIN DULANY surveyed agreeable to an article of agreement entered into by said DULANY & MOSS dated 20 July 1808 beginning at "A" several white oak & hickory saplings standing in or near the line of MATTHEWS' Patent, a supposed corner of sd. FRENCH'S Patent, running thence with his lines reversed North 5° West 28 Poles to

"B" two chesnut saplings blazed supposed corner of sd. Patent, thence South 78° West 70 poles to

INDEX OF PERSONS

INDEX OF PERSONS

INDEX OF PERSONS

INDEX OF PERSONS

INDEX OF PERSONS

INDEX OF PERSONS

INDEX OF PERSONS

INDEX OF PERSONS

INDEX OF PERSONS

INDEX OF PERSONS

INDEX OF SLAVES

INDEX OF LOCATIONS

INDEX OF LOCATIONS